Almighty God,
Father of our Lord Jesus Christ,
grant, we pray,
that we might be grounded and settled
in your truth
by the coming of your Holy Spirit
into our hearts.

What we do not know,
reveal to us;
what is lacking within us,
make complete;
that which we do know,
confirm in us;
and keep us blameless in your service,
through Jesus Christ our Lord.

Amen.

IMMERSE™
——— The Reading Bible ———

PROPHETS

Tyndale House Publishers, Inc.
Carol Stream, Illinois

CREATED IN ALLIANCE WITH

**INSTITUTE FOR
BIBLE READING**

Library of Congress Cataloging-in-Publication Data

Names: Tyndale House Publishers.
Title: Prophets.
Other titles: Bible. Prophets. English. New Living Translation. 2018.
Description: Carol Stream, Illinois : Tyndale House Publishers, Inc., 2018. |
  Series: Immerse: the reading Bible
Identifiers: LCCN 2017055092 | ISBN 9781496424167 (sc)
Classification: LCC BS1503 .N49 2018 | DDC 224/.0520834—dc23 LC record available at
  https://lccn.loc.gov/2017055092

Printed in the United States of America

24	23	22	21	20	19	18
7	6	5	4	3	2	1

CONTENTS

——— ✛ ———

This volume presents the First Testament prophets in
groupings that generally represent four historical periods.
The first grouping includes prophets who spoke to God's
people before the fall of Israel's northern kingdom.

——— ✛ ———

The second grouping includes prophets who spoke after
the fall of the northern kingdom of Israel but before
the fall of the southern kingdom of Judah.

——— ✛ ———

The third grouping includes prophets ministering around
the time of Jerusalem's destruction, when the people of
Judah were being taken away into Babylonian exile.

———— ✝ ————

The fourth grouping includes books that, for the most part, represent prophetic ministry after the remnant of God's people returned from Babylonian exile.

—— *Welcome to* ——

I M M E R S E
The Bible Reading Experience

The Bible is a great gift. The Creator of all things entered into our human story and spoke to us. He inspired people over many centuries to shape words into books that reveal his mind, bringing wisdom into our lives and light to our paths. But God's biggest intention for the Bible is to invite us into its Story. What God wants for us, more than anything else, is that we make the Bible's great drama of restoration and new life the story of our lives, too.

The appropriate way to receive a gift like this is to come to know the Bible deeply, to lose ourselves in it precisely so that we can find ourselves in it. In other words, we need to immerse ourselves in it—to read God's words at length and without distraction, to read with deeper historical and literary perspective, and to read through the Bible with friends in a regular three-year rhythm. *Immerse: The Bible Reading Experience* has been specially designed for this purpose.

Immerse: The Reading Bible presents each book of the Bible without the distractions of chapter and verse markers, subject headers, or footnotes—all later historical additions to the text. The *Holy Bible*, New Living Translation, is presented in a single-column format with easy-to-read type. To provide meaningful perspective, book introductions give historical and literary context, and the books are often reordered chronologically or grouped with books that share similar ancient audiences. Every feature in this unique Bible enhances the opportunity for readers to engage with God's words in simple clarity.

A more complete explanation of this unique Bible presentation can be found in the articles that begin on page 445 at the back of this volume.

—— *Introduction to* ——

PROPHETS

THE BIBLE TELLS THE STORY of how God chose the people of Israel for the sake of restoring the whole world. He entered into a series of covenants with Abraham and his descendants in order to move them closer and closer to this goal of being a life-giving blessing to all peoples.

But over and over again, the ancient Israelites failed to honor their covenant obligations to God. The Law of Moses insisted that they give the LORD their exclusive allegiance, but they repeatedly turned to worship other gods. The Law provided numerous safeguards for the poor and vulnerable, but the people frequently exploited the weakest of their citizens. In short, Israel failed to be the light to the nations that God was calling them to be.

But God was determined to keep working with this imperfect nation to achieve his goal. So God sent special messengers—the prophets—to call the people back to him. The messages of many of these prophets have been collected and preserved for us, and they now comprise nearly a third of the Bible's First Testament.

The prophets play the role of covenant mediators, calling the people to be loyal to their covenant with the LORD. Many of the prophets frame their arguments as "covenant lawsuits" against the people. The prophet Micah, for example, announces at one point, "Listen to the LORD's complaint! He has a case against his people." The prophets establish in their arguments that the people have become unfaithful to God by failing to keep their covenant commitments.

This is why the prophets typically begin their messages with warnings, followed by the announcement of necessary consequences for disobedience. But judgment is never the LORD's final word for Israel. Difficult messages of correction and judgment transform into visions of restoration and flourishing life. The prophets see a new future for

Israel—and the world—based solely on God's good promises and his covenant faithfulness.

The prophets themselves were more street preachers than the authors of books, normally proclaiming the LORD's messages at the gates of Jerusalem and the Temple. They usually spoke in oracles, which were recorded and serve as the basic literary unit for most of the prophetic books. Prophetic oracles are poems that convey a single idea through several strategies.

The prophets often used visual metaphors from the natural world to help their listeners imagine or picture their messages. Sometimes the metaphors came directly from the prophets' dramatic visions from God, which cannot easily be described in human terms. At other times, the metaphors were drawn from the prophets' own circumstances or experiences.

Some oracles were based on the repetition of key ideas—"litanies" (or lists) that drive home an essential point. Amos, for example, describes five different misfortunes that God had brought upon his people and says after each one, "But still you would not return to me." Prophetic language is typically strong and evokes powerful emotions because so much was at stake in these interventions with Israel.

Some of the prophets set their oracles to music. This was another way they could ensure that their message would spread and be remembered. Isaiah, for example, introduces one oracle with, "I will sing for the one I love a song about his vineyard." This particular oracle presents an extended metaphor, describing Israel as a well-tended vineyard that failed to produce the fruit the Keeper wanted: the justice and righteousness that God had been cultivating in them.

We present these books of the prophets in an order that follows their general historical sequence. As Israel journeys from the time of the empire of Assyria, through the period of the rule of Babylon and then Persia, to the return of the people to their homeland, the prophets are present to speak into Israel's various historical situations. The collections cannot all be dated precisely. Jonah and Joel are particularly difficult to locate historically, so they are placed last and can be read in view of the larger prophetic tradition.

As Israel's wayfaring continues through the centuries, the prophets relentlessly remind the people of their true calling. Even through the dark abyss of exile and the loss of land and home, their hope for the future remains. This story is God's, and at the end of the day he will act to save his people—and his world.

IMMERSED IN AMOS

IN THE FIRST HALF of the eighth century BC, the northern kingdom of Israel reached its greatest heights of prosperity and strength under the long reign of Jeroboam II. Israel's leaders and nobles reveled in the glory and power of their economic success and military prowess. They believed that this reflected God's favor and blessings upon them. After all, didn't they bring lavish offerings to their gods at the temple in Bethel, which was the king's sanctuary and a national place of worship, as well as at other shrines such as in Gilgal and Dan?

But their self-satisfaction was disturbed by the words of a shepherd from a small town in the southern kingdom: "The temples of Israel will be destroyed; I will bring the dynasty of King Jeroboam to a sudden end." Why did the prophet Amos bring these dire words to the people? In the midst of their comfort and wealth, the LORD had seen the truth: "They trample helpless people in the dust and shove the oppressed out of the way." Israel's brash self-assurance was built on idolatrous worship, gross injustice, and mistreatment of the poor. So God sent his messenger to warn the northern kingdom of their coming judgment and demise.

The leaders of Israel gave Amos's warning all the attention they felt it deserved: They threw him out of the kingdom and told him to take his message back to Judah where he'd come from. So Amos left, but his prophecies were written down to preserve them as an ongoing witness against the injustices that would doom the northern kingdom. He became the earliest of the "writing prophets," whose words have been collected for us in the Bible.

The book of Amos begins by establishing the credibility of his warnings. Its superscription specifies that he received his message "two years before the earthquake." Amos had predicted this: "The earth will tremble for your deeds, and everyone will mourn. The ground will rise like the Nile River at floodtime; it will heave up, then sink again." And when this earthquake came, it was devastating. Geologists have found evidence at multiple sites of widespread and sudden destruction consistent with a massive earthquake late in the reign of Jeroboam II.

After this opening assertion that God truly is speaking through Amos, the book relays a cycle of oracles against the nations that immediately surround Israel. The prophet first announces judgment against these nations, and then, in the seventh oracle, turns to speak against the southern kingdom of Judah. The listeners in the northern kingdom likely would have expected this to be the final oracle, and they would have cheered the condemnation of their neighbors and their closest rivals in Judah. But Amos has been drawing a target with Israel at the center, and he delivers his longest denunciation against the northern kingdom of Israel. Because of their wanton luxury, oppression of the poor, and idolatry, they will be defeated and destroyed.

The rest of the book reinforces this message. It consists of loosely organized and sometimes interwoven short oracles that take up the same themes: Idolatry, injustice, oppression, and debauchery will bring God's judgment, no matter how strong Israel's army or enthusiastic its religious services.

As part of this message of judgment, Amos also relays a series of visions given to him by God that metaphorically depict the coming punishment. These visions are juxtaposed with an account of the expulsion of Amos from the northern kingdom, showing that the people have rejected both God's message and God's genuine messenger.

The final oracle is the most devastating of all. In it God dismisses the Israelites as his covenant people, saying that the exodus from Egypt should not make them feel more special than any other nation: "'Are you Israelites more important to me than the Ethiopians?' asks the LORD. 'I brought Israel out of Egypt, but I also brought the Philistines from Crete and led the Arameans out of Kir. I, the Sovereign LORD, am watching this sinful nation of Israel. I will destroy it from the face of the earth.'"

But then, in a pattern we will see again and again, the epilogue expresses renewed hope for the future. Amos, the earliest of the prophets, sets a template that God's later messengers will also follow. There will be judgment on God's people because of injustice and unfaithfulness, but then a promised restoration will come through the mercy and love of God. The covenant will prevail: God will reinstate himself as King and heal his land.

AMOS

+

This message was given to Amos, a shepherd from the town of Tekoa in Judah. He received this message in visions two years before the earthquake, when Uzziah was king of Judah and Jeroboam II, the son of Jehoash, was king of Israel.

This is what he saw and heard:

"The LORD's voice will roar from Zion
and thunder from Jerusalem!
The lush pastures of the shepherds will dry up;
the grass on Mount Carmel will wither and die."

+

This is what the LORD says:

"The people of Damascus have sinned again and again,
and I will not let them go unpunished!
They beat down my people in Gilead
as grain is threshed with iron sledges.
So I will send down fire on King Hazael's palace,
and the fortresses of King Ben-hadad will be destroyed.
I will break down the gates of Damascus
and slaughter the people in the valley of Aven.
I will destroy the ruler in Beth-eden,
and the people of Aram will go as captives to Kir,"
says the LORD.

This is what the LORD says:

"The people of Gaza have sinned again and again,
and I will not let them go unpunished!
They sent whole villages into exile,
selling them as slaves to Edom.

So I will send down fire on the walls of Gaza,
    and all its fortresses will be destroyed.
I will slaughter the people of Ashdod
    and destroy the king of Ashkelon.
Then I will turn to attack Ekron,
    and the few Philistines still left will be killed,"
    says the Sovereign LORD.

This is what the LORD says:

"The people of Tyre have sinned again and again,
    and I will not let them go unpunished!
They broke their treaty of brotherhood with Israel,
    selling whole villages as slaves to Edom.
So I will send down fire on the walls of Tyre,
    and all its fortresses will be destroyed."

This is what the LORD says:

"The people of Edom have sinned again and again,
    and I will not let them go unpunished!
They chased down their relatives, the Israelites, with swords,
    showing them no mercy.
In their rage, they slashed them continually
    and were unrelenting in their anger.
So I will send down fire on Teman,
    and the fortresses of Bozrah will be destroyed."

This is what the LORD says:

"The people of Ammon have sinned again and again,
    and I will not let them go unpunished!
When they attacked Gilead to extend their borders,
    they ripped open pregnant women with their swords.
So I will send down fire on the walls of Rabbah,
    and all its fortresses will be destroyed.
The battle will come upon them with shouts,
    like a whirlwind in a mighty storm.
And their king and his princes will go into exile together,"
    says the LORD.

This is what the LORD says:

"The people of Moab have sinned again and again,
    and I will not let them go unpunished!

They desecrated the bones of Edom's king,
  burning them to ashes.
So I will send down fire on the land of Moab,
  and all the fortresses in Kerioth will be destroyed.
The people will fall in the noise of battle,
  as the warriors shout and the ram's horn sounds.
And I will destroy their king
  and slaughter all their princes,"
  says the LORD.

This is what the LORD says:

"The people of Judah have sinned again and again,
  and I will not let them go unpunished!
They have rejected the instruction of the LORD,
  refusing to obey his decrees.
They have been led astray by the same lies
  that deceived their ancestors.
So I will send down fire on Judah,
  and all the fortresses of Jerusalem will be destroyed."

This is what the LORD says:

"The people of Israel have sinned again and again,
  and I will not let them go unpunished!
They sell honorable people for silver
  and poor people for a pair of sandals.
They trample helpless people in the dust
  and shove the oppressed out of the way.
Both father and son sleep with the same woman,
  corrupting my holy name.
At their religious festivals,
  they lounge in clothing their debtors put up as security.
In the house of their gods,
  they drink wine bought with unjust fines.

"But as my people watched,
  I destroyed the Amorites,
though they were as tall as cedars
  and as strong as oaks.
I destroyed the fruit on their branches
  and dug out their roots.
It was I who rescued you from Egypt
  and led you through the desert for forty years,

so you could possess the land of the Amorites.
I chose some of your sons to be prophets
    and others to be Nazirites.
Can you deny this, my people of Israel?"
    asks the LORD.
"But you caused the Nazirites to sin by making them drink wine,
    and you commanded the prophets, 'Shut up!'

"So I will make you groan
    like a wagon loaded down with sheaves of grain.
Your fastest runners will not get away.
    The strongest among you will become weak.
Even mighty warriors will be unable to save themselves.
    The archers will not stand their ground.
The swiftest runners won't be fast enough to escape.
    Even those riding horses won't be able to save themselves.
On that day the most courageous of your fighting men
    will drop their weapons and run for their lives,"
    says the LORD.

+

Listen to this message that the LORD has spoken against you, O people of Israel—against the entire family I rescued from Egypt:

"From among all the families on the earth,
    I have been intimate with you alone.
That is why I must punish you
    for all your sins."

Can two people walk together
    without agreeing on the direction?
Does a lion ever roar in a thicket
    without first finding a victim?
Does a young lion growl in its den
    without first catching its prey?
Does a bird ever get caught in a trap
    that has no bait?
Does a trap spring shut
    when there's nothing to catch?
When the ram's horn blows a warning,
    shouldn't the people be alarmed?
Does disaster come to a city
    unless the LORD has planned it?

Indeed, the Sovereign LORD never does anything
    until he reveals his plans to his servants the prophets.

The lion has roared—
    so who isn't frightened?
The Sovereign LORD has spoken—
    so who can refuse to proclaim his message?

Announce this to the leaders of Philistia
    and to the great ones of Egypt:
"Take your seats now on the hills around Samaria,
    and witness the chaos and oppression in Israel."

"My people have forgotten how to do right,"
    says the LORD.
"Their fortresses are filled with wealth
    taken by theft and violence.
Therefore," says the Sovereign LORD,
    "an enemy is coming!
He will surround them and shatter their defenses.
    Then he will plunder all their fortresses."

This is what the LORD says:

"A shepherd who tries to rescue a sheep from a lion's mouth
    will recover only two legs or a piece of an ear.
So it will be for the Israelites in Samaria lying on luxurious beds,
    and for the people of Damascus reclining on couches.

"Now listen to this, and announce it throughout all Israel," says the Lord,
the LORD God of Heaven's Armies.

"On the very day I punish Israel for its sins,
    I will destroy the pagan altars at Bethel.
The horns of the altar will be cut off
    and fall to the ground.
And I will destroy the beautiful homes of the wealthy—
    their winter mansions and their summer houses, too—
all their palaces filled with ivory,"
    says the LORD.

Listen to me, you fat cows
    living in Samaria,
you women who oppress the poor

and crush the needy,
and who are always calling to your husbands,
  "Bring us another drink!"
The Sovereign LORD has sworn this by his holiness:
"The time will come when you will be led away
  with hooks in your noses.
Every last one of you will be dragged away
  like a fish on a hook!
You will be led out through the ruins of the wall;
  you will be thrown from your fortresses,"
  says the LORD.

"Go ahead and offer sacrifices to the idols at Bethel.
  Keep on disobeying at Gilgal.
Offer sacrifices each morning,
  and bring your tithes every three days.
Present your bread made with yeast
  as an offering of thanksgiving.
Then give your extra voluntary offerings
  so you can brag about it everywhere!
This is the kind of thing you Israelites love to do,"
  says the Sovereign LORD.

"I brought hunger to every city
  and famine to every town.
But still you would not return to me,"
  says the LORD.

"I kept the rain from falling
  when your crops needed it the most.
I sent rain on one town
  but withheld it from another.
Rain fell on one field,
  while another field withered away.
People staggered from town to town looking for water,
  but there was never enough.
But still you would not return to me,"
  says the LORD.

"I struck your farms and vineyards with blight and mildew.
  Locusts devoured all your fig and olive trees.
But still you would not return to me,"
  says the LORD.

"I sent plagues on you
  like the plagues I sent on Egypt long ago.
I killed your young men in war
  and led all your horses away.
  The stench of death filled the air!
But still you would not return to me,"
  says the LORD.

"I destroyed some of your cities,
  as I destroyed Sodom and Gomorrah.
Those of you who survived
  were like charred sticks pulled from a fire.
But still you would not return to me,"
  says the LORD.

"Therefore, I will bring upon you all the disasters I have announced.
  Prepare to meet your God in judgment, you people of Israel!"

For the LORD is the one who shaped the mountains,
  stirs up the winds, and reveals his thoughts to mankind.
He turns the light of dawn into darkness
  and treads on the heights of the earth.
  The LORD God of Heaven's Armies is his name!

Listen, you people of Israel! Listen to this funeral song I am singing:

"The virgin Israel has fallen,
  never to rise again!
She lies abandoned on the ground,
  with no one to help her up."

The Sovereign LORD says:

"When a city sends a thousand men to battle,
  only a hundred will return.
When a town sends a hundred,
  only ten will come back alive."

Now this is what the LORD says to the family of Israel:

"Come back to me and live!
Don't worship at the pagan altars at Bethel;
  don't go to the shrines at Gilgal or Beersheba.
For the people of Gilgal will be dragged off into exile,

and the people of Bethel will be reduced to nothing."
Come back to the LORD and live!
Otherwise, he will roar through Israel like a fire,
    devouring you completely.
Your gods in Bethel
    won't be able to quench the flames.

You twist justice, making it a bitter pill for the oppressed.
    You treat the righteous like dirt.

It is the LORD who created the stars,
    the Pleiades and Orion.
He turns darkness into morning
    and day into night.
He draws up water from the oceans
    and pours it down as rain on the land.
    The LORD is his name!
With blinding speed and power he destroys the strong,
    crushing all their defenses.

How you hate honest judges!
    How you despise people who tell the truth!

You trample the poor,
    stealing their grain through taxes and unfair rent.
Therefore, though you build beautiful stone houses,
    you will never live in them.
Though you plant lush vineyards,
    you will never drink wine from them.
For I know the vast number of your sins
    and the depth of your rebellions.

You oppress good people by taking bribes
    and deprive the poor of justice in the courts.
So those who are smart keep their mouths shut,
    for it is an evil time.

Do what is good and run from evil
    so that you may live!
Then the LORD God of Heaven's Armies will be your helper,
    just as you have claimed.
Hate evil and love what is good;

turn your courts into true halls of justice.
Perhaps even yet the LORD God of Heaven's Armies
    will have mercy on the remnant of his people.

Therefore, this is what the Lord, the LORD God of Heaven's Armies, says:

"There will be crying in all the public squares
    and mourning in every street.
Call for the farmers to weep with you,
    and summon professional mourners to wail.
There will be wailing in every vineyard,
    for I will destroy them all,"
    says the LORD.

What sorrow awaits you who say,
    "If only the day of the LORD were here!"
You have no idea what you are wishing for.
    That day will bring darkness, not light.
In that day you will be like a man who runs from a lion—
    only to meet a bear.
Escaping from the bear, he leans his hand against a wall in his house—
    and he's bitten by a snake.
Yes, the day of the LORD will be dark and hopeless,
    without a ray of joy or hope.

"I hate all your show and pretense—
    the hypocrisy of your religious festivals and solemn assemblies.
I will not accept your burnt offerings and grain offerings.
    I won't even notice all your choice peace offerings.
Away with your noisy hymns of praise!
    I will not listen to the music of your harps.
Instead, I want to see a mighty flood of justice,
    an endless river of righteous living.

"Was it to me you were bringing sacrifices and offerings during the forty years in the wilderness, Israel? No, you served your pagan gods—Sakkuth your king god and Kaiwan your star god—the images you made for yourselves. So I will send you into exile, to a land east of Damascus," says the LORD, whose name is the God of Heaven's Armies.

What sorrow awaits you who lounge in luxury in Jerusalem,
    and you who feel secure in Samaria!

You are famous and popular in Israel,
    and people go to you for help.
But go over to Calneh
    and see what happened there.
Then go to the great city of Hamath
    and down to the Philistine city of Gath.
You are no better than they were,
    and look at how they were destroyed.
You push away every thought of coming disaster,
    but your actions only bring the day of judgment closer.
How terrible for you who sprawl on ivory beds
    and lounge on your couches,
eating the meat of tender lambs from the flock
    and of choice calves fattened in the stall.
You sing trivial songs to the sound of the harp
    and fancy yourselves to be great musicians like David.
You drink wine by the bowlful
    and perfume yourselves with fragrant lotions.
    You care nothing about the ruin of your nation.
Therefore, you will be the first to be led away as captives.
    Suddenly, all your parties will end.

The Sovereign LORD has sworn by his own name, and this is what he, the
LORD God of Heaven's Armies, says:

"I despise the arrogance of Israel,
    and I hate their fortresses.
I will give this city
    and everything in it to their enemies."

(If there are ten men left in one house, they will all die. And when a relative
who is responsible to dispose of the dead goes into the house to carry out
the bodies, he will ask the last survivor, "Is anyone else with you?" When
the person begins to swear, "No, by . . . ," he will interrupt and say, "Stop!
Don't even mention the name of the LORD.")

When the LORD gives the command,
    homes both great and small will be smashed to pieces.

Can horses gallop over boulders?
    Can oxen be used to plow them?
But that's how foolish you are when you turn justice into poison
    and the sweet fruit of righteousness into bitterness.

And you brag about your conquest of Lo-debar.
  You boast, "Didn't we take Karnaim by our own strength?"

"O people of Israel, I am about to bring an enemy nation against you,"
  says the LORD God of Heaven's Armies.
"They will oppress you throughout your land—
  from Lebo-hamath in the north
  to the Arabah Valley in the south."

+

The Sovereign LORD showed me a vision. I saw him preparing to send a vast swarm of locusts over the land. This was after the king's share had been harvested from the fields and as the main crop was coming up. In my vision the locusts ate every green plant in sight. Then I said, "O Sovereign LORD, please forgive us or we will not survive, for Israel is so small."

So the LORD relented from this plan. "I will not do it," he said.

Then the Sovereign LORD showed me another vision. I saw him preparing to punish his people with a great fire. The fire had burned up the depths of the sea and was devouring the entire land. Then I said, "O Sovereign LORD, please stop or we will not survive, for Israel is so small."

Then the LORD relented from this plan, too. "I will not do that either," said the Sovereign LORD.

Then he showed me another vision. I saw the Lord standing beside a wall that had been built using a plumb line. He was using a plumb line to see if it was still straight. And the LORD said to me, "Amos, what do you see?"

I answered, "A plumb line."

And the Lord replied, "I will test my people with this plumb line. I will no longer ignore all their sins. The pagan shrines of your ancestors will be ruined, and the temples of Israel will be destroyed; I will bring the dynasty of King Jeroboam to a sudden end."

Then Amaziah, the priest of Bethel, sent a message to Jeroboam, king of Israel: "Amos is hatching a plot against you right here on your very doorstep! What he is saying is intolerable. He is saying, 'Jeroboam will soon be killed, and the people of Israel will be sent away into exile.'"

Then Amaziah sent orders to Amos: "Get out of here, you prophet! Go on back to the land of Judah, and earn your living by prophesying there! Don't bother us with your prophecies here in Bethel. This is the king's sanctuary and the national place of worship!"

But Amos replied, "I'm not a professional prophet, and I was never trained to be one. I'm just a shepherd, and I take care of sycamore-fig trees. But the LORD called me away from my flock and told me, 'Go and prophesy to my people in Israel.' Now then, listen to this message from the LORD:

"You say,
'Don't prophesy against Israel.
   Stop preaching against my people.'
But this is what the LORD says:
'Your wife will become a prostitute in this city,
   and your sons and daughters will be killed.
Your land will be divided up,
   and you yourself will die in a foreign land.
And the people of Israel will certainly become captives in exile,
   far from their homeland.'"

Then the Sovereign LORD showed me another vision. In it I saw a basket filled with ripe fruit. "What do you see, Amos?" he asked.

I replied, "A basket full of ripe fruit."

Then the LORD said, "Like this fruit, Israel is ripe for punishment! I will not delay their punishment again. In that day the singing in the temple will turn to wailing. Dead bodies will be scattered everywhere. They will be carried out of the city in silence. I, the Sovereign LORD, have spoken!"

Listen to this, you who rob the poor
   and trample down the needy!
You can't wait for the Sabbath day to be over
   and the religious festivals to end
   so you can get back to cheating the helpless.
You measure out grain with dishonest measures
   and cheat the buyer with dishonest scales.
And you mix the grain you sell
   with chaff swept from the floor.
Then you enslave poor people
   for one piece of silver or a pair of sandals.

Now the LORD has sworn this oath
   by his own name, the Pride of Israel:
"I will never forget
   the wicked things you have done!
The earth will tremble for your deeds,
   and everyone will mourn.

The ground will rise like the Nile River at floodtime;
   it will heave up, then sink again.

"In that day," says the Sovereign LORD,
"I will make the sun go down at noon
   and darken the earth while it is still day.
I will turn your celebrations into times of mourning
   and your singing into weeping.
You will wear funeral clothes
   and shave your heads to show your sorrow—
as if your only son had died.
   How very bitter that day will be!

"The time is surely coming," says the Sovereign LORD,
   "when I will send a famine on the land—
not a famine of bread or water
   but of hearing the words of the LORD.
People will stagger from sea to sea
   and wander from border to border
searching for the word of the LORD,
   but they will not find it.
Beautiful girls and strong young men
   will grow faint in that day,
   thirsting for the LORD's word.
And those who swear by the shameful idols of Samaria—
   who take oaths in the name of the god of Dan
   and make vows in the name of the god of Beersheba—
they will all fall down,
   never to rise again."

Then I saw a vision of the Lord standing beside the altar. He said,

"Strike the tops of the Temple columns,
   so that the foundation will shake.
Bring down the roof
   on the heads of the people below.
I will kill with the sword those who survive.
   No one will escape!

"Even if they dig down to the place of the dead,
   I will reach down and pull them up.
Even if they climb up into the heavens,
   I will bring them down.

Even if they hide at the very top of Mount Carmel,
  I will search them out and capture them.
Even if they hide at the bottom of the ocean,
  I will send the sea serpent after them to bite them.
Even if their enemies drive them into exile,
  I will command the sword to kill them there.
I am determined to bring disaster upon them
  and not to help them."

The Lord, the LORD of Heaven's Armies,
  touches the land and it melts,
  and all its people mourn.
The ground rises like the Nile River at floodtime,
  and then it sinks again.
The LORD's home reaches up to the heavens,
  while its foundation is on the earth.
He draws up water from the oceans
  and pours it down as rain on the land.
  The LORD is his name!

"Are you Israelites more important to me
  than the Ethiopians?" asks the LORD.
"I brought Israel out of Egypt,
  but I also brought the Philistines from Crete
  and led the Arameans out of Kir.

"I, the Sovereign LORD,
  am watching this sinful nation of Israel.
I will destroy it
  from the face of the earth.

+

But I will never completely destroy the family of Israel,"
  says the LORD.
"For I will give the command
  and will shake Israel along with the other nations
as grain is shaken in a sieve,
  yet not one true kernel will be lost.
But all the sinners will die by the sword—
  all those who say, 'Nothing bad will happen to us.'

"In that day I will restore the fallen house of David.
  I will repair its damaged walls.

From the ruins I will rebuild it
   and restore its former glory.
And Israel will possess what is left of Edom
   and all the nations I have called to be mine."
The LORD has spoken,
   and he will do these things.

"The time will come," says the LORD,
"when the grain and grapes will grow faster
   than they can be harvested.
Then the terraced vineyards on the hills of Israel
   will drip with sweet wine!
I will bring my exiled people of Israel
   back from distant lands,
and they will rebuild their ruined cities
   and live in them again.
They will plant vineyards and gardens;
   they will eat their crops and drink their wine.
I will firmly plant them there
   in their own land.
They will never again be uprooted
   from the land I have given them,"
   says the LORD your God.

IMMERSED IN HOSEA

AMOS WAS NOT the only prophet who was rebuffed by the people of the northern kingdom of Israel. Toward the end of Jeroboam II's reign, a man named Hosea also tried to bring a warning from God against their injustice and idolatry. But the people called him "crazy" and a fool, and they plotted against him. Despite this strong hostility and opposition, Hosea's messages and prophecies were recorded and collected, and they have come down to us today in this book.

The book of Hosea has two parts. The first is set during the stable and prosperous years of Jeroboam II's reign. Hosea refers to the grain, wine, olive oil, silver, and gold that were abundant in those years. The second (and longer) part of the book describes the three chaotic decades following Jeroboam II's death when four of the final six northern kings were assassinated, creating social instability, economic distress, and shifting dependence on foreign powers.

But both parts of the book deliver the same message, which is both ominous and hopeful at the same time. Because Israel has strayed so far from God, plunging into immoral idol worship and violating the requirements of justice from the Law of Moses, nothing but a fresh start will restore its covenant relationship with the LORD. The people must be taken into exile so that in their isolation they may come to know God once again.

In the first part of the book, this scenario is dramatized in Hosea's own life. God tells Hosea to marry a woman who will be unfaithful to him, just as the Israelites have been unfaithful to their covenant God. But even though his wife abandons him, Hosea is told to take her back again. (He has to buy her back from slavery in order to accomplish this.) After a season of abstinence, Hosea then acts as her husband again. In the same way, God will reclaim his role as Israel's true husband: "I will win her back once again. I will lead her into the desert and speak tenderly to her there. . . . She will give herself to me there, as she did long ago when she was young, when I freed her from her captivity in Egypt."

The second part of the book opens with a stunning presentation of a classic covenant lawsuit:

- First, Israel is called to court: "Hear the word of the LORD, O people of Israel! The LORD has brought charges against you."
- Next, the charges are brought: "There is no faithfulness, no kindness, no knowledge of God in your land. You make vows and break them; you kill and steal and commit adultery. There is violence everywhere—one murder after another."
- Then the sentence is pronounced: "That is why your land is in mourning, and everyone is wasting away. Even the wild animals, the birds of the sky, and the fish of the sea are disappearing."

The people of Israel have failed to remain faithful in their covenant relationship with God, and the consequences include the undoing of creation itself. Part of Israel's failure involved embracing the debauched fertility cult of Baal, which the people had unfortunately become addicted to. Instead of looking to Baal for life and prosperity, the people should have looked only to the Creator himself as the true source of life. But now, in their disobedience, they would experience the desert of exile and destruction.

Hosea highlights key events of Israel's earlier covenant history, especially the Exodus, to inspire the people to renew their relationship with God and begin living out their story in the present. At one point Hosea takes a step back from delivering prophecies in God's name in order to appeal personally to his fellow Israelites, "Come, let us return to the LORD." If the people would return, then the LORD's promises of restoration given through Hosea would be realized: "I will heal you of your faithlessness; my love will know no bounds, for my anger will be gone forever."

HOSEA

<hr/>

The LORD gave this message to Hosea son of Beeri during the years when Uzziah, Jotham, Ahaz, and Hezekiah were kings of Judah, and Jeroboam son of Jehoash was king of Israel.

✦ ✦ ✦

When the LORD first began speaking to Israel through Hosea, he said to him, "Go and marry a prostitute, so that some of her children will be conceived in prostitution. This will illustrate how Israel has acted like a prostitute by turning against the LORD and worshiping other gods."

So Hosea married Gomer, the daughter of Diblaim, and she became pregnant and gave Hosea a son. And the LORD said, "Name the child Jezreel, for I am about to punish King Jehu's dynasty to avenge the murders he committed at Jezreel. In fact, I will bring an end to Israel's independence. I will break its military power in the Jezreel Valley."

Soon Gomer became pregnant again and gave birth to a daughter. And the LORD said to Hosea, "Name your daughter Lo-ruhamah—'Not loved'—for I will no longer show love to the people of Israel or forgive them. But I will show love to the people of Judah. I will free them from their enemies—not with weapons and armies or horses and charioteers, but by my power as the LORD their God."

After Gomer had weaned Lo-ruhamah, she again became pregnant and gave birth to a second son. And the LORD said, "Name him Lo-ammi—'Not my people'—for Israel is not my people, and I am not their God.

"Yet the time will come when Israel's people will be like the sands of the seashore—too many to count! Then, at the place where they were told, 'You are not my people,' it will be said, 'You are children of the living God.' Then the people of Judah and Israel will unite together. They will choose one leader for themselves, and they will return from exile together. What a day that will be—the day of Jezreel—when God will again plant his people in his land.

"In that day you will call your brothers Ammi—'My people.' And you will call your sisters Ruhamah—'The ones I love.'

"But now bring charges against Israel—your mother—
　　for she is no longer my wife,
　　and I am no longer her husband.
Tell her to remove the prostitute's makeup from her face
　　and the clothing that exposes her breasts.
Otherwise, I will strip her as naked
　　as she was on the day she was born.
I will leave her to die of thirst,
　　as in a dry and barren wilderness.
And I will not love her children,
　　for they were conceived in prostitution.
Their mother is a shameless prostitute
　　and became pregnant in a shameful way.
She said, 'I'll run after other lovers
　　and sell myself to them for food and water,
for clothing of wool and linen,
　　and for olive oil and drinks.'

"For this reason I will fence her in with thornbushes.
　　I will block her path with a wall
　　to make her lose her way.
When she runs after her lovers,
　　she won't be able to catch them.
She will search for them
　　but not find them.
Then she will think,
'I might as well return to my husband,
　　for I was better off with him than I am now.'
She doesn't realize it was I who gave her everything
　　　she has—
　　the grain, the new wine, the olive oil;
I even gave her silver and gold.
　　But she gave all my gifts to Baal.

"But now I will take back the ripened grain and new wine
　　I generously provided each harvest season.
I will take away the wool and linen clothing
　　I gave her to cover her nakedness.
I will strip her naked in public,
　　while all her lovers look on.

No one will be able
    to rescue her from my hands.
I will put an end to her annual festivals,
    her new moon celebrations, and her Sabbath days—
    all her appointed festivals.
I will destroy her grapevines and fig trees,
    things she claims her lovers gave her.
I will let them grow into tangled thickets,
    where only wild animals will eat the fruit.
I will punish her for all those times
    when she burned incense to her images of Baal,
when she put on her earrings and jewels
    and went out to look for her lovers
but forgot all about me,"
    says the LORD.

"But then I will win her back once again.
    I will lead her into the desert
    and speak tenderly to her there.
I will return her vineyards to her
    and transform the Valley of Trouble into a gateway of hope.
She will give herself to me there,
    as she did long ago when she was young,
    when I freed her from her captivity in Egypt.
When that day comes," says the LORD,
    "you will call me 'my husband'
    instead of 'my master.'
O Israel, I will wipe the many names of Baal from your lips,
    and you will never mention them again.
On that day I will make a covenant
    with all the wild animals and the birds of the sky
and the animals that scurry along the ground
    so they will not harm you.
I will remove all weapons of war from the land,
    all swords and bows,
so you can live unafraid
    in peace and safety.
I will make you my wife forever,
    showing you righteousness and justice,
    unfailing love and compassion.
I will be faithful to you and make you mine,
    and you will finally know me as the LORD.

"In that day, I will answer,"
  says the LORD.
"I will answer the sky as it pleads for clouds.
  And the sky will answer the earth with rain.
Then the earth will answer the thirsty cries
  of the grain, the grapevines, and the olive trees.
And they in turn will answer,
  'Jezreel'—'God plants!'
At that time I will plant a crop of Israelites
  and raise them for myself.
I will show love
  to those I called 'Not loved.'
And to those I called 'Not my people,'
  I will say, 'Now you are my people.'
And they will reply, 'You are our God!'"

+

Then the LORD said to me, "Go and love your wife again, even though she commits adultery with another lover. This will illustrate that the LORD still loves Israel, even though the people have turned to other gods and love to worship them."

So I bought her back for fifteen pieces of silver and five bushels of barley and a measure of wine. Then I said to her, "You must live in my house for many days and stop your prostitution. During this time, you will not have sexual relations with anyone, not even with me."

This shows that Israel will go a long time without a king or prince, and without sacrifices, sacred pillars, priests, or even idols! But afterward the people will return and devote themselves to the LORD their God and to David's descendant, their king. In the last days, they will tremble in awe of the LORD and of his goodness.

+ + +

Hear the word of the LORD, O people of Israel!
  The LORD has brought charges against you, saying:
"There is no faithfulness, no kindness,
  no knowledge of God in your land.
You make vows and break them;
  you kill and steal and commit adultery.
There is violence everywhere—
  one murder after another.

That is why your land is in mourning,
   and everyone is wasting away.
Even the wild animals, the birds of the sky,
   and the fish of the sea are disappearing.

"Don't point your finger at someone else
   and try to pass the blame!
My complaint, you priests,
   is with you.
So you will stumble in broad daylight,
   and your false prophets will fall with you in the night.
   And I will destroy Israel, your mother.
My people are being destroyed
   because they don't know me.
Since you priests refuse to know me,
   I refuse to recognize you as my priests.
Since you have forgotten the laws of your God,
   I will forget to bless your children.
The more priests there are,
   the more they sin against me.
They have exchanged the glory of God
   for the shame of idols.

"When the people bring their sin offerings, the priests
    get fed.
   So the priests are glad when the people sin!
'And what the priests do, the people also do.'
   So now I will punish both priests and people
   for their wicked deeds.
They will eat and still be hungry.
   They will play the prostitute and gain nothing from it,
for they have deserted the LORD
   to worship other gods.
Wine has robbed my people
   of their understanding.

"They ask a piece of wood for advice!
   They think a stick can tell them the future!
Longing after idols
   has made them foolish.
They have played the prostitute,
   serving other gods and deserting their God.
They offer sacrifices to idols on the mountaintops.

They go up into the hills to burn incense
in the pleasant shade of oaks, poplars, and terebinth trees.

"That is why your daughters turn to prostitution,
and your daughters-in-law commit adultery.
But why should I punish them
for their prostitution and adultery?
For your men are doing the same thing,
sinning with whores and shrine prostitutes.
O foolish people! You refuse to understand,
so you will be destroyed.

"Though you, Israel, are a prostitute,
may Judah not be guilty of such things.
Do not join the false worship at Gilgal or Beth-aven,
and do not take oaths there in the LORD's name.
Israel is stubborn,
like a stubborn heifer.
So should the LORD feed her
like a lamb in a lush pasture?
Leave Israel alone,
because she is married to idolatry.
When the rulers of Israel finish their drinking,
off they go to find some prostitutes.
They love shame more than honor.
So a mighty wind will sweep them away.
Their sacrifices to idols will bring them shame.

"Hear this, you priests.
Pay attention, you leaders of Israel.
Listen, you members of the royal family.
Judgment has been handed down against you.
For you have led the people into a snare
by worshiping the idols at Mizpah and Tabor.
You have dug a deep pit to trap them at Acacia Grove.
But I will settle with you for what you have done.
I know what you are like, O Ephraim.
You cannot hide yourself from me, O Israel.
You have left me as a prostitute leaves her husband;
you are utterly defiled.
Your deeds won't let you return to your God.
You are a prostitute through and through,
and you do not know the LORD.

"The arrogance of Israel testifies against her;
　　Israel and Ephraim will stumble under their load of guilt.
　　Judah, too, will fall with them.
When they come with their flocks and herds
　　to offer sacrifices to the LORD,
they will not find him,
　　because he has withdrawn from them.
They have betrayed the honor of the LORD,
　　bearing children that are not his.
Now their false religion will devour them
　　along with their wealth.

"Sound the alarm in Gibeah!
　　Blow the trumpet in Ramah!
Raise the battle cry in Beth-aven!
　　Lead on into battle, O warriors of Benjamin!
One thing is certain, Israel:
　　On your day of punishment,
　　you will become a heap of rubble.

The leaders of Judah have become like thieves.
　　So I will pour my anger on them like a waterfall.

"The people of Israel will be crushed and broken by my
　　　judgment
　　because they are determined to worship idols.
I will destroy Israel as a moth consumes wool.
　　I will make Judah as weak as rotten wood.

"When Israel and Judah saw how sick they were,
　　Israel turned to Assyria—
to the great king there—
　　but he could neither help nor cure them.
I will be like a lion to Israel,
　　like a strong young lion to Judah.
　　I will tear them to pieces!
I will carry them off,
　　and no one will be left to rescue them.
Then I will return to my place
　　until they admit their guilt and turn to me.
For as soon as trouble comes,
　　they will earnestly search for me."

"Come, let us return to the LORD.
He has torn us to pieces;
  now he will heal us.
He has injured us;
  now he will bandage our wounds.
In just a short time he will restore us,
  so that we may live in his presence.
Oh, that we might know the LORD!
  Let us press on to know him.
He will respond to us as surely as the arrival of dawn
  or the coming of rains in early spring."

"O Israel and Judah,
  what should I do with you?" asks the LORD.
"For your love vanishes like the morning mist
  and disappears like dew in the sunlight.
I sent my prophets to cut you to pieces—
  to slaughter you with my words,
  with judgments as inescapable as light.
I want you to show love,
  not offer sacrifices.
I want you to know me
  more than I want burnt offerings.

"But like Adam, you broke my covenant
  and betrayed my trust.
Gilead is a city of sinners,
  tracked with footprints of blood.
Priests form bands of robbers,
  waiting in ambush for their victims.
They murder travelers along the road to Shechem
  and practice every kind of sin.
Yes, I have seen something horrible in Ephraim and Israel:
  My people are defiled by prostituting themselves with
    other gods!

"O Judah, a harvest of punishment is also waiting for you,
  though I wanted to restore the fortunes of my people.
I want to heal Israel, but its sins are too great.
  Samaria is filled with liars.
Thieves are on the inside
  and bandits on the outside!

Its people don't realize
    that I am watching them.
Their sinful deeds are all around them,
    and I see them all.

"The people entertain the king with their wickedness,
    and the princes laugh at their lies.
They are all adulterers,
    always aflame with lust.
They are like an oven that is kept hot
    while the baker is kneading the dough.
On royal holidays, the princes get drunk with wine,
    carousing with those who mock them.
Their hearts are like an oven
    blazing with intrigue.
Their plot smolders through the night,
    and in the morning it breaks out like a raging fire.
Burning like an oven,
    they consume their leaders.
They kill their kings one after another,
    and no one cries to me for help.

"The people of Israel mingle with godless foreigners,
    making themselves as worthless as a half-baked cake!
Worshiping foreign gods has sapped their strength,
    but they don't even know it.
Their hair is gray,
    but they don't realize they're old and weak.
Their arrogance testifies against them,
    yet they don't return to the LORD their God
    or even try to find him.

"The people of Israel have become like silly, witless doves,
    first calling to Egypt, then flying to Assyria for help.
But as they fly about,
    I will throw my net over them
and bring them down like a bird from the sky.
    I will punish them for all the evil they do.

"What sorrow awaits those who have deserted me!
    Let them die, for they have rebelled against me.
I wanted to redeem them,
    but they have told lies about me.

They do not cry out to me with sincere hearts.
    Instead, they sit on their couches and wail.
They cut themselves, begging foreign gods for grain and
        new wine,
    and they turn away from me.
I trained them and made them strong,
    yet now they plot evil against me.
They look everywhere except to the Most High.
    They are as useless as a crooked bow.
Their leaders will be killed by their enemies
    because of their insolence toward me.
Then the people of Egypt
    will laugh at them.

"Sound the alarm!
    The enemy descends like an eagle on the people of the LORD,
for they have broken my covenant
    and revolted against my law.
Now Israel pleads with me,
    'Help us, for you are our God!'
But it is too late.
The people of Israel have rejected what is good,
    and now their enemies will chase after them.
The people have appointed kings without my consent,
    and princes without my approval.
By making idols for themselves from their silver and gold,
    they have brought about their own destruction.

"O Samaria, I reject this calf—
    this idol you have made.
My fury burns against you.
    How long will you be incapable of innocence?
This calf you worship, O Israel,
    was crafted by your own hands!
It is not God!
    Therefore, it must be smashed to bits.

"They have planted the wind
    and will harvest the whirlwind.
The stalks of grain wither
    and produce nothing to eat.
And even if there is any grain,
    foreigners will eat it.

"The people of Israel have been swallowed up;
    they lie among the nations like an old discarded pot.
Like a wild donkey looking for a mate,
    they have gone up to Assyria.
The people of Israel have sold themselves—
    sold themselves to many lovers.
But though they have sold themselves to many allies,
    I will now gather them together for judgment.
Then they will writhe
    under the burden of the great king.

"Israel has built many altars to take away sin,
    but these very altars became places for sinning!
Even though I gave them all my laws,
    they act as if those laws don't apply to them.
The people love to offer sacrifices to me,
    feasting on the meat,
    but I do not accept their sacrifices.
I will hold my people accountable for their sins,
    and I will punish them.
    They will return to Egypt.
Israel has forgotten its Maker and built great palaces,
    and Judah has fortified its cities.
Therefore, I will send down fire on their cities
    and will burn up their fortresses."

O people of Israel,
    do not rejoice as other nations do.
For you have been unfaithful to your God,
    hiring yourselves out like prostitutes,
    worshiping other gods on every threshing floor.
So now your harvests will be too small to feed you.
    There will be no grapes for making new wine.
You may no longer stay here in the Lord's land.
    Instead, you will return to Egypt,
and in Assyria you will eat food
    that is ceremonially unclean.
There you will make no offerings of wine to the Lord.
    None of your sacrifices there will please him.
They will be unclean, like food touched by a person in mourning.
    All who present such sacrifices will be defiled.
They may eat this food themselves,

but they may not offer it to the LORD.
What then will you do on festival days?
    How will you observe the LORD's festivals?
Even if you escape destruction from Assyria,
    Egypt will conquer you, and Memphis will bury you.
Nettles will take over your treasures of silver;
    thistles will invade your ruined homes.

The time of Israel's punishment has come;
    the day of payment is here.
    Soon Israel will know this all too well.
Because of your great sin and hostility,
    you say, "The prophets are crazy
    and the inspired men are fools!"
The prophet is a watchman over Israel for my God,
    yet traps are laid for him wherever he goes.
    He faces hostility even in the house of God.
The things my people do are as depraved
    as what they did in Gibeah long ago.
God will not forget.
    He will surely punish them for their sins.

+

The LORD says, "O Israel, when I first found you,
    it was like finding fresh grapes in the desert.
When I saw your ancestors,
    it was like seeing the first ripe figs of the season.
But then they deserted me for Baal-peor,
    giving themselves to that shameful idol.
Soon they became vile,
    as vile as the god they worshiped.
The glory of Israel will fly away like a bird,
    for your children will not be born
or grow in the womb
    or even be conceived.
Even if you do have children who grow up,
    I will take them from you.
It will be a terrible day when I turn away
    and leave you alone.
I have watched Israel become as beautiful as Tyre.
    But now Israel will bring out her children for slaughter."

O LORD, what should I request for your people?
    I will ask for wombs that don't give birth
    and breasts that give no milk.

The LORD says, "All their wickedness began at Gilgal;
    there I began to hate them.
I will drive them from my land
    because of their evil actions.
I will love them no more
    because all their leaders are rebels.
The people of Israel are struck down.
    Their roots are dried up,
    and they will bear no more fruit.
And if they give birth,
    I will slaughter their beloved children."

My God will reject the people of Israel
    because they will not listen or obey.
They will be wanderers,
    homeless among the nations.

How prosperous Israel is—
    a luxuriant vine loaded with fruit.
But the richer the people get,
    the more pagan altars they build.
The more bountiful their harvests,
    the more beautiful their sacred pillars.
The hearts of the people are fickle;
    they are guilty and must be punished.
The LORD will break down their altars
    and smash their sacred pillars.
Then they will say, "We have no king
    because we didn't fear the LORD.
But even if we had a king,
    what could he do for us anyway?"
They spout empty words
    and make covenants they don't intend to keep.
So injustice springs up among them
    like poisonous weeds in a farmer's field.

The people of Samaria tremble in fear
    for their calf idol at Beth-aven,
    and they mourn for it.

Though its priests rejoice over it,
  its glory will be stripped away.
This idol will be carted away to Assyria,
  a gift to the great king there.
Ephraim will be ridiculed and Israel will be shamed,
  because its people have trusted in this idol.
Samaria and its king will be cut off;
  they will float away like driftwood on an ocean wave.
And the pagan shrines of Aven, the place of Israel's sin, will crumble.
  Thorns and thistles will grow up around their altars.
They will beg the mountains, "Bury us!"
  and plead with the hills, "Fall on us!"

The LORD says, "O Israel, ever since Gibeah,
  there has been only sin and more sin!
You have made no progress whatsoever.
  Was it not right that the wicked men of Gibeah were attacked?
Now whenever it fits my plan,
  I will attack you, too.
I will call out the armies of the nations
  to punish you for your multiplied sins.

"Israel is like a trained heifer treading out the grain—
  an easy job she loves.
  But I will put a heavy yoke on her tender neck.
I will force Judah to pull the plow
  and Israel to break up the hard ground.
I said, 'Plant the good seeds of righteousness,
  and you will harvest a crop of love.
Plow up the hard ground of your hearts,
  for now is the time to seek the LORD,
that he may come
  and shower righteousness upon you.'

"But you have cultivated wickedness
  and harvested a thriving crop of sins.
You have eaten the fruit of lies—
  trusting in your military might,
believing that great armies
  could make your nation safe.
Now the terrors of war
  will rise among your people.
All your fortifications will fall,

just as when Shalman destroyed Beth-arbel.
Even mothers and children
   were dashed to death there.
You will share that fate, Bethel,
   because of your great wickedness.
When the day of judgment dawns,
   the king of Israel will be completely
     destroyed.

"When Israel was a child, I loved him,
   and I called my son out of Egypt.
But the more I called to him,
   the farther he moved from me,
offering sacrifices to the images of Baal
   and burning incense to idols.
I myself taught Israel how to walk,
   leading him along by the hand.
But he doesn't know or even care
   that it was I who took care of him.
I led Israel along
   with my ropes of kindness and love.
I lifted the yoke from his neck,
   and I myself stooped to feed him.

"But since my people refuse to return to me,
   they will return to Egypt
   and will be forced to serve Assyria.
War will swirl through their cities;
   their enemies will crash through their gates.
They will destroy them,
   trapping them in their own evil plans.
For my people are determined to desert me.
They call me the Most High,
   but they don't truly honor me.

"Oh, how can I give you up, Israel?
   How can I let you go?
How can I destroy you like Admah
   or demolish you like Zeboiim?
My heart is torn within me,
   and my compassion overflows.
No, I will not unleash my fierce anger.
   I will not completely destroy Israel,

for I am God and not a mere mortal.
  I am the Holy One living among you,
  and I will not come to destroy.
For someday the people will follow me.
  I, the Lord, will roar like a lion.
And when I roar,
  my people will return trembling from the west.
Like a flock of birds, they will come from Egypt.
  Trembling like doves, they will return from Assyria.
And I will bring them home again,"
  says the Lord.

Israel surrounds me with lies and deceit,
  but Judah still obeys God
  and is faithful to the Holy One.
The people of Israel feed on the wind;
  they chase after the east wind all day long.
They pile up lies and violence;
  they are making an alliance with Assyria
  while sending olive oil to buy support from Egypt.

Now the Lord is bringing charges against Judah.
  He is about to punish Jacob for all his deceitful ways,
  and pay him back for all he has done.
Even in the womb,
  Jacob struggled with his brother;
when he became a man,
  he even fought with God.
Yes, he wrestled with the angel and won.
  He wept and pleaded for a blessing from him.
There at Bethel he met God face to face,
  and God spoke to him—
the Lord God of Heaven's Armies,
  the Lord is his name!
So now, come back to your God.
  Act with love and justice,
  and always depend on him.

But no, the people are like crafty merchants
  selling from dishonest scales—
  they love to cheat.
Israel boasts, "I am rich!
  I've made a fortune all by myself!

No one has caught me cheating!
    My record is spotless!"

"But I am the LORD your God,
    who rescued you from slavery in Egypt.
And I will make you live in tents again,
    as you do each year at the Festival of Shelters.
I sent my prophets to warn you
    with many visions and parables."

But the people of Gilead are worthless
    because of their idol worship.
And in Gilgal, too, they sacrifice bulls;
        their altars are lined up like the heaps of stone
        along the edges of a plowed field.
Jacob fled to the land of Aram,
    and there he earned a wife by tending sheep.
Then by a prophet
    the LORD brought Jacob's descendants out of Egypt;
and by that prophet
    they were protected.
But the people of Israel
    have bitterly provoked the LORD,
so their Lord will now sentence them to death
    in payment for their sins.

When the tribe of Ephraim spoke,
    the people shook with fear,
        for that tribe was important in Israel.
But the people of Ephraim sinned by worshiping Baal
    and thus sealed their destruction.
Now they continue to sin by making silver idols,
    images shaped skillfully with human hands.
"Sacrifice to these," they cry,
    "and kiss the calf idols!"
Therefore, they will disappear like the morning mist,
    like dew in the morning sun,
like chaff blown by the wind,
    like smoke from a chimney.

"I have been the LORD your God
    ever since I brought you out of Egypt.
You must acknowledge no God but me,
    for there is no other savior.

I took care of you in the wilderness,
in that dry and thirsty land.
But when you had eaten and were satisfied,
you became proud and forgot me.
So now I will attack you like a lion,
like a leopard that lurks along the road.
Like a bear whose cubs have been taken away,
I will tear out your heart.
I will devour you like a hungry lioness
and mangle you like a wild animal.

"You are about to be destroyed, O Israel—
yes, by me, your only helper.
Now where is your king?
Let him save you!
Where are all the leaders of the land,
the king and the officials you demanded of me?
In my anger I gave you kings,
and in my fury I took them away.

"Ephraim's guilt has been collected,
and his sin has been stored up for punishment.
Pain has come to the people
like the pain of childbirth,
but they are like a child
who resists being born.
The moment of birth has arrived,
but they stay in the womb!

"Should I ransom them from the grave?
Should I redeem them from death?
O death, bring on your terrors!
O grave, bring on your plagues!
For I will not take pity on them.
Ephraim was the most fruitful of all his brothers,
but the east wind—a blast from the LORD—
will arise in the desert.
All their flowing springs will run dry,
and all their wells will disappear.
Every precious thing they own
will be plundered and carried away.
The people of Samaria
must bear the consequences of their guilt
because they rebelled against their God.

They will be killed by an invading army,
  their little ones dashed to death against the ground,
  their pregnant women ripped open by swords."

Return, O Israel, to the LORD your God,
  for your sins have brought you down.
Bring your confessions, and return to the LORD.
  Say to him,
"Forgive all our sins and graciously receive us,
  so that we may offer you our praises.
Assyria cannot save us,
  nor can our warhorses.
Never again will we say to the idols we have made,
  'You are our gods.'
No, in you alone
  do the orphans find mercy."

The LORD says,
"Then I will heal you of your faithlessness;
  my love will know no bounds,
  for my anger will be gone forever.
I will be to Israel
  like a refreshing dew from heaven.
Israel will blossom like the lily;
  it will send roots deep into the soil
  like the cedars in Lebanon.
Its branches will spread out like beautiful olive trees,
  as fragrant as the cedars of Lebanon.
My people will again live under my shade.
  They will flourish like grain and blossom like grapevines.
  They will be as fragrant as the wines of Lebanon.

"O Israel, stay away from idols!
  I am the one who answers your prayers and cares for you.
I am like a tree that is always green;
  all your fruit comes from me."

✢ ✢ ✢

Let those who are wise understand these things.
  Let those with discernment listen carefully.
The paths of the LORD are true and right,
  and righteous people live by walking in them.
  But in those paths sinners stumble and fall.

THE NAME MICAH means "Who is like Yahweh?" So it shouldn't come as a surprise that Micah's short book of prophetic oracles focuses on God's unique character, especially in the context of his covenant relationship with his people.

Because God is holy and wants his people to be a light to the world, Micah warns his compatriots in Judah that God is about to judge and punish them for their unfaithfulness. Like the people of the northern kingdom of Israel, the people of Judah were exploiting the poor, violating the protections for the vulnerable built into the Law of Moses. "How can I tolerate your merchants who use dishonest scales and weights?" God asks through Micah. "The rich among you have become wealthy through extortion and violence." And so, Micah warns, "Mount Zion will be plowed like an open field; Jerusalem will be reduced to ruins!"

But Micah's messages do not end with judgment. The LORD of the covenant is above all else the God who offers forgiveness, compassion, and loyalty to his people. Micah emphatically affirms that God will keep his promises to heal and restore. Once again in the prophets, hope gets the final word.

Micah's collection of oracles is organized into three groups—not chronologically but thematically. Each group begins with prophecies of ruin before presenting hopeful promises of restoration. An example of the message of judgment can be found at the beginning of the third set of oracles. Here Micah uses the prophetic technique of the "covenant lawsuit," as Hosea did, in which God brings the people to trial for breaking their covenant with him: "Listen to the LORD's complaint!" Micah says. "He has a case against his people."

God reviews earlier biblical stories to show that he has consistently protected the people and provided for them. In response, Micah wonders aloud what compensation they can possibly offer back to God. The people clearly believe that all they need to do is offer sacrifices, and they complain about even having to do that. But what the LORD really requires is this: "to do what is right, to love mercy, and to walk humbly with your God."

Disaster ultimately does arrive during the reign of Hezekiah, as the Assyrians invade Judah after conquering and destroying the northern kingdom of Israel. In response to the Assyrian invasion, Micah declares about King David's birthplace, "You, O Bethlehem Ephrathah, are only a small village among all the people of Judah. Yet a ruler of Israel, whose origins are in the distant past, will come from you on my behalf." The immediate reference is to Hezekiah, a godly king in the line of David whose trust in the LORD would turn back the Assyrian invasion in Judah. But the author of the Gospel of Matthew looks back to this passage and sees a reference to Jesus the Messiah, who was also born in Bethlehem, the City of David.

The prophets often speak to both the present and the future in such passages, creating a longing for God's ultimate redemption and the restoration of all things. Micah speaks of a hope that looks beyond the current generation and foresees that after the people of Judah are exiled to Babylon, they will be brought back in a great deliverance not unlike the Exodus. God promises, "I will do mighty miracles for you, like those I did when I rescued you from slavery in Egypt."

Perhaps the most marvelous oracle in the whole book is placed right at its center, in the middle of the second group of oracles, just as the theme changes from ruin to restoration: "In the last days, the mountain of the LORD's house will be the highest of all," Micah envisions, "and people from all over the world will stream there to worship. People from many nations will come and say, 'Come, let us go up to the mountain of the LORD, to the house of Jacob's God. There he will teach us his ways, and we will walk in his paths.'"

Israel's story will determine the world's story. The vision of God's salvation spreading over the whole earth is a bright light that shines forth from the whole prophetic collection, pointing to the glorious culmination of the Bible's story in Jesus the Messiah.

MICAH

---✢---

The LORD gave this message to Micah of Moresheth during the years when
Jotham, Ahaz, and Hezekiah were kings of Judah. The visions he saw concerned both Samaria and Jerusalem.

✢ ✢ ✢

Attention! Let all the people of the world listen!
    Let the earth and everything in it hear.
The Sovereign LORD is making accusations against you;
    the Lord speaks from his holy Temple.
Look! The LORD is coming!
    He leaves his throne in heaven
    and tramples the heights of the earth.
The mountains melt beneath his feet
    and flow into the valleys
like wax in a fire,
    like water pouring down a hill.
And why is this happening?
    Because of the rebellion of Israel—
    yes, the sins of the whole nation.
Who is to blame for Israel's rebellion?
    Samaria, its capital city!
Where is the center of idolatry in Judah?
    In Jerusalem, its capital!

"So I, the LORD, will make the city of Samaria
    a heap of ruins.
Her streets will be plowed up
    for planting vineyards.
I will roll the stones of her walls into the valley below,
    exposing her foundations.
All her carved images will be smashed.
    All her sacred treasures will be burned.

These things were bought with the money
   earned by her prostitution,
and they will now be carried away
   to pay prostitutes elsewhere."

Therefore, I will mourn and lament.
   I will walk around barefoot and naked.
I will howl like a jackal
   and moan like an owl.
For my people's wound
   is too deep to heal.
It has reached into Judah,
   even to the gates of Jerusalem.

Don't tell our enemies in Gath;
   don't weep at all.
You people in Beth-leaphrah,
   roll in the dust to show your despair.
You people in Shaphir,
   go as captives into exile—naked and ashamed.
The people of Zaanan
   dare not come outside their walls.
The people of Beth-ezel mourn,
   for their house has no support.
The people of Maroth anxiously wait for relief,
   but only bitterness awaits them
as the LORD's judgment reaches
   even to the gates of Jerusalem.

Harness your chariot horses and flee,
   you people of Lachish.
You were the first city in Judah
   to follow Israel in her rebellion,
   and you led Jerusalem into sin.
Send farewell gifts to Moresheth-gath;
   there is no hope of saving it.
The town of Aczib
   has deceived the kings of Israel.
O people of Mareshah,
   I will bring a conqueror to capture your town.
And the leaders of Israel
   will go to Adullam.

Oh, people of Judah, shave your heads in sorrow,
    for the children you love will be snatched away.
Make yourselves as bald as a vulture,
    for your little ones will be exiled to distant lands.

What sorrow awaits you who lie awake at night,
    thinking up evil plans.
You rise at dawn and hurry to carry them out,
    simply because you have the power to do so.
When you want a piece of land,
    you find a way to seize it.
When you want someone's house,
    you take it by fraud and violence.
You cheat a man of his property,
    stealing his family's inheritance.

But this is what the LORD says:
"I will reward your evil with evil;
    you won't be able to pull your neck out of the
        noose.
You will no longer walk around proudly,
    for it will be a terrible time."

In that day your enemies will make fun of you
    by singing this song of despair about you:
    "We are finished,
        completely ruined!
    God has confiscated our land,
        taking it from us.
    He has given our fields
        to those who betrayed us."
Others will set your boundaries then,
    and the LORD's people will have no say
    in how the land is divided.

"Don't say such things,"
    the people respond.
"Don't prophesy like that.
    Such disasters will never come our way!"

Should you talk that way, O family of Israel?
    Will the LORD's Spirit have patience with such
        behavior?

If you would do what is right,
    you would find my words comforting.
Yet to this very hour
    my people rise against me like an enemy!
You steal the shirts right off the backs
    of those who trusted you,
making them as ragged as men
    returning from battle.
You have evicted women from their pleasant homes
    and forever stripped their children of all that God
        would give them.
Up! Begone!
    This is no longer your land and home,
for you have filled it with sin
    and ruined it completely.

Suppose a prophet full of lies would say to you,
    "I'll preach to you the joys of wine and alcohol!"
That's just the kind of prophet you would like!

+

"Someday, O Israel, I will gather you;
    I will gather the remnant who are left.
I will bring you together again like sheep in
      a pen,
    like a flock in its pasture.
Yes, your land will again
    be filled with noisy crowds!
Your leader will break out
    and lead you out of exile,
out through the gates of the enemy cities,
    back to your own land.
Your king will lead you;
    the LORD himself will guide you."

+ + +

I said, "Listen, you leaders of Israel!
    You are supposed to know right from wrong,
but you are the very ones
    who hate good and love evil.

You skin my people alive
    and tear the flesh from their bones.
Yes, you eat my people's flesh,
    strip off their skin,
    and break their bones.
You chop them up
    like meat for the cooking pot.
Then you beg the LORD for help in times of trouble!
    Do you really expect him to answer?
After all the evil you have done,
    he won't even look at you!"

This is what the LORD says:
    "You false prophets are leading my people astray!
You promise peace for those who give you food,
    but you declare war on those who refuse to feed you.
Now the night will close around you,
    cutting off all your visions.
Darkness will cover you,
    putting an end to your predictions.
The sun will set for you prophets,
    and your day will come to an end.
Then you seers will be put to shame,
    and you fortune-tellers will be disgraced.
And you will cover your faces
    because there is no answer from God."

But as for me, I am filled with power—
    with the Spirit of the LORD.
I am filled with justice and strength
    to boldly declare Israel's sin and rebellion.

Listen to me, you leaders of Israel!
    You hate justice and twist all that is right.
You are building Jerusalem
    on a foundation of murder and corruption.
You rulers make decisions based on bribes;
    you priests teach God's laws only for a price;
you prophets won't prophesy unless you are paid.
    Yet all of you claim to depend on the LORD.
"No harm can come to us," you say,
    "for the LORD is here among us."

Because of you, Mount Zion will be plowed like an open field;
    Jerusalem will be reduced to ruins!
A thicket will grow on the heights
    where the Temple now stands.

+

In the last days, the mountain of the LORD's house
    will be the highest of all—
    the most important place on earth.
It will be raised above the other hills,
    and people from all over the world will stream there
        to worship.
People from many nations will come and say,
"Come, let us go up to the mountain of the LORD,
    to the house of Jacob's God.
There he will teach us his ways,
    and we will walk in his paths."
For the LORD's teaching will go out from Zion;
    his word will go out from Jerusalem.
The LORD will mediate between peoples
    and will settle disputes between strong nations far away.
They will hammer their swords into plowshares
    and their spears into pruning hooks.
Nation will no longer fight against nation,
    nor train for war anymore.
Everyone will live in peace and prosperity,
    enjoying their own grapevines and fig trees,
    for there will be nothing to fear.
The LORD of Heaven's Armies
    has made this promise!
Though the nations around us follow their idols,
    we will follow the LORD our God forever and ever.

"In that coming day," says the LORD,
"I will gather together those who are lame,
    those who have been exiles,
    and those whom I have filled with grief.
Those who are weak will survive as a remnant;
    those who were exiles will become a strong nation.
Then I, the LORD, will rule from Jerusalem
    as their king forever."

As for you, Jerusalem,
    the citadel of God's people,
your royal might and power
    will come back to you again.
The kingship will be restored
    to my precious Jerusalem.

But why are you now screaming in terror?
    Have you no king to lead you?
Have your wise people all died?
    Pain has gripped you like a woman in childbirth.
Writhe and groan like a woman in labor,
    you people of Jerusalem,
for now you must leave this city
    to live in the open country.
You will soon be sent in exile
    to distant Babylon.
But the LORD will rescue you there;
    he will redeem you from the grip of your enemies.

Now many nations have gathered against you.
    "Let her be desecrated," they say.
    "Let us see the destruction of Jerusalem."
But they do not know the LORD's thoughts
    or understand his plan.
These nations don't know
    that he is gathering them together
to be beaten and trampled
    like sheaves of grain on a threshing floor.
"Rise up and crush the nations, O Jerusalem!"
    says the LORD.
"For I will give you iron horns and bronze hooves,
    so you can trample many nations to pieces.
You will present their stolen riches to the LORD,
    their wealth to the Lord of all the earth."

Mobilize! Marshal your troops!
    The enemy is laying siege to Jerusalem.
They will strike Israel's leader
    in the face with a rod.

But you, O Bethlehem Ephrathah,
    are only a small village among all the people of Judah.

Yet a ruler of Israel,
    whose origins are in the distant past,
    will come from you on my behalf.
The people of Israel will be abandoned to their enemies
    until the woman in labor gives birth.
Then at last his fellow countrymen
    will return from exile to their own land.
And he will stand to lead his flock with the LORD's strength,
    in the majesty of the name of the LORD his God.
Then his people will live there undisturbed,
    for he will be highly honored around the world.
    And he will be the source of peace.

When the Assyrians invade our land
    and break through our defenses,
we will appoint seven rulers to watch over us,
    eight princes to lead us.
They will rule Assyria with drawn swords
    and enter the gates of the land of Nimrod.
He will rescue us from the Assyrians
    when they pour over the borders to invade our land.

Then the remnant left in Israel
    will take their place among the nations.
They will be like dew sent by the LORD
    or like rain falling on the grass,
which no one can hold back
    and no one can restrain.
The remnant left in Israel
    will take their place among the nations.
They will be like a lion among the animals of the forest,
    like a strong young lion among flocks of sheep and goats,
pouncing and tearing as they go
    with no rescuer in sight.
The people of Israel will stand up to their foes,
    and all their enemies will be wiped out.

"In that day," says the LORD,
"I will slaughter your horses
    and destroy your chariots.
I will tear down your walls
    and demolish your defenses.

I will put an end to all witchcraft,
  and there will be no more fortune-tellers.
I will destroy all your idols and sacred pillars,
  so you will never again worship the work of your own hands.
I will abolish your idol shrines with their Asherah poles
  and destroy your pagan cities.
I will pour out my vengeance
  on all the nations that refuse to obey me."

✛ ✛ ✛

Listen to what the LORD is saying:

"Stand up and state your case against me.
  Let the mountains and hills be called to witness your complaints.
And now, O mountains,
  listen to the LORD's complaint!
He has a case against his people.
  He will bring charges against Israel.

"O my people, what have I done to you?
  What have I done to make you tired of me?
  Answer me!
For I brought you out of Egypt
  and redeemed you from slavery.
  I sent Moses, Aaron, and Miriam to help you.
Don't you remember, my people,
  how King Balak of Moab tried to have you cursed
  and how Balaam son of Beor blessed you instead?
And remember your journey from Acacia Grove to Gilgal,
  when I, the LORD, did everything I could
  to teach you about my faithfulness."

What can we bring to the LORD?
  Should we bring him burnt offerings?
Should we bow before God Most High
  with offerings of yearling calves?
Should we offer him thousands of rams
  and ten thousand rivers of olive oil?
Should we sacrifice our firstborn children
  to pay for our sins?

No, O people, the LORD has told you what is good,
  and this is what he requires of you:

to do what is right, to love mercy,
    and to walk humbly with your God.

Fear the LORD if you are wise!
    His voice calls to everyone in Jerusalem:
"The armies of destruction are coming;
    the LORD is sending them.
What shall I say about the homes of the wicked
    filled with treasures gained by cheating?
What about the disgusting practice
    of measuring out grain with dishonest measures?
How can I tolerate your merchants
    who use dishonest scales and weights?
The rich among you have become wealthy
    through extortion and violence.
Your citizens are so used to lying
    that their tongues can no longer tell the truth.

"Therefore, I will wound you!
    I will bring you to ruin for all your sins.
You will eat but never have enough.
    Your hunger pangs and emptiness will remain.
And though you try to save your money,
    it will come to nothing in the end.
You will save a little,
    but I will give it to those who conquer you.
You will plant crops
    but not harvest them.
You will press your olives
    but not get enough oil to anoint yourselves.
You will trample the grapes
    but get no juice to make your wine.
You keep only the laws of evil King Omri;
    you follow only the example of wicked King Ahab!
Therefore, I will make an example of you,
    bringing you to complete ruin.
You will be treated with contempt,
    mocked by all who see you."

How miserable I am!
I feel like the fruit picker after the harvest
    who can find nothing to eat.

Not a cluster of grapes or a single early fig
    can be found to satisfy my hunger.
The godly people have all disappeared;
    not one honest person is left on the earth.
They are all murderers,
    setting traps even for their own brothers.
Both their hands are equally skilled at doing evil!
    Officials and judges alike demand bribes.
The people with influence get what they want,
    and together they scheme to twist justice.
Even the best of them is like a brier;
    the most honest is as dangerous as a hedge of thorns.
But your judgment day is coming swiftly now.
    Your time of punishment is here, a time of confusion.
Don't trust anyone—
    not your best friend or even your wife!
For the son despises his father.
    The daughter defies her mother.
The daughter-in-law defies her mother-in-law.
    Your enemies are right in your own household!

+

As for me, I look to the LORD for help.
    I wait confidently for God to save me,
    and my God will certainly hear me.
Do not gloat over me, my enemies!
    For though I fall, I will rise again.
Though I sit in darkness,
    the LORD will be my light.
I will be patient as the LORD punishes me,
    for I have sinned against him.
But after that, he will take up my case
    and give me justice for all I have suffered from my enemies.
The LORD will bring me into the light,
    and I will see his righteousness.
Then my enemies will see that the LORD is on my side.
    They will be ashamed that they taunted me, saying,
"So where is the LORD—
    that God of yours?"
With my own eyes I will see their downfall;
    they will be trampled like mud in the streets.

In that day, Israel, your cities will be rebuilt,
    and your borders will be extended.
People from many lands will come and honor you—
    from Assyria all the way to the towns of Egypt,
from Egypt all the way to the Euphrates River,
    and from distant seas and mountains.
But the land will become empty and desolate
    because of the wickedness of those who live there.

O Lord, protect your people with your shepherd's staff;
    lead your flock, your special possession.
Though they live alone in a thicket
    on the heights of Mount Carmel,
let them graze in the fertile pastures of Bashan and Gilead
    as they did long ago.

"Yes," says the Lord,
    "I will do mighty miracles for you,
like those I did when I rescued you
    from slavery in Egypt."

All the nations of the world will stand amazed
    at what the Lord will do for you.
They will be embarrassed
    at their feeble power.
They will cover their mouths in silent awe,
    deaf to everything around them.
Like snakes crawling from their holes,
    they will come out to meet the Lord our God.
They will fear him greatly,
    trembling in terror at his presence.

Where is another God like you,
    who pardons the guilt of the remnant,
    overlooking the sins of his special people?
You will not stay angry with your people forever,
    because you delight in showing unfailing love.
Once again you will have compassion on us.
    You will trample our sins under your feet
    and throw them into the depths of the ocean!
You will show us your faithfulness and unfailing love
    as you promised to our ancestors Abraham and Jacob long ago.

IMMERSED IN ISAIAH

THE PROPHET ISAIAH was a contemporary of Micah, but his book contains twelve times as much material. It addresses many other nations besides Judah—the entire creation, in fact—and also a variety of significant periods in Israel's covenant history, even beyond the prophet's lifetime.

While Isaiah is a long book to read, it is foundational for seeing how God's relationship with humanity moves forward from the earlier covenants to the new covenant introduced by Jesus. New Testament writers quote from Isaiah more often than any other book except Psalms.

The collection of Isaiah's oracles has eight major parts:

The first part (pp. 57-78) is set during a significant crisis in Judah's history. Israel and Syria (also known as Aram) have invaded Judah, and they intend to replace King Ahaz with a puppet king of their own. The LORD uses this occasion to file a covenant lawsuit against the people of Judah for the same injustice and insincere worship that doomed the northern kingdom of Israel. In the midst of the disaster, Isaiah foresees the birth of a godly king who will establish justice and bring peace to the land. While these oracles initially envision King Hezekiah, they also point to the long-term story of the coming Messiah.

The oracles in the second part of the book (pp. 78-95) address other nations and speak to future developments: the coming campaigns of the Assyrians, the rise of Babylon, the conquest of Judah, and the exile and return of God's people.

In both the third (pp. 95-101) and fifth (pp. 114-116) parts, the perspective expands beyond individual nations. And in these sections, as is so often done in the prophets, Isaiah first describes ruin but then turns to restoration. This vision ultimately merges with the anticipated return of the Judean exiles and reveals the connection between the rescue of God's people and the renewal of God's good world:

Even the wilderness and desert will be glad in those days.
The wasteland will rejoice and blossom with spring crocuses.
Yes, there will be an abundance of flowers
and singing and joy! . . .

Those who have been ransomed by the LORD will return.
They will enter Jerusalem singing,
crowned with everlasting joy.

In between these two sections, the fourth part of the book (pp. 101-113) presents six oracles that announce "what sorrow awaits" Israel and Judah. These oracles come from the twenty-year period between Assyria's conquest of Israel and its invasion of Judah.

The narratives in the sixth part of the book (pp. 116-123) describe how God brought miraculous deliverance from the Assyrians when King Hezekiah trusted in him. However, they also foreshadow the eventual Babylonian conquest and exile.

The seventh part (pp. 123-155) describes a time in Babylon, over 150 years later. The Persian ruler Cyrus is about to conquer the Babylonians, and his policy in other lands is to allow exiled populations to return home. These long oracles are some of the most beautiful and encouraging in all of Scripture, assuring God's people that his promise to end their exile will surely be accomplished as intended. These oracles also introduce a figure referred to as God's "servant." This servant has a complex identity, likely referring initially to God's people through whom God will continue to work to bring about his purposes. Ultimately, these servant songs point to the future Messiah who will bring deliverance from the deepest exile of all—that of sin and death.

The final part of the book (pp. 155-175) speaks to an even later period, after the return from exile. Once again the people of Judah need to be warned against injustice, oppression, and idolatrous worship. But these oracles also look beyond the return from exile to a restoration that is cosmic in scope. God's glory will radiate from Jerusalem in a fresh and powerful way, and Jerusalem will be a place of great joy in a "new heavens and new earth."

And so the book of Isaiah, which begins at a time when God's covenant with David was gravely threatened, traces the grand sweep of redemptive history and points forward to the climactic covenant brought by David's greatest descendant and to the inauguration of the new creation.

ISAIAH

✛

These are the visions that Isaiah son of Amoz saw concerning Judah and Jerusalem. He saw these visions during the years when Uzziah, Jotham, Ahaz, and Hezekiah were kings of Judah.

✛ ✛ ✛

Listen, O heavens! Pay attention, earth!
　　This is what the LORD says:
"The children I raised and cared for
　　have rebelled against me.
Even an ox knows its owner,
　　and a donkey recognizes its master's care—
but Israel doesn't know its master.
　　My people don't recognize my care for them."

Oh, what a sinful nation they are—
　　loaded down with a burden of guilt.
They are evil people,
　　corrupt children who have rejected the LORD.
They have despised the Holy One of Israel
　　and turned their backs on him.

Why do you continue to invite punishment?
　　Must you rebel forever?
Your head is injured,
　　and your heart is sick.
You are battered from head to foot—
　　covered with bruises, welts, and infected wounds—
　　without any soothing ointments or bandages.
Your country lies in ruins,
　　and your towns are burned.
Foreigners plunder your fields before your eyes
　　and destroy everything they see.

Beautiful Jerusalem stands abandoned
   like a watchman's shelter in a vineyard,
like a lean-to in a cucumber field after the harvest,
   like a helpless city under siege.
If the LORD of Heaven's Armies
   had not spared a few of us,
we would have been wiped out like Sodom,
   destroyed like Gomorrah.

Listen to the LORD, you leaders of "Sodom."
   Listen to the law of our God, people of "Gomorrah."
"What makes you think I want all your sacrifices?"
   says the LORD.
"I am sick of your burnt offerings of rams
   and the fat of fattened cattle.
I get no pleasure from the blood
   of bulls and lambs and goats.
When you come to worship me,
   who asked you to parade through my courts with all your
      ceremony?
Stop bringing me your meaningless gifts;
   the incense of your offerings disgusts me!
As for your celebrations of the new moon and the Sabbath
   and your special days for fasting—
they are all sinful and false.
   I want no more of your pious meetings.
I hate your new moon celebrations and your annual festivals.
   They are a burden to me. I cannot stand them!
When you lift up your hands in prayer, I will not look.
   Though you offer many prayers, I will not listen,
      for your hands are covered with the blood of innocent victims.
Wash yourselves and be clean!
   Get your sins out of my sight.
   Give up your evil ways.
Learn to do good.
   Seek justice.
Help the oppressed.
   Defend the cause of orphans.
   Fight for the rights of widows.

"Come now, let's settle this,"
   says the LORD.

"Though your sins are like scarlet,
    I will make them as white as snow.
Though they are red like crimson,
    I will make them as white as wool.
If you will only obey me,
    you will have plenty to eat.
But if you turn away and refuse to listen,
    you will be devoured by the sword of your
        enemies.
    I, the LORD, have spoken!"

See how Jerusalem, once so faithful,
    has become a prostitute.
Once the home of justice and righteousness,
    she is now filled with murderers.
Once like pure silver,
    you have become like worthless slag.
Once so pure,
    you are now like watered-down wine.
Your leaders are rebels,
    the companions of thieves.
All of them love bribes
    and demand payoffs,
but they refuse to defend the cause of orphans
    or fight for the rights of widows.

Therefore, the Lord, the LORD of Heaven's Armies,
    the Mighty One of Israel, says,
"I will take revenge on my enemies
    and pay back my foes!
I will raise my fist against you.
    I will melt you down and skim off your slag.
    I will remove all your impurities.
Then I will give you good judges again
    and wise counselors like you used to have.
Then Jerusalem will again be called the Home of Justice
    and the Faithful City."

Zion will be restored by justice;
    those who repent will be revived by righteousness.
But rebels and sinners will be completely destroyed,
    and those who desert the LORD will be consumed.

You will be ashamed of your idol worship
 in groves of sacred oaks.
You will blush because you worshiped
 in gardens dedicated to idols.
You will be like a great tree with withered leaves,
 like a garden without water.
The strongest among you will disappear like straw;
 their evil deeds will be the spark that sets it on fire.
They and their evil works will burn up together,
 and no one will be able to put out the fire.

This is a vision that Isaiah son of Amoz saw concerning Judah and Jerusalem:

In the last days, the mountain of the LORD's house
 will be the highest of all—
 the most important place on earth.
It will be raised above the other hills,
 and people from all over the world will stream there to worship.
People from many nations will come and say,
"Come, let us go up to the mountain of the LORD,
 to the house of Jacob's God.
There he will teach us his ways,
 and we will walk in his paths."
For the LORD's teaching will go out from Zion;
 his word will go out from Jerusalem.
The LORD will mediate between nations
 and will settle international disputes.
They will hammer their swords into plowshares
 and their spears into pruning hooks.
Nation will no longer fight against nation,
 nor train for war anymore.
Come, descendants of Jacob,
 let us walk in the light of the LORD!

For the LORD has rejected his people,
 the descendants of Jacob,
because they have filled their land with practices from the East
 and with sorcerers, as the Philistines do.
 They have made alliances with pagans.
Israel is full of silver and gold;
 there is no end to its treasures.

Their land is full of warhorses;
  there is no end to its chariots.
Their land is full of idols;
  the people worship things they have made
  with their own hands.
So now they will be humbled,
  and all will be brought low—
  do not forgive them.
Crawl into caves in the rocks.
  Hide in the dust
from the terror of the LORD
  and the glory of his majesty.
Human pride will be brought down,
  and human arrogance will be humbled.
Only the LORD will be exalted
  on that day of judgment.

For the LORD of Heaven's Armies
  has a day of reckoning.
He will punish the proud and mighty
  and bring down everything that is exalted.
He will cut down the tall cedars of Lebanon
  and all the mighty oaks of Bashan.
He will level all the high mountains
  and all the lofty hills.
He will break down every high tower
  and every fortified wall.
He will destroy all the great trading ships
  and every magnificent vessel.
Human pride will be humbled,
  and human arrogance will be brought down.
Only the LORD will be exalted
  on that day of judgment.

Idols will completely disappear.
When the LORD rises to shake the earth,
  his enemies will crawl into holes in the ground.
They will hide in caves in the rocks
  from the terror of the LORD
  and the glory of his majesty.
On that day of judgment they will abandon the gold and silver idols
  they made for themselves to worship.

They will leave their gods to the rodents and bats,
   while they crawl away into caverns
   and hide among the jagged rocks in the cliffs.
They will try to escape the terror of the LORD
   and the glory of his majesty
   as he rises to shake the earth.
Don't put your trust in mere humans.
   They are as frail as breath.
   What good are they?

The Lord, the LORD of Heaven's Armies,
   will take away from Jerusalem and Judah
everything they depend on:
   every bit of bread
   and every drop of water,
all their heroes and soldiers,
   judges and prophets,
   fortune-tellers and elders,
army officers and high officials,
   advisers, skilled sorcerers, and astrologers.

I will make boys their leaders,
   and toddlers their rulers.
People will oppress each other—
   man against man,
   neighbor against neighbor.
Young people will insult their elders,
   and vulgar people will sneer at the honorable.

In those days a man will say to his brother,
"Since you have a coat, you be our leader!
   Take charge of this heap of ruins!"
But he will reply,
   "No! I can't help.
I don't have any extra food or clothes.
   Don't put me in charge!"

For Jerusalem will stumble,
   and Judah will fall,
because they speak out against the LORD and refuse to obey him.
   They provoke him to his face.
The very look on their faces gives them away.
   They display their sin like the people of Sodom

and don't even try to hide it.
They are doomed!
 They have brought destruction upon themselves.

Tell the godly that all will be well for them.
 They will enjoy the rich reward they have earned!
But the wicked are doomed,
 for they will get exactly what they deserve.

Childish leaders oppress my people,
 and women rule over them.
O my people, your leaders mislead you;
 they send you down the wrong road.

The LORD takes his place in court
 and presents his case against his people.
The LORD comes forward to pronounce judgment
 on the elders and rulers of his people:
"You have ruined Israel, my vineyard.
 Your houses are filled with things stolen from the poor.
How dare you crush my people,
 grinding the faces of the poor into the dust?"
 demands the Lord, the LORD of Heaven's Armies.

The LORD says, "Beautiful Zion is haughty:
craning her elegant neck,
 flirting with her eyes,
walking with dainty steps,
 tinkling her ankle bracelets.
So the Lord will send scabs on her head;
 the LORD will make beautiful Zion bald."

On that day of judgment
 the Lord will strip away everything that makes her
  beautiful:
ornaments, headbands, crescent necklaces,
 earrings, bracelets, and veils;
scarves, ankle bracelets, sashes,
 perfumes, and charms;
rings, jewels,
 party clothes, gowns, capes, and purses;
mirrors, fine linen garments,
 head ornaments, and shawls.

Instead of smelling of sweet perfume, she will stink.
    She will wear a rope for a sash,
    and her elegant hair will fall out.
She will wear rough burlap instead of rich robes.
    Shame will replace her beauty.
The men of the city will be killed with the sword,
    and her warriors will die in battle.
The gates of Zion will weep and mourn.
    The city will be like a ravaged woman,
    huddled on the ground.

In that day so few men will be left that seven women will fight for each man, saying, "Let us all marry you! We will provide our own food and clothing. Only let us take your name so we won't be mocked as old maids."

But in that day, the branch of the LORD
    will be beautiful and glorious;
the fruit of the land will be the pride and glory
    of all who survive in Israel.
All who remain in Zion
    will be a holy people—
those who survive the destruction of Jerusalem
    and are recorded among the living.
The Lord will wash the filth from beautiful Zion
    and cleanse Jerusalem of its bloodstains
    with the hot breath of fiery judgment.
Then the LORD will provide shade for Mount Zion
    and all who assemble there.
He will provide a canopy of cloud during the day
    and smoke and flaming fire at night,
    covering the glorious land.
It will be a shelter from daytime heat
    and a hiding place from storms and rain.

Now I will sing for the one I love
    a song about his vineyard:
My beloved had a vineyard
    on a rich and fertile hill.
He plowed the land, cleared its stones,
    and planted it with the best vines.
In the middle he built a watchtower
    and carved a winepress in the nearby rocks.

Then he waited for a harvest of sweet grapes,
  but the grapes that grew were bitter.

Now, you people of Jerusalem and Judah,
  you judge between me and my vineyard.
What more could I have done for my vineyard
  that I have not already done?
When I expected sweet grapes,
  why did my vineyard give me bitter grapes?

Now let me tell you
  what I will do to my vineyard:
I will tear down its hedges
  and let it be destroyed.
I will break down its walls
  and let the animals trample it.
I will make it a wild place
  where the vines are not pruned and the ground
    is not hoed,
  a place overgrown with briers and thorns.
I will command the clouds
  to drop no rain on it.

The nation of Israel is the vineyard of the LORD of Heaven's Armies.
  The people of Judah are his pleasant garden.
He expected a crop of justice,
  but instead he found oppression.
He expected to find righteousness,
  but instead he heard cries of violence.

What sorrow for you who buy up house after house and field after
    field,
  until everyone is evicted and you live alone in the land.
But I have heard the LORD of Heaven's Armies
  swear a solemn oath:
"Many houses will stand deserted;
  even beautiful mansions will be empty.
Ten acres of vineyard will not produce even six gallons of wine.
  Ten baskets of seed will yield only one basket of grain."

What sorrow for those who get up early in the morning
  looking for a drink of alcohol
and spend long evenings drinking wine
  to make themselves flaming drunk.

They furnish wine and lovely music at their grand parties—
    lyre and harp, tambourine and flute—
but they never think about the LORD
    or notice what he is doing.

So my people will go into exile far away
    because they do not know me.
Those who are great and honored will starve,
    and the common people will die of thirst.
The grave is licking its lips in anticipation,
    opening its mouth wide.
The great and the lowly
    and all the drunken mob will be swallowed up.
Humanity will be destroyed, and people brought down;
    even the arrogant will lower their eyes in humiliation.
But the LORD of Heaven's Armies will be exalted by his justice.
    The holiness of God will be displayed by his righteousness.
In that day lambs will find good pastures,
    and fattened sheep and young goats will feed among the ruins.

What sorrow for those who drag their sins behind them
    with ropes made of lies,
    who drag wickedness behind them like a cart!
They even mock God and say,
    "Hurry up and do something!
    We want to see what you can do.
Let the Holy One of Israel carry out his plan,
    for we want to know what it is."

What sorrow for those who say
    that evil is good and good is evil,
that dark is light and light is dark,
    that bitter is sweet and sweet is bitter.
What sorrow for those who are wise in their own eyes
    and think themselves so clever.
What sorrow for those who are heroes at drinking wine
    and boast about all the alcohol they can hold.
They take bribes to let the wicked go free,
    and they punish the innocent.

Therefore, just as fire licks up stubble
    and dry grass shrivels in the flame,
so their roots will rot
    and their flowers wither.

For they have rejected the law of the LORD of Heaven's Armies;
　　they have despised the word of the Holy One of Israel.
That is why the LORD's anger burns against his people,
　　and why he has raised his fist to crush them.
The mountains tremble,
　　and the corpses of his people litter the streets like garbage.
But even then the LORD's anger is not satisfied.
　　His fist is still poised to strike!

He will send a signal to distant nations far away
　　and whistle to those at the ends of the earth.
　　They will come racing toward Jerusalem.
They will not get tired or stumble.
　　They will not stop for rest or sleep.
Not a belt will be loose,
　　not a sandal strap broken.
Their arrows will be sharp
　　and their bows ready for battle.
Sparks will fly from their horses' hooves,
　　and the wheels of their chariots will spin like a whirlwind.
They will roar like lions,
　　like the strongest of lions.
Growling, they will pounce on their victims and carry them off,
　　and no one will be there to rescue them.
They will roar over their victims on that day of destruction
　　like the roaring of the sea.
If someone looks across the land,
　　only darkness and distress will be seen;
　　even the light will be darkened by clouds.

+

It was in the year King Uzziah died that I saw the Lord. He was sitting on a lofty throne, and the train of his robe filled the Temple. Attending him were mighty seraphim, each having six wings. With two wings they covered their faces, with two they covered their feet, and with two they flew. They were calling out to each other,

　　"Holy, holy, holy is the LORD of Heaven's Armies!
　　　The whole earth is filled with his glory!"

Their voices shook the Temple to its foundations, and the entire building was filled with smoke.

Then I said, "It's all over! I am doomed, for I am a sinful man. I have filthy lips, and I live among a people with filthy lips. Yet I have seen the King, the LORD of Heaven's Armies."

Then one of the seraphim flew to me with a burning coal he had taken from the altar with a pair of tongs. He touched my lips with it and said, "See, this coal has touched your lips. Now your guilt is removed, and your sins are forgiven."

Then I heard the Lord asking, "Whom should I send as a messenger to this people? Who will go for us?"

I said, "Here I am. Send me."

And he said, "Yes, go, and say to this people,

'Listen carefully, but do not understand.
    Watch closely, but learn nothing.'
Harden the hearts of these people.
    Plug their ears and shut their eyes.
That way, they will not see with their eyes,
    nor hear with their ears,
nor understand with their hearts
    and turn to me for healing."

Then I said, "Lord, how long will this go on?"
And he replied,

"Until their towns are empty,
    their houses are deserted,
    and the whole country is a wasteland;
until the LORD has sent everyone away,
    and the entire land of Israel lies deserted.
If even a tenth—a remnant—survive,
    it will be invaded again and burned.
But as a terebinth or oak tree leaves a stump when it is cut down,
    so Israel's stump will be a holy seed."

When Ahaz, son of Jotham and grandson of Uzziah, was king of Judah, King Rezin of Syria and Pekah son of Remaliah, the king of Israel, set out to attack Jerusalem. However, they were unable to carry out their plan.

The news had come to the royal court of Judah: "Syria is allied with Israel against us!" So the hearts of the king and his people trembled with fear, like trees shaking in a storm.

Then the LORD said to Isaiah, "Take your son Shear-jashub and go out to meet King Ahaz. You will find him at the end of the aqueduct that feeds water into the upper pool, near the road leading to the field where cloth

is washed. Tell him to stop worrying. Tell him he doesn't need to fear the
fierce anger of those two burned-out embers, King Rezin of Syria and Pekah son of Remaliah. Yes, the kings of Syria and Israel are plotting against
him, saying, 'We will attack Judah and capture it for ourselves. Then we
will install the son of Tabeel as Judah's king.' But this is what the Sovereign
LORD says:

> "This invasion will never happen;
>   it will never take place;
> for Syria is no stronger than its capital, Damascus,
>   and Damascus is no stronger than its king, Rezin.
> As for Israel, within sixty-five years
>   it will be crushed and completely destroyed.
> Israel is no stronger than its capital, Samaria,
>   and Samaria is no stronger than its king, Pekah son of Remaliah.
> Unless your faith is firm,
>   I cannot make you stand firm."

Later, the LORD sent this message to King Ahaz: "Ask the LORD your
God for a sign of confirmation, Ahaz. Make it as difficult as you want—as
high as heaven or as deep as the place of the dead."

But the king refused. "No," he said, "I will not test the LORD like that."

Then Isaiah said, "Listen well, you royal family of David! Isn't it enough
to exhaust human patience? Must you exhaust the patience of my God as
well? All right then, the Lord himself will give you the sign. Look! The
virgin will conceive a child! She will give birth to a son and will call him
Immanuel (which means 'God is with us'). By the time this child is old
enough to choose what is right and reject what is wrong, he will be eating
yogurt and honey. For before the child is that old, the lands of the two
kings you fear so much will both be deserted.

"Then the LORD will bring things on you, your nation, and your family
unlike anything since Israel broke away from Judah. He will bring the king
of Assyria upon you!"

In that day the LORD will whistle for the army of southern Egypt and
for the army of Assyria. They will swarm around you like flies and bees.
They will come in vast hordes and settle in the fertile areas and also in the
desolate valleys, caves, and thorny places. In that day the Lord will hire a
"razor" from beyond the Euphrates River—the king of Assyria—and use
it to shave off everything: your land, your crops, and your people.

In that day a farmer will be fortunate to have a cow and two sheep or
goats left. Nevertheless, there will be enough milk for everyone because
so few people will be left in the land. They will eat their fill of yogurt

and honey. In that day the lush vineyards, now worth 1,000 pieces of silver, will become patches of briers and thorns. The entire land will become a vast expanse of briers and thorns, a hunting ground overrun by wildlife. No one will go to the fertile hillsides where the gardens once grew, for briers and thorns will cover them. Cattle, sheep, and goats will graze there.

Then the LORD said to me, "Make a large signboard and clearly write this name on it: Maher-shalal-hash-baz." I asked Uriah the priest and Zechariah son of Jeberekiah, both known as honest men, to witness my doing this.

Then I slept with my wife, and she became pregnant and gave birth to a son. And the LORD said, "Call him Maher-shalal-hash-baz. For before this child is old enough to say 'Papa' or 'Mama,' the king of Assyria will carry away both the abundance of Damascus and the riches of Samaria."

Then the LORD spoke to me again and said, "My care for the people of Judah is like the gently flowing waters of Shiloah, but they have rejected it. They are rejoicing over what will happen to King Rezin and King Pekah. Therefore, the Lord will overwhelm them with a mighty flood from the Euphrates River—the king of Assyria and all his glory. This flood will overflow all its channels and sweep into Judah until it is chin deep. It will spread its wings, submerging your land from one end to the other, O Immanuel.

"Huddle together, you nations, and be terrified.
    Listen, all you distant lands.
Prepare for battle, but you will be crushed!
    Yes, prepare for battle, but you will be crushed!
Call your councils of war, but they will be worthless.
    Develop your strategies, but they will not succeed.
    For God is with us!"

The LORD has given me a strong warning not to think like everyone else does. He said,

"Don't call everything a conspiracy, like they do,
    and don't live in dread of what frightens them.
Make the LORD of Heaven's Armies holy in your life.
    He is the one you should fear.
He is the one who should make you tremble.
    He will keep you safe.
But to Israel and Judah
    he will be a stone that makes people stumble,
    a rock that makes them fall.

And for the people of Jerusalem
　he will be a trap and a snare.
Many will stumble and fall,
　never to rise again.
　They will be snared and captured."

Preserve the teaching of God;
　entrust his instructions to those who follow me.
I will wait for the LORD,
　who has turned away from the descendants
　　of Jacob.
　I will put my hope in him.

I and the children the LORD has given me serve as signs and warnings to Israel from the LORD of Heaven's Armies who dwells in his Temple on Mount Zion.

Someone may say to you, "Let's ask the mediums and those who consult the spirits of the dead. With their whisperings and mutterings, they will tell us what to do." But shouldn't people ask God for guidance? Should the living seek guidance from the dead?

Look to God's instructions and teachings! People who contradict his word are completely in the dark. They will go from one place to another, weary and hungry. And because they are hungry, they will rage and curse their king and their God. They will look up to heaven and down at the earth, but wherever they look, there will be trouble and anguish and dark despair. They will be thrown out into the darkness.

Nevertheless, that time of darkness and despair will not go on forever. The land of Zebulun and Naphtali will be humbled, but there will be a time in the future when Galilee of the Gentiles, which lies along the road that runs between the Jordan and the sea, will be filled with glory.

The people who walk in darkness
　will see a great light.
For those who live in a land of deep darkness,
　a light will shine.
You will enlarge the nation of Israel,
　and its people will rejoice.
They will rejoice before you
　as people rejoice at the harvest
　and like warriors dividing the plunder.
For you will break the yoke of their slavery
　and lift the heavy burden from their shoulders.

You will break the oppressor's rod,
    just as you did when you destroyed the army of Midian.
The boots of the warrior
    and the uniforms bloodstained by war
will all be burned.
    They will be fuel for the fire.

For a child is born to us,
    a son is given to us.
The government will rest on his shoulders.
    And he will be called:
Wonderful Counselor, Mighty God,
    Everlasting Father, Prince of Peace.
His government and its peace
    will never end.
He will rule with fairness and justice from the throne of his
      ancestor David
    for all eternity.
The passionate commitment of the LORD of Heaven's Armies
    will make this happen!

+

The Lord has spoken out against Jacob;
    his judgment has fallen upon Israel.
And the people of Israel and Samaria,
    who spoke with such pride and arrogance,
    will soon know it.
They said, "We will replace the broken bricks of our ruins with
      finished stone,
    and replant the felled sycamore-fig trees with cedars."

But the LORD will bring Rezin's enemies against Israel
    and stir up all their foes.
The Syrians from the east and the Philistines from the west
    will bare their fangs and devour Israel.
But even then the LORD's anger will not be satisfied.
    His fist is still poised to strike.

For after all this punishment, the people will still not repent.
    They will not seek the LORD of Heaven's Armies.
Therefore, in a single day the LORD will destroy both the head and
      the tail,
    the noble palm branch and the lowly reed.

The leaders of Israel are the head,
  and the lying prophets are the tail.
For the leaders of the people have misled them.
  They have led them down the path of destruction.
That is why the Lord takes no pleasure in the young men
  and shows no mercy even to the widows and orphans.
For they are all wicked hypocrites,
  and they all speak foolishness.
But even then the Lord's anger will not be satisfied.
  His fist is still poised to strike.

This wickedness is like a brushfire.
  It burns not only briers and thorns
but also sets the forests ablaze.
  Its burning sends up clouds of smoke.
The land will be blackened
  by the fury of the Lord of Heaven's Armies.
The people will be fuel for the fire,
  and no one will spare even his own brother.
They will attack their neighbor on the right
  but will still be hungry.
They will devour their neighbor on the left
  but will not be satisfied.
In the end they will even eat their own children.
Manasseh will feed on Ephraim,
  Ephraim will feed on Manasseh,
  and both will devour Judah.
But even then the Lord's anger will not be satisfied.
  His fist is still poised to strike.

What sorrow awaits the unjust judges
  and those who issue unfair laws.
They deprive the poor of justice
  and deny the rights of the needy among my people.
They prey on widows
  and take advantage of orphans.

What will you do when I punish you,
  when I send disaster upon you from a distant land?
To whom will you turn for help?
  Where will your treasures be safe?
You will stumble along as prisoners
  or lie among the dead.

But even then the LORD's anger will not be satisfied.
   His fist is still poised to strike.

"What sorrow awaits Assyria, the rod of my anger.
   I use it as a club to express my anger.
I am sending Assyria against a godless nation,
   against a people with whom I am angry.
Assyria will plunder them,
   trampling them like dirt beneath its feet.
But the king of Assyria will not understand that he is my tool;
   his mind does not work that way.
His plan is simply to destroy,
   to cut down nation after nation.
He will say,
   'Each of my princes will soon be a king.
We destroyed Calno just as we did Carchemish.
   Hamath fell before us as Arpad did.
   And we destroyed Samaria just as we did Damascus.
Yes, we have finished off many a kingdom
   whose gods were greater than those in Jerusalem and Samaria.
So we will defeat Jerusalem and her gods,
   just as we destroyed Samaria with hers.'"

After the Lord has used the king of Assyria to accomplish his purposes on Mount Zion and in Jerusalem, he will turn against the king of Assyria and punish him—for he is proud and arrogant. He boasts,

"By my own powerful arm I have done this.
   With my own shrewd wisdom I planned it.
I have broken down the defenses of nations
   and carried off their treasures.
   I have knocked down their kings like a bull.
I have robbed their nests of riches
   and gathered up kingdoms as a farmer gathers eggs.
No one can even flap a wing against me
   or utter a peep of protest."

But can the ax boast greater power than the person who uses it?
   Is the saw greater than the person who saws?
Can a rod strike unless a hand moves it?
   Can a wooden cane walk by itself?
Therefore, the Lord, the LORD of Heaven's Armies,
   will send a plague among Assyria's proud troops,
   and a flaming fire will consume its glory.

The LORD, the Light of Israel, will be a fire;
　　the Holy One will be a flame.
He will devour the thorns and briers with fire,
　　burning up the enemy in a single night.
The LORD will consume Assyria's glory
　　like a fire consumes a forest in a fruitful land;
　　it will waste away like sick people in a plague.
Of all that glorious forest, only a few trees will
　　　　survive—
　　so few that a child could count them!

In that day the remnant left in Israel,
　　the survivors in the house of Jacob,
will no longer depend on allies
　　who seek to destroy them.
But they will faithfully trust the LORD,
　　the Holy One of Israel.
A remnant will return;
　　yes, the remnant of Jacob will return to the Mighty God.
But though the people of Israel are as numerous
　　as the sand of the seashore,
only a remnant of them will return.
　　The LORD has rightly decided to destroy his people.
Yes, the Lord, the LORD of Heaven's Armies,
　　has already decided to destroy the entire land.

So this is what the Lord, the LORD of Heaven's Armies, says: "O my
people in Zion, do not be afraid of the Assyrians when they oppress you
with rod and club as the Egyptians did long ago. In a little while my anger
against you will end, and then my anger will rise up to destroy them." The
LORD of Heaven's Armies will lash them with his whip, as he did when
Gideon triumphed over the Midianites at the rock of Oreb, or when the
LORD's staff was raised to drown the Egyptian army in the sea.

In that day the LORD will end the bondage of his people.
　　He will break the yoke of slavery
　　and lift it from their shoulders.

Look, the Assyrians are now at Aiath.
　　They are passing through Migron
　　and are storing their equipment at Micmash.
They are crossing the pass
　　and are camping at Geba.
Fear strikes the town of Ramah.

All the people of Gibeah, the hometown of Saul,
  are running for their lives.
Scream in terror,
  you people of Gallim!
Shout out a warning to Laishah.
  Oh, poor Anathoth!
There go the people of Madmenah, all fleeing.
  The citizens of Gebim are trying to hide.
The enemy stops at Nob for the rest of that day.
  He shakes his fist at beautiful Mount Zion, the mountain
    of Jerusalem.

But look! The Lord, the LORD of Heaven's Armies,
  will chop down the mighty tree of Assyria with great power!
He will cut down the proud.
  That lofty tree will be brought down.
He will cut down the forest trees with an ax.
  Lebanon will fall to the Mighty One.

Out of the stump of David's family will grow a shoot—
  yes, a new Branch bearing fruit from the old root.
And the Spirit of the LORD will rest on him—
  the Spirit of wisdom and understanding,
the Spirit of counsel and might,
  the Spirit of knowledge and the fear of the LORD.
He will delight in obeying the LORD.
  He will not judge by appearance
  nor make a decision based on hearsay.
He will give justice to the poor
  and make fair decisions for the exploited.
The earth will shake at the force of his word,
  and one breath from his mouth will destroy the wicked.
He will wear righteousness like a belt
  and truth like an undergarment.

In that day the wolf and the lamb will live together;
  the leopard will lie down with the baby goat.
The calf and the yearling will be safe with the lion,
  and a little child will lead them all.
The cow will graze near the bear.
  The cub and the calf will lie down together.
  The lion will eat hay like a cow.
The baby will play safely near the hole of a cobra.

Yes, a little child will put its hand in a nest of deadly snakes without
    harm.
Nothing will hurt or destroy in all my holy mountain,
    for as the waters fill the sea,
    so the earth will be filled with people who know the LORD.

In that day the heir to David's throne
    will be a banner of salvation to all the world.
The nations will rally to him,
    and the land where he lives will be a glorious place.
In that day the Lord will reach out his hand a second time
    to bring back the remnant of his people—
those who remain in Assyria and northern Egypt;
    in southern Egypt, Ethiopia, and Elam;
    in Babylonia, Hamath, and all the distant coastlands.
He will raise a flag among the nations
    and assemble the exiles of Israel.
He will gather the scattered people of Judah
    from the ends of the earth.

Then at last the jealousy between Israel and Judah will end.
    They will not be rivals anymore.
They will join forces to swoop down on Philistia to the west.
    Together they will attack and plunder the nations to the east.
They will occupy the lands of Edom and Moab,
    and Ammon will obey them.
The LORD will make a dry path through the gulf of the Red Sea.
    He will wave his hand over the Euphrates River,
sending a mighty wind to divide it into seven streams
    so it can easily be crossed on foot.
He will make a highway for the remnant of his people,
    the remnant coming from Assyria,
just as he did for Israel long ago
    when they returned from Egypt.

In that day you will sing:
    "I will praise you, O LORD!
You were angry with me, but not any more.
    Now you comfort me.
See, God has come to save me.
    I will trust in him and not be afraid.
The LORD GOD is my strength and my song;
    he has given me victory."

With joy you will drink deeply
   from the fountain of salvation!
In that wonderful day you will sing:
   "Thank the LORD! Praise his name!
Tell the nations what he has done.
   Let them know how mighty he is!
Sing to the LORD, for he has done wonderful things.
   Make known his praise around the world.
Let all the people of Jerusalem shout his praise with joy!
   For great is the Holy One of Israel who lives among you."

+ + +

Isaiah son of Amoz received this message concerning the destruction of
Babylon:

"Raise a signal flag on a bare hilltop.
   Call up an army against Babylon.
Wave your hand to encourage them
   as they march into the palaces of the high and mighty.
I, the LORD, have dedicated these soldiers for this task.
   Yes, I have called mighty warriors to express my anger,
   and they will rejoice when I am exalted."

Hear the noise on the mountains!
   Listen, as the vast armies march!
It is the noise and shouting of many nations.
   The LORD of Heaven's Armies has called this army
     together.
They come from distant countries,
   from beyond the farthest horizons.
They are the LORD's weapons to carry out his anger.
   With them he will destroy the whole land.

Scream in terror, for the day of the LORD has arrived—
   the time for the Almighty to destroy.
Every arm is paralyzed with fear.
   Every heart melts,
   and people are terrified.
Pangs of anguish grip them,
   like those of a woman in labor.
They look helplessly at one another,
   their faces aflame with fear.

For see, the day of the LORD is coming—
   the terrible day of his fury and fierce anger.
The land will be made desolate,
   and all the sinners destroyed with it.
The heavens will be black above them;
   the stars will give no light.
The sun will be dark when it rises,
   and the moon will provide no light.

"I, the LORD, will punish the world for its evil
   and the wicked for their sin.
I will crush the arrogance of the proud
   and humble the pride of the mighty.
I will make people scarcer than gold—
   more rare than the fine gold of Ophir.
For I will shake the heavens.
   The earth will move from its place
when the LORD of Heaven's Armies displays his wrath
   in the day of his fierce anger."

Everyone in Babylon will run about like a hunted gazelle,
   like sheep without a shepherd.
They will try to find their own people
   and flee to their own land.
Anyone who is captured will be cut down—
   run through with a sword.
Their little children will be dashed to death before their eyes.
   Their homes will be sacked, and their wives will be raped.

"Look, I will stir up the Medes against Babylon.
   They cannot be tempted by silver
   or bribed with gold.
The attacking armies will shoot down the young men with arrows.
   They will have no mercy on helpless babies
   and will show no compassion for children."

Babylon, the most glorious of kingdoms,
   the flower of Chaldean pride,
will be devastated like Sodom and Gomorrah
   when God destroyed them.
Babylon will never be inhabited again.
   It will remain empty for generation after generation.
Nomads will refuse to camp there,
   and shepherds will not bed down their sheep.

Desert animals will move into the ruined city,
   and the houses will be haunted by howling creatures.
Owls will live among the ruins,
   and wild goats will go there to dance.
Hyenas will howl in its fortresses,
   and jackals will make dens in its luxurious palaces.
Babylon's days are numbered;
   its time of destruction will soon arrive.

But the LORD will have mercy on the descendants of Jacob. He will choose
Israel as his special people once again. He will bring them back to settle
once again in their own land. And people from many different nations will
come and join them there and unite with the people of Israel. The nations
of the world will help the people of Israel to return, and those who come
to live in the LORD's land will serve them. Those who captured Israel will
themselves be captured, and Israel will rule over its enemies.

In that wonderful day when the LORD gives his people rest from sorrow
and fear, from slavery and chains, you will taunt the king of Babylon. You
will say,

"The mighty man has been destroyed.
   Yes, your insolence is ended.
For the LORD has crushed your wicked power
   and broken your evil rule.
You struck the people with endless blows of rage
   and held the nations in your angry grip
   with unrelenting tyranny.
But finally the earth is at rest and quiet.
   Now it can sing again!
Even the trees of the forest—
   the cypress trees and the cedars of Lebanon—
   sing out this joyous song:
'Since you have been cut down,
   no one will come now to cut us down!'

"In the place of the dead there is excitement
   over your arrival.
The spirits of world leaders and mighty kings long dead
   stand up to see you.
With one voice they all cry out,
   'Now you are as weak as we are!
Your might and power were buried with you.
   The sound of the harp in your palace has ceased.

Now maggots are your sheet,
    and worms your blanket.'

"How you are fallen from heaven,
    O shining star, son of the morning!
You have been thrown down to the earth,
    you who destroyed the nations of the world.
For you said to yourself,
    'I will ascend to heaven and set my throne above God's stars.
I will preside on the mountain of the gods
    far away in the north.
I will climb to the highest heavens
    and be like the Most High.'
Instead, you will be brought down to the place of the dead,
    down to its lowest depths.
Everyone there will stare at you and ask,
'Can this be the one who shook the earth
    and made the kingdoms of the world tremble?
Is this the one who destroyed the world
    and made it into a wasteland?
Is this the king who demolished the world's greatest cities
    and had no mercy on his prisoners?'

"The kings of the nations lie in stately glory,
    each in his own tomb,
but you will be thrown out of your grave
    like a worthless branch.
Like a corpse trampled underfoot,
    you will be dumped into a mass grave
    with those killed in battle.
You will descend to the pit.
    You will not be given a proper burial,
for you have destroyed your nation
    and slaughtered your people.
The descendants of such an evil person
    will never again receive honor.
Kill this man's children!
    Let them die because of their father's sins!
They must not rise and conquer the earth,
    filling the world with their cities."

This is what the LORD of Heaven's Armies says:
    "I, myself, have risen against Babylon!

I will destroy its children and its children's children,"
   says the LORD.
"I will make Babylon a desolate place of owls,
   filled with swamps and marshes.
I will sweep the land with the broom of destruction.
   I, the LORD of Heaven's Armies, have spoken!"

+

The LORD of Heaven's Armies has sworn this oath:

"It will all happen as I have planned.
   It will be as I have decided.
I will break the Assyrians when they are in Israel;
   I will trample them on my mountains.
My people will no longer be their slaves
   nor bow down under their heavy loads.
I have a plan for the whole earth,
   a hand of judgment upon all the nations.
The LORD of Heaven's Armies has spoken—
   who can change his plans?
When his hand is raised,
   who can stop him?"

+

This message came to me the year King Ahaz died:

Do not rejoice, you Philistines,
   that the rod that struck you is broken—
   that the king who attacked you is dead.
For from that snake a more poisonous snake will be born,
   a fiery serpent to destroy you!
I will feed the poor in my pasture;
   the needy will lie down in peace.
But as for you, I will wipe you out with famine
   and destroy the few who remain.
Wail at the gates! Weep in the cities!
   Melt with fear, you Philistines!
A powerful army comes like smoke from the north.
   Each soldier rushes forward eager to fight.

What should we tell the Philistine messengers? Tell them,

"The LORD has built Jerusalem;
   its walls will give refuge to his oppressed people."

+

This message came to me concerning Moab:

In one night the town of Ar will be leveled,
    and the city of Kir will be destroyed.
Your people will go to their temple in Dibon to mourn.
    They will go to their sacred shrines to weep.
They will wail for the fate of Nebo and Medeba,
    shaving their heads in sorrow and cutting off their beards.
They will wear burlap as they wander the streets.
    From every home and public square will come the sound of wailing.
The people of Heshbon and Elealeh will cry out;
    their voices will be heard as far away as Jahaz!
The bravest warriors of Moab will cry out in utter terror.
    They will be helpless with fear.

My heart weeps for Moab.
    Its people flee to Zoar and Eglath-shelishiyah.
Weeping, they climb the road to Luhith.
    Their cries of distress can be heard all along the road
        to Horonaim.
Even the waters of Nimrim are dried up!
    The grassy banks are scorched.
The tender plants are gone;
    nothing green remains.
The people grab their possessions
    and carry them across the Ravine of Willows.
A cry of distress echoes through the land of Moab
    from one end to the other—
    from Eglaim to Beer-elim.
The stream near Dibon runs red with blood,
    but I am still not finished with Dibon!
Lions will hunt down the survivors—
    both those who try to escape
    and those who remain behind.

Send lambs from Sela as tribute
    to the ruler of the land.
Send them through the desert
    to the mountain of beautiful Zion.
The women of Moab are left like homeless birds
    at the shallow crossings of the Arnon River.

"Help us," they cry.
    "Defend us against our enemies.
Protect us from their relentless attack.
    Do not betray us now that we have escaped.
Let our refugees stay among you.
    Hide them from our enemies until the terror is past."

When oppression and destruction have ended
    and enemy raiders have disappeared,
then God will establish one of David's descendants as king.
    He will rule with mercy and truth.
He will always do what is just
    and be eager to do what is right.

We have heard about proud Moab—
    about its pride and arrogance and rage.
    But all that boasting has disappeared.
The entire land of Moab weeps.
    Yes, everyone in Moab mourns
for the cakes of raisins from Kir-hareseth.
    They are all gone now.
The farms of Heshbon are abandoned;
    the vineyards at Sibmah are deserted.
The rulers of the nations have broken down Moab—
    that beautiful grapevine.
Its tendrils spread north as far as the town of Jazer
    and trailed eastward into the wilderness.
Its shoots reached so far west
    that they crossed over the Dead Sea.

So now I weep for Jazer and the vineyards of Sibmah;
    my tears will flow for Heshbon and Elealeh.
There are no more shouts of joy
    over your summer fruits and harvest.
Gone now is the gladness,
    gone the joy of harvest.
There will be no singing in the vineyards,
    no more happy shouts,
no treading of grapes in the winepresses.
    I have ended all their harvest joys.
My heart's cry for Moab is like a lament on a harp.
    I am filled with anguish for Kir-hareseth.
The people of Moab will worship at their pagan shrines,

but it will do them no good.
They will cry to the gods in their temples,
    but no one will be able to save them.

The Lord has already said these things about Moab in the past. But now the Lord says, "Within three years, counting each day, the glory of Moab will be ended. From its great population, only a feeble few will be left alive."

✛

This message came to me concerning Damascus:

"Look, the city of Damascus will disappear!
    It will become a heap of ruins.
The towns of Aroer will be deserted.
    Flocks will graze in the streets and lie down undisturbed,
    with no one to chase them away.
The fortified towns of Israel will also be destroyed,
    and the royal power of Damascus will end.
All that remains of Syria
    will share the fate of Israel's departed glory,"
    declares the Lord of Heaven's Armies.

"In that day Israel's glory will grow dim;
    its robust body will waste away.
The whole land will look like a grainfield
    after the harvesters have gathered the grain.
It will be desolate,
    like the fields in the valley of Rephaim after the harvest.
Only a few of its people will be left,
    like stray olives left on a tree after the harvest.
Only two or three remain in the highest branches,
    four or five scattered here and there on the limbs,"
    declares the Lord, the God of Israel.

Then at last the people will look to their Creator
    and turn their eyes to the Holy One of Israel.
They will no longer look to their idols for help
    or worship what their own hands have made.
They will never again bow down to their Asherah poles
    or worship at the pagan shrines they have built.
Their largest cities will be like a deserted forest,
    like the land the Hivites and Amorites abandoned
when the Israelites came here so long ago.

It will be utterly desolate.
Why? Because you have turned from the God who can save you.
    You have forgotten the Rock who can hide you.
So you may plant the finest grapevines
    and import the most expensive seedlings.
They may sprout on the day you set them out;
    yes, they may blossom on the very morning you plant them,
but you will never pick any grapes from them.
    Your only harvest will be a load of grief and unrelieved pain.

Listen! The armies of many nations
    roar like the roaring of the sea.
Hear the thunder of the mighty forces
    as they rush forward like thundering waves.
But though they thunder like breakers on a beach,
    God will silence them, and they will run away.
They will flee like chaff scattered by the wind,
    like a tumbleweed whirling before a storm.
In the evening Israel waits in terror,
    but by dawn its enemies are dead.
This is the just reward of those who plunder us,
    a fitting end for those who destroy us.

+

Listen, Ethiopia—land of fluttering sails
    that lies at the headwaters of the Nile,
that sends ambassadors
    in swift boats down the river.

Go, swift messengers!
Take a message to a tall, smooth-skinned people,
    who are feared far and wide
for their conquests and destruction,
    and whose land is divided by rivers.

All you people of the world,
    everyone who lives on the earth—
when I raise my battle flag on the mountain, look!
    When I blow the ram's horn, listen!
For the LORD has told me this:
"I will watch quietly from my dwelling place—
    as quietly as the heat rises on a summer day,

or as the morning dew forms during the harvest."
Even before you begin your attack,
   while your plans are ripening like grapes,
the LORD will cut off your new growth with pruning shears.
   He will snip off and discard your spreading branches.
Your mighty army will be left dead in the fields
   for the mountain vultures and wild animals.
The vultures will tear at the corpses all summer.
   The wild animals will gnaw at the bones all winter.

At that time the LORD of Heaven's Armies will receive gifts
   from this land divided by rivers,
from this tall, smooth-skinned people,
   who are feared far and wide for their conquests and destruction.
They will bring the gifts to Jerusalem,
   where the LORD of Heaven's Armies dwells.

+

This message came to me concerning Egypt:

Look! The LORD is advancing against Egypt,
   riding on a swift cloud.
The idols of Egypt tremble.
   The hearts of the Egyptians melt with fear.

"I will make Egyptian fight against Egyptian—
   brother against brother,
neighbor against neighbor,
   city against city,
   province against province.
The Egyptians will lose heart,
   and I will confuse their plans.
They will plead with their idols for wisdom
   and call on spirits, mediums, and those who consult the spirits
     of the dead.
I will hand Egypt over
   to a hard, cruel master.
A fierce king will rule them,"
   says the Lord, the LORD of Heaven's Armies.

The waters of the Nile will fail to rise and flood the fields.
   The riverbed will be parched and dry.
The canals of the Nile will dry up,

and the streams of Egypt will stink
   with rotting reeds and rushes.
All the greenery along the riverbank
   and all the crops along the river
   will dry up and blow away.
The fishermen will lament for lack of work.
   Those who cast hooks into the Nile will groan,
   and those who use nets will lose heart.
There will be no flax for the harvesters,
   no thread for the weavers.
They will be in despair,
   and all the workers will be sick at heart.

What fools are the officials of Zoan!
   Their best counsel to the king of Egypt is stupid and wrong.
Will they still boast to Pharaoh of their wisdom?
   Will they dare brag about all their wise ancestors?
Where are your wise counselors, Pharaoh?
   Let them tell you what God plans,
   what the LORD of Heaven's Armies is going to do to Egypt.
The officials of Zoan are fools,
   and the officials of Memphis are deluded.
The leaders of the people
   have led Egypt astray.
The LORD has sent a spirit of foolishness on them,
   so all their suggestions are wrong.
They cause Egypt to stagger
   like a drunk in his vomit.
There is nothing Egypt can do.
   All are helpless—
the head and the tail,
   the noble palm branch and the lowly reed.

In that day the Egyptians will be as weak as women. They will cower in fear beneath the upraised fist of the LORD of Heaven's Armies. Just to speak the name of Israel will terrorize them, for the LORD of Heaven's Armies has laid out his plans against them.

In that day five of Egypt's cities will follow the LORD of Heaven's Armies. They will even begin to speak Hebrew, the language of Canaan. One of these cities will be Heliopolis, the City of the Sun.

In that day there will be an altar to the LORD in the heart of Egypt, and there will be a monument to the LORD at its border. It will be a sign and a witness that the LORD of Heaven's Armies is worshiped in the land of

Egypt. When the people cry to the LORD for help against those who oppress them, he will send them a savior who will rescue them. The LORD will make himself known to the Egyptians. Yes, they will know the LORD and will give their sacrifices and offerings to him. They will make a vow to the LORD and will keep it. The LORD will strike Egypt, and then he will bring healing. For the Egyptians will turn to the LORD, and he will listen to their pleas and heal them.

In that day Egypt and Assyria will be connected by a highway. The Egyptians and Assyrians will move freely between their lands, and they will both worship God. In that day Israel will be the third, along with Egypt and Assyria, a blessing in the midst of the earth. For the LORD of Heaven's Armies will say, "Blessed be Egypt, my people. Blessed be Assyria, the land I have made. Blessed be Israel, my special possession!"

✦

In the year when King Sargon of Assyria sent his commander in chief to capture the Philistine city of Ashdod, the LORD told Isaiah son of Amoz, "Take off the burlap you have been wearing, and remove your sandals." Isaiah did as he was told and walked around naked and barefoot.

Then the LORD said, "My servant Isaiah has been walking around naked and barefoot for the last three years. This is a sign—a symbol of the terrible troubles I will bring upon Egypt and Ethiopia. For the king of Assyria will take away the Egyptians and Ethiopians as prisoners. He will make them walk naked and barefoot, both young and old, their buttocks bared, to the shame of Egypt. Then the Philistines will be thrown into panic, for they counted on the power of Ethiopia and boasted of their allies in Egypt! They will say, 'If this can happen to Egypt, what chance do we have? We were counting on Egypt to protect us from the king of Assyria.'"

✦

This message came to me concerning Babylon—the desert by the sea:

Disaster is roaring down on you from the desert,
    like a whirlwind sweeping in from the Negev.
I see a terrifying vision:
    I see the betrayer betraying,
    the destroyer destroying.
Go ahead, you Elamites and Medes,
    attack and lay siege.
I will make an end

to all the groaning Babylon caused.
My stomach aches and burns with pain.
  Sharp pangs of anguish are upon me,
  like those of a woman in labor.
I grow faint when I hear what God is planning;
  I am too afraid to look.
My mind reels and my heart races.
  I longed for evening to come,
  but now I am terrified of the dark.

Look! They are preparing a great feast.
  They are spreading rugs for people to sit on.
  Everyone is eating and drinking.
But quick! Grab your shields and prepare for battle.
  You are being attacked!

Meanwhile, the Lord said to me,
"Put a watchman on the city wall.
  Let him shout out what he sees.
He should look for chariots
  drawn by pairs of horses,
and for riders on donkeys and camels.
  Let the watchman be fully alert."

Then the watchman called out,
"Day after day I have stood on the watchtower, my lord.
  Night after night I have remained at my post.
Now at last—look!
Here comes a man in a chariot
  with a pair of horses!"
Then the watchman said,
  "Babylon is fallen, fallen!
All the idols of Babylon
  lie broken on the ground!"
O my people, threshed and winnowed,
  I have told you everything the LORD of Heaven's Armies has said,
  everything the God of Israel has told me.

+

This message came to me concerning Edom:

Someone from Edom keeps calling to me,
  "Watchman, how much longer until morning?

When will the night be over?"
The watchman replies,
"Morning is coming, but night will soon return.
If you wish to ask again, then come back and ask."

+

This message came to me concerning Arabia:

O caravans from Dedan,
    hide in the deserts of Arabia.
O people of Tema,
    bring water to these thirsty people,
    food to these weary refugees.
They have fled from the sword,
    from the drawn sword,
from the bent bow
    and the terrors of battle.

The Lord said to me, "Within a year, counting each day, all the glory of Kedar will come to an end. Only a few of its courageous archers will survive. I, the LORD, the God of Israel, have spoken!"

+

This message came to me concerning Jerusalem—the Valley of Vision:

What is happening?
    Why is everyone running to the rooftops?
The whole city is in a terrible uproar.
    What do I see in this reveling city?
Bodies are lying everywhere,
    killed not in battle but by famine and disease.
All your leaders have fled.
    They surrendered without resistance.
The people tried to slip away,
    but they were captured, too.
That's why I said, "Leave me alone to weep;
    do not try to comfort me.
Let me cry for my people
    as I watch them being destroyed."

Oh, what a day of crushing defeat!
    What a day of confusion and terror

brought by the Lord, the LORD of Heaven's Armies,
   upon the Valley of Vision!
The walls of Jerusalem have been broken,
   and cries of death echo from the mountainsides.
Elamites are the archers,
   with their chariots and charioteers.
   The men of Kir hold up the shields.
Chariots fill your beautiful valleys,
   and charioteers storm your gates.
Judah's defenses have been stripped away.
   You run to the armory for your weapons.
You inspect the breaks in the walls of Jerusalem.
   You store up water in the lower pool.
You survey the houses and tear some down
   for stone to strengthen the walls.
Between the city walls, you build a reservoir
   for water from the old pool.
But you never ask for help from the One who did all this.
   You never considered the One who planned this long ago.

At that time the Lord, the LORD of Heaven's Armies,
   called you to weep and mourn.
He told you to shave your heads in sorrow for your sins
   and to wear clothes of burlap to show your remorse.
But instead, you dance and play;
   you slaughter cattle and kill sheep.
   You feast on meat and drink wine.
You say, "Let's feast and drink,
   for tomorrow we die!"

The LORD of Heaven's Armies has revealed this to me: "Till the day you die, you will never be forgiven for this sin." That is the judgment of the Lord, the LORD of Heaven's Armies.

This is what the Lord, the LORD of Heaven's Armies, said to me: "Confront Shebna, the palace administrator, and give him this message:

"Who do you think you are,
   and what are you doing here,
building a beautiful tomb for yourself—
   a monument high up in the rock?
For the LORD is about to hurl you away, mighty man.
   He is going to grab you,

crumple you into a ball,
    and toss you away into a distant, barren land.
There you will die,
    and your glorious chariots will be broken and useless.
    You are a disgrace to your master!

"Yes, I will drive you out of office," says the LORD. "I will pull you down from your high position. And then I will call my servant Eliakim son of Hilkiah to replace you. I will dress him in your royal robes and will give him your title and your authority. And he will be a father to the people of Jerusalem and Judah. I will give him the key to the house of David—the highest position in the royal court. When he opens doors, no one will be able to close them; when he closes doors, no one will be able to open them. He will bring honor to his family name, for I will drive him firmly in place like a nail in the wall. They will give him great responsibility, and he will bring honor to even the lowliest members of his family."

But the LORD of Heaven's Armies also says: "The time will come when I will pull out the nail that seemed so firm. It will come out and fall to the ground. Everything it supports will fall with it. I, the LORD, have spoken!"

+

This message came to me concerning Tyre:

Wail, you trading ships of Tarshish,
    for the harbor and houses of Tyre are gone!
The rumors you heard in Cyprus
    are all true.
Mourn in silence, you people of the coast
    and you merchants of Sidon.
Your traders crossed the sea,
    sailing over deep waters.
They brought you grain from Egypt
    and harvests from along the Nile.
You were the marketplace of the world.

But now you are put to shame, city of Sidon,
    for Tyre, the fortress of the sea, says,
"Now I am childless;
    I have no sons or daughters."
When Egypt hears the news about Tyre,
    there will be great sorrow.

Send word now to Tarshish!
  Wail, you people who live in distant lands!
Is this silent ruin all that is left of your once joyous city?
  What a long history was yours!
  Think of all the colonists you sent to distant places.

Who has brought this disaster on Tyre,
  that great creator of kingdoms?
Her traders were all princes,
  her merchants were nobles.
The LORD of Heaven's Armies has done it
  to destroy your pride
  and bring low all earth's nobility.
Come, people of Tarshish,
  sweep over the land like the flooding Nile,
  for Tyre is defenseless.
The LORD held out his hand over the sea
  and shook the kingdoms of the earth.
He has spoken out against Phoenicia,
  ordering that her fortresses be destroyed.
He says, "Never again will you rejoice,
  O daughter of Sidon, for you have been
    crushed.
Even if you flee to Cyprus,
  you will find no rest."

Look at the land of Babylonia—
  the people of that land are gone!
The Assyrians have handed Babylon over
  to the wild animals of the desert.
They have built siege ramps against its walls,
  torn down its palaces,
  and turned it to a heap of rubble.

Wail, you ships of Tarshish,
  for your harbor is destroyed!

For seventy years, the length of a king's life, Tyre will be forgotten. But
then the city will come back to life as in the song about the prostitute:

Take a harp and walk the streets,
  you forgotten harlot.
Make sweet melody and sing your songs
  so you will be remembered again.

Yes, after seventy years the LORD will revive Tyre. But she will be no different than she was before. She will again be a prostitute to all kingdoms around the world. But in the end her profits will be given to the LORD. Her wealth will not be hoarded but will provide good food and fine clothing for the LORD's priests.

+ + +

Look! The LORD is about to destroy the earth
　　and make it a vast wasteland.
He devastates the surface of the earth
　　and scatters the people.
Priests and laypeople,
　　servants and masters,
　　maids and mistresses,
　　buyers and sellers,
　　lenders and borrowers,
　　bankers and debtors—none will be spared.
The earth will be completely emptied and looted.
　　The LORD has spoken!

The earth mourns and dries up,
　　and the land wastes away and withers.
　　Even the greatest people on earth waste away.
The earth suffers for the sins of its people,
　　for they have twisted God's instructions,
violated his laws,
　　and broken his everlasting covenant.
Therefore, a curse consumes the earth.
　　Its people must pay the price for their sin.
They are destroyed by fire,
　　and only a few are left alive.
The grapevines waste away,
　　and there is no new wine.
　　All the merrymakers sigh and mourn.
The cheerful sound of tambourines is stilled;
　　the happy cries of celebration are heard no more.
　　The melodious chords of the harp are silent.
Gone are the joys of wine and song;
　　alcoholic drink turns bitter in the mouth.
The city writhes in chaos;
　　every home is locked to keep out intruders.
Mobs gather in the streets, crying out for wine.

Joy has turned to gloom.
Gladness has been banished from the land.
The city is left in ruins,
its gates battered down.
Throughout the earth the story is the same—
only a remnant is left,
like the stray olives left on the tree
or the few grapes left on the vine after harvest.

But all who are left shout and sing for joy.
Those in the west praise the LORD's majesty.
In eastern lands, give glory to the LORD.
In the lands beyond the sea, praise the name of the LORD, the God
of Israel.
We hear songs of praise from the ends of the earth,
songs that give glory to the Righteous One!

But my heart is heavy with grief.
Weep for me, for I wither away.
Deceit still prevails,
and treachery is everywhere.
Terror and traps and snares will be your lot,
you people of the earth.
Those who flee in terror will fall into a trap,
and those who escape the trap will be caught in a snare.

Destruction falls like rain from the heavens;
the foundations of the earth shake.
The earth has broken up.
It has utterly collapsed;
it is violently shaken.
The earth staggers like a drunk.
It trembles like a tent in a storm.
It falls and will not rise again,
for the guilt of its rebellion is very heavy.

In that day the LORD will punish the gods in the heavens
and the proud rulers of the nations on earth.
They will be rounded up and put in prison.
They will be shut up in prison
and will finally be punished.
Then the glory of the moon will wane,
and the brightness of the sun will fade,
for the LORD of Heaven's Armies will rule on Mount Zion.

He will rule in great glory in Jerusalem,
in the sight of all the leaders of his people.

+

O Lord, I will honor and praise your name,
for you are my God.
You do such wonderful things!
You planned them long ago,
and now you have accomplished them.
You turn mighty cities into heaps of ruins.
Cities with strong walls are turned to rubble.
Beautiful palaces in distant lands disappear
and will never be rebuilt.
Therefore, strong nations will declare your glory;
ruthless nations will fear you.

But you are a tower of refuge to the poor, O Lord,
a tower of refuge to the needy in distress.
You are a refuge from the storm
and a shelter from the heat.
For the oppressive acts of ruthless people
are like a storm beating against a wall,
or like the relentless heat of the desert.
But you silence the roar of foreign nations.
As the shade of a cloud cools relentless heat,
so the boastful songs of ruthless people are stilled.

In Jerusalem, the Lord of Heaven's Armies
will spread a wonderful feast
for all the people of the world.
It will be a delicious banquet
with clear, well-aged wine and choice meat.
There he will remove the cloud of gloom,
the shadow of death that hangs over the earth.
He will swallow up death forever!
The Sovereign Lord will wipe away all tears.
He will remove forever all insults and mockery
against his land and people.
The Lord has spoken!

In that day the people will proclaim,
"This is our God!

We trusted in him, and he saved us!
This is the Lord, in whom we trusted.
    Let us rejoice in the salvation he brings!"
For the Lord's hand of blessing will rest on Jerusalem.
    But Moab will be crushed.
    It will be like straw trampled down and left to rot.
God will push down Moab's people
    as a swimmer pushes down water with his hands.
He will end their pride
    and all their evil works.
The high walls of Moab will be demolished.
    They will be brought down to the ground,
    down into the dust.

In that day, everyone in the land of Judah will sing this song:

Our city is strong!
    We are surrounded by the walls of God's salvation.
Open the gates to all who are righteous;
    allow the faithful to enter.
You will keep in perfect peace
    all who trust in you,
    all whose thoughts are fixed on you!
Trust in the Lord always,
    for the Lord God is the eternal Rock.
He humbles the proud
    and brings down the arrogant city.
    He brings it down to the dust.
The poor and oppressed trample it underfoot,
    and the needy walk all over it.

But for those who are righteous,
    the way is not steep and rough.
You are a God who does what is right,
    and you smooth out the path ahead of them.
Lord, we show our trust in you by obeying your laws;
    our heart's desire is to glorify your name.
In the night I search for you;
    in the morning I earnestly seek you.
For only when you come to judge the earth
    will people learn what is right.
Your kindness to the wicked
    does not make them do good.

Although others do right, the wicked keep doing wrong
 and take no notice of the LORD's majesty.
O LORD, they pay no attention to your upraised fist.
 Show them your eagerness to defend your people.
Then they will be ashamed.
 Let your fire consume your enemies.

LORD, you will grant us peace;
 all we have accomplished is really from you.
O LORD our God, others have ruled us,
 but you alone are the one we worship.
Those we served before are dead and gone.
 Their departed spirits will never return!
You attacked them and destroyed them,
 and they are long forgotten.
O LORD, you have made our nation great;
 yes, you have made us great.
You have extended our borders,
 and we give you the glory!

LORD, in distress we searched for you.
 We prayed beneath the burden of your discipline.
Just as a pregnant woman
 writhes and cries out in pain as she gives birth,
 so were we in your presence, LORD.
We, too, writhe in agony,
 but nothing comes of our suffering.
We have not given salvation to the earth,
 nor brought life into the world.
But those who die in the LORD will live;
 their bodies will rise again!
Those who sleep in the earth
 will rise up and sing for joy!
For your life-giving light will fall like dew
 on your people in the place of the dead!

Go home, my people,
 and lock your doors!
Hide yourselves for a little while
 until the LORD's anger has passed.
Look! The LORD is coming from heaven
 to punish the people of the earth for their sins.
The earth will no longer hide those who have been killed.
 They will be brought out for all to see.

In that day the LORD will take his terrible, swift sword and punish Levi-
athan, the swiftly moving serpent, the coiling, writhing serpent. He will
kill the dragon of the sea.

"In that day,
 sing about the fruitful vineyard.
I, the LORD, will watch over it,
 watering it carefully.
Day and night I will watch so no one can harm it.
 My anger will be gone.
If I find briers and thorns growing,
 I will attack them;
I will burn them up—
 unless they turn to me for help.
Let them make peace with me;
 yes, let them make peace with me."
The time is coming when Jacob's descendants will
  take root.
 Israel will bud and blossom
 and fill the whole earth with fruit!

Has the LORD struck Israel
 as he struck her enemies?
Has he punished her
 as he punished them?
No, but he exiled Israel to call her to account.
 She was exiled from her land
 as though blown away in a storm from the east.
The LORD did this to purge Israel's wickedness,
 to take away all her sin.
As a result, all the pagan altars will be crushed to dust.
 No Asherah pole or pagan shrine will be left standing.
The fortified towns will be silent and empty,
 the houses abandoned, the streets overgrown with weeds.
Calves will graze there,
 chewing on twigs and branches.
The people are like the dead branches of a tree,
 broken off and used for kindling beneath the cooking pots.
Israel is a foolish and stupid nation,
 for its people have turned away from God.
Therefore, the one who made them
 will show them no pity or mercy.

Yet the time will come when the LORD will gather them together like handpicked grain. One by one he will gather them—from the Euphrates River in the east to the Brook of Egypt in the west. In that day the great trumpet will sound. Many who were dying in exile in Assyria and Egypt will return to Jerusalem to worship the LORD on his holy mountain.

+ + +

What sorrow awaits the proud city of Samaria—
    the glorious crown of the drunks of Israel.
It sits at the head of a fertile valley,
    but its glorious beauty will fade like a flower.
It is the pride of a people
    brought down by wine.
For the Lord will send a mighty army against it.
    Like a mighty hailstorm and a torrential rain,
they will burst upon it like a surging flood
    and smash it to the ground.
The proud city of Samaria—
    the glorious crown of the drunks of Israel—
will be trampled beneath its enemies' feet.
It sits at the head of a fertile valley,
    but its glorious beauty will fade like a flower.
Whoever sees it will snatch it up,
    as an early fig is quickly picked and eaten.

Then at last the LORD of Heaven's Armies
    will himself be Israel's glorious crown.
He will be the pride and joy
    of the remnant of his people.
He will give a longing for justice
    to their judges.
He will give great courage
    to their warriors who stand at the gates.

Now, however, Israel is led by drunks
    who reel with wine and stagger with alcohol.
The priests and prophets stagger with alcohol
    and lose themselves in wine.
They reel when they see visions
    and stagger as they render decisions.
Their tables are covered with vomit;
    filth is everywhere.

"Who does the LORD think we are?" they ask.
  "Why does he speak to us like this?
Are we little children,
  just recently weaned?
He tells us everything over and over—
one line at a time,
  one line at a time,
a little here,
  and a little there!"

So now God will have to speak to his people
  through foreign oppressors who speak a strange
    language!
God has told his people,
"Here is a place of rest;
  let the weary rest here.
This is a place of quiet rest."
  But they would not listen.
So the LORD will spell out his message for them again,
one line at a time,
  one line at a time,
a little here,
  and a little there,
so that they will stumble and fall.
  They will be injured, trapped, and captured.

Therefore, listen to this message from the LORD,
  you scoffing rulers in Jerusalem.
You boast, "We have struck a bargain to cheat death
  and have made a deal to dodge the grave.
The coming destruction can never touch us,
  for we have built a strong refuge made of lies and
    deception."

Therefore, this is what the Sovereign LORD says:
"Look! I am placing a foundation stone in Jerusalem,
  a firm and tested stone.
It is a precious cornerstone that is safe to build on.
  Whoever believes need never be shaken.
I will test you with the measuring line of justice
  and the plumb line of righteousness.
Since your refuge is made of lies,
  a hailstorm will knock it down.

Since it is made of deception,
　　a flood will sweep it away.
I will cancel the bargain you made to cheat death,
　　and I will overturn your deal to dodge the grave.
When the terrible enemy sweeps through,
　　you will be trampled into the ground.
Again and again that flood will come,
　　morning after morning,
day and night,
　　until you are carried away."

This message will bring terror to your people.
The bed you have made is too short to lie on.
　　The blankets are too narrow to cover you.
The LORD will come as he did against the Philistines at Mount
　　　Perazim
　　and against the Amorites at Gibeon.
He will come to do a strange thing;
　　he will come to do an unusual deed:
For the Lord, the LORD of Heaven's Armies,
　　has plainly said that he is determined to crush the
　　　whole land.
So scoff no more,
　　or your punishment will be even greater.

Listen to me;
　　listen, and pay close attention.
Does a farmer always plow and never sow?
　　Is he forever cultivating the soil and never planting?
Does he not finally plant his seeds—
　　black cumin, cumin, wheat, barley, and emmer wheat—
each in its proper way,
　　and each in its proper place?
The farmer knows just what to do,
　　for God has given him understanding.
A heavy sledge is never used to thresh black cumin;
　　rather, it is beaten with a light stick.
A threshing wheel is never rolled on cumin;
　　instead, it is beaten lightly with a flail.
Grain for bread is easily crushed,
　　so he doesn't keep on pounding it.
He threshes it under the wheels of a cart,
　　but he doesn't pulverize it.

The LORD of Heaven's Armies is a wonderful teacher,
   and he gives the farmer great wisdom.

"What sorrow awaits Ariel, the City of David.
   Year after year you celebrate your feasts.
Yet I will bring disaster upon you,
   and there will be much weeping and sorrow.
For Jerusalem will become what her name Ariel means—
   an altar covered with blood.
I will be your enemy,
   surrounding Jerusalem and attacking its walls.
I will build siege towers
   and destroy it.
Then deep from the earth you will speak;
   from low in the dust your words will come.
Your voice will whisper from the ground
   like a ghost conjured up from the grave.

"But suddenly, your ruthless enemies will be crushed
   like the finest of dust.
Your many attackers will be driven away
   like chaff before the wind.
Suddenly, in an instant,
   I, the LORD of Heaven's Armies, will act for you
with thunder and earthquake and great noise,
   with whirlwind and storm and consuming fire.
All the nations fighting against Jerusalem
   will vanish like a dream!
Those who are attacking her walls
   will vanish like a vision in the night.
A hungry person dreams of eating
   but wakes up still hungry.
A thirsty person dreams of drinking
   but is still faint from thirst when morning comes.
So it will be with your enemies,
   with those who attack Mount Zion."

Are you amazed and incredulous?
   Don't you believe it?
Then go ahead and be blind.
   You are stupid, but not from wine!
   You stagger, but not from liquor!

For the LORD has poured out on you a spirit of deep sleep.
He has closed the eyes of your prophets and visionaries.

All the future events in this vision are like a sealed book to them. When
you give it to those who can read, they will say, "We can't read it because
it is sealed." When you give it to those who cannot read, they will say, "We
don't know how to read."

And so the Lord says,
"These people say they are mine.
They honor me with their lips,
but their hearts are far from me.
And their worship of me
is nothing but man-made rules learned by rote.
Because of this, I will once again astound these hypocrites
with amazing wonders.
The wisdom of the wise will pass away,
and the intelligence of the intelligent will disappear."

What sorrow awaits those who try to hide their plans from
the LORD,
who do their evil deeds in the dark!
"The LORD can't see us," they say.
"He doesn't know what's going on!"
How foolish can you be?
He is the Potter, and he is certainly greater than you, the clay!
Should the created thing say of the one who made it,
"He didn't make me"?
Does a jar ever say,
"The potter who made me is stupid"?

Soon—and it will not be very long—
the forests of Lebanon will become a fertile field,
and the fertile field will yield bountiful crops.
In that day the deaf will hear words read from a book,
and the blind will see through the gloom and darkness.
The humble will be filled with fresh joy from the LORD.
The poor will rejoice in the Holy One of Israel.
The scoffer will be gone,
the arrogant will disappear,
and those who plot evil will be killed.
Those who convict the innocent
by their false testimony will disappear.

A similar fate awaits those who use trickery to pervert justice
    and who tell lies to destroy the innocent.

That is why the LORD, who redeemed Abraham, says to the people of
Israel,

"My people will no longer be ashamed
    or turn pale with fear.
For when they see their many children
    and all the blessings I have given them,
they will recognize the holiness of the Holy One of Jacob.
    They will stand in awe of the God of Israel.
Then the wayward will gain understanding,
    and complainers will accept instruction.

"What sorrow awaits my rebellious children,"
    says the LORD.
"You make plans that are contrary to mine.
    You make alliances not directed by my Spirit,
    thus piling up your sins.
For without consulting me,
    you have gone down to Egypt for help.
You have put your trust in Pharaoh's protection.
    You have tried to hide in his shade.
But by trusting Pharaoh, you will be humiliated,
    and by depending on him, you will be disgraced.
For though his power extends to Zoan
    and his officials have arrived in Hanes,
all who trust in him will be ashamed.
    He will not help you.
    Instead, he will disgrace you."

This message came to me concerning the animals in the Negev:

The caravan moves slowly
    across the terrible desert to Egypt—
donkeys weighed down with riches
    and camels loaded with treasure—
    all to pay for Egypt's protection.
They travel through the wilderness,
    a place of lionesses and lions,
    a place where vipers and poisonous snakes live.
All this, and Egypt will give you nothing in return.
    Egypt's promises are worthless!

Therefore, I call her Rahab—
  the Harmless Dragon.

Now go and write down these words.
  Write them in a book.
They will stand until the end of time
  as a witness
that these people are stubborn rebels
  who refuse to pay attention to the LORD's instructions.
They tell the seers,
  "Stop seeing visions!"
They tell the prophets,
  "Don't tell us what is right.
Tell us nice things.
  Tell us lies.
Forget all this gloom.
  Get off your narrow path.
Stop telling us about your
  'Holy One of Israel.'"

This is the reply of the Holy One of Israel:

"Because you despise what I tell you
  and trust instead in oppression and lies,
calamity will come upon you suddenly—
  like a bulging wall that bursts and falls.
In an instant it will collapse
  and come crashing down.
You will be smashed like a piece of pottery—
  shattered so completely that
there won't be a piece big enough
  to carry coals from a fireplace
  or a little water from the well."

This is what the Sovereign LORD,
  the Holy One of Israel, says:
"Only in returning to me
  and resting in me will you be saved.
In quietness and confidence is your strength.
  But you would have none of it.
You said, 'No, we will get our help from Egypt.
  They will give us swift horses for riding into battle.'
But the only swiftness you are going to see
  is the swiftness of your enemies chasing you!

One of them will chase a thousand of you.
    Five of them will make all of you flee.
You will be left like a lonely flagpole on a hill
    or a tattered banner on a distant mountaintop."

So the LORD must wait for you to come to him
    so he can show you his love and compassion.
For the LORD is a faithful God.
    Blessed are those who wait for his help.

O people of Zion, who live in Jerusalem,
    you will weep no more.
He will be gracious if you ask for help.
    He will surely respond to the sound of your cries.
Though the Lord gave you adversity for food
    and suffering for drink,
he will still be with you to teach you.
    You will see your teacher with your own eyes.
Your own ears will hear him.
    Right behind you a voice will say,
"This is the way you should go,"
    whether to the right or to the left.
Then you will destroy all your silver idols
    and your precious gold images.
You will throw them out like filthy rags,
    saying to them, "Good riddance!"

Then the LORD will bless you with rain at planting time. There will be
wonderful harvests and plenty of pastureland for your livestock. The oxen
and donkeys that till the ground will eat good grain, its chaff blown away
by the wind. In that day, when your enemies are slaughtered and the towers fall, there will be streams of water flowing down every mountain and
hill. The moon will be as bright as the sun, and the sun will be seven times
brighter—like the light of seven days in one! So it will be when the LORD
begins to heal his people and cure the wounds he gave them.

Look! The LORD is coming from far away,
    burning with anger,
    surrounded by thick, rising smoke.
His lips are filled with fury;
    his words consume like fire.
His hot breath pours out like a flood
    up to the neck of his enemies.

He will sift out the proud nations for destruction.
  He will bridle them and lead them away to ruin.

But the people of God will sing a song of joy,
  like the songs at the holy festivals.
You will be filled with joy,
  as when a flutist leads a group of pilgrims
to Jerusalem, the mountain of the LORD—
  to the Rock of Israel.
And the LORD will make his majestic voice heard.
  He will display the strength of his mighty arm.
It will descend with devouring flames,
  with cloudbursts, thunderstorms, and huge hailstones.
At the LORD's command, the Assyrians will be shattered.
  He will strike them down with his royal scepter.
And as the LORD strikes them with his rod of punishment,
  his people will celebrate with tambourines and harps.
  Lifting his mighty arm, he will fight the Assyrians.
Topheth—the place of burning—
  has long been ready for the Assyrian king;
  the pyre is piled high with wood.
The breath of the LORD, like fire from a volcano,
  will set it ablaze.

What sorrow awaits those who look to Egypt for help,
  trusting their horses, chariots, and charioteers
and depending on the strength of human armies
  instead of looking to the LORD,
  the Holy One of Israel.
In his wisdom, the LORD will send great disaster;
  he will not change his mind.
He will rise against the wicked
  and against their helpers.
For these Egyptians are mere humans, not God!
  Their horses are puny flesh, not mighty spirits!
When the LORD raises his fist against them,
  those who help will stumble,
and those being helped will fall.
  They will all fall down and die together.

But this is what the LORD has told me:

"When a strong young lion
  stands growling over a sheep it has killed,

it is not frightened by the shouts and noise
    of a whole crowd of shepherds.
In the same way, the LORD of Heaven's Armies
    will come down and fight on Mount Zion.
The LORD of Heaven's Armies will hover over Jerusalem
    and protect it like a bird protecting its nest.
He will defend and save the city;
    he will pass over it and rescue it."

Though you are such wicked rebels, my people, come and return to the LORD. I know the glorious day will come when each of you will throw away the gold idols and silver images your sinful hands have made.

"The Assyrians will be destroyed,
    but not by the swords of men.
The sword of God will strike them,
    and they will panic and flee.
The strong young Assyrians
    will be taken away as captives.
Even the strongest will quake with terror,
    and princes will flee when they see your battle flags,"
says the LORD, whose fire burns in Zion,
    whose flame blazes from Jerusalem.

Look, a righteous king is coming!
    And honest princes will rule under him.
Each one will be like a shelter from the wind
    and a refuge from the storm,
like streams of water in the desert
    and the shadow of a great rock in a parched land.

Then everyone who has eyes will be able to see the truth,
    and everyone who has ears will be able to hear it.
Even the hotheads will be full of sense and understanding.
    Those who stammer will speak out plainly.
In that day ungodly fools will not be heroes.
    Scoundrels will not be respected.
For fools speak foolishness
    and make evil plans.
They practice ungodliness
    and spread false teachings about the LORD.
They deprive the hungry of food
    and give no water to the thirsty.
The smooth tricks of scoundrels are evil.

They plot crooked schemes.
They lie to convict the poor,
    even when the cause of the poor is just.
But generous people plan to do what is generous,
    and they stand firm in their generosity.

Listen, you women who lie around in ease.
    Listen to me, you who are so smug.
In a short time—just a little more than a year—
    you careless ones will suddenly begin to care.
For your fruit crops will fail,
    and the harvest will never take place.
Tremble, you women of ease;
    throw off your complacency.
Strip off your pretty clothes,
    and put on burlap to show your grief.
Beat your breasts in sorrow for your bountiful farms
    and your fruitful grapevines.
For your land will be overgrown with thorns and briers.
    Your joyful homes and happy towns will be gone.
The palace and the city will be deserted,
    and busy towns will be empty.
Wild donkeys will frolic and flocks will graze
    in the empty forts and watchtowers
until at last the Spirit is poured out
    on us from heaven.
Then the wilderness will become a fertile field,
    and the fertile field will yield bountiful crops.

Justice will rule in the wilderness
    and righteousness in the fertile field.
And this righteousness will bring peace.
    Yes, it will bring quietness and confidence forever.
My people will live in safety, quietly at home.
    They will be at rest.
Even if the forest should be destroyed
    and the city torn down,
the Lord will greatly bless his people.
    Wherever they plant seed, bountiful crops will spring up.
    Their cattle and donkeys will graze freely.

What sorrow awaits you Assyrians, who have destroyed others
    but have never been destroyed yourselves.

You betray others,
    but you have never been betrayed.
When you are done destroying,
    you will be destroyed.
When you are done betraying,
    you will be betrayed.
But LORD, be merciful to us,
    for we have waited for you.
Be our strong arm each day
    and our salvation in times of trouble.
The enemy runs at the sound of your voice.
    When you stand up, the nations flee!
Just as caterpillars and locusts strip the fields and vines,
    so the fallen army of Assyria will be stripped!

Though the LORD is very great and lives in heaven,
    he will make Jerusalem his home of justice and
        righteousness.
In that day he will be your sure foundation,
    providing a rich store of salvation, wisdom, and knowledge.
    The fear of the LORD will be your treasure.

But now your brave warriors weep in public.
    Your ambassadors of peace cry in bitter disappointment.
Your roads are deserted;
    no one travels them anymore.
The Assyrians have broken their peace treaty
    and care nothing for the promises they made before
        witnesses.
    They have no respect for anyone.
The land of Israel wilts in mourning.
    Lebanon withers with shame.
The plain of Sharon is now a wilderness.
    Bashan and Carmel have been plundered.

But the LORD says: "Now I will stand up.
    Now I will show my power and might.
You Assyrians produce nothing but dry grass and stubble.
    Your own breath will turn to fire and consume you.
Your people will be burned up completely,
    like thornbushes cut down and tossed in a fire.
Listen to what I have done, you nations far away!
    And you that are near, acknowledge my might!"

The sinners in Jerusalem shake with fear.
   Terror seizes the godless.
"Who can live with this devouring fire?" they cry.
   "Who can survive this all-consuming fire?"
Those who are honest and fair,
   who refuse to profit by fraud,
   who stay far away from bribes,
who refuse to listen to those who plot murder,
   who shut their eyes to all enticement to do wrong—
these are the ones who will dwell on high.
   The rocks of the mountains will be their fortress.
Food will be supplied to them,
   and they will have water in abundance.

Your eyes will see the king in all his splendor,
   and you will see a land that stretches into the distance.
You will think back to this time of terror, asking,
"Where are the Assyrian officers
   who counted our towers?
Where are the bookkeepers
   who recorded the plunder taken from our fallen city?"
You will no longer see these fierce, violent people
   with their strange, unknown language.

Instead, you will see Zion as a place of holy festivals.
   You will see Jerusalem, a city quiet and secure.
It will be like a tent whose ropes are taut
   and whose stakes are firmly fixed.
The Lord will be our Mighty One.
   He will be like a wide river of protection
that no enemy can cross,
   that no enemy ship can sail upon.
For the Lord is our judge,
   our lawgiver, and our king.
   He will care for us and save us.
The enemies' sails hang loose
   on broken masts with useless tackle.
Their treasure will be divided by the people of God.
   Even the lame will take their share!
The people of Israel will no longer say,
   "We are sick and helpless,"
   for the Lord will forgive their sins.

+ + +

Come here and listen, O nations of the earth.
  Let the world and everything in it hear my words.
For the LORD is enraged against the nations.
  His fury is against all their armies.
He will completely destroy them,
  dooming them to slaughter.
Their dead will be left unburied,
  and the stench of rotting bodies will fill the land.
  The mountains will flow with their blood.
The heavens above will melt away
  and disappear like a rolled-up scroll.
The stars will fall from the sky
  like withered leaves from a grapevine,
  or shriveled figs from a fig tree.

And when my sword has finished its work in the heavens,
  it will fall upon Edom,
  the nation I have marked for destruction.
The sword of the LORD is drenched with blood
  and covered with fat—
with the blood of lambs and goats,
  with the fat of rams prepared for sacrifice.
Yes, the LORD will offer a sacrifice in the city of Bozrah.
  He will make a mighty slaughter in Edom.
Even men as strong as wild oxen will die—
  the young men alongside the veterans.
The land will be soaked with blood
  and the soil enriched with fat.

For it is the day of the LORD's revenge,
  the year when Edom will be paid back for all it did to Israel.
The streams of Edom will be filled with burning pitch,
  and the ground will be covered with fire.
This judgment on Edom will never end;
  the smoke of its burning will rise forever.
The land will lie deserted from generation to generation.
  No one will live there anymore.
It will be haunted by the desert owl and the screech owl,
  the great owl and the raven.
For God will measure that land carefully;
  he will measure it for chaos and destruction.

It will be called the Land of Nothing,
   and all its nobles will soon be gone.
Thorns will overrun its palaces;
   nettles and thistles will grow in its forts.
The ruins will become a haunt for jackals
   and a home for owls.
Desert animals will mingle there with hyenas,
   their howls filling the night.
Wild goats will bleat at one another among the ruins,
   and night creatures will come there to rest.
There the owl will make her nest and lay her eggs.
   She will hatch her young and cover them with her wings.
And the buzzards will come,
   each one with its mate.

Search the book of the LORD,
   and see what he will do.
Not one of these birds and animals will be missing,
   and none will lack a mate,
for the LORD has promised this.
   His Spirit will make it all come true.
He has surveyed and divided the land
   and deeded it over to those creatures.
They will possess it forever,
   from generation to generation.

Even the wilderness and desert will be glad in those days.
   The wasteland will rejoice and blossom with spring crocuses.
Yes, there will be an abundance of flowers
   and singing and joy!
The deserts will become as green as the mountains of Lebanon,
   as lovely as Mount Carmel or the plain of Sharon.
There the LORD will display his glory,
   the splendor of our God.
With this news, strengthen those who have tired hands,
   and encourage those who have weak knees.
Say to those with fearful hearts,
   "Be strong, and do not fear,
for your God is coming to destroy your enemies.
   He is coming to save you."

And when he comes, he will open the eyes of the blind
   and unplug the ears of the deaf.

The lame will leap like a deer,
  and those who cannot speak will sing for joy!
Springs will gush forth in the wilderness,
  and streams will water the wasteland.
The parched ground will become a pool,
  and springs of water will satisfy the thirsty land.
Marsh grass and reeds and rushes will flourish
  where desert jackals once lived.

And a great road will go through that once deserted land.
  It will be named the Highway of Holiness.
Evil-minded people will never travel on it.
  It will be only for those who walk in God's ways;
  fools will never walk there.
Lions will not lurk along its course,
  nor any other ferocious beasts.
There will be no other dangers.
  Only the redeemed will walk on it.
Those who have been ransomed by the LORD will return.
  They will enter Jerusalem singing,
  crowned with everlasting joy.
Sorrow and mourning will disappear,
  and they will be filled with joy and gladness.

+ + +

In the fourteenth year of King Hezekiah's reign, King Sennacherib of Assyria came to attack the fortified towns of Judah and conquered them. Then the king of Assyria sent his chief of staff from Lachish with a huge army to confront King Hezekiah in Jerusalem. The Assyrians took up a position beside the aqueduct that feeds water into the upper pool, near the road leading to the field where cloth is washed.

These are the officials who went out to meet with them: Eliakim son of Hilkiah, the palace administrator; Shebna the court secretary; and Joah son of Asaph, the royal historian.

Then the Assyrian king's chief of staff told them to give this message to Hezekiah:

"This is what the great king of Assyria says: What are you trusting
in that makes you so confident? Do you think that mere words can
substitute for military skill and strength? Who are you counting on,
that you have rebelled against me? On Egypt? If you lean on Egypt, it

will be like a reed that splinters beneath your weight and pierces your hand. Pharaoh, the king of Egypt, is completely unreliable!

"But perhaps you will say to me, 'We are trusting in the LORD our God!' But isn't he the one who was insulted by Hezekiah? Didn't Hezekiah tear down his shrines and altars and make everyone in Judah and Jerusalem worship only at the altar here in Jerusalem?

"I'll tell you what! Strike a bargain with my master, the king of Assyria. I will give you 2,000 horses if you can find that many men to ride on them! With your tiny army, how can you think of challenging even the weakest contingent of my master's troops, even with the help of Egypt's chariots and charioteers? What's more, do you think we have invaded your land without the LORD's direction? The LORD himself told us, 'Attack this land and destroy it!'"

Then Eliakim, Shebna, and Joah said to the Assyrian chief of staff, "Please speak to us in Aramaic, for we understand it well. Don't speak in Hebrew, for the people on the wall will hear."

But Sennacherib's chief of staff replied, "Do you think my master sent this message only to you and your master? He wants all the people to hear it, for when we put this city under siege, they will suffer along with you. They will be so hungry and thirsty that they will eat their own dung and drink their own urine."

Then the chief of staff stood and shouted in Hebrew to the people on the wall, "Listen to this message from the great king of Assyria! This is what the king says: Don't let Hezekiah deceive you. He will never be able to rescue you. Don't let him fool you into trusting in the LORD by saying, 'The LORD will surely rescue us. This city will never fall into the hands of the Assyrian king!'

"Don't listen to Hezekiah! These are the terms the king of Assyria is offering: Make peace with me—open the gates and come out. Then each of you can continue eating from your own grapevine and fig tree and drinking from your own well. Then I will arrange to take you to another land like this one—a land of grain and new wine, bread and vineyards.

"Don't let Hezekiah mislead you by saying, 'The LORD will rescue us!' Have the gods of any other nations ever saved their people from the king of Assyria? What happened to the gods of Hamath and Arpad? And what about the gods of Sepharvaim? Did any god rescue Samaria from my power? What god of any nation has ever been able to save its people from my power? So what makes you think that the LORD can rescue Jerusalem from me?"

But the people were silent and did not utter a word because Hezekiah had commanded them, "Do not answer him."

Then Eliakim son of Hilkiah, the palace administrator; Shebna the court secretary; and Joah son of Asaph, the royal historian, went back to Hezekiah. They tore their clothes in despair, and they went in to see the king and told him what the Assyrian chief of staff had said.

When King Hezekiah heard their report, he tore his clothes and put on burlap and went into the Temple of the LORD. And he sent Eliakim the palace administrator, Shebna the court secretary, and the leading priests, all dressed in burlap, to the prophet Isaiah son of Amoz. They told him, "This is what King Hezekiah says: Today is a day of trouble, insults, and disgrace. It is like when a child is ready to be born, but the mother has no strength to deliver the baby. But perhaps the LORD your God has heard the Assyrian chief of staff, sent by the king to defy the living God, and will punish him for his words. Oh, pray for those of us who are left!"

After King Hezekiah's officials delivered the king's message to Isaiah, the prophet replied, "Say to your master, 'This is what the LORD says: Do not be disturbed by this blasphemous speech against me from the Assyrian king's messengers. Listen! I myself will move against him, and the king will receive a message that he is needed at home. So he will return to his land, where I will have him killed with a sword.'"

Meanwhile, the Assyrian chief of staff left Jerusalem and went to consult the king of Assyria, who had left Lachish and was attacking Libnah.

Soon afterward King Sennacherib received word that King Tirhakah of Ethiopia was leading an army to fight against him. Before leaving to meet the attack, he sent messengers back to Hezekiah in Jerusalem with this message:

"This message is for King Hezekiah of Judah. Don't let your God, in whom you trust, deceive you with promises that Jerusalem will not be captured by the king of Assyria. You know perfectly well what the kings of Assyria have done wherever they have gone. They have completely destroyed everyone who stood in their way! Why should you be any different? Have the gods of other nations rescued them—such nations as Gozan, Haran, Rezeph, and the people of Eden who were in Tel-assar? My predecessors destroyed them all! What happened to the king of Hamath and the king of Arpad? What happened to the kings of Sepharvaim, Hena, and Ivvah?"

After Hezekiah received the letter from the messengers and read it, he went up to the LORD's Temple and spread it out before the LORD. And Hezekiah prayed this prayer before the LORD: "O LORD of Heaven's Armies, God of Israel, you are enthroned between the mighty cherubim! You alone are God of all the kingdoms of the earth. You alone created the heavens and the earth. Bend down, O LORD, and listen! Open your eyes,

O LORD, and see! Listen to Sennacherib's words of defiance against the living God.

"It is true, LORD, that the kings of Assyria have destroyed all these nations. And they have thrown the gods of these nations into the fire and burned them. But of course the Assyrians could destroy them! They were not gods at all—only idols of wood and stone shaped by human hands. Now, O LORD our God, rescue us from his power; then all the kingdoms of the earth will know that you alone, O LORD, are God."

Then Isaiah son of Amoz sent this message to Hezekiah: "This is what the LORD, the God of Israel, says: Because you prayed about King Sennacherib of Assyria, the LORD has spoken this word against him:

"The virgin daughter of Zion
   despises you and laughs at you.
The daughter of Jerusalem
   shakes her head in derision as you flee.

"Whom have you been defying and ridiculing?
   Against whom did you raise your voice?
At whom did you look with such haughty eyes?
   It was the Holy One of Israel!
By your messengers you have defied the Lord.
   You have said, 'With my many chariots
I have conquered the highest mountains—
   yes, the remotest peaks of Lebanon.
I have cut down its tallest cedars
   and its finest cypress trees.
I have reached its farthest heights
   and explored its deepest forests.
I have dug wells in many foreign lands
   and refreshed myself with their water.
With the sole of my foot,
   I stopped up all the rivers of Egypt!'

"But have you not heard?
   I decided this long ago.
Long ago I planned it,
   and now I am making it happen.
I planned for you to crush fortified cities
   into heaps of rubble.
That is why their people have so little power
   and are so frightened and confused.
They are as weak as grass,

as easily trampled as tender green shoots.
They are like grass sprouting on a housetop,
    scorched before it can grow lush and tall.

"But I know you well—
    where you stay
and when you come and go.
    I know the way you have raged against me.
And because of your raging against me
    and your arrogance, which I have heard for myself,
I will put my hook in your nose
    and my bit in your mouth.
I will make you return
    by the same road on which you came."

Then Isaiah said to Hezekiah, "Here is the proof that what I say is true:

"This year you will eat only what grows up by itself,
    and next year you will eat what springs up from that.
But in the third year you will plant crops and harvest them;
    you will tend vineyards and eat their fruit.
And you who are left in Judah,
    who have escaped the ravages of the siege,
will put roots down in your own soil
    and grow up and flourish.
For a remnant of my people will spread out from Jerusalem,
    a group of survivors from Mount Zion.
The passionate commitment of the LORD of Heaven's Armies
    will make this happen!

"And this is what the LORD says about the king of Assyria:

"'His armies will not enter Jerusalem.
    They will not even shoot an arrow at it.
They will not march outside its gates with their shields
    nor build banks of earth against its walls.
The king will return to his own country
    by the same road on which he came.
He will not enter this city,'
    says the LORD.
'For my own honor and for the sake of my servant David,
    I will defend this city and protect it.'"

That night the angel of the LORD went out to the Assyrian camp and killed 185,000 Assyrian soldiers. When the surviving Assyrians woke up the next morning, they found corpses everywhere. Then King Sennacherib of Assyria broke camp and returned to his own land. He went home to his capital of Nineveh and stayed there.

One day while he was worshiping in the temple of his god Nisroch, his sons Adrammelech and Sharezer killed him with their swords. They then escaped to the land of Ararat, and another son, Esarhaddon, became the next king of Assyria.

+

About that time Hezekiah became deathly ill, and the prophet Isaiah son of Amoz went to visit him. He gave the king this message: "This is what the LORD says: 'Set your affairs in order, for you are going to die. You will not recover from this illness.'"

When Hezekiah heard this, he turned his face to the wall and prayed to the LORD, "Remember, O LORD, how I have always been faithful to you and have served you single-mindedly, always doing what pleases you." Then he broke down and wept bitterly.

Then this message came to Isaiah from the LORD: "Go back to Hezekiah and tell him, 'This is what the LORD, the God of your ancestor David, says: I have heard your prayer and seen your tears. I will add fifteen years to your life, and I will rescue you and this city from the king of Assyria. Yes, I will defend this city.

"'And this is the sign from the LORD to prove that he will do as he promised: I will cause the sun's shadow to move ten steps backward on the sundial of Ahaz!'" So the shadow on the sundial moved backward ten steps.

When King Hezekiah was well again, he wrote this poem:

> I said, "In the prime of my life,
> must I now enter the place of the dead?
> Am I to be robbed of the rest of my years?"
> I said, "Never again will I see the LORD GOD
> while still in the land of the living.
> Never again will I see my friends
> or be with those who live in this world.
> My life has been blown away
> like a shepherd's tent in a storm.
> It has been cut short,
> as when a weaver cuts cloth from a loom.
> Suddenly, my life was over.
> I waited patiently all night,
> but I was torn apart as though by lions.

Suddenly, my life was over.
Delirious, I chattered like a swallow or a crane,
and then I moaned like a mourning dove.
My eyes grew tired of looking to heaven for help.
I am in trouble, Lord. Help me!"

But what could I say?
For he himself sent this sickness.
Now I will walk humbly throughout my years
because of this anguish I have felt.
Lord, your discipline is good,
for it leads to life and health.
You restore my health
and allow me to live!
Yes, this anguish was good for me,
for you have rescued me from death
and forgiven all my sins.
For the dead cannot praise you;
they cannot raise their voices in praise.
Those who go down to the grave
can no longer hope in your faithfulness.
Only the living can praise you as I do today.
Each generation tells of your faithfulness
to the next.
Think of it—the LORD is ready to heal me!
I will sing his praises with instruments
every day of my life
in the Temple of the LORD.

Isaiah had said to Hezekiah's servants, "Make an ointment from figs and spread it over the boil, and Hezekiah will recover."

And Hezekiah had asked, "What sign will prove that I will go to the Temple of the LORD?"

Soon after this, Merodach-baladan son of Baladan, king of Babylon, sent Hezekiah his best wishes and a gift. He had heard that Hezekiah had been very sick and that he had recovered. Hezekiah was delighted with the Babylonian envoys and showed them everything in his treasure-houses—the silver, the gold, the spices, and the aromatic oils. He also took them to see his armory and showed them everything in his royal treasuries! There was nothing in his palace or kingdom that Hezekiah did not show them.

Then Isaiah the prophet went to King Hezekiah and asked him, "What did those men want? Where were they from?"

Hezekiah replied, "They came from the distant land of Babylon."

"What did they see in your palace?" asked Isaiah.

"They saw everything," Hezekiah replied. "I showed them everything I own—all my royal treasuries."

Then Isaiah said to Hezekiah, "Listen to this message from the LORD of Heaven's Armies: 'The time is coming when everything in your palace—all the treasures stored up by your ancestors until now—will be carried off to Babylon. Nothing will be left,' says the LORD. 'Some of your very own sons will be taken away into exile. They will become eunuchs who will serve in the palace of Babylon's king.'"

Then Hezekiah said to Isaiah, "This message you have given me from the LORD is good." For the king was thinking, "At least there will be peace and security during my lifetime."

+ + +

"Comfort, comfort my people,"
    says your God.
"Speak tenderly to Jerusalem.
Tell her that her sad days are gone
    and her sins are pardoned.
Yes, the LORD has punished her twice over
    for all her sins."

Listen! It's the voice of someone shouting,
"Clear the way through the wilderness
    for the LORD!
Make a straight highway through the wasteland
    for our God!
Fill in the valleys,
    and level the mountains and hills.
Straighten the curves,
    and smooth out the rough places.
Then the glory of the LORD will be revealed,
    and all people will see it together.
    The LORD has spoken!"

A voice said, "Shout!"
    I asked, "What should I shout?"

"Shout that people are like the grass.
    Their beauty fades as quickly
    as the flowers in a field.

The grass withers and the flowers fade
 beneath the breath of the Lord.
 And so it is with people.
The grass withers and the flowers fade,
 but the word of our God stands forever."

O Zion, messenger of good news,
 shout from the mountaintops!
Shout it louder, O Jerusalem.
 Shout, and do not be afraid.
Tell the towns of Judah,
 "Your God is coming!"
Yes, the Sovereign Lord is coming in power.
 He will rule with a powerful arm.
 See, he brings his reward with him as he comes.
He will feed his flock like a shepherd.
 He will carry the lambs in his arms,
holding them close to his heart.
 He will gently lead the mother sheep with their young.

Who else has held the oceans in his hand?
 Who has measured off the heavens with his fingers?
Who else knows the weight of the earth
 or has weighed the mountains and hills on a scale?
Who is able to advise the Spirit of the Lord?
 Who knows enough to give him advice or teach him?
Has the Lord ever needed anyone's advice?
 Does he need instruction about what is good?
Did someone teach him what is right
 or show him the path of justice?

No, for all the nations of the world
 are but a drop in the bucket.
They are nothing more
 than dust on the scales.
He picks up the whole earth
 as though it were a grain of sand.
All the wood in Lebanon's forests
 and all Lebanon's animals would not be enough
 to make a burnt offering worthy of our God.
The nations of the world are worth nothing to him.
 In his eyes they count for less than nothing—
 mere emptiness and froth.

To whom can you compare God?
What image can you find to resemble him?
Can he be compared to an idol formed in a mold,
overlaid with gold, and decorated with silver chains?
Or if people are too poor for that,
they might at least choose wood that won't decay
and a skilled craftsman
to carve an image that won't fall down!

Haven't you heard? Don't you understand?
Are you deaf to the words of God—
the words he gave before the world began?
Are you so ignorant?
God sits above the circle of the earth.
The people below seem like grasshoppers to him!
He spreads out the heavens like a curtain
and makes his tent from them.
He judges the great people of the world
and brings them all to nothing.
They hardly get started, barely taking root,
when he blows on them and they wither.
The wind carries them off like chaff.

"To whom will you compare me?
Who is my equal?" asks the Holy One.

Look up into the heavens.
Who created all the stars?
He brings them out like an army, one after another,
calling each by its name.
Because of his great power and incomparable strength,
not a single one is missing.
O Jacob, how can you say the LORD does not see your troubles?
O Israel, how can you say God ignores your rights?
Have you never heard?
Have you never understood?
The LORD is the everlasting God,
the Creator of all the earth.
He never grows weak or weary.
No one can measure the depths of his understanding.
He gives power to the weak
and strength to the powerless.
Even youths will become weak and tired,
and young men will fall in exhaustion.

But those who trust in the LORD will find new strength.
    They will soar high on wings like eagles.
They will run and not grow weary.
    They will walk and not faint.

+

"Listen in silence before me, you lands beyond the sea.
    Bring your strongest arguments.
Come now and speak.
    The court is ready for your case.

"Who has stirred up this king from the east,
    rightly calling him to God's service?
Who gives this man victory over many nations
    and permits him to trample their kings underfoot?
With his sword, he reduces armies to dust.
    With his bow, he scatters them like chaff before the wind.
He chases them away and goes on safely,
    though he is walking over unfamiliar ground.
Who has done such mighty deeds,
    summoning each new generation from the beginning of time?
It is I, the LORD, the First and the Last.
    I alone am he."

The lands beyond the sea watch in fear.
    Remote lands tremble and mobilize for war.
The idol makers encourage one another,
    saying to each other, "Be strong!"
The carver encourages the goldsmith,
    and the molder helps at the anvil.
    "Good," they say. "It's coming along fine."
Carefully they join the parts together,
    then fasten the thing in place so it won't fall over.

"But as for you, Israel my servant,
    Jacob my chosen one,
    descended from Abraham my friend,
I have called you back from the ends of the earth,
    saying, 'You are my servant.'
For I have chosen you
    and will not throw you away.
Don't be afraid, for I am with you.
    Don't be discouraged, for I am your God.

I will strengthen you and help you.
  I will hold you up with my victorious right hand.

"See, all your angry enemies lie there,
  confused and humiliated.
Anyone who opposes you will die
  and come to nothing.
You will look in vain
  for those who tried to conquer you.
Those who attack you
  will come to nothing.
For I hold you by your right hand—
  I, the LORD your God.
And I say to you,
  'Don't be afraid. I am here to help you.
Though you are a lowly worm, O Jacob,
  don't be afraid, people of Israel, for I will help you.
I am the LORD, your Redeemer.
  I am the Holy One of Israel.'
You will be a new threshing instrument
  with many sharp teeth.
You will tear your enemies apart,
  making chaff of mountains.
You will toss them into the air,
  and the wind will blow them all away;
  a whirlwind will scatter them.
Then you will rejoice in the LORD.
  You will glory in the Holy One of Israel.

"When the poor and needy search for water and there is none,
  and their tongues are parched from thirst,
then I, the LORD, will answer them.
  I, the God of Israel, will never abandon them.
I will open up rivers for them on the high plateaus.
  I will give them fountains of water in the valleys.
I will fill the desert with pools of water.
  Rivers fed by springs will flow across the parched ground.
I will plant trees in the barren desert—
  cedar, acacia, myrtle, olive, cypress, fir, and pine.
I am doing this so all who see this miracle
  will understand what it means—
that it is the LORD who has done this,
  the Holy One of Israel who created it.

"Present the case for your idols,"
  says the LORD.
"Let them show what they can do,"
  says the King of Israel.
"Let them try to tell us what happened long ago
  so that we may consider the evidence.
Or let them tell us what the future holds,
  so we can know what's going to happen.
Yes, tell us what will occur in the days ahead.
  Then we will know you are gods.
In fact, do anything—good or bad!
  Do something that will amaze and frighten us.
But no! You are less than nothing and can do nothing at all.
  Those who choose you pollute themselves.

"But I have stirred up a leader who will approach from the north.
  From the east he will call on my name.
I will give him victory over kings and princes.
  He will trample them as a potter treads on clay.

"Who told you from the beginning
  that this would happen?
Who predicted this,
  making you admit that he was right?
  No one said a word!
I was the first to tell Zion,
  'Look! Help is on the way!'
  I will send Jerusalem a messenger with good news.
Not one of your idols told you this.
  Not one gave any answer when I asked.
See, they are all foolish, worthless things.
  All your idols are as empty as the wind.

+

"Look at my servant, whom I strengthen.
  He is my chosen one, who pleases me.
I have put my Spirit upon him.
  He will bring justice to the nations.
He will not shout
  or raise his voice in public.
He will not crush the weakest reed
  or put out a flickering candle.

He will bring justice to all who have been wronged.
He will not falter or lose heart
    until justice prevails throughout the earth.
    Even distant lands beyond the sea will wait for his instruction."

God, the LORD, created the heavens and stretched them out.
    He created the earth and everything in it.
He gives breath to everyone,
    life to everyone who walks the earth.
And it is he who says,
"I, the LORD, have called you to demonstrate my righteousness.
    I will take you by the hand and guard you,
and I will give you to my people, Israel,
    as a symbol of my covenant with them.
And you will be a light to guide the nations.
    You will open the eyes of the blind.
You will free the captives from prison,
    releasing those who sit in dark dungeons.

"I am the LORD; that is my name!
    I will not give my glory to anyone else,
    nor share my praise with carved idols.
Everything I prophesied has come true,
    and now I will prophesy again.
I will tell you the future before it happens."

Sing a new song to the LORD!
    Sing his praises from the ends of the earth!
Sing, all you who sail the seas,
    all you who live in distant coastlands.
Join in the chorus, you desert towns;
    let the villages of Kedar rejoice!
Let the people of Sela sing for joy;
    shout praises from the mountaintops!
Let the whole world glorify the LORD;
    let it sing his praise.
The LORD will march forth like a mighty hero;
    he will come out like a warrior, full of fury.
He will shout his battle cry
    and crush all his enemies.

He will say, "I have long been silent;
    yes, I have restrained myself.

But now, like a woman in labor,
  I will cry and groan and pant.
I will level the mountains and hills
  and blight all their greenery.
I will turn the rivers into dry land
  and will dry up all the pools.
I will lead blind Israel down a new path,
  guiding them along an unfamiliar way.
I will brighten the darkness before them
  and smooth out the road ahead of them.
Yes, I will indeed do these things;
  I will not forsake them.
But those who trust in idols,
  who say, 'You are our gods,'
  will be turned away in shame.

"Listen, you who are deaf!
  Look and see, you blind!
Who is as blind as my own people, my servant?
  Who is as deaf as my messenger?
Who is as blind as my chosen people,
  the servant of the LORD?
You see and recognize what is right
  but refuse to act on it.
You hear with your ears,
  but you don't really listen."

Because he is righteous,
  the LORD has exalted his glorious law.
But his own people have been robbed and plundered,
  enslaved, imprisoned, and trapped.
They are fair game for anyone
  and have no one to protect them,
  no one to take them back home.

Who will hear these lessons from the past
  and see the ruin that awaits you in the future?
Who allowed Israel to be robbed and hurt?
  It was the LORD, against whom we sinned,
for the people would not walk in his path,
  nor would they obey his law.
Therefore, he poured out his fury on them
  and destroyed them in battle.

They were enveloped in flames,
    but they still refused to understand.
They were consumed by fire,
    but they did not learn their lesson.

But now, O Jacob, listen to the LORD who created you.
    O Israel, the one who formed you says,
"Do not be afraid, for I have ransomed you.
    I have called you by name; you are mine.
When you go through deep waters,
    I will be with you.
When you go through rivers of difficulty,
    you will not drown.
When you walk through the fire of oppression,
    you will not be burned up;
    the flames will not consume you.
For I am the LORD, your God,
    the Holy One of Israel, your Savior.
I gave Egypt as a ransom for your freedom;
    I gave Ethiopia and Seba in your place.
Others were given in exchange for you.
    I traded their lives for yours
because you are precious to me.
    You are honored, and I love you.

"Do not be afraid, for I am with you.
    I will gather you and your children from east and west.
I will say to the north and south,
    'Bring my sons and daughters back to Israel
    from the distant corners of the earth.
Bring all who claim me as their God,
    for I have made them for my glory.
    It was I who created them.'"

Bring out the people who have eyes but are blind,
    who have ears but are deaf.
Gather the nations together!
    Assemble the peoples of the world!
Which of their idols has ever foretold such things?
    Which can predict what will happen tomorrow?
Where are the witnesses of such predictions?
    Who can verify that they spoke the truth?

"But you are my witnesses, O Israel!" says the LORD.
  "You are my servant.
You have been chosen to know me, believe in me,
  and understand that I alone am God.
There is no other God—
  there never has been, and there never will be.
I, yes I, am the LORD,
  and there is no other Savior.
First I predicted your rescue,
  then I saved you and proclaimed it to the world.
No foreign god has ever done this.
  You are witnesses that I am the only God,"
  says the LORD.
"From eternity to eternity I am God.
  No one can snatch anyone out of my hand.
  No one can undo what I have done."

+

This is what the LORD says—your Redeemer, the Holy One of Israel:

"For your sakes I will send an army against Babylon,
  forcing the Babylonians to flee in those ships they are so proud of.
I am the LORD, your Holy One,
  Israel's Creator and King.
I am the LORD, who opened a way through the waters,
  making a dry path through the sea.
I called forth the mighty army of Egypt
  with all its chariots and horses.
I drew them beneath the waves, and they drowned,
  their lives snuffed out like a smoldering candlewick.

"But forget all that—
  it is nothing compared to what I am going to do.
For I am about to do something new.
  See, I have already begun! Do you not see it?
I will make a pathway through the wilderness.
  I will create rivers in the dry wasteland.
The wild animals in the fields will thank me,
  the jackals and owls, too,
  for giving them water in the desert.
Yes, I will make rivers in the dry wasteland
  so my chosen people can be refreshed.

I have made Israel for myself,
    and they will someday honor me before the whole world.

"But, dear family of Jacob, you refuse to ask for my help.
    You have grown tired of me, O Israel!
You have not brought me sheep or goats for burnt offerings.
    You have not honored me with sacrifices,
though I have not burdened and wearied you
    with requests for grain offerings and frankincense.
You have not brought me fragrant calamus
    or pleased me with the fat from sacrifices.
Instead, you have burdened me with your sins
    and wearied me with your faults.

"I—yes, I alone—will blot out your sins for my own sake
    and will never think of them again.
Let us review the situation together,
    and you can present your case to prove your innocence.
From the very beginning, your first ancestor sinned against me;
    all your leaders broke my laws.
That is why I have disgraced your priests;
    I have decreed complete destruction for Jacob
    and shame for Israel.

"But now, listen to me, Jacob my servant,
    Israel my chosen one.
The LORD who made you and helps you says:
Do not be afraid, O Jacob, my servant,
    O dear Israel, my chosen one.
For I will pour out water to quench your thirst
    and to irrigate your parched fields.
And I will pour out my Spirit on your descendants,
    and my blessing on your children.
They will thrive like watered grass,
    like willows on a riverbank.
Some will proudly claim, 'I belong to the LORD.'
    Others will say, 'I am a descendant of Jacob.'
Some will write the LORD's name on their hands
    and will take the name of Israel as their own."

This is what the LORD says—Israel's King and Redeemer, the LORD of
Heaven's Armies:

"I am the First and the Last;
  there is no other God.
Who is like me?
  Let him step forward and prove to you his power.
Let him do as I have done since ancient times
  when I established a people and explained its future.
Do not tremble; do not be afraid.
  Did I not proclaim my purposes for you long ago?
You are my witnesses—is there any other God?
  No! There is no other Rock—not one!"

How foolish are those who manufacture idols.
  These prized objects are really worthless.
The people who worship idols don't know this,
  so they are all put to shame.
Who but a fool would make his own god—
  an idol that cannot help him one bit?
All who worship idols will be disgraced
  along with all these craftsmen—mere humans—
  who claim they can make a god.
They may all stand together,
  but they will stand in terror and shame.

The blacksmith stands at his forge to make a sharp tool,
  pounding and shaping it with all his might.
His work makes him hungry and weak.
  It makes him thirsty and faint.
Then the wood-carver measures a block of wood
  and draws a pattern on it.
He works with chisel and plane
  and carves it into a human figure.
He gives it human beauty
  and puts it in a little shrine.
He cuts down cedars;
  he selects the cypress and the oak;
he plants the pine in the forest
  to be nourished by the rain.
Then he uses part of the wood to make a fire.
  With it he warms himself and bakes his bread.
Then—yes, it's true—he takes the rest of it
  and makes himself a god to worship!
He makes an idol
  and bows down in front of it!

He burns part of the tree to roast his meat
  and to keep himself warm.
  He says, "Ah, that fire feels good."
Then he takes what's left
  and makes his god: a carved idol!
He falls down in front of it,
  worshiping and praying to it.
"Rescue me!" he says.
  "You are my god!"

Such stupidity and ignorance!
  Their eyes are closed, and they cannot see.
  Their minds are shut, and they cannot think.
The person who made the idol never stops to reflect,
  "Why, it's just a block of wood!
I burned half of it for heat
  and used it to bake my bread and roast my meat.
How can the rest of it be a god?
  Should I bow down to worship a piece of wood?"
The poor, deluded fool feeds on ashes.
  He trusts something that can't help him at all.
Yet he cannot bring himself to ask,
  "Is this idol that I'm holding in my hand a lie?"

"Pay attention, O Jacob,
  for you are my servant, O Israel.
I, the LORD, made you,
  and I will not forget you.
I have swept away your sins like a cloud.
  I have scattered your offenses like the morning mist.
Oh, return to me,
  for I have paid the price to set you free."

Sing, O heavens, for the LORD has done this wondrous thing.
  Shout for joy, O depths of the earth!
Break into song,
  O mountains and forests and every tree!
For the LORD has redeemed Jacob
  and is glorified in Israel.

+

This is what the LORD says—
  your Redeemer and Creator:

"I am the LORD, who made all things.
  I alone stretched out the heavens.
Who was with me
  when I made the earth?
I expose the false prophets as liars
  and make fools of fortune-tellers.
I cause the wise to give bad advice,
  thus proving them to be fools.
But I carry out the predictions of my prophets!
  By them I say to Jerusalem, 'People will live here again,'
and to the towns of Judah, 'You will be rebuilt;
  I will restore all your ruins!'
When I speak to the rivers and say, 'Dry up!'
  they will be dry.
When I say of Cyrus, 'He is my shepherd,'
  he will certainly do as I say.
He will command, 'Rebuild Jerusalem';
  he will say, 'Restore the Temple.'"

This is what the LORD says to Cyrus, his anointed one,
  whose right hand he will empower.
Before him, mighty kings will be paralyzed with fear.
  Their fortress gates will be opened,
  never to shut again.
This is what the LORD says:

"I will go before you, Cyrus,
  and level the mountains.
I will smash down gates of bronze
  and cut through bars of iron.
And I will give you treasures hidden in the darkness—
  secret riches.
I will do this so you may know that I am the LORD,
  the God of Israel, the one who calls you by name.

"And why have I called you for this work?
  Why did I call you by name when you did not know me?
It is for the sake of Jacob my servant,
  Israel my chosen one.
I am the LORD;
  there is no other God.
I have equipped you for battle,
  though you don't even know me,

so all the world from east to west
  will know there is no other God.
I am the LORD, and there is no other.
  I create the light and make the darkness.
I send good times and bad times.
  I, the LORD, am the one who does these things.

"Open up, O heavens,
  and pour out your righteousness.
Let the earth open wide
  so salvation and righteousness can sprout up together.
  I, the LORD, created them.

"What sorrow awaits those who argue with their Creator.
  Does a clay pot argue with its maker?
Does the clay dispute with the one who shapes it, saying,
  'Stop, you're doing it wrong!'
Does the pot exclaim,
  'How clumsy can you be?'
How terrible it would be if a newborn baby said to its father,
  'Why was I born?'
or if it said to its mother,
  'Why did you make me this way?'"

This is what the LORD says—
  the Holy One of Israel and your Creator:
"Do you question what I do for my children?
  Do you give me orders about the work of my hands?
I am the one who made the earth
  and created people to live on it.
With my hands I stretched out the heavens.
  All the stars are at my command.
I will raise up Cyrus to fulfill my righteous purpose,
  and I will guide his actions.
He will restore my city and free my captive people—
  without seeking a reward!
  I, the LORD of Heaven's Armies, have spoken!"

This is what the LORD says:

"You will rule the Egyptians,
  the Ethiopians, and the Sabeans.
They will come to you with all their merchandise,
  and it will all be yours.

They will follow you as prisoners in chains.
    They will fall to their knees in front of you and say,
'God is with you, and he is the only God.
    There is no other.'"

Truly, O God of Israel, our Savior,
    you work in mysterious ways.
All craftsmen who make idols will be humiliated.
    They will all be disgraced together.
But the LORD will save the people of Israel
    with eternal salvation.
Throughout everlasting ages,
    they will never again be humiliated and disgraced.

For the LORD is God,
    and he created the heavens and earth
    and put everything in place.
He made the world to be lived in,
    not to be a place of empty chaos.
"I am the LORD," he says,
    "and there is no other.
I publicly proclaim bold promises.
    I do not whisper obscurities in some dark corner.
I would not have told the people of Israel to seek me
    if I could not be found.
I, the LORD, speak only what is true
    and declare only what is right.

"Gather together and come,
    you fugitives from surrounding nations.
What fools they are who carry around their wooden idols
    and pray to gods that cannot save!
Consult together, argue your case.
    Get together and decide what to say.
Who made these things known so long ago?
    What idol ever told you they would happen?
Was it not I, the LORD?
    For there is no other God but me,
a righteous God and Savior.
    There is none but me.
Let all the world look to me for salvation!
    For I am God; there is no other.
I have sworn by my own name;

I have spoken the truth,
and I will never go back on my word:
Every knee will bend to me,
and every tongue will declare allegiance to me."
The people will declare,
"The LORD is the source of all my righteousness and strength."
And all who were angry with him
will come to him and be ashamed.
In the LORD all the generations of Israel will be justified,
and in him they will boast.

+

Bel and Nebo, the gods of Babylon,
bow as they are lowered to the ground.
They are being hauled away on ox carts.
The poor beasts stagger under the weight.
Both the idols and their owners are bowed down.
The gods cannot protect the people,
and the people cannot protect the gods.
They go off into captivity together.

"Listen to me, descendants of Jacob,
all you who remain in Israel.
I have cared for you since you were born.
Yes, I carried you before you were born.
I will be your God throughout your lifetime—
until your hair is white with age.
I made you, and I will care for you.
I will carry you along and save you.

"To whom will you compare me?
Who is my equal?
Some people pour out their silver and gold
and hire a craftsman to make a god from it.
Then they bow down and worship it!
They carry it around on their shoulders,
and when they set it down, it stays there.
It can't even move!
And when someone prays to it, there is no answer.
It can't rescue anyone from trouble.

"Do not forget this! Keep it in mind!
Remember this, you guilty ones.

Remember the things I have done in the past.
  For I alone am God!
  I am God, and there is none like me.
Only I can tell you the future
  before it even happens.
Everything I plan will come to pass,
  for I do whatever I wish.
I will call a swift bird of prey from the east—
  a leader from a distant land to come and do my bidding.
I have said what I would do,
  and I will do it.

"Listen to me, you stubborn people
  who are so far from doing right.
For I am ready to set things right,
  not in the distant future, but right now!
I am ready to save Jerusalem
  and show my glory to Israel.

+

"Come down, virgin daughter of Babylon, and sit in the dust.
  For your days of sitting on a throne have ended.
O daughter of Babylonia, never again will you be
  the lovely princess, tender and delicate.
Take heavy millstones and grind flour.
  Remove your veil, and strip off your robe.
  Expose yourself to public view.
You will be naked and burdened with shame.
  I will take vengeance against you without pity."

Our Redeemer, whose name is the LORD of Heaven's Armies,
  is the Holy One of Israel.

"O beautiful Babylon, sit now in darkness and silence.
  Never again will you be known as the queen of kingdoms.
For I was angry with my chosen people
  and punished them by letting them fall into your hands.
But you, Babylon, showed them no mercy.
  You oppressed even the elderly.
You said, 'I will reign forever as queen of the world!'
  You did not reflect on your actions
  or think about their consequences.

"Listen to this, you pleasure-loving kingdom,
    living at ease and feeling secure.
You say, 'I am the only one, and there is no other.
    I will never be a widow or lose my children.'
Well, both these things will come upon you in a moment:
    widowhood and the loss of your children.
Yes, these calamities will come upon you,
    despite all your witchcraft and magic.

"You felt secure in your wickedness.
    'No one sees me,' you said.
But your 'wisdom' and 'knowledge' have led you astray,
    and you said, 'I am the only one, and there is no other.'
So disaster will overtake you,
    and you won't be able to charm it away.
Calamity will fall upon you,
    and you won't be able to buy your way out.
A catastrophe will strike you suddenly,
    one for which you are not prepared.

"Now use your magical charms!
    Use the spells you have worked at all these years!
Maybe they will do you some good.
    Maybe they can make someone afraid of you.
All the advice you receive has made you tired.
    Where are all your astrologers,
those stargazers who make predictions each month?
    Let them stand up and save you from what the future holds.
But they are like straw burning in a fire;
    they cannot save themselves from the flame.
You will get no help from them at all;
    their hearth is no place to sit for warmth.
And all your friends,
    those with whom you've done business since childhood,
will go their own ways,
    turning a deaf ear to your cries.

✢

"Listen to me, O family of Jacob,
    you who are called by the name of Israel
    and born into the family of Judah.
Listen, you who take oaths in the name of the LORD

and call on the God of Israel.
You don't keep your promises,
    even though you call yourself the holy city
and talk about depending on the God of Israel,
    whose name is the LORD of Heaven's Armies.
Long ago I told you what was going to happen.
    Then suddenly I took action,
    and all my predictions came true.
For I know how stubborn and obstinate you are.
    Your necks are as unbending as iron.
    Your heads are as hard as bronze.
That is why I told you what would happen;
    I told you beforehand what I was going to do.
Then you could never say, 'My idols did it.
    My wooden image and metal god commanded it to happen!'
You have heard my predictions and seen them fulfilled,
    but you refuse to admit it.
Now I will tell you new things,
    secrets you have not yet heard.
They are brand new, not things from the past.
    So you cannot say, 'We knew that all the time!'

"Yes, I will tell you of things that are entirely new,
    things you never heard of before.
For I know so well what traitors you are.
    You have been rebels from birth.
Yet for my own sake and for the honor of my name,
    I will hold back my anger and not wipe you out.
I have refined you, but not as silver is refined.
    Rather, I have refined you in the furnace of suffering.
I will rescue you for my sake—
    yes, for my own sake!
I will not let my reputation be tarnished,
    and I will not share my glory with idols!

"Listen to me, O family of Jacob,
    Israel my chosen one!
I alone am God,
    the First and the Last.
It was my hand that laid the foundations of the earth,
    my right hand that spread out the heavens above.
When I call out the stars,
    they all appear in order."

Have any of your idols ever told you this?
　　Come, all of you, and listen:
The LORD has chosen Cyrus as his ally.
　　He will use him to put an end to the empire of Babylon
　　and to destroy the Babylonian armies.

"I have said it: I am calling Cyrus!
　　I will send him on this errand and will help him succeed.
Come closer, and listen to this.
　　From the beginning I have told you plainly what would happen."

And now the Sovereign LORD and his Spirit
　　have sent me with this message.
This is what the LORD says—
　　your Redeemer, the Holy One of Israel:
"I am the LORD your God,
　　who teaches you what is good for you
　　and leads you along the paths you should follow.
Oh, that you had listened to my commands!
　　Then you would have had peace flowing like a gentle river
　　and righteousness rolling over you like waves in the sea.
Your descendants would have been like the sands along the
　　　　seashore—
　　too many to count!
There would have been no need for your destruction,
　　or for cutting off your family name."

Yet even now, be free from your captivity!
　　Leave Babylon and the Babylonians.
Sing out this message!
　　Shout it to the ends of the earth!
The LORD has redeemed his servants,
　　the people of Israel.
They were not thirsty
　　when he led them through the desert.
He divided the rock,
　　and water gushed out for them to drink.
"But there is no peace for the wicked,"
　　says the LORD.

✢

Listen to me, all you in distant lands!
　　Pay attention, you who are far away!

The Lord called me before my birth;
    from within the womb he called me by name.
He made my words of judgment as sharp as a sword.
    He has hidden me in the shadow of his hand.
    I am like a sharp arrow in his quiver.

He said to me, "You are my servant, Israel,
    and you will bring me glory."

I replied, "But my work seems so useless!
    I have spent my strength for nothing and to no purpose.
Yet I leave it all in the Lord's hand;
    I will trust God for my reward."

And now the Lord speaks—
    the one who formed me in my mother's womb to be his servant,
    who commissioned me to bring Israel back to him.
The Lord has honored me,
    and my God has given me strength.
He says, "You will do more than restore the people of Israel to me.
    I will make you a light to the Gentiles,
    and you will bring my salvation to the ends of the earth."

The Lord, the Redeemer
    and Holy One of Israel,
says to the one who is despised and rejected by the nations,
    to the one who is the servant of rulers:
"Kings will stand at attention when you pass by.
    Princes will also bow low
because of the Lord, the faithful one,
    the Holy One of Israel, who has chosen you."

+

This is what the Lord says:

"At just the right time, I will respond to you.
    On the day of salvation I will help you.
I will protect you and give you to the people
    as my covenant with them.
Through you I will reestablish the land of Israel
    and assign it to its own people again.
I will say to the prisoners, 'Come out in freedom,'
    and to those in darkness, 'Come into the light.'

They will be my sheep, grazing in green pastures
  and on hills that were previously bare.
They will neither hunger nor thirst.
  The searing sun will not reach them anymore.
For the LORD in his mercy will lead them;
  he will lead them beside cool waters.
And I will make my mountains into level paths for them.
  The highways will be raised above the valleys.
See, my people will return from far away,
  from lands to the north and west,
  and from as far south as Egypt."

Sing for joy, O heavens!
  Rejoice, O earth!
  Burst into song, O mountains!
For the LORD has comforted his people
  and will have compassion on them in their suffering.

Yet Jerusalem says, "The LORD has deserted us;
  the Lord has forgotten us."

"Never! Can a mother forget her nursing child?
  Can she feel no love for the child she has borne?
But even if that were possible,
  I would not forget you!
See, I have written your name on the palms of my hands.
  Always in my mind is a picture of Jerusalem's walls in ruins.
Soon your descendants will come back,
  and all who are trying to destroy you will go away.
Look around you and see,
  for all your children will come back to you.
As surely as I live," says the LORD,
  "they will be like jewels or bridal ornaments for you to display.

"Even the most desolate parts of your abandoned land
  will soon be crowded with your people.
Your enemies who enslaved you
  will be far away.
The generations born in exile will return and say,
  'We need more room! It's crowded here!'
Then you will think to yourself,
  'Who has given me all these descendants?
For most of my children were killed,
  and the rest were carried away into exile.

I was left here all alone.
  Where did all these people come from?
Who bore these children?
  Who raised them for me?'"

This is what the Sovereign LORD says:
  "See, I will give a signal to the godless nations.
They will carry your little sons back to you in their arms;
  they will bring your daughters on their shoulders.
Kings and queens will serve you
  and care for all your needs.
They will bow to the earth before you
  and lick the dust from your feet.
Then you will know that I am the LORD.
  Those who trust in me will never be put to shame."

Who can snatch the plunder of war from the hands of a warrior?
  Who can demand that a tyrant let his captives go?
But the LORD says,
"The captives of warriors will be released,
  and the plunder of tyrants will be retrieved.
For I will fight those who fight you,
  and I will save your children.
I will feed your enemies with their own flesh.
  They will be drunk with rivers of their own blood.
All the world will know that I, the LORD,
  am your Savior and your Redeemer,
  the Mighty One of Israel."

This is what the LORD says:

"Was your mother sent away because I divorced her?
  Did I sell you as slaves to my creditors?
No, you were sold because of your sins.
  And your mother, too, was taken because of your sins.
Why was no one there when I came?
  Why didn't anyone answer when I called?
Is it because I have no power to rescue?
  No, that is not the reason!
For I can speak to the sea and make it dry up!
  I can turn rivers into deserts covered with dying fish.
I dress the skies in darkness,
  covering them with clothes of mourning."

+

The Sovereign LORD has given me his words of wisdom,
  so that I know how to comfort the weary.
Morning by morning he wakens me
  and opens my understanding to his will.
The Sovereign LORD has spoken to me,
  and I have listened.
  I have not rebelled or turned away.
I offered my back to those who beat me
  and my cheeks to those who pulled out my beard.
I did not hide my face
  from mockery and spitting.

Because the Sovereign LORD helps me,
  I will not be disgraced.
Therefore, I have set my face like a stone,
  determined to do his will.
  And I know that I will not be put to shame.
He who gives me justice is near.
  Who will dare to bring charges against me now?
Where are my accusers?
  Let them appear!
See, the Sovereign LORD is on my side!
  Who will declare me guilty?
All my enemies will be destroyed
  like old clothes that have been eaten by moths!

Who among you fears the LORD
  and obeys his servant?
If you are walking in darkness,
  without a ray of light,
trust in the LORD
  and rely on your God.
But watch out, you who live in your own light
  and warm yourselves by your own fires.
This is the reward you will receive from me:
  You will soon fall down in great torment.

+

"Listen to me, all who hope for deliverance—
  all who seek the LORD!

Consider the rock from which you were cut,
    the quarry from which you were mined.
Yes, think about Abraham, your ancestor,
    and Sarah, who gave birth to your nation.
Abraham was only one man when I called him.
    But when I blessed him, he became a great nation."

The LORD will comfort Israel again
    and have pity on her ruins.
Her desert will blossom like Eden,
    her barren wilderness like the garden of the LORD.
Joy and gladness will be found there.
    Songs of thanksgiving will fill the air.

"Listen to me, my people.
    Hear me, Israel,
for my law will be proclaimed,
    and my justice will become a light to the nations.
My mercy and justice are coming soon.
    My salvation is on the way.
    My strong arm will bring justice to the nations.
All distant lands will look to me
    and wait in hope for my powerful arm.
Look up to the skies above,
    and gaze down on the earth below.
For the skies will disappear like smoke,
    and the earth will wear out like a piece of clothing.
The people of the earth will die like flies,
    but my salvation lasts forever.
    My righteous rule will never end!

"Listen to me, you who know right from wrong,
    you who cherish my law in your hearts.
Do not be afraid of people's scorn,
    nor fear their insults.
For the moth will devour them as it devours clothing.
    The worm will eat at them as it eats wool.
But my righteousness will last forever.
    My salvation will continue from generation to generation."

+

Wake up, wake up, O LORD! Clothe yourself with strength!
    Flex your mighty right arm!

Rouse yourself as in the days of old
  when you slew Egypt, the dragon of the Nile.
Are you not the same today,
  the one who dried up the sea,
making a path of escape through the depths
  so that your people could cross over?
Those who have been ransomed by the LORD will return.
  They will enter Jerusalem singing,
  crowned with everlasting joy.
Sorrow and mourning will disappear,
  and they will be filled with joy and gladness.

"I, yes I, am the one who comforts you.
  So why are you afraid of mere humans,
  who wither like the grass and disappear?
Yet you have forgotten the LORD, your Creator,
  the one who stretched out the sky like a canopy
  and laid the foundations of the earth.
Will you remain in constant dread of human oppressors?
  Will you continue to fear the anger of your enemies?
Where is their fury and anger now?
  It is gone!
Soon all you captives will be released!
  Imprisonment, starvation, and death will not be your fate!
For I am the LORD your God,
  who stirs up the sea, causing its waves to roar.
  My name is the LORD of Heaven's Armies.
And I have put my words in your mouth
  and hidden you safely in my hand.
I stretched out the sky like a canopy
  and laid the foundations of the earth.
I am the one who says to Israel,
  'You are my people!'"

Wake up, wake up, O Jerusalem!
  You have drunk the cup of the LORD's fury.
You have drunk the cup of terror,
  tipping out its last drops.
Not one of your children is left alive
  to take your hand and guide you.
These two calamities have fallen on you:
  desolation and destruction, famine and war.
And who is left to sympathize with you?

Who is left to comfort you?
For your children have fainted and lie in the streets,
   helpless as antelopes caught in a net.
The Lord has poured out his fury;
   God has rebuked them.

But now listen to this, you afflicted ones
   who sit in a drunken stupor,
     though not from drinking wine.
This is what the Sovereign Lord,
   your God and Defender, says:
"See, I have taken the terrible cup from your hands.
   You will drink no more of my fury.
Instead, I will hand that cup to your tormentors,
   those who said, 'We will trample you into the dust
   and walk on your backs.'"

Wake up, wake up, O Zion!
   Clothe yourself with strength.
Put on your beautiful clothes, O holy city of Jerusalem,
   for unclean and godless people will enter your gates no longer.
Rise from the dust, O Jerusalem.
   Sit in a place of honor.
Remove the chains of slavery from your neck,
   O captive daughter of Zion.
For this is what the Lord says:
"When I sold you into exile,
   I received no payment.
Now I can redeem you
   without having to pay for you."

This is what the Sovereign Lord says: "Long ago my people chose to
live in Egypt. Now they are oppressed by Assyria. What is this?" asks the
Lord. "Why are my people enslaved again? Those who rule them shout in
exultation. My name is blasphemed all day long. But I will reveal my name
to my people, and they will come to know its power. Then at last they will
recognize that I am the one who speaks to them."

How beautiful on the mountains
   are the feet of the messenger who brings good news,
the good news of peace and salvation,
   the news that the God of Israel reigns!
The watchmen shout and sing with joy,
   for before their very eyes

they see the LORD returning to Jerusalem.
Let the ruins of Jerusalem break into joyful song,
   for the LORD has comforted his people.
   He has redeemed Jerusalem.
The LORD has demonstrated his holy power
   before the eyes of all the nations.
All the ends of the earth will see
   the victory of our God.

Get out! Get out and leave your captivity,
   where everything you touch is unclean.
Get out of there and purify yourselves,
   you who carry home the sacred objects of the LORD.
You will not leave in a hurry,
   running for your lives.
For the LORD will go ahead of you;
   yes, the God of Israel will protect you from behind.

✢

See, my servant will prosper;
   he will be highly exalted.
But many were amazed when they saw him.
    His face was so disfigured he seemed hardly human,
   and from his appearance, one would scarcely know he was a man.
And he will startle many nations.
    Kings will stand speechless in his presence.
For they will see what they had not been told;
   they will understand what they had not heard about.

Who has believed our message?
    To whom has the LORD revealed his powerful arm?
My servant grew up in the LORD's presence like a tender green shoot,
   like a root in dry ground.
There was nothing beautiful or majestic about his appearance,
   nothing to attract us to him.
He was despised and rejected—
   a man of sorrows, acquainted with deepest grief.
We turned our backs on him and looked the other way.
   He was despised, and we did not care.

Yet it was our weaknesses he carried;
   it was our sorrows that weighed him down.

And we thought his troubles were a punishment from God,
    a punishment for his own sins!
But he was pierced for our rebellion,
    crushed for our sins.
He was beaten so we could be whole.
    He was whipped so we could be healed.
All of us, like sheep, have strayed away.
    We have left God's paths to follow our own.
Yet the LORD laid on him
    the sins of us all.

He was oppressed and treated harshly,
    yet he never said a word.
He was led like a lamb to the slaughter.
    And as a sheep is silent before the shearers,
    he did not open his mouth.
Unjustly condemned,
    he was led away.
No one cared that he died without descendants,
    that his life was cut short in midstream.
But he was struck down
    for the rebellion of my people.
He had done no wrong
    and had never deceived anyone.
But he was buried like a criminal;
    he was put in a rich man's grave.

But it was the LORD's good plan to crush him
    and cause him grief.
Yet when his life is made an offering for sin,
    he will have many descendants.
He will enjoy a long life,
    and the LORD's good plan will prosper in his hands.
When he sees all that is accomplished by his anguish,
    he will be satisfied.
And because of his experience,
    my righteous servant will make it possible
for many to be counted righteous,
    for he will bear all their sins.
I will give him the honors of a victorious soldier,
    because he exposed himself to death.
He was counted among the rebels.
    He bore the sins of many and interceded for rebels.

+

"Sing, O childless woman,
  you who have never given birth!
Break into loud and joyful song, O Jerusalem,
  you who have never been in labor.
For the desolate woman now has more children
  than the woman who lives with her husband,"
    says the LORD.
"Enlarge your house; build an addition.
  Spread out your home, and spare no expense!
For you will soon be bursting at the seams.
  Your descendants will occupy other nations
  and resettle the ruined cities.

"Fear not; you will no longer live in shame.
  Don't be afraid; there is no more disgrace for you.
You will no longer remember the shame of your youth
  and the sorrows of widowhood.
For your Creator will be your husband;
  the LORD of Heaven's Armies is his name!
He is your Redeemer, the Holy One of Israel,
  the God of all the earth.
For the LORD has called you back from your grief—
  as though you were a young wife abandoned by her husband,"
    says your God.
"For a brief moment I abandoned you,
  but with great compassion I will take you back.
In a burst of anger I turned my face away for a little while.
  But with everlasting love I will have compassion on you,"
    says the LORD, your Redeemer.

"Just as I swore in the time of Noah
  that I would never again let a flood cover the earth,
so now I swear
  that I will never again be angry and punish you.
For the mountains may move
  and the hills disappear,
but even then my faithful love for you will remain.
  My covenant of blessing will never be broken,"
    says the LORD, who has mercy on you.

"O storm-battered city,
  troubled and desolate!

I will rebuild you with precious jewels
  and make your foundations from lapis lazuli.
I will make your towers of sparkling rubies,
  your gates of shining gems,
  and your walls of precious stones.
I will teach all your children,
  and they will enjoy great peace.
You will be secure under a government that is just and fair.
  Your enemies will stay far away.
You will live in peace,
  and terror will not come near.
If any nation comes to fight you,
  it is not because I sent them.
  Whoever attacks you will go down in defeat.

"I have created the blacksmith
  who fans the coals beneath the forge
and makes the weapons of destruction.
  And I have created the armies that destroy.
But in that coming day
  no weapon turned against you will succeed.
You will silence every voice
  raised up to accuse you.
These benefits are enjoyed by the servants of the LORD;
  their vindication will come from me.
  I, the LORD, have spoken!

+

"Is anyone thirsty?
  Come and drink—
  even if you have no money!
Come, take your choice of wine or milk—
  it's all free!
Why spend your money on food that does not give you strength?
  Why pay for food that does you no good?
Listen to me, and you will eat what is good.
  You will enjoy the finest food.

"Come to me with your ears wide open.
  Listen, and you will find life.
I will make an everlasting covenant with you.
  I will give you all the unfailing love I promised to David.

See how I used him to display my power among the peoples.
  I made him a leader among the nations.
You also will command nations you do not know,
  and peoples unknown to you will come running to obey,
because I, the LORD your God,
  the Holy One of Israel, have made you glorious."

Seek the LORD while you can find him.
  Call on him now while he is near.
Let the wicked change their ways
  and banish the very thought of doing wrong.
Let them turn to the LORD that he may have mercy on them.
  Yes, turn to our God, for he will forgive generously.

"My thoughts are nothing like your thoughts," says the LORD.
  "And my ways are far beyond anything you could imagine.
For just as the heavens are higher than the earth,
  so my ways are higher than your ways
  and my thoughts higher than your thoughts.

"The rain and snow come down from the heavens
  and stay on the ground to water the earth.
They cause the grain to grow,
  producing seed for the farmer
  and bread for the hungry.
It is the same with my word.
  I send it out, and it always produces fruit.
It will accomplish all I want it to,
  and it will prosper everywhere I send it.
You will live in joy and peace.
  The mountains and hills will burst into song,
  and the trees of the field will clap their hands!
Where once there were thorns, cypress trees will grow.
  Where nettles grew, myrtles will sprout up.
These events will bring great honor to the LORD's name;
  they will be an everlasting sign of his power and love."

✢ ✢ ✢

This is what the LORD says:

"Be just and fair to all.
  Do what is right and good,
for I am coming soon to rescue you

and to display my righteousness among you.
Blessed are all those
   who are careful to do this.
Blessed are those who honor my Sabbath days of rest
   and keep themselves from doing wrong.

"Don't let foreigners who commit themselves to the LORD say,
   'The LORD will never let me be part of his people.'
And don't let the eunuchs say,
   'I'm a dried-up tree with no children and no future.'
For this is what the LORD says:
I will bless those eunuchs
   who keep my Sabbath days holy
and who choose to do what pleases me
   and commit their lives to me.
I will give them—within the walls of my house—
   a memorial and a name
   far greater than sons and daughters could give.
For the name I give them is an everlasting one.
   It will never disappear!

"I will also bless the foreigners who commit themselves to the LORD,
   who serve him and love his name,
who worship him and do not desecrate the Sabbath day of rest,
   and who hold fast to my covenant.
I will bring them to my holy mountain of Jerusalem
   and will fill them with joy in my house of prayer.
I will accept their burnt offerings and sacrifices,
   because my Temple will be called a house of prayer for all nations.
For the Sovereign LORD,
   who brings back the outcasts of Israel, says:
I will bring others, too,
   besides my people Israel."

Come, wild animals of the field!
   Come, wild animals of the forest!
   Come and devour my people!
For the leaders of my people—
   the LORD's watchmen, his shepherds—
   are blind and ignorant.
They are like silent watchdogs
   that give no warning when danger comes.
They love to lie around, sleeping and dreaming.

Like greedy dogs, they are never satisfied.
They are ignorant shepherds,
   all following their own path
   and intent on personal gain.
"Come," they say, "let's get some wine and have a party.
   Let's all get drunk.
Then tomorrow we'll do it again
   and have an even bigger party!"

Good people pass away;
   the godly often die before their time.
   But no one seems to care or wonder why.
No one seems to understand
   that God is protecting them from the evil to come.
For those who follow godly paths
   will rest in peace when they die.

"But you—come here, you witches' children,
   you offspring of adulterers and prostitutes!
Whom do you mock,
   making faces and sticking out your tongues?
   You children of sinners and liars!
You worship your idols with great passion
   beneath the oaks and under every green tree.
You sacrifice your children down in the valleys,
   among the jagged rocks in the cliffs.
Your gods are the smooth stones in the valleys.
   You worship them with liquid offerings and grain offerings.
They, not I, are your inheritance.
   Do you think all this makes me happy?
You have committed adultery on every high mountain.
   There you have worshiped idols
   and have been unfaithful to me.
You have put pagan symbols
   on your doorposts and behind your doors.
You have left me
   and climbed into bed with these detestable gods.
You have committed yourselves to them.
   You love to look at their naked bodies.
You have gone to Molech
   with olive oil and many perfumes,
sending your agents far and wide,
   even to the world of the dead.

You grew weary in your search,
    but you never gave up.
Desire gave you renewed strength,
    and you did not grow weary.

"Are you afraid of these idols?
    Do they terrify you?
Is that why you have lied to me
    and forgotten me and my words?
Is it because of my long silence
    that you no longer fear me?
Now I will expose your so-called good deeds.
    None of them will help you.
Let's see if your idols can save you
    when you cry to them for help.
Why, a puff of wind can knock them down!
    If you just breathe on them, they fall over!
But whoever trusts in me will inherit the land
    and possess my holy mountain."

God says, "Rebuild the road!
    Clear away the rocks and stones
    so my people can return from captivity."
The high and lofty one who lives in eternity,
    the Holy One, says this:
"I live in the high and holy place
    with those whose spirits are contrite and humble.
I restore the crushed spirit of the humble
    and revive the courage of those with repentant hearts.
For I will not fight against you forever;
    I will not always be angry.
If I were, all people would pass away—
    all the souls I have made.
I was angry,
    so I punished these greedy people.
I withdrew from them,
    but they kept going on their own stubborn way.
I have seen what they do,
    but I will heal them anyway!
    I will lead them.
I will comfort those who mourn,
    bringing words of praise to their lips.

May they have abundant peace, both near and far,"
     says the LORD, who heals them.
"But those who still reject me are like the restless sea,
     which is never still
     but continually churns up mud and dirt.
There is no peace for the wicked,"
     says my God.

"Shout with the voice of a trumpet blast.
     Shout aloud! Don't be timid.
Tell my people Israel of their sins!
     Yet they act so pious!
They come to the Temple every day
     and seem delighted to learn all about me.
They act like a righteous nation
     that would never abandon the laws of its God.
They ask me to take action on their behalf,
     pretending they want to be near me.
'We have fasted before you!' they say.
     'Why aren't you impressed?
We have been very hard on ourselves,
     and you don't even notice it!'

"I will tell you why!" I respond.
     "It's because you are fasting to please yourselves.
Even while you fast,
     you keep oppressing your workers.
What good is fasting
     when you keep on fighting and quarreling?
This kind of fasting
     will never get you anywhere with me.
You humble yourselves
     by going through the motions of penance,
bowing your heads
     like reeds bending in the wind.
You dress in burlap
     and cover yourselves with ashes.
Is this what you call fasting?
     Do you really think this will please the LORD?

"No, this is the kind of fasting I want:
Free those who are wrongly imprisoned;
     lighten the burden of those who work for you.

Let the oppressed go free,
  and remove the chains that bind people.
Share your food with the hungry,
  and give shelter to the homeless.
Give clothes to those who need them,
  and do not hide from relatives who need your help.

"Then your salvation will come like the dawn,
  and your wounds will quickly heal.
Your godliness will lead you forward,
  and the glory of the LORD will protect you from behind.
Then when you call, the LORD will answer.
  'Yes, I am here,' he will quickly reply.

"Remove the heavy yoke of oppression.
  Stop pointing your finger and spreading vicious rumors!
Feed the hungry,
  and help those in trouble.
Then your light will shine out from the darkness,
  and the darkness around you will be as bright as noon.
The LORD will guide you continually,
  giving you water when you are dry
  and restoring your strength.
You will be like a well-watered garden,
  like an ever-flowing spring.
Some of you will rebuild the deserted ruins of your cities.
  Then you will be known as a rebuilder of walls
  and a restorer of homes.

"Keep the Sabbath day holy.
  Don't pursue your own interests on that day,
but enjoy the Sabbath
  and speak of it with delight as the LORD's holy day.
Honor the Sabbath in everything you do on that day,
  and don't follow your own desires or talk idly.
Then the LORD will be your delight.
  I will give you great honor
and satisfy you with the inheritance I promised to your ancestor Jacob.
  I, the LORD, have spoken!"

Listen! The LORD's arm is not too weak to save you,
  nor is his ear too deaf to hear you call.
It's your sins that have cut you off from God.

Because of your sins, he has turned away
   and will not listen anymore.
Your hands are the hands of murderers,
   and your fingers are filthy with sin.
Your lips are full of lies,
   and your mouth spews corruption.

No one cares about being fair and honest.
   The people's lawsuits are based on lies.
They conceive evil deeds
   and then give birth to sin.
They hatch deadly snakes
   and weave spiders' webs.
Whoever eats their eggs will die;
   whoever cracks them will hatch a viper.
Their webs can't be made into clothing,
   and nothing they do is productive.
All their activity is filled with sin,
   and violence is their trademark.
Their feet run to do evil,
   and they rush to commit murder.
They think only about sinning.
   Misery and destruction always follow them.
They don't know where to find peace
   or what it means to be just and good.
They have mapped out crooked roads,
   and no one who follows them knows a moment's peace.

So there is no justice among us,
   and we know nothing about right living.
We look for light but find only darkness.
   We look for bright skies but walk in gloom.
We grope like the blind along a wall,
   feeling our way like people without eyes.
Even at brightest noontime,
   we stumble as though it were dark.
Among the living,
   we are like the dead.
We growl like hungry bears;
   we moan like mournful doves.
We look for justice, but it never comes.
   We look for rescue, but it is far away from us.
For our sins are piled up before God

and testify against us.
Yes, we know what sinners we are.
We know we have rebelled and have denied the Lord.
We have turned our backs on our God.
We know how unfair and oppressive we have been,
carefully planning our deceitful lies.
Our courts oppose the righteous,
and justice is nowhere to be found.
Truth stumbles in the streets,
and honesty has been outlawed.
Yes, truth is gone,
and anyone who renounces evil is attacked.

The Lord looked and was displeased
to find there was no justice.
He was amazed to see that no one intervened
to help the oppressed.
So he himself stepped in to save them with his strong arm,
and his justice sustained him.
He put on righteousness as his body armor
and placed the helmet of salvation on his head.
He clothed himself with a robe of vengeance
and wrapped himself in a cloak of divine passion.
He will repay his enemies for their evil deeds.
His fury will fall on his foes.
He will pay them back even to the ends of the earth.
In the west, people will respect the name of the Lord;
in the east, they will glorify him.
For he will come like a raging flood tide
driven by the breath of the Lord.

"The Redeemer will come to Jerusalem
to buy back those in Israel
who have turned from their sins,"
says the Lord.

"And this is my covenant with them," says the Lord. "My Spirit will not leave them, and neither will these words I have given you. They will be on your lips and on the lips of your children and your children's children forever. I, the Lord, have spoken!

"Arise, Jerusalem! Let your light shine for all to see.
For the glory of the Lord rises to shine on you.

Darkness as black as night covers all the nations of the earth,
    but the glory of the LORD rises and appears over you.
All nations will come to your light;
    mighty kings will come to see your radiance.

"Look and see, for everyone is coming home!
    Your sons are coming from distant lands;
    your little daughters will be carried home.
Your eyes will shine,
    and your heart will thrill with joy,
for merchants from around the world will come to you.
    They will bring you the wealth of many lands.
Vast caravans of camels will converge on you,
    the camels of Midian and Ephah.
The people of Sheba will bring gold and frankincense
    and will come worshiping the LORD.
The flocks of Kedar will be given to you,
    and the rams of Nebaioth will be brought for my altars.
I will accept their offerings,
    and I will make my Temple glorious.

"And what do I see flying like clouds to Israel,
    like doves to their nests?
They are ships from the ends of the earth,
    from lands that trust in me,
    led by the great ships of Tarshish.
They are bringing the people of Israel home from
      far away,
    carrying their silver and gold.
They will honor the LORD your God,
    the Holy One of Israel,
    for he has filled you with splendor.

"Foreigners will come to rebuild your towns,
    and their kings will serve you.
For though I have destroyed you in my anger,
    I will now have mercy on you through my grace.
Your gates will stay open day and night
    to receive the wealth of many lands.
The kings of the world will be led as captives
    in a victory procession.
For the nations that refuse to serve you
    will be destroyed.

"The glory of Lebanon will be yours—
    the forests of cypress, fir, and pine—
to beautify my sanctuary.
    My Temple will be glorious!
The descendants of your tormentors
    will come and bow before you.
Those who despised you
    will kiss your feet.
They will call you the City of the LORD,
    and Zion of the Holy One of Israel.

"Though you were once despised and hated,
    with no one traveling through you,
I will make you beautiful forever,
    a joy to all generations.
Powerful kings and mighty nations
    will satisfy your every need,
as though you were a child
    nursing at the breast of a queen.
You will know at last that I, the LORD,
    am your Savior and your Redeemer,
    the Mighty One of Israel.
I will exchange your bronze for gold,
    your iron for silver,
your wood for bronze,
    and your stones for iron.
I will make peace your leader
    and righteousness your ruler.
Violence will disappear from your land;
    the desolation and destruction of war will end.
Salvation will surround you like city walls,
    and praise will be on the lips of all who enter there.

"No longer will you need the sun to shine by day,
    nor the moon to give its light by night,
for the LORD your God will be your everlasting light,
    and your God will be your glory.
Your sun will never set;
    your moon will not go down.
For the LORD will be your everlasting light.
    Your days of mourning will come to an end.
All your people will be righteous.
  · They will possess their land forever,

for I will plant them there with my own hands
  in order to bring myself glory.
The smallest family will become a thousand people,
  and the tiniest group will become a mighty nation.
  At the right time, I, the LORD, will make it happen."

The Spirit of the Sovereign LORD is upon me,
  for the LORD has anointed me
  to bring good news to the poor.
He has sent me to comfort the brokenhearted
  and to proclaim that captives will be released
  and prisoners will be freed.
He has sent me to tell those who mourn
  that the time of the LORD's favor has come,
  and with it, the day of God's anger against their enemies.
To all who mourn in Israel,
  he will give a crown of beauty for ashes,
a joyous blessing instead of mourning,
  festive praise instead of despair.
In their righteousness, they will be like great oaks
  that the LORD has planted for his own glory.

They will rebuild the ancient ruins,
  repairing cities destroyed long ago.
They will revive them,
  though they have been deserted for many generations.
Foreigners will be your servants.
  They will feed your flocks
and plow your fields
  and tend your vineyards.
You will be called priests of the LORD,
  ministers of our God.
You will feed on the treasures of the nations
  and boast in their riches.
Instead of shame and dishonor,
  you will enjoy a double share of honor.
You will possess a double portion of prosperity in your land,
  and everlasting joy will be yours.

"For I, the LORD, love justice.
  I hate robbery and wrongdoing.
I will faithfully reward my people for their suffering
  and make an everlasting covenant with them.

Their descendants will be recognized
  and honored among the nations.
Everyone will realize that they are a people
  the LORD has blessed."

I am overwhelmed with joy in the LORD my God!
  For he has dressed me with the clothing of salvation
  and draped me in a robe of righteousness.
I am like a bridegroom dressed for his wedding
  or a bride with her jewels.
The Sovereign LORD will show his justice to the nations
    of the world.
  Everyone will praise him!
His righteousness will be like a garden in early spring,
  with plants springing up everywhere.

Because I love Zion,
  I will not keep still.
Because my heart yearns for Jerusalem,
  I cannot remain silent.
I will not stop praying for her
  until her righteousness shines like the dawn,
  and her salvation blazes like a burning torch.
The nations will see your righteousness.
  World leaders will be blinded by your glory.
And you will be given a new name
  by the LORD's own mouth.
The LORD will hold you in his hand for all to see—
  a splendid crown in the hand of God.
Never again will you be called "The Forsaken City"
  or "The Desolate Land."
Your new name will be "The City of God's Delight"
  and "The Bride of God,"
for the LORD delights in you
  and will claim you as his bride.
Your children will commit themselves to you, O Jerusalem,
  just as a young man commits himself to his bride.
Then God will rejoice over you
  as a bridegroom rejoices over his bride.

O Jerusalem, I have posted watchmen on your walls;
  they will pray day and night, continually.
  Take no rest, all you who pray to the LORD.

Give the Lord no rest until he completes his work,
    until he makes Jerusalem the pride of the earth.
The Lord has sworn to Jerusalem by his own strength:
    "I will never again hand you over to your enemies.
Never again will foreign warriors come
    and take away your grain and new wine.
You raised the grain, and you will eat it,
    praising the Lord.
Within the courtyards of the Temple,
    you yourselves will drink the wine you have pressed."

Go out through the gates!
    Prepare the highway for my people to return!
Smooth out the road; pull out the boulders;
    raise a flag for all the nations to see.
The Lord has sent this message to every land:
    "Tell the people of Israel,
'Look, your Savior is coming.
    See, he brings his reward with him as he comes.'"
They will be called "The Holy People"
    and "The People Redeemed by the Lord."
And Jerusalem will be known as "The Desirable Place"
    and "The City No Longer Forsaken."

Who is this who comes from Edom,
    from the city of Bozrah,
    with his clothing stained red?
Who is this in royal robes,
    marching in his great strength?

"It is I, the Lord, announcing your salvation!
    It is I, the Lord, who has the power to save!"

Why are your clothes so red,
    as if you have been treading out grapes?

"I have been treading the winepress alone;
    no one was there to help me.
In my anger I have trampled my enemies
    as if they were grapes.
In my fury I have trampled my foes.
    Their blood has stained my clothes.
For the time has come for me to avenge my people,
    to ransom them from their oppressors.

I was amazed to see that no one intervened
   to help the oppressed.
So I myself stepped in to save them with my strong arm,
   and my wrath sustained me.
I crushed the nations in my anger
   and made them stagger and fall to the ground,
   spilling their blood upon the earth."

I will tell of the LORD's unfailing love.
   I will praise the LORD for all he has done.
I will rejoice in his great goodness to Israel,
   which he has granted according to his mercy and love.
He said, "They are my very own people.
   Surely they will not betray me again."
   And he became their Savior.
In all their suffering he also suffered,
   and he personally rescued them.
In his love and mercy he redeemed them.
   He lifted them up and carried them
   through all the years.
But they rebelled against him
   and grieved his Holy Spirit.
So he became their enemy
   and fought against them.

Then they remembered those days of old
   when Moses led his people out of Egypt.
They cried out, "Where is the one who brought Israel through the sea,
   with Moses as their shepherd?
Where is the one who sent his Holy Spirit
   to be among his people?
Where is the one whose power was displayed
   when Moses lifted up his hand—
the one who divided the sea before them,
   making himself famous forever?
Where is the one who led them through the bottom of the sea?
   They were like fine stallions
   racing through the desert, never stumbling.
As with cattle going down into a peaceful valley,
   the Spirit of the LORD gave them rest.
You led your people, LORD,
   and gained a magnificent reputation."

LORD, look down from heaven;
  look from your holy, glorious home, and see us.
Where is the passion and the might
  you used to show on our behalf?
  Where are your mercy and compassion now?
Surely you are still our Father!
  Even if Abraham and Jacob would disown us,
LORD, you would still be our Father.
  You are our Redeemer from ages past.
LORD, why have you allowed us to turn from your path?
  Why have you given us stubborn hearts so we no longer fear you?
Return and help us, for we are your servants,
  the tribes that are your special possession.
How briefly your holy people possessed your holy place,
  and now our enemies have destroyed it.
Sometimes it seems as though we never belonged to you,
  as though we had never been known as your people.

Oh, that you would burst from the heavens and come down!
  How the mountains would quake in your presence!
As fire causes wood to burn
  and water to boil,
your coming would make the nations tremble.
  Then your enemies would learn the reason for your fame!
When you came down long ago,
  you did awesome deeds beyond our highest expectations.
  And oh, how the mountains quaked!
For since the world began,
  no ear has heard
and no eye has seen a God like you,
  who works for those who wait for him!
You welcome those who gladly do good,
  who follow godly ways.
But you have been very angry with us,
  for we are not godly.
We are constant sinners;
  how can people like us be saved?
We are all infected and impure with sin.
  When we display our righteous deeds,
  they are nothing but filthy rags.
Like autumn leaves, we wither and fall,
  and our sins sweep us away like the wind.

Yet no one calls on your name
    or pleads with you for mercy.
Therefore, you have turned away from us
    and turned us over to our sins.

And yet, O LORD, you are our Father.
    We are the clay, and you are the potter.
    We all are formed by your hand.
Don't be so angry with us, LORD.
    Please don't remember our sins forever.
Look at us, we pray,
    and see that we are all your people.
Your holy cities are destroyed.
    Zion is a wilderness;
    yes, Jerusalem is a desolate ruin.
The holy and beautiful Temple
    where our ancestors praised you
has been burned down,
    and all the things of beauty are destroyed.
After all this, LORD, must you still refuse to help us?
    Will you continue to be silent and punish us?

The LORD says,

    "I was ready to respond, but no one asked for help.
        I was ready to be found, but no one was looking for me.
    I said, 'Here I am, here I am!'
        to a nation that did not call on my name.
    All day long I opened my arms to a rebellious people.
        But they follow their own evil paths
        and their own crooked schemes.
    All day long they insult me to my face
        by worshiping idols in their sacred gardens.
        They burn incense on pagan altars.
    At night they go out among the graves,
        worshiping the dead.
    They eat the flesh of pigs
        and make stews with other forbidden foods.
    Yet they say to each other,
        'Don't come too close or you will defile me!
        I am holier than you!'
    These people are a stench in my nostrils,
        an acrid smell that never goes away.

"Look, my decree is written out in front of me:
    I will not stand silent;
I will repay them in full!
    Yes, I will repay them—
both for their own sins
    and for those of their ancestors,"
        says the LORD.
"For they also burned incense on the mountains
    and insulted me on the hills.
    I will pay them back in full!

"But I will not destroy them all,"
    says the LORD.
"For just as good grapes are found among a cluster of bad ones
    (and someone will say, 'Don't throw them all away—
    some of those grapes are good!'),
so I will not destroy all Israel.
    For I still have true servants there.
I will preserve a remnant of the people of Israel
    and of Judah to possess my land.
Those I choose will inherit it,
    and my servants will live there.
The plain of Sharon will again be filled with flocks
    for my people who have searched for me,
    and the valley of Achor will be a place to pasture herds.

"But because the rest of you have forsaken the LORD
    and have forgotten his Temple,
and because you have prepared feasts to honor the god of Fate
    and have offered mixed wine to the god of Destiny,
now I will 'destine' you for the sword.
    All of you will bow down before the executioner.
For when I called, you did not answer.
    When I spoke, you did not listen.
You deliberately sinned—before my very eyes—
    and chose to do what you know I despise."

Therefore, this is what the Sovereign LORD says:
"My servants will eat,
    but you will starve.
My servants will drink,
    but you will be thirsty.
My servants will rejoice,
    but you will be sad and ashamed.

My servants will sing for joy,
  but you will cry in sorrow and despair.
Your name will be a curse word among my people,
  for the Sovereign LORD will destroy you
  and will call his true servants by another name.
All who invoke a blessing or take an oath
  will do so by the God of truth.
For I will put aside my anger
  and forget the evil of earlier days.

"Look! I am creating new heavens and a new earth,
  and no one will even think about the old ones anymore.
Be glad; rejoice forever in my creation!
  And look! I will create Jerusalem as a place of happiness.
  Her people will be a source of joy.
I will rejoice over Jerusalem
  and delight in my people.
And the sound of weeping and crying
  will be heard in it no more.

"No longer will babies die when only a few days old.
  No longer will adults die before they have lived a full life.
No longer will people be considered old at one hundred!
  Only the cursed will die that young!
In those days people will live in the houses they build
  and eat the fruit of their own vineyards.
Unlike the past, invaders will not take their houses
  and confiscate their vineyards.
For my people will live as long as trees,
  and my chosen ones will have time to enjoy their hard-won gains.
They will not work in vain,
  and their children will not be doomed to misfortune.
For they are people blessed by the LORD,
  and their children, too, will be blessed.
I will answer them before they even call to me.
  While they are still talking about their needs,
  I will go ahead and answer their prayers!
The wolf and the lamb will feed together.
  The lion will eat hay like a cow.
  But the snakes will eat dust.
In those days no one will be hurt or destroyed on my holy mountain.
  I, the LORD, have spoken!"

This is what the LORD says:

"Heaven is my throne,
   and the earth is my footstool.
Could you build me a temple as good as that?
   Could you build me such a resting place?
My hands have made both heaven and earth;
   they and everything in them are mine.
   I, the LORD, have spoken!

"I will bless those who have humble and contrite hearts,
   who tremble at my word.
But those who choose their own ways—
   delighting in their detestable sins—
   will not have their offerings accepted.
When such people sacrifice a bull,
   it is no more acceptable than a human sacrifice.
When they sacrifice a lamb,
   it's as though they had sacrificed a dog!
When they bring an offering of grain,
   they might as well offer the blood of a pig.
When they burn frankincense,
   it's as if they had blessed an idol.
I will send them great trouble—
   all the things they feared.
For when I called, they did not answer.
   When I spoke, they did not listen.
They deliberately sinned before my very eyes
   and chose to do what they know I despise."

Hear this message from the LORD,
   all you who tremble at his words:
"Your own people hate you
   and throw you out for being loyal to my name.
'Let the LORD be honored!' they scoff.
   'Be joyful in him!'
   But they will be put to shame.
What is all the commotion in the city?
   What is that terrible noise from the Temple?
It is the voice of the LORD
   taking vengeance against his enemies.

"Before the birth pains even begin,
   Jerusalem gives birth to a son.

Who has ever seen anything as strange as this?
    Who ever heard of such a thing?
Has a nation ever been born in a single day?
    Has a country ever come forth in a mere moment?
But by the time Jerusalem's birth pains begin,
    her children will be born.
Would I ever bring this nation to the point of birth
    and then not deliver it?" asks the Lord.
"No! I would never keep this nation from being born,"
    says your God.

"Rejoice with Jerusalem!
    Be glad with her, all you who love her
    and all you who mourn for her.
Drink deeply of her glory
    even as an infant drinks at its mother's comforting breasts."

This is what the Lord says:
"I will give Jerusalem a river of peace and prosperity.
    The wealth of the nations will flow to her.
Her children will be nursed at her breasts,
    carried in her arms, and held on her lap.
I will comfort you there in Jerusalem
    as a mother comforts her child."

When you see these things, your heart will rejoice.
    You will flourish like the grass!
Everyone will see the Lord's hand of blessing on his servants—
    and his anger against his enemies.
See, the Lord is coming with fire,
    and his swift chariots roar like a whirlwind.
He will bring punishment with the fury of his anger
    and the flaming fire of his hot rebuke.
The Lord will punish the world by fire
    and by his sword.
He will judge the earth,
    and many will be killed by him.

"Those who 'consecrate' and 'purify' themselves in a sacred garden
with its idol in the center—feasting on pork and rats and other detestable
meats—will come to a terrible end," says the Lord. "I can see what they are doing, and I know what they are thinking. So
I will gather all nations and peoples together, and they will see my glory.
I will perform a sign among them. And I will send those who survive to

be messengers to the nations—to Tarshish, to the Libyans and Lydians (who are famous as archers), to Tubal and Greece, and to all the lands beyond the sea that have not heard of my fame or seen my glory. There they will declare my glory to the nations. They will bring the remnant of your people back from every nation. They will bring them to my holy mountain in Jerusalem as an offering to the LORD. They will ride on horses, in chariots and wagons, and on mules and camels," says the LORD. "And I will appoint some of them to be my priests and Levites. I, the LORD, have spoken!

"As surely as my new heavens and earth will remain,
    so will you always be my people,
with a name that will never disappear,"
    says the LORD.
"All humanity will come to worship me
    from week to week
    and from month to month.
And as they go out, they will see
    the dead bodies of those who have rebelled against me.
For the worms that devour them will never die,
    and the fire that burns them will never go out.
All who pass by
    will view them with utter horror."

IMMERSED IN ZEPHANIAH

ZEPHANIAH'S ORACLES for the people of Judah were uttered nearly three-quarters of a century after the days of Micah and Isaiah. In the intervening years, Hezekiah's successors—Manasseh and Amon—had tried to appease their Assyrian overlords by serving Assyrian gods and suppressing the LORD's true priests and prophets. But the power of Assyria eventually declined, and its hold on subject nations weakened. This allowed nations like Judah to regain some of their independence, which enabled the true prophets once again to speak freely for the LORD.

One of those prophets, Zephaniah, warned the complacent people of Judah—who thought, "the LORD will do nothing to [us], either good or bad"—that they needed to return to God with urgency. They had little time left, as the fearsome "day of the LORD"—the time when the LORD would come and punish the unfaithful—was fast approaching.

Amos, Isaiah, and later prophets also speak of the "day of the LORD" as a time of judgment. Because God is a God of justice and peace, at some point he must intervene to judge and set things right. The flourishing of creation requires the destruction of evil. In the New Testament, more light is shed on the "day of the LORD," as we learn that it also involves God's breaking into the present creation to inaugurate his new creation. But here in Zephaniah's short book, we already see the "day of the LORD" described as both a warning of imminent disaster and a vision of future restoration.

By now King Josiah, who had begun to reign as a child, was old enough to assert himself. He carried out extensive religious reforms, which included wiping out the worship of pagan gods, restoring the Temple in Jerusalem, and leading the people to renew their covenant with the LORD. We know from the accounts of his life recorded in Samuel–Kings and Chronicles that he was prompted to do this largely by the rediscovery of the Book of the Law in the Temple.

But Josiah was no doubt also influenced by Zephaniah's warnings, particularly since the prophet was a direct descendant of Hezekiah and probably also a member of the royal court. "Act now, before the fierce fury of the LORD falls," Zephaniah urged. "Seek to do what is right and to live humbly. Perhaps even yet the LORD will protect you." By heeding this call, the people were spared at least for another generation.

The oracles of Zephaniah are organized into three groups. A similar phrase occurs at the end of the first and second groups, marking off the three parts of the book: "For the whole land will be devoured by the fire of his jealousy."

As in Micah, the book's ultimate movement is from ruin to restoration; but in this case, it takes place over the course of the book as a whole, rather than within each group of oracles. The three groups together predict judgment on Judah and Jerusalem, then judgment on other nations, and finally the restoration of Judah and Jerusalem. (This pattern also shapes other prophetic books, such as Ezekiel.) Zephaniah is careful to emphasize that only the "lowly and humble" will share in the great renewal.

The book ends with a vision similar to the one at the end of Isaiah, with God's holy city rebuilt and thriving once again. Addressing Jerusalem directly, Zephaniah says the LORD himself will come to live there: "On that day the announcement to Jerusalem will be, 'Cheer up, Zion! Don't be afraid! For the LORD your God is living among you. He is a mighty savior. He will take delight in you with gladness. With his love, he will calm all your fears. He will rejoice over you with joyful songs.'"

ZEPHANIAH

✛

The Lord gave this message to Zephaniah when Josiah son of Amon was king of Judah. Zephaniah was the son of Cushi, son of Gedaliah, son of Amariah, son of Hezekiah.

✛

"I will sweep away everything
  from the face of the earth," says the Lord.
"I will sweep away people and animals alike.
  I will sweep away the birds of the sky and the fish in the sea.
I will reduce the wicked to heaps of rubble,
  and I will wipe humanity from the face of the earth," says the Lord.
"I will crush Judah and Jerusalem with my fist
  and destroy every last trace of their Baal worship.
I will put an end to all the idolatrous priests,
  so that even the memory of them will disappear.
For they go up to their roofs
  and bow down to the sun, moon, and stars.
They claim to follow the Lord,
  but then they worship Molech, too.
And I will destroy those who used to worship me
  but now no longer do.
They no longer ask for the Lord's guidance
  or seek my blessings."

Stand in silence in the presence of the Sovereign Lord,
  for the awesome day of the Lord's judgment is near.
The Lord has prepared his people for a great slaughter
  and has chosen their executioners.
"On that day of judgment,"
  says the Lord,
"I will punish the leaders and princes of Judah
  and all those following pagan customs.

Yes, I will punish those who participate in pagan worship ceremonies,
    and those who fill their masters' houses with violence and deceit.

"On that day," says the LORD,
    "a cry of alarm will come from the Fish Gate
and echo throughout the New Quarter of the city.
    And a great crash will sound from the hills.
Wail in sorrow, all you who live in the market area,
    for all the merchants and traders will be destroyed.

"I will search with lanterns in Jerusalem's darkest corners
    to punish those who sit complacent in their sins.
They think the LORD will do nothing to them,
    either good or bad.
So their property will be plundered,
    their homes will be ransacked.
They will build new homes
    but never live in them.
They will plant vineyards
    but never drink wine from them.

"That terrible day of the LORD is near.
    Swiftly it comes—
a day of bitter tears,
    a day when even strong men will cry out.
It will be a day when the LORD's anger is poured out—
    a day of terrible distress and anguish,
a day of ruin and desolation,
    a day of darkness and gloom,
a day of clouds and blackness,
    a day of trumpet calls and battle cries.
Down go the walled cities
    and the strongest battlements!

"Because you have sinned against the LORD,
    I will make you grope around like the blind.
Your blood will be poured into the dust,
    and your bodies will lie rotting on the ground."

Your silver and gold will not save you
    on that day of the LORD's anger.
For the whole land will be devoured
    by the fire of his jealousy.
He will make a terrifying end
    of all the people on earth.

+

Gather together—yes, gather together,
  you shameless nation.
Gather before judgment begins,
  before your time to repent is blown away like chaff.
Act now, before the fierce fury of the LORD falls
  and the terrible day of the LORD's anger begins.
Seek the LORD, all who are humble,
  and follow his commands.
Seek to do what is right
  and to live humbly.
Perhaps even yet the LORD will protect you—
  protect you from his anger on that day of destruction.

Gaza and Ashkelon will be abandoned,
  Ashdod and Ekron torn down.
And what sorrow awaits you Philistines
  who live along the coast and in the land of Canaan,
  for this judgment is against you, too!
The LORD will destroy you
  until not one of you is left.
The Philistine coast will become a wilderness pasture,
  a place of shepherd camps
  and enclosures for sheep and goats.
The remnant of the tribe of Judah will pasture there.
  They will rest at night in the abandoned houses in Ashkelon.
For the LORD their God will visit his people in kindness
  and restore their prosperity again.

"I have heard the taunts of the Moabites
  and the insults of the Ammonites,
mocking my people
  and invading their borders.
Now, as surely as I live,"
  says the LORD of Heaven's Armies, the God of Israel,
"Moab and Ammon will be destroyed—
  destroyed as completely as Sodom and Gomorrah.
Their land will become a place of stinging nettles,
  salt pits, and eternal desolation.
The remnant of my people will plunder them
  and take their land."

They will receive the wages of their pride,
    for they have scoffed at the people of the LORD of Heaven's Armies.
The LORD will terrify them
    as he destroys all the gods in the land.
Then nations around the world will worship the LORD,
    each in their own land.

"You Ethiopians will also be slaughtered
    by my sword," says the LORD.

And the LORD will strike the lands of the north with his fist,
    destroying the land of Assyria.
He will make its great capital, Nineveh, a desolate wasteland,
    parched like a desert.
The proud city will become a pasture for flocks and herds,
    and all sorts of wild animals will settle there.
The desert owl and screech owl will roost on its ruined columns,
    their calls echoing through the gaping windows.
Rubble will block all the doorways,
    and the cedar paneling will be exposed to the weather.
This is the boisterous city,
    once so secure.
"I am the greatest!" it boasted.
    "No other city can compare with me!"
But now, look how it has become an utter ruin,
    a haven for wild animals.
Everyone passing by will laugh in derision
    and shake a defiant fist.

What sorrow awaits rebellious, polluted Jerusalem,
    the city of violence and crime!
No one can tell it anything;
    it refuses all correction.
It does not trust in the LORD
    or draw near to its God.
Its leaders are like roaring lions
    hunting for their victims.
Its judges are like ravenous wolves at evening time,
    who by dawn have left no trace of their prey.
Its prophets are arrogant liars seeking their own gain.
    Its priests defile the Temple by disobeying God's
        instructions.

But the Lord is still there in the city,
    and he does no wrong.
Day by day he hands down justice,
    and he does not fail.
    But the wicked know no shame.

"I have wiped out many nations,
    devastating their fortress walls and towers.
Their streets are now deserted;
    their cities lie in silent ruin.
There are no survivors—
    none at all.
I thought, 'Surely they will have reverence for me now!
    Surely they will listen to my warnings.
Then I won't need to strike again,
    destroying their homes.'
But no, they get up early
    to continue their evil deeds.
Therefore, be patient," says the Lord.
    "Soon I will stand and accuse these evil nations.
For I have decided to gather the kingdoms of the earth
    and pour out my fiercest anger and fury on them.
All the earth will be devoured
    by the fire of my jealousy.

✦

"Then I will purify the speech of all people,
    so that everyone can worship the Lord together.
My scattered people who live beyond the rivers of Ethiopia
    will come to present their offerings.
On that day you will no longer need to be ashamed,
    for you will no longer be rebels against me.
I will remove all proud and arrogant people from among you.
    There will be no more haughtiness on my holy mountain.
Those who are left will be the lowly and humble,
    for it is they who trust in the name of the Lord.
The remnant of Israel will do no wrong;
    they will never tell lies or deceive one another.
They will eat and sleep in safety,
    and no one will make them afraid."

Sing, O daughter of Zion;
    shout aloud, O Israel!
Be glad and rejoice with all your heart,
    O daughter of Jerusalem!
For the Lord will remove his hand of judgment
    and will disperse the armies of your enemy.
And the Lord himself, the King of Israel,
    will live among you!
At last your troubles will be over,
    and you will never again fear disaster.
On that day the announcement to Jerusalem will be,
    "Cheer up, Zion! Don't be afraid!
For the Lord your God is living among you.
    He is a mighty savior.
He will take delight in you with gladness.
    With his love, he will calm all your fears.
    He will rejoice over you with joyful songs."

"I will gather you who mourn for the appointed festivals;
    you will be disgraced no more.
And I will deal severely with all who have oppressed you.
    I will save the weak and helpless ones;
I will bring together
    those who were chased away.
I will give glory and fame to my former exiles,
    wherever they have been mocked and shamed.
On that day I will gather you together
    and bring you home again.
I will give you a good name, a name of distinction,
    among all the nations of the earth,
as I restore your fortunes before their very eyes.
    I, the Lord, have spoken!"

VERY LITTLE IS KNOWN about the prophet Nahum. We are given no details of his personal life other than that he "lived in Elkosh," a city whose location is unknown today. Since he shows brilliant skill with words, we do know that he was educated and literate. The historical situation he refers to in his messages is also clear.

Nahum's five oracles describe the fall of the city of Nineveh, capital of the Assyrian Empire, an event that happened in 612 BC. The messages celebrate this event as an expression of God's just rule over the world, specifically his judgment against an oppressive people. Nahum highlights the Assyrians' oppression by asking, "Where can anyone be found who has not suffered from your continual cruelty?"

The first oracle in the book is most likely a song because its lines begin with the consecutive letters of the first half of the Hebrew alphabet. (This literary device appears in several of the psalms.) The oracle praises God as both just and merciful, echoing the language God used to describe himself to Moses at Mount Sinai: "The LORD is slow to get angry, but . . . he never lets the guilty go unpunished." This provides the context for what's said in the other four oracles in the book, which describe God's judgment against Nineveh.

The second oracle draws a series of contrasts by speaking alternately to Assyria and Judah. For example, the temples and gods of Assyria will be destroyed, but Judah will again be free to celebrate its own religious festivals. Here we get a brief glimpse of an essential truth of the gospel: When the "messenger is coming over the mountains with good news," a crucial part of the announcement is that God's enemies have been defeated.

The third oracle is a poetic depiction of the battle in which Nineveh was conquered. It's here that the prophet Nahum particularly exhibits his special ability with words. He first develops an extended image of bright colors and gleaming light to portray a formidable coalition of nations on the attack. He then alludes to the way Nineveh's river floods and destroys part of its wall, creating a breach that allows the siege forces to enter. He uses the image of receding floodwaters to represent the Assyrian army and population fleeing the onslaught. When Nahum says at the end that the city is "plundered, empty, and ruined," he begins with a short Hebrew word, adds a letter to make the next word, and adds another letter for the third, thus using the lengthening sound in each successive word to represent the spreading disaster.

The fourth oracle details the crimes for which Assyria has been judged and punished. Like a "den filled with young lions," it has been cruelly violent. And like a prostitute or "mistress of deadly charms," it has "enticed the nations," forcing subject peoples to worship its false gods.

The last oracle in the book, which probably comes from a time shortly before Nineveh fell, warns the Assyrians not to be complacent and think that their capital cannot be conquered. It reminds them that fifty years earlier, their own emperor went all the way to Egypt and captured the supposedly impregnable city of Thebes, which was "protected by the river on all sides, walled in by water."

This final oracle is a fitting ending to the book. It serves as a caution to any other nation, including Judah, that might think it can never be conquered. The implied warning is that only fidelity to the God of justice and mercy will keep a nation secure. The supposed strength of any empire cannot stand when God's judgment arrives.

NAHUM

+

This message concerning Nineveh came as a vision to Nahum, who lived
in Elkosh.

The LORD is a jealous God,
  filled with vengeance and rage.
He takes revenge on all who oppose him
  and continues to rage against his enemies!
The LORD is slow to get angry, but his power is great,
  and he never lets the guilty go unpunished.
He displays his power in the whirlwind and the storm.
  The billowing clouds are the dust beneath his feet.
At his command the oceans dry up,
  and the rivers disappear.
The lush pastures of Bashan and Carmel fade,
  and the green forests of Lebanon wither.
In his presence the mountains quake,
  and the hills melt away;
the earth trembles,
  and its people are destroyed.
Who can stand before his fierce anger?
  Who can survive his burning fury?
His rage blazes forth like fire,
  and the mountains crumble to dust in his presence.

The LORD is good,
  a strong refuge when trouble comes.
  He is close to those who trust in him.
But he will sweep away his enemies
  in an overwhelming flood.
He will pursue his foes
  into the darkness of night.

Why are you scheming against the LORD?
　　He will destroy you with one blow;
　　he won't need to strike twice!
His enemies, tangled like thornbushes
　　and staggering like drunks,
　　will be burned up like dry stubble in a field.
Who is this wicked counselor of yours
　　who plots evil against the LORD?

This is what the LORD says:
"Though the Assyrians have many allies,
　　they will be destroyed and disappear.
O my people, I have punished you before,
　　but I will not punish you again.
Now I will break the yoke of bondage from your neck
　　and tear off the chains of Assyrian oppression."

And this is what the LORD says concerning the Assyrians in Nineveh:
"You will have no more children to carry on your name.
　　I will destroy all the idols in the temples of your gods.
I am preparing a grave for you
　　because you are despicable!"

Look! A messenger is coming over the mountains with good news!
　　He is bringing a message of peace.
Celebrate your festivals, O people of Judah,
　　and fulfill all your vows,
for your wicked enemies will never invade your land again.
　　They will be completely destroyed!

Your enemy is coming to crush you, Nineveh.
　　Man the ramparts! Watch the roads!
　　Prepare your defenses! Call out your forces!

Even though the destroyer has destroyed Judah,
　　the LORD will restore its honor.
Israel's vine has been stripped of branches,
　　but he will restore its splendor.

Shields flash red in the sunlight!
　　See the scarlet uniforms of the valiant troops!
Watch as their glittering chariots move into position,
　　with a forest of spears waving above them.
The chariots race recklessly along the streets
　　and rush wildly through the squares.

They flash like firelight
  and move as swiftly as lightning.
The king shouts to his officers;
  they stumble in their haste,
  rushing to the walls to set up their defenses.
The river gates have been torn open!
  The palace is about to collapse!
Nineveh's exile has been decreed,
  and all the servant girls mourn its capture.
They moan like doves
  and beat their breasts in sorrow.
Nineveh is like a leaking water reservoir!
  The people are slipping away.
"Stop, stop!" someone shouts,
  but no one even looks back.
Loot the silver!
  Plunder the gold!
There's no end to Nineveh's treasures—
  its vast, uncounted wealth.
Soon the city is plundered, empty, and ruined.
  Hearts melt and knees shake.
The people stand aghast,
  their faces pale and trembling.

Where now is that great Nineveh,
  that den filled with young lions?
It was a place where people—like lions and their cubs—
  walked freely and without fear.
The lion tore up meat for his cubs
  and strangled prey for his mate.
He filled his den with prey,
  his caverns with his plunder.

"I am your enemy!"
  says the LORD of Heaven's Armies.
"Your chariots will soon go up in smoke.
  Your young men will be killed in battle.
Never again will you plunder conquered nations.
  The voices of your proud messengers will be heard no more."

What sorrow awaits Nineveh,
  the city of murder and lies!
She is crammed with wealth

and is never without victims.
Hear the crack of whips,
    the rumble of wheels!
Horses' hooves pound,
    and chariots clatter wildly.
See the flashing swords and glittering spears
    as the charioteers charge past!
There are countless casualties,
    heaps of bodies—
so many bodies that
    people stumble over them.
All this because Nineveh,
    the beautiful and faithless city,
mistress of deadly charms,
    enticed the nations with her beauty.
She taught them all her magic,
    enchanting people everywhere.

"I am your enemy!"
    says the Lord of Heaven's Armies.
"And now I will lift your skirts
    and show all the earth your nakedness and shame.
I will cover you with filth
    and show the world how vile you really are.
All who see you will shrink back and say,
    'Nineveh lies in ruins.
Where are the mourners?'
    Does anyone regret your destruction?"

Are you any better than the city of Thebes,
    situated on the Nile River, surrounded by water?
She was protected by the river on all sides,
    walled in by water.
Ethiopia and the land of Egypt
    gave unlimited assistance.
The nations of Put and Libya
    were among her allies.
Yet Thebes fell,
    and her people were led away as captives.
Her babies were dashed to death
    against the stones of the streets.
Soldiers threw dice to get Egyptian officers as servants.
    All their leaders were bound in chains.

And you, Nineveh, will also stagger like a drunkard.
   You will hide for fear of the attacking enemy.
All your fortresses will fall.
   They will be devoured like the ripe figs
that fall into the mouths
   of those who shake the trees.
Your troops will be as weak
   and helpless as women.
The gates of your land will be opened wide to the enemy
   and set on fire and burned.
Get ready for the siege!
   Store up water!
   Strengthen the defenses!
Go into the pits to trample clay,
   and pack it into molds,
      making bricks to repair the walls.

But the fire will devour you;
   the sword will cut you down.
The enemy will consume you like locusts,
   devouring everything they see.
There will be no escape,
   even if you multiply like swarming locusts.
Your merchants have multiplied
   until they outnumber the stars.
But like a swarm of locusts,
   they strip the land and fly away.
Your guards and officials are also like swarming locusts
   that crowd together in the hedges on a cold day.
But like locusts that fly away when the sun comes up,
   all of them will fly away and disappear.

Your shepherds are asleep, O Assyrian king;
   your princes lie dead in the dust.
Your people are scattered across the mountains
   with no one to gather them together.
There is no healing for your wound;
   your injury is fatal.
All who hear of your destruction
   will clap their hands for joy.
Where can anyone be found
   who has not suffered from your continual cruelty?

IMMERSED IN HABAKKUK

HABAKKUK LIVED AROUND the same time as Nahum, in the period when the Babylonian Empire was gaining ascendancy over the Assyrians. We're told nothing explicit about the prophet himself, but we do have some intriguing clues about his identity.

The contents of the book of Habakkuk are presented in a unique style, quite different from the other prophetic books. Rather than bringing a message from God to the people, Habakkuk engages in a dialogue with God. He also includes a song, complete with musical notations. His opening complaint to God resembles the opening of a lament psalm, a literary form used by God's people, especially after the Exile, to express deep sorrow.

As the book opens, Habakkuk is identified as a prophet. At that time, the term *prophet* could be applied to certain Levites who served in the Temple. They were responsible to "proclaim God's messages to the accompaniment of lyres, harps, and cymbals," as Chronicles puts it. Given the character of his compositions and his identifying title, Habakkuk may well have been one of the Temple musicians. We get a further suggestion of this when he ends his dialogue with God by accepting the difficult things he's heard: "The LORD is in his holy Temple. Let all the earth be silent before him." This could indicate the prophet's close ties to the Temple and that his messages were spoken and recorded there.

Habakkuk begins by complaining that the people of Judah are using their reprieve from Assyrian domination to engage in renewed injustice and violence against the vulnerable. God responds that, as a consequence, he will soon allow the Babylonians to subjugate the kingdom of Judah.

But Habakkuk protests that the Babylonians are just as cruel and idolatrous as the Assyrians—and far worse than the people of Judah whom God is about to judge. The prophet asks, "Should you be silent while the wicked swallow up people more righteous than they?" God assures Habakkuk that the Babylonians themselves will be judged and punished for their own sins in due time: "This vision is for a future time. It describes the end, and it will be fulfilled. If it seems slow in coming, wait patiently, for it will surely take place." The LORD then announces a series of woes against the Babylonians. Five times God promises that "sorrow awaits" them for their violence, extortion, and idolatry.

In response, Habakkuk quietly and confidently accepts what God has said and then composes a song. In the song, he first reviews God's past deeds of deliverance. He portrays these in terms of a *theophany* (a description of God coming down to earth in great power), a literary device also found in many of the psalms. Even though all seems lost at the moment, the history of God's previous demonstrations of mercy brings hope. Habakkuk sings of what the LORD has already done, resting in the knowledge of the redemption that is surely coming again:

I have heard all about you, LORD.
   I am filled with awe by your amazing works.
In this time of our deep need,
   help us again as you did in years gone by.

HABAKKUK

✝

This is the message that the prophet Habakkuk received in a vision.

✝

How long, O LORD, must I call for help?
   But you do not listen!
"Violence is everywhere!" I cry,
   but you do not come to save.
Must I forever see these evil deeds?
   Why must I watch all this misery?
Wherever I look,
   I see destruction and violence.
I am surrounded by people
   who love to argue and fight.
The law has become paralyzed,
   and there is no justice in the courts.
The wicked far outnumber the righteous,
   so that justice has become perverted.

The LORD replied,

"Look around at the nations;
   look and be amazed!
For I am doing something in your own day,
   something you wouldn't believe
   even if someone told you about it.
I am raising up the Babylonians,
   a cruel and violent people.
They will march across the world
   and conquer other lands.
They are notorious for their cruelty
   and do whatever they like.

Their horses are swifter than cheetahs
and fiercer than wolves at dusk.
Their charioteers charge from far away.
Like eagles, they swoop down to devour their prey.

"On they come, all bent on violence.
Their hordes advance like a desert wind,
sweeping captives ahead of them like sand.
They scoff at kings and princes
and scorn all their fortresses.
They simply pile ramps of earth
against their walls and capture them!
They sweep past like the wind
and are gone.
But they are deeply guilty,
for their own strength is their god."

O Lord my God, my Holy One, you who are eternal—
surely you do not plan to wipe us out?
O Lord, our Rock, you have sent these Babylonians
to correct us,
to punish us for our many sins.
But you are pure and cannot stand the sight of evil.
Will you wink at their treachery?
Should you be silent while the wicked
swallow up people more righteous than they?

Are we only fish to be caught and killed?
Are we only sea creatures that have no leader?
Must we be strung up on their hooks
and caught in their nets while they rejoice and celebrate?
Then they will worship their nets
and burn incense in front of them.
"These nets are the gods who have made us rich!"
they will claim.
Will you let them get away with this forever?
Will they succeed forever in their heartless
conquests?

I will climb up to my watchtower
and stand at my guardpost.
There I will wait to see what the Lord says
and how he will answer my complaint.

Then the LORD said to me,

"Write my answer plainly on tablets,
   so that a runner can carry the correct message
      to others.
This vision is for a future time.
   It describes the end, and it will be fulfilled.
If it seems slow in coming, wait patiently,
   for it will surely take place.
   It will not be delayed.

"Look at the proud!
   They trust in themselves, and their lives are crooked.
   But the righteous will live by their faithfulness to God.
Wealth is treacherous,
   and the arrogant are never at rest.
They open their mouths as wide as the grave,
   and like death, they are never satisfied.
In their greed they have gathered up many nations
   and swallowed many peoples.

"But soon their captives will taunt them.
   They will mock them, saying,
'What sorrow awaits you thieves!
   Now you will get what you deserve!
You've become rich by extortion,
   but how much longer can this go on?'
Suddenly, your debtors will take action.
   They will turn on you and take all you have,
   while you stand trembling and helpless.
Because you have plundered many nations,
   now all the survivors will plunder you.
You committed murder throughout the countryside
   and filled the towns with violence.

"What sorrow awaits you who build big houses
   with money gained dishonestly!
You believe your wealth will buy security,
   putting your family's nest beyond the reach of danger.
But by the murders you committed,
   you have shamed your name and forfeited your lives.
The very stones in the walls cry out against you,
   and the beams in the ceilings echo the complaint.

"What sorrow awaits you who build cities
　　with money gained through murder and corruption!
Has not the LORD of Heaven's Armies promised
　　that the wealth of nations will turn to ashes?
They work so hard,
　　but all in vain!
For as the waters fill the sea,
　　the earth will be filled with an awareness
　　of the glory of the LORD.

"What sorrow awaits you who make your neighbors drunk!
　　You force your cup on them
　　so you can gloat over their shameful nakedness.
But soon it will be your turn to be disgraced.
　　Come, drink and be exposed!
Drink from the cup of the LORD's judgment,
　　and all your glory will be turned to shame.
You cut down the forests of Lebanon.
　　Now you will be cut down.
You destroyed the wild animals,
　　so now their terror will be yours.
You committed murder throughout the countryside
　　and filled the towns with violence.

"What good is an idol carved by man,
　　or a cast image that deceives you?
How foolish to trust in your own creation—
　　a god that can't even talk!
What sorrow awaits you who say to wooden idols,
　　'Wake up and save us!'
To speechless stone images you say,
　　'Rise up and teach us!'
　　Can an idol tell you what to do?
They may be overlaid with gold and silver,
　　but they are lifeless inside.
But the LORD is in his holy Temple.
　　Let all the earth be silent before him."

+

This prayer was sung by the prophet Habakkuk:

I have heard all about you, LORD.
　　I am filled with awe by your amazing works.

In this time of our deep need,
  help us again as you did in years gone by.
And in your anger,
  remember your mercy.

I see God moving across the deserts from Edom,
  the Holy One coming from Mount Paran.
His brilliant splendor fills the heavens,
  and the earth is filled with his praise.
His coming is as brilliant as the sunrise.
  Rays of light flash from his hands,
  where his awesome power is hidden.
Pestilence marches before him;
  plague follows close behind.
When he stops, the earth shakes.
  When he looks, the nations tremble.
He shatters the everlasting mountains
  and levels the eternal hills.
  He is the Eternal One!
I see the people of Cushan in distress,
  and the nation of Midian trembling in terror.

Was it in anger, LORD, that you struck the rivers
  and parted the sea?
Were you displeased with them?
  No, you were sending your chariots of salvation!
You brandished your bow
  and your quiver of arrows.
  You split open the earth with flowing rivers.
The mountains watched and trembled.
  Onward swept the raging waters.
The mighty deep cried out,
  lifting its hands in submission.
The sun and moon stood still in the sky
  as your brilliant arrows flew
  and your glittering spear flashed.

You marched across the land in anger
  and trampled the nations in your fury.
You went out to rescue your chosen people,
  to save your anointed ones.
You crushed the heads of the wicked
  and stripped their bones from head to toe.

With his own weapons,
   you destroyed the chief of those
who rushed out like a whirlwind,
   thinking Israel would be easy prey.
You trampled the sea with your horses,
   and the mighty waters piled high.

I trembled inside when I heard this;
   my lips quivered with fear.
My legs gave way beneath me,
   and I shook in terror.
I will wait quietly for the coming day
   when disaster will strike the people who invade us.
Even though the fig trees have no blossoms,
   and there are no grapes on the vines;
even though the olive crop fails,
   and the fields lie empty and barren;
even though the flocks die in the fields,
   and the cattle barns are empty,
yet I will rejoice in the LORD!
   I will be joyful in the God of my salvation!
The Sovereign LORD is my strength!
   He makes me as surefooted as a deer,
   able to tread upon the heights.

(For the choir director: This prayer is to be accompanied by stringed instruments.)

IMMERSED IN JEREMIAH

THE BOOK OF JEREMIAH is the longest book within the Prophets, containing oracles and stories drawn from a period of more than thirty years. But a single historical situation looms over the whole book: The Babylonian Empire threatens and then destroys Jerusalem, leading to the exile of its people. This constitutes the single biggest crisis that God's people had ever encountered.

God calls Jeremiah to be a prophet when he is still young (Jeremiah actually protests that he's "too young"), and God tells him to renew the warning that earlier prophets had sounded. The people of Judah confidently think they will never be conquered because the LORD has made his home in the Jerusalem Temple. But Jeremiah warns them: "Do you really think you can steal, murder, commit adultery, lie, and burn incense to Baal and all those other new gods of yours, and then come here and stand before me in my Temple and chant, 'We are safe!'—only to go right back to all those evils again?"

But the more Jeremiah insists that disaster is imminent, the more the leaders and people resist him. He is mocked and hated and even accused of treason against the nation. Finally, he is thrown in prison, where he nearly dies. But through it all—even in the midst of deep depression—Jeremiah faithfully fulfills his calling. For the LORD had told him, "Today I appoint you to stand up against nations and kingdoms. Some you must uproot and tear down, destroy and overthrow. Others you must build up and plant."

The material in the book of Jeremiah is organized into four major parts, each marked off at the end by a reference to Jeremiah's words being written down and then read. The first part is a collection of his oracles about Judah (pp. 203-254), spoken at different points in his career.

In the second part of the book (pp. 254-274), Jeremiah recounts stories and messages related to events in Jerusalem during the reigns of Jehoiakim and Zedekiah in the years just before the final Babylonian invasion. More stories like these make up the third part of the book (pp. 274-284), where they concentrate on the final years of the kingdom of Judah and the destruction of Jerusalem.

Like many of the prophets, Jeremiah also proclaims messages about other nations. These oracles are collected in the last section (pp. 284-308), where a message predicting Babylon's eventual downfall has the last word among Jeremiah's messages. (At some point, the introduction to these oracles to the nations became separated from the actual messages and was placed earlier in the book. In this edition we've reunited the introduction with the oracles themselves.)

After "the end of Jeremiah's messages," the book concludes with an epilogue that describes in terrible detail the fall of Jerusalem and the destruction of the Temple. This epilogue closely matches the description at the end of the book of Samuel–Kings.

Even though the book closes with an account of the tragic demise of the kingdom of Judah, a bright hope for God's people still lives at its center. A special oracle called the "book of comfort" (pp. 260-265) is placed in the middle of the second section, which puts it right in the center of Jeremiah's book as a whole. Here the LORD promises that because his love for his people is everlasting, he will bring them back from exile: "I will bring them from the north and from the distant corners of the earth. . . . A great company will return! Tears of joy will stream down their faces, and I will lead them home with great care."

God told Jeremiah that his words would both "tear down" and "build up and plant." And so it is fitting that in the center of the book, God promises that he "will make a new covenant with the people of Israel and Judah." God is going to put his instructions deep within them, transforming them from the inside out. The rebellion of Adam has been living in the hearts of God's people. But a new day is promised, a day of forgiveness and renewal, when all God's hopes and dreams for Israel will be realized. This is the great future that moves the Bible's great story forward.

JEREMIAH

✣

These are the words of Jeremiah son of Hilkiah, one of the priests from the town of Anathoth in the land of Benjamin. The LORD first gave messages to Jeremiah during the thirteenth year of the reign of Josiah son of Amon, king of Judah. The LORD's messages continued throughout the reign of King Jehoiakim, Josiah's son, until the eleventh year of the reign of King Zedekiah, another of Josiah's sons. In August of that eleventh year the people of Jerusalem were taken away as captives.

✚ ✚ ✚

The LORD gave me this message:

> "I knew you before I formed you in your mother's womb.
>   Before you were born I set you apart
>   and appointed you as my prophet to the nations."

"O Sovereign LORD," I said, "I can't speak for you! I'm too young!"

The LORD replied, "Don't say, 'I'm too young,' for you must go wherever I send you and say whatever I tell you. And don't be afraid of the people, for I will be with you and will protect you. I, the LORD, have spoken!"

Then the LORD reached out and touched my mouth and said,

> "Look, I have put my words in your mouth!
> Today I appoint you to stand up
>   against nations and kingdoms.
> Some you must uproot and tear down,
>   destroy and overthrow.
> Others you must build up
>   and plant."

Then the LORD said to me, "Look, Jeremiah! What do you see?"

And I replied, "I see a branch from an almond tree."

And the LORD said, "That's right, and it means that I am watching, and I will certainly carry out all my plans."

Then the LORD spoke to me again and asked, "What do you see now?"
And I replied, "I see a pot of boiling water, spilling from the north."

"Yes," the LORD said, "for terror from the north will boil out on the people of this land. Listen! I am calling the armies of the kingdoms of the north to come to Jerusalem. I, the LORD, have spoken!

> "They will set their thrones
>   at the gates of the city.
> They will attack its walls
>   and all the other towns of Judah.
> I will pronounce judgment
>   on my people for all their evil—
> for deserting me and burning incense to other gods.
>   Yes, they worship idols made with their own hands!
>
> "Get up and prepare for action.
>   Go out and tell them everything I tell you to say.
> Do not be afraid of them,
>   or I will make you look foolish in front of them.
> For see, today I have made you strong
>   like a fortified city that cannot be captured,
>   like an iron pillar or a bronze wall.
> You will stand against the whole land—
>   the kings, officials, priests, and people of Judah.
> They will fight you, but they will fail.
>   For I am with you, and I will take care of you.
>   I, the LORD, have spoken!"

+

The LORD gave me another message. He said, "Go and shout this message to Jerusalem. This is what the LORD says:

> "I remember how eager you were to please me
>   as a young bride long ago,
> how you loved me and followed me
>   even through the barren wilderness.
> In those days Israel was holy to the LORD,
>   the first of his children.
> All who harmed his people were declared guilty,
>   and disaster fell on them.
>   I, the LORD, have spoken!"

Listen to the word of the LORD, people of Jacob—all you families of Israel! This is what the LORD says:

"What did your ancestors find wrong with me
   that led them to stray so far from me?
They worshiped worthless idols,
   only to become worthless themselves.
They did not ask, 'Where is the LORD
   who brought us safely out of Egypt
and led us through the barren wilderness—
   a land of deserts and pits,
a land of drought and death,
   where no one lives or even travels?'

"And when I brought you into a fruitful land
   to enjoy its bounty and goodness,
you defiled my land and
   corrupted the possession I had promised you.
The priests did not ask,
   'Where is the LORD?'
Those who taught my word ignored me,
   the rulers turned against me,
and the prophets spoke in the name of Baal,
   wasting their time on worthless idols.
Therefore, I will bring my case against you,"
   says the LORD.
"I will even bring charges against your children's children
   in the years to come.

"Go west and look in the land of Cyprus;
   go east and search through the land of Kedar.
Has anyone ever heard of anything
   as strange as this?
Has any nation ever traded its gods for new ones,
   even though they are not gods at all?
Yet my people have exchanged their glorious God
   for worthless idols!
The heavens are shocked at such a thing
   and shrink back in horror and dismay,"
   says the LORD.
"For my people have done two evil things:
They have abandoned me—
   the fountain of living water.

And they have dug for themselves cracked cisterns
    that can hold no water at all!

"Why has Israel become a slave?
    Why has he been carried away as plunder?
Strong lions have roared against him,
    and the land has been destroyed.
The towns are now in ruins,
    and no one lives in them anymore.
Egyptians, marching from their cities of Memphis and Tahpanhes,
    have destroyed Israel's glory and power.
And you have brought this upon yourselves
    by rebelling against the LORD your God,
    even though he was leading you on the way!

"What have you gained by your alliances with Egypt
    and your covenants with Assyria?
What good to you are the streams of the Nile
    or the waters of the Euphrates River?
Your wickedness will bring its own punishment.
    Your turning from me will shame you.
You will see what an evil, bitter thing it is
    to abandon the LORD your God and not to fear him.
    I, the Lord, the LORD of Heaven's Armies, have spoken!

"Long ago I broke the yoke that oppressed you
    and tore away the chains of your slavery,
but still you said,
    'I will not serve you.'
On every hill and under every green tree,
    you have prostituted yourselves by bowing down to idols.
But I was the one who planted you,
    choosing a vine of the purest stock—the very best.
    How did you grow into this corrupt wild vine?
No amount of soap or lye can make you clean.
    I still see the stain of your guilt.
    I, the Sovereign LORD, have spoken!

"You say, 'That's not true!
    I haven't worshiped the images of Baal!'
But how can you say that?
    Go and look in any valley in the land!
Face the awful sins you have done.
    You are like a restless female camel

desperately searching for a mate.
You are like a wild donkey,
  sniffing the wind at mating time.
Who can restrain her lust?
  Those who desire her don't need to search,
  for she goes running to them!
When will you stop running?
  When will you stop panting after other gods?
But you say, 'Save your breath.
  I'm in love with these foreign gods,
  and I can't stop loving them now!'

"Israel is like a thief
  who feels shame only when he gets caught.
They, their kings, officials, priests, and prophets—
  all are alike in this.
To an image carved from a piece of wood they say,
  'You are my father.'
To an idol chiseled from a block of stone they say,
  'You are my mother.'
They turn their backs on me,
  but in times of trouble they cry out to me,
  'Come and save us!'
But why not call on these gods you have made?
  When trouble comes, let them save you if they can!
For you have as many gods
  as there are towns in Judah.
Why do you accuse me of doing wrong?
  You are the ones who have rebelled,"
  says the LORD.
"I have punished your children,
  but they did not respond to my discipline.
You yourselves have killed your prophets
  as a lion kills its prey.

"O my people, listen to the words of the LORD!
  Have I been like a desert to Israel?
  Have I been to them a land of darkness?
Why then do my people say, 'At last we are free
    from God!
  We don't need him anymore!'
Does a young woman forget her jewelry,
  or a bride her wedding dress?

Yet for years on end
   my people have forgotten me.

"How you plot and scheme to win your lovers.
   Even an experienced prostitute could learn from you!
Your clothing is stained with the blood of the innocent and the poor,
   though you didn't catch them breaking into your houses!
And yet you say,
'I have done nothing wrong.
   Surely God isn't angry with me!'
But now I will punish you severely
   because you claim you have not sinned.
First here, then there—
   you flit from one ally to another asking for help.
But your new friends in Egypt will let you down,
   just as Assyria did before.
In despair, you will be led into exile
   with your hands on your heads,
for the LORD has rejected the nations you trust.
   They will not help you at all.

"If a man divorces a woman
   and she goes and marries someone else,
he will not take her back again,
   for that would surely corrupt the land.
But you have prostituted yourself with many lovers,
   so why are you trying to come back to me?"
   says the LORD.
"Look at the shrines on every hilltop.
   Is there any place you have not been defiled
   by your adultery with other gods?
You sit like a prostitute beside the road waiting for a customer.
   You sit alone like a nomad in the desert.
You have polluted the land with your prostitution
   and your wickedness.
That's why even the spring rains have failed.
   For you are a brazen prostitute and completely shameless.
Yet you say to me,
'Father, you have been my guide since my youth.
Surely you won't be angry forever!
   Surely you can forget about it!'
So you talk,
   but you keep on doing all the evil you can."

+

During the reign of King Josiah, the LORD said to me, "Have you seen what fickle Israel has done? Like a wife who commits adultery, Israel has worshiped other gods on every hill and under every green tree. I thought, 'After she has done all this, she will return to me.' But she did not return, and her faithless sister Judah saw this. She saw that I divorced faithless Israel because of her adultery. But that treacherous sister Judah had no fear, and now she, too, has left me and given herself to prostitution. Israel treated it all so lightly—she thought nothing of committing adultery by worshiping idols made of wood and stone. So now the land has been polluted. But despite all this, her faithless sister Judah has never sincerely returned to me. She has only pretended to be sorry. I, the LORD, have spoken!"

Then the LORD said to me, "Even faithless Israel is less guilty than treacherous Judah! Therefore, go and give this message to Israel. This is what the LORD says:

"O Israel, my faithless people,
    come home to me again,
for I am merciful.
    I will not be angry with you forever.
Only acknowledge your guilt.
    Admit that you rebelled against the LORD your God
and committed adultery against him
    by worshiping idols under every green tree.
Confess that you refused to listen to my voice.
    I, the LORD, have spoken!

"Return home, you wayward children,"
    says the LORD,
    "for I am your master.
I will bring you back to the land of Israel—
    one from this town and two from that family—
    from wherever you are scattered.
And I will give you shepherds after my own heart,
    who will guide you with knowledge and understanding.

"And when your land is once more filled with people," says the LORD, "you will no longer wish for 'the good old days' when you possessed the Ark of the LORD's Covenant. You will not miss those days or even remember them, and there will be no need to rebuild the Ark. In that day Jerusalem will be known as 'The Throne of the LORD.' All nations will come there to honor the LORD. They will no longer stubbornly follow their own evil desires. In those days the people of Judah and Israel will return together from exile in the north. They will return to the land I gave your ancestors as an inheritance forever.

"I thought to myself,
  'I would love to treat you as my own children!'
I wanted nothing more than to give you this beautiful land—
  the finest possession in the world.
I looked forward to your calling me 'Father,'
  and I wanted you never to turn from me.
But you have been unfaithful to me, you people of Israel!
  You have been like a faithless wife who leaves her husband.
  I, the LORD, have spoken."

Voices are heard high on the windswept mountains,
  the weeping and pleading of Israel's people.
For they have chosen crooked paths
  and have forgotten the LORD their God.

"My wayward children," says the LORD,
  "come back to me, and I will heal your wayward hearts."

"Yes, we're coming," the people reply,
  "for you are the LORD our God.
Our worship of idols on the hills
  and our religious orgies on the mountains
  are a delusion.
Only in the LORD our God
  will Israel ever find salvation.
From childhood we have watched
  as everything our ancestors worked for—
their flocks and herds, their sons and daughters—
  was squandered on a delusion.
Let us now lie down in shame
  and cover ourselves with dishonor,
for we and our ancestors have sinned
  against the LORD our God.
From our childhood to this day
  we have never obeyed him."

"O Israel," says the LORD,
  "if you wanted to return to me, you could.
You could throw away your detestable idols
  and stray away no more.

Then when you swear by my name, saying,
  'As surely as the LORD lives,'
you could do so
  with truth, justice, and righteousness.
Then you would be a blessing to the nations of the world,
  and all people would come and praise my name."

This is what the LORD says to the people of Judah and Jerusalem:

"Plow up the hard ground of your hearts!
  Do not waste your good seed among thorns.
O people of Judah and Jerusalem,
  surrender your pride and power.
Change your hearts before the LORD,
  or my anger will burn like an unquenchable fire
  because of all your sins.

"Shout to Judah, and broadcast to Jerusalem!
  Tell them to sound the alarm throughout the land:
'Run for your lives!
  Flee to the fortified cities!'
Raise a signal flag as a warning for Jerusalem:
  'Flee now! Do not delay!'
For I am bringing terrible destruction upon you
  from the north."

A lion stalks from its den,
  a destroyer of nations.
It has left its lair and is headed your way.
  It's going to devastate your land!
Your towns will lie in ruins,
  with no one living in them anymore.
So put on clothes of mourning
  and weep with broken hearts,
for the fierce anger of the LORD
  is still upon us.

"In that day," says the LORD,
  "the king and the officials will tremble in fear.
The priests will be struck with horror,
  and the prophets will be appalled."

Then I said, "O Sovereign LORD,
  the people have been deceived by what you said,

for you promised peace for Jerusalem.
But the sword is held at their throats!"

The time is coming when the LORD will say
to the people of Jerusalem,
"My dear people, a burning wind is blowing in from the desert,
and it's not a gentle breeze useful for winnowing grain.
It is a roaring blast sent by me!
Now I will pronounce your destruction!"

Our enemy rushes down on us like storm clouds!
His chariots are like whirlwinds.
His horses are swifter than eagles.
How terrible it will be, for we are doomed!
O Jerusalem, cleanse your heart
that you may be saved.
How long will you harbor
your evil thoughts?
Your destruction has been announced
from Dan and the hill country of Ephraim.

"Warn the surrounding nations
and announce this to Jerusalem:
The enemy is coming from a distant land,
raising a battle cry against the towns of Judah.
They surround Jerusalem like watchmen around a field,
for my people have rebelled against me,"
says the LORD.
"Your own actions have brought this upon you.
This punishment is bitter, piercing you to the heart!"

My heart, my heart—I writhe in pain!
My heart pounds within me! I cannot be still.
For I have heard the blast of enemy trumpets
and the roar of their battle cries.
Waves of destruction roll over the land,
until it lies in complete desolation.
Suddenly my tents are destroyed;
in a moment my shelters are crushed.
How long must I see the battle flags
and hear the trumpets of war?

"My people are foolish
and do not know me," says the LORD.

"They are stupid children
　who have no understanding.
They are clever enough at doing wrong,
　but they have no idea how to do right!"

I looked at the earth, and it was empty and formless.
　I looked at the heavens, and there was no light.
I looked at the mountains and hills,
　and they trembled and shook.
I looked, and all the people were gone.
　All the birds of the sky had flown away.
I looked, and the fertile fields had become a wilderness.
　The towns lay in ruins,
　crushed by the LORD's fierce anger.

This is what the LORD says:
"The whole land will be ruined,
　but I will not destroy it completely.
The earth will mourn
　and the heavens will be draped in black
because of my decree against my people.
　I have made up my mind and will not change it."

At the noise of charioteers and archers,
　the people flee in terror.
They hide in the bushes
　and run for the mountains.
All the towns have been abandoned—
　not a person remains!
What are you doing,
　you who have been plundered?
Why do you dress up in beautiful clothing
　and put on gold jewelry?
Why do you brighten your eyes with mascara?
　Your primping will do you no good!
The allies who were your lovers
　despise you and seek to kill you.

I hear a cry, like that of a woman in labor,
　the groans of a woman giving birth to her first child.
It is beautiful Jerusalem
　gasping for breath and crying out,
　"Help! I'm being murdered!"

"Run up and down every street in Jerusalem," says the LORD.
  "Look high and low; search throughout the city!
If you can find even one just and honest person,
  I will not destroy the city.
But even when they are under oath,
  saying, 'As surely as the LORD lives,'
  they are still telling lies!"

LORD, you are searching for honesty.
You struck your people,
  but they paid no attention.
You crushed them,
  but they refused to be corrected.
They are determined, with faces set like stone;
  they have refused to repent.

Then I said, "But what can we expect from the poor?
  They are ignorant.
They don't know the ways of the LORD.
  They don't understand God's laws.
So I will go and speak to their leaders.
  Surely they know the ways of the LORD
  and understand God's laws."
But the leaders, too, as one man,
  had thrown off God's yoke
  and broken his chains.
So now a lion from the forest will attack them;
  a wolf from the desert will pounce on them.
A leopard will lurk near their towns,
  tearing apart any who dare to venture out.
For their rebellion is great,
  and their sins are many.

"How can I pardon you?
  For even your children have turned from me.
They have sworn by gods that are not gods at all!
  I fed my people until they were full.
But they thanked me by committing adultery
  and lining up at the brothels.
They are well-fed, lusty stallions,
  each neighing for his neighbor's wife.
Should I not punish them for this?" says the LORD.
  "Should I not avenge myself against such a nation?

"Go down the rows of the vineyards and destroy the grapevines,
　　leaving a scattered few alive.
Strip the branches from the vines,
　　for these people do not belong to the Lord.
The people of Israel and Judah
　　are full of treachery against me,"
　　says the Lord.
"They have lied about the Lord
　　and said, 'He won't bother us!
No disasters will come upon us.
　　There will be no war or famine.
God's prophets are all windbags
　　who don't really speak for him.
　　Let their predictions of disaster fall on themselves!'"

Therefore, this is what the Lord God of Heaven's Armies says:

"Because the people are talking like this,
　　my messages will flame out of your mouth
　　and burn the people like kindling wood.
O Israel, I will bring a distant nation against you,"
　　says the Lord.
"It is a mighty nation,
　　an ancient nation,
a people whose language you do not know,
　　whose speech you cannot understand.
Their weapons are deadly;
　　their warriors are mighty.
They will devour the food of your harvest;
　　they will devour your sons and daughters.
They will devour your flocks and herds;
　　they will devour your grapes and figs.
And they will destroy your fortified towns,
　　which you think are so safe.

"Yet even in those days I will not blot you out completely," says the
Lord. "And when your people ask, 'Why did the Lord our God do all
this to us?' you must reply, 'You rejected him and gave yourselves to foreign gods in your own land. Now you will serve foreigners in a land that
is not your own.'

"Make this announcement to Israel,
　　and say this to Judah:
Listen, you foolish and senseless people,

with eyes that do not see
and ears that do not hear.
Have you no respect for me?
Why don't you tremble in my presence?
I, the LORD, define the ocean's sandy shoreline
as an everlasting boundary that the waters cannot cross.
The waves may toss and roar,
but they can never pass the boundaries I set.
But my people have stubborn and rebellious hearts.
They have turned away and abandoned me.
They do not say from the heart,
'Let us live in awe of the LORD our God,
for he gives us rain each spring and fall,
assuring us of a harvest when the time is right.'
Your wickedness has deprived you of these wonderful blessings.
Your sin has robbed you of all these good things.

"Among my people are wicked men
who lie in wait for victims like a hunter hiding in a blind.
They continually set traps
to catch people.
Like a cage filled with birds,
their homes are filled with evil plots.
And now they are great and rich.
They are fat and sleek,
and there is no limit to their wicked deeds.
They refuse to provide justice to orphans
and deny the rights of the poor.
Should I not punish them for this?" says the LORD.
"Should I not avenge myself against such a nation?
A horrible and shocking thing
has happened in this land—
the prophets give false prophecies,
and the priests rule with an iron hand.
Worse yet, my people like it that way!
But what will you do when the end comes?

"Run for your lives, you people of Benjamin!
Get out of Jerusalem!
Sound the alarm in Tekoa!
Send up a signal at Beth-hakkerem!
A powerful army is coming from the north,
coming with disaster and destruction.

O Jerusalem, you are my beautiful and delicate daughter—
    but I will destroy you!
Enemies will surround you, like shepherds camped around the city.
    Each chooses a place for his troops to devour.
They shout, 'Prepare for battle!
    Attack at noon!'
'No, it's too late; the day is fading,
    and the evening shadows are falling.'
'Well then, let's attack at night
    and destroy her palaces!'"

This is what the LORD of Heaven's Armies says:
"Cut down the trees for battering rams.
    Build siege ramps against the walls of Jerusalem.
This is the city to be punished,
    for she is wicked through and through.
She spouts evil like a fountain.
    Her streets echo with the sounds of violence and
        destruction.
    I always see her sickness and sores.
Listen to this warning, Jerusalem,
    or I will turn from you in disgust.
Listen, or I will turn you into a heap of ruins,
    a land where no one lives."

This is what the LORD of Heaven's Armies says:
"Even the few who remain in Israel
    will be picked over again,
as when a harvester checks each vine a second time
    to pick the grapes that were missed."

To whom can I give warning?
    Who will listen when I speak?
Their ears are closed,
    and they cannot hear.
They scorn the word of the LORD.
    They don't want to listen at all.
So now I am filled with the LORD's fury.
    Yes, I am tired of holding it in!

"I will pour out my fury on children playing in the streets
    and on gatherings of young men,
on husbands and wives
    and on those who are old and gray.

Their homes will be turned over to their enemies,
  as will their fields and their wives.
For I will raise my powerful fist
  against the people of this land,"
  says the LORD.
"From the least to the greatest,
  their lives are ruled by greed.
From prophets to priests,
  they are all frauds.
They offer superficial treatments
  for my people's mortal wound.
They give assurances of peace
  when there is no peace.
Are they ashamed of their disgusting actions?
  Not at all—they don't even know how to blush!
Therefore, they will lie among the slaughtered.
  They will be brought down when I punish them,"
  says the LORD.

This is what the LORD says:
"Stop at the crossroads and look around.
  Ask for the old, godly way, and walk in it.
Travel its path, and you will find rest for your souls.
  But you reply, 'No, that's not the road we want!'
I posted watchmen over you who said,
  'Listen for the sound of the alarm.'
But you replied,
  'No! We won't pay attention!'

"Therefore, listen to this, all you nations.
  Take note of my people's situation.
Listen, all the earth!
  I will bring disaster on my people.
It is the fruit of their own schemes,
  because they refuse to listen to me.
  They have rejected my word.
There's no use offering me sweet frankincense from Sheba.
  Keep your fragrant calamus imported from distant lands!
I will not accept your burnt offerings.
  Your sacrifices have no pleasing aroma for me."

Therefore, this is what the LORD says:
  "I will put obstacles in my people's path.

Fathers and sons will both fall over them.
   Neighbors and friends will die together."

This is what the LORD says:
"Look! A great army coming from the north!
   A great nation is rising against you from far-off lands.
They are armed with bows and spears.
   They are cruel and show no mercy.
They sound like a roaring sea
   as they ride forward on horses.
They are coming in battle formation,
   planning to destroy you, beautiful Jerusalem."

We have heard reports about the enemy,
   and we wring our hands in fright.
Pangs of anguish have gripped us,
   like those of a woman in labor.
Don't go out to the fields!
   Don't travel on the roads!
The enemy's sword is everywhere
   and terrorizes us at every turn!
Oh, my people, dress yourselves in burlap
   and sit among the ashes.
Mourn and weep bitterly, as for the loss of an only son.
   For suddenly the destroying armies will be upon you!

"Jeremiah, I have made you a tester of metals,
   that you may determine the quality of my people.
They are the worst kind of rebel,
   full of slander.
They are as hard as bronze and iron,
   and they lead others into corruption.
The bellows fiercely fan the flames
   to burn out the corruption.
But it does not purify them,
   for the wickedness remains.
I will label them 'Rejected Silver,'
   for I, the LORD, am discarding them."

The LORD gave another message to Jeremiah. He said, "Go to the entrance of the LORD's Temple, and give this message to the people: 'O Judah, listen to this message from the LORD! Listen to it, all of you who worship here! This is what the LORD of Heaven's Armies, the God of Israel, says:

"'Even now, if you quit your evil ways, I will let you stay in your own land. But don't be fooled by those who promise you safety simply because the LORD's Temple is here. They chant, "The LORD's Temple is here! The LORD's Temple is here!" But I will be merciful only if you stop your evil thoughts and deeds and start treating each other with justice; only if you stop exploiting foreigners, orphans, and widows; only if you stop your murdering; and only if you stop harming yourselves by worshiping idols. Then I will let you stay in this land that I gave to your ancestors to keep forever.

"'Don't be fooled into thinking that you will never suffer because the Temple is here. It's a lie! Do you really think you can steal, murder, commit adultery, lie, and burn incense to Baal and all those other new gods of yours, and then come here and stand before me in my Temple and chant, "We are safe!"—only to go right back to all those evils again? Don't you yourselves admit that this Temple, which bears my name, has become a den of thieves? Surely I see all the evil going on there. I, the LORD, have spoken!

"'Go now to the place at Shiloh where I once put the Tabernacle that bore my name. See what I did there because of all the wickedness of my people, the Israelites. While you were doing these wicked things, says the LORD, I spoke to you about it repeatedly, but you would not listen. I called out to you, but you refused to answer. So just as I destroyed Shiloh, I will now destroy this Temple that bears my name, this Temple that you trust in for help, this place that I gave to you and your ancestors. And I will send you out of my sight into exile, just as I did your relatives, the people of Israel.'

"Pray no more for these people, Jeremiah. Do not weep or pray for them, and don't beg me to help them, for I will not listen to you. Don't you see what they are doing throughout the towns of Judah and in the streets of Jerusalem? No wonder I am so angry! Watch how the children gather wood and the fathers build sacrificial fires. See how the women knead dough and make cakes to offer to the Queen of Heaven. And they pour out liquid offerings to their other idol gods! Am I the one they are hurting?" asks the LORD. "Most of all, they hurt themselves, to their own shame."

So this is what the Sovereign LORD says: "I will pour out my terrible fury on this place. Its people, animals, trees, and crops will be consumed by the unquenchable fire of my anger."

This is what the LORD of Heaven's Armies, the God of Israel, says: "Take your burnt offerings and your other sacrifices and eat them yourselves! When I led your ancestors out of Egypt, it was not burnt offerings and sacrifices I wanted from them. This is what I told them: 'Obey me, and I will be your God, and you will be my people. Do everything as I say, and all will be well!'

"But my people would not listen to me. They kept doing whatever they wanted, following the stubborn desires of their evil hearts. They went backward instead of forward. From the day your ancestors left Egypt until now, I have continued to send my servants, the prophets—day in and day out. But my people have not listened to me or even tried to hear. They have been stubborn and sinful—even worse than their ancestors.

"Tell them all this, but do not expect them to listen. Shout out your warnings, but do not expect them to respond. Say to them, 'This is the nation whose people will not obey the LORD their God and who refuse to be taught. Truth has vanished from among them; it is no longer heard on their lips. Shave your head in mourning, and weep alone on the mountains. For the LORD has rejected and forsaken this generation that has provoked his fury.'

"The people of Judah have sinned before my very eyes," says the LORD. "They have set up their abominable idols right in the Temple that bears my name, defiling it. They have built pagan shrines at Topheth, the garbage dump in the valley of Ben-Hinnom, and there they burn their sons and daughters in the fire. I have never commanded such a horrible deed; it never even crossed my mind to command such a thing! So beware, for the time is coming," says the LORD, "when that garbage dump will no longer be called Topheth or the valley of Ben-Hinnom, but the Valley of Slaughter. They will bury the bodies in Topheth until there is no more room for them. The bodies of my people will be food for the vultures and wild animals, and no one will be left to scare them away. I will put an end to the happy singing and laughter in the streets of Jerusalem. The joyful voices of bridegrooms and brides will no longer be heard in the towns of Judah. The land will lie in complete desolation.

"In that day," says the LORD, "the enemy will break open the graves of the kings and officials of Judah, and the graves of the priests, prophets, and common people of Jerusalem. They will spread out their bones on the ground before the sun, moon, and stars—the gods my people have loved, served, and worshiped. Their bones will not be gathered up again or buried but will be scattered on the ground like manure. And the people of this evil nation who survive will wish to die rather than live where I will send them. I, the LORD of Heaven's Armies, have spoken!

"Jeremiah, say to the people, 'This is what the LORD says:

"'When people fall down, don't they get up again?
When they discover they're on the wrong road, don't they turn back?

Then why do these people stay on their self-destructive path?
  Why do the people of Jerusalem refuse to turn back?
They cling tightly to their lies
  and will not turn around.
I listen to their conversations
  and don't hear a word of truth.
Is anyone sorry for doing wrong?
  Does anyone say, "What a terrible thing I have done"?
No! All are running down the path of sin
  as swiftly as a horse galloping into battle!
Even the stork that flies across the sky
  knows the time of her migration,
as do the turtledove, the swallow, and the crane.
  They all return at the proper time each year.
But not my people!
  They do not know the LORD's laws.

"'How can you say, "We are wise because we have the word of the
    LORD,"
  when your teachers have twisted it by writing lies?
These wise teachers will fall
  into the trap of their own foolishness,
for they have rejected the word of the LORD.
  Are they so wise after all?
I will give their wives to others
  and their farms to strangers.
From the least to the greatest,
  their lives are ruled by greed.
Yes, even my prophets and priests are like that.
  They are all frauds.
They offer superficial treatments
  for my people's mortal wound.
They give assurances of peace
  when there is no peace.
Are they ashamed of these disgusting actions?
  Not at all—they don't even know how to blush!
Therefore, they will lie among the slaughtered.
  They will be brought down when I punish them,
  says the LORD.
I will surely consume them.
  There will be no more harvests of figs and grapes.
Their fruit trees will all die.

Whatever I gave them will soon be gone.
I, the LORD, have spoken!'

"Then the people will say,
'Why should we wait here to die?
Come, let's go to the fortified towns and die there.
For the LORD our God has decreed our destruction
and has given us a cup of poison to drink
because we sinned against the LORD.
We hoped for peace, but no peace came.
We hoped for a time of healing, but found only terror.'

"The snorting of the enemies' warhorses can be heard
all the way from the land of Dan in the north!
The neighing of their stallions makes the whole land tremble.
They are coming to devour the land and everything in it—
cities and people alike.
I will send these enemy troops among you
like poisonous snakes you cannot charm.
They will bite you, and you will die.
I, the LORD, have spoken!"

My grief is beyond healing;
my heart is broken.
Listen to the weeping of my people;
it can be heard all across the land.
"Has the LORD abandoned Jerusalem?" the people ask.
"Is her King no longer there?"

"Oh, why have they provoked my anger with their carved idols
and their worthless foreign gods?" says the LORD.

"The harvest is finished,
and the summer is gone," the people cry,
"yet we are not saved!"

I hurt with the hurt of my people.
I mourn and am overcome with grief.
Is there no medicine in Gilead?
Is there no physician there?
Why is there no healing
for the wounds of my people?

If only my head were a pool of water
and my eyes a fountain of tears,

I would weep day and night
    for all my people who have been slaughtered.
Oh, that I could go away and forget my people
    and live in a travelers' shack in the desert.
For they are all adulterers—
    a pack of treacherous liars.

"My people bend their tongues like bows
    to shoot out lies.
They refuse to stand up for the truth.
    They only go from bad to worse.
They do not know me,"
    says the LORD.

"Beware of your neighbor!
    Don't even trust your brother!
For brother takes advantage of brother,
    and friend slanders friend.
They all fool and defraud each other;
    no one tells the truth.
With practiced tongues they tell lies;
    they wear themselves out with all their sinning.
They pile lie upon lie
    and utterly refuse to acknowledge me,"
    says the LORD.

Therefore, this is what the LORD of Heaven's Armies says:
"See, I will melt them down in a crucible
    and test them like metal.
What else can I do with my people?
    For their tongues shoot lies like poisoned arrows.
They speak friendly words to their neighbors
    while scheming in their heart to kill them.
Should I not punish them for this?" says the LORD.
    "Should I not avenge myself against such a nation?"

I will weep for the mountains
    and wail for the wilderness pastures.
For they are desolate and empty of life;
    the lowing of cattle is heard no more;
    the birds and wild animals have all fled.

"I will make Jerusalem into a heap of ruins," says the LORD.
    "It will be a place haunted by jackals.

The towns of Judah will be ghost towns,
    with no one living in them."

Who is wise enough to understand all this? Who has been instructed by the LORD and can explain it to others? Why has the land been so ruined that no one dares to travel through it?

The LORD replies, "This has happened because my people have abandoned my instructions; they have refused to obey what I said. Instead, they have stubbornly followed their own desires and worshiped the images of Baal, as their ancestors taught them. So now, this is what the LORD of Heaven's Armies, the God of Israel, says: Look! I will feed them with bitterness and give them poison to drink. I will scatter them around the world, in places they and their ancestors never heard of, and even there I will chase them with the sword until I have destroyed them completely."

This is what the LORD of Heaven's Armies says:
"Consider all this, and call for the mourners.
    Send for the women who mourn at funerals.
Quick! Begin your weeping!
    Let the tears flow from your eyes.
Hear the people of Jerusalem crying in despair,
    'We are ruined! We are completely humiliated!
We must leave our land,
    because our homes have been torn down.'"

Listen, you women, to the words of the LORD;
    open your ears to what he has to say.
Teach your daughters to wail;
    teach one another how to lament.
For death has crept in through our windows
    and has entered our mansions.
It has killed off the flower of our youth:
    Children no longer play in the streets,
    and young men no longer gather in the squares.

This is what the LORD says:
"Bodies will be scattered across the fields like clumps of manure,
    like bundles of grain after the harvest.
    No one will be left to bury them."

This is what the LORD says:
"Don't let the wise boast in their wisdom,
    or the powerful boast in their power,
    or the rich boast in their riches.

But those who wish to boast
   should boast in this alone:
that they truly know me and understand that I am
    the LORD
  who demonstrates unfailing love
  and who brings justice and righteousness to the earth,
and that I delight in these things.
   I, the LORD, have spoken!

"A time is coming," says the LORD, "when I will punish all those who are circumcised in body but not in spirit—the Egyptians, Edomites, Ammonites, Moabites, the people who live in the desert in remote places, and yes, even the people of Judah. And like all these pagan nations, the people of Israel also have uncircumcised hearts."

Hear the word that the LORD speaks to you, O Israel! This is what the LORD says:

"Do not act like the other nations,
  who try to read their future in the stars.
Do not be afraid of their predictions,
  even though other nations are terrified by them.
Their ways are futile and foolish.
  They cut down a tree, and a craftsman carves an idol.
They decorate it with gold and silver
  and then fasten it securely with hammer and nails
  so it won't fall over.
Their gods are like
  helpless scarecrows in a cucumber field!
They cannot speak,
  and they need to be carried because they cannot walk.
Do not be afraid of such gods,
  for they can neither harm you nor do you any good."

LORD, there is no one like you!
  For you are great, and your name is full of power.
Who would not fear you, O King of nations?
  That title belongs to you alone!
Among all the wise people of the earth
  and in all the kingdoms of the world,
  there is no one like you.

People who worship idols are stupid and foolish.
  The things they worship are made of wood!

They bring beaten sheets of silver from Tarshish
    and gold from Uphaz,
and they give these materials to skillful craftsmen
    who make their idols.
Then they dress these gods in royal blue and purple robes
    made by expert tailors.
But the LORD is the only true God.
    He is the living God and the everlasting King!
The whole earth trembles at his anger.
    The nations cannot stand up to his wrath.

Say this to those who worship other gods: "Your so-called gods, who did not make the heavens and earth, will vanish from the earth and from under the heavens."

But the LORD made the earth by his power,
    and he preserves it by his wisdom.
With his own understanding
    he stretched out the heavens.
When he speaks in the thunder,
    the heavens roar with rain.
He causes the clouds to rise over the earth.
    He sends the lightning with the rain
    and releases the wind from his storehouses.
The whole human race is foolish and has no knowledge!
    The craftsmen are disgraced by the idols they make,
for their carefully shaped works are a fraud.
    These idols have no breath or power.
Idols are worthless; they are ridiculous lies!
    On the day of reckoning they will all be
        destroyed.
But the God of Israel is no idol!
    He is the Creator of everything that exists,
including Israel, his own special possession.
    The LORD of Heaven's Armies is his name!

Pack your bags and prepare to leave;
    the siege is about to begin.
For this is what the LORD says:
"Suddenly, I will fling out
    all you who live in this land.
I will pour great troubles upon you,
    and at last you will feel my anger."

My wound is severe,
> and my grief is great.
My sickness is incurable,
> but I must bear it.
My home is gone,
> and no one is left to help me rebuild it.
My children have been taken away,
> and I will never see them again.
The shepherds of my people have lost their senses.
> They no longer seek wisdom from the LORD.
Therefore, they fail completely,
> and their flocks are scattered.
Listen! Hear the terrifying roar of great armies
> as they roll down from the north.
The towns of Judah will be destroyed
> and become a haunt for jackals.

I know, LORD, that our lives are not our own.
> We are not able to plan our own course.
So correct me, LORD, but please be gentle.
> Do not correct me in anger, for I would die.
Pour out your wrath on the nations that refuse to acknowledge you—
> on the peoples that do not call upon your name.
For they have devoured your people Israel;
> they have devoured and consumed them,
> making the land a desolate wilderness.

+

The LORD gave another message to Jeremiah. He said, "Remind the people of Judah and Jerusalem about the terms of my covenant with them. Say to them, 'This is what the LORD, the God of Israel, says: Cursed is anyone who does not obey the terms of my covenant! For I said to your ancestors when I brought them out of the iron-smelting furnace of Egypt, "If you obey me and do whatever I command you, then you will be my people, and I will be your God." I said this so I could keep my promise to your ancestors to give you a land flowing with milk and honey—the land you live in today.'"

Then I replied, "Amen, LORD! May it be so."

Then the LORD said, "Broadcast this message in the streets of Jerusalem. Go from town to town throughout the land and say, 'Remember the ancient covenant, and do everything it requires. For I solemnly warned your ancestors when I brought them out of Egypt, "Obey me!" I have repeated this warning over and over to this day, but your ancestors did not listen or even pay attention. Instead, they stubbornly followed their own evil desires. And because they refused to obey, I brought upon them all the curses described in this covenant.'"

Again the LORD spoke to me and said, "I have discovered a conspiracy against me among the people of Judah and Jerusalem. They have returned to the sins of their ancestors. They have refused to listen to me and are worshiping other gods. Israel and Judah have both broken the covenant I made with their ancestors. Therefore, this is what the LORD says: I am going to bring calamity upon them, and they will not escape. Though they beg for mercy, I will not listen to their cries. Then the people of Judah and Jerusalem will pray to their idols and burn incense before them. But the idols will not save them when disaster strikes! Look now, people of Judah; you have as many gods as you have towns. You have as many altars of shame—altars for burning incense to your god Baal—as there are streets in Jerusalem.

"Pray no more for these people, Jeremiah. Do not weep or pray for them, for I will not listen to them when they cry out to me in distress.

> "What right do my beloved people have to come to my Temple,
>   when they have done so many immoral things?
> Can their vows and sacrifices prevent their destruction?
>   They actually rejoice in doing evil!
> I, the LORD, once called them a thriving olive tree,
>   beautiful to see and full of good fruit.
> But now I have sent the fury of their enemies
>   to burn them with fire,
>   leaving them charred and broken.

"I, the LORD of Heaven's Armies, who planted this olive tree, have ordered it destroyed. For the people of Israel and Judah have done evil, arousing my anger by burning incense to Baal."

Then the LORD told me about the plots my enemies were making against me. I was like a lamb being led to the slaughter. I had no idea that they were planning to kill me! "Let's destroy this man and all his words," they said. "Let's cut him down, so his name will be forgotten forever."

> O LORD of Heaven's Armies,
> you make righteous judgments,
>   and you examine the deepest thoughts and secrets.
> Let me see your vengeance against them,
>   for I have committed my cause to you.

This is what the LORD says about the men of Anathoth who wanted me dead. They had said, "We will kill you if you do not stop prophesying in the LORD's name." So this is what the LORD of Heaven's Armies says about them: "I will punish them! Their young men will die in battle, and their boys and girls will starve to death. Not one of these plotters from Anathoth will survive, for I will bring disaster upon them when their time of punishment comes."

LORD, you always give me justice
    when I bring a case before you.
So let me bring you this complaint:
Why are the wicked so prosperous?
    Why are evil people so happy?
You have planted them,
    and they have taken root and prospered.
Your name is on their lips,
    but you are far from their hearts.
But as for me, LORD, you know my heart.
    You see me and test my thoughts.
Drag these people away like sheep to be butchered!
    Set them aside to be slaughtered!

How long must this land mourn?
    Even the grass in the fields has withered.
The wild animals and birds have disappeared
    because of the evil in the land.
For the people have said,
    "The LORD doesn't see what's ahead for us!"

"If racing against mere men makes you tired,
    how will you race against horses?
If you stumble and fall on open ground,
    what will you do in the thickets near the Jordan?
Even your brothers, members of your own family,
    have turned against you.
    They plot and raise complaints against you.
Do not trust them,
    no matter how pleasantly they speak.

"I have abandoned my people, my special possession.
    I have surrendered my dearest ones to their enemies.
My chosen people have roared at me like a lion of the forest,
    so I have treated them with contempt.

My chosen people act like speckled vultures,
　but they themselves are surrounded by vultures.
　Bring on the wild animals to pick their corpses clean!

"Many rulers have ravaged my vineyard,
　trampling down the vines
　and turning all its beauty into a barren
　　wilderness.
They have made it an empty wasteland;
　I hear its mournful cry.
The whole land is desolate,
　and no one even cares.
On all the bare hilltops,
　destroying armies can be seen.
The sword of the LORD devours people
　from one end of the nation to the other.
　No one will escape!
My people have planted wheat
　but are harvesting thorns.
They have worn themselves out,
　but it has done them no good.
They will harvest a crop of shame
　because of the fierce anger of the LORD."

Now this is what the LORD says: "I will uproot from their land all the evil nations reaching out for the possession I gave my people Israel. And I will uproot Judah from among them. But afterward I will return and have compassion on all of them. I will bring them home to their own lands again, each nation to its own possession. And if these nations truly learn the ways of my people, and if they learn to swear by my name, saying, 'As surely as the LORD lives' (just as they taught my people to swear by the name of Baal), then they will be given a place among my people. But any nation who refuses to obey me will be uprooted and destroyed. I, the LORD, have spoken!"

✝

This is what the LORD said to me: "Go and buy a linen loincloth and put it on, but do not wash it." So I bought the loincloth as the LORD directed me, and I put it on.

Then the LORD gave me another message: "Take the linen loincloth you are wearing, and go to the Euphrates River. Hide it there in a hole in the rocks." So I went and hid it by the Euphrates as the LORD had instructed me.

A long time afterward the LORD said to me, "Go back to the Euphrates and get the loincloth I told you to hide there." So I went to the Euphrates and dug it out of the hole where I had hidden it. But now it was rotting and falling apart. The loincloth was good for nothing.

Then I received this message from the LORD: "This is what the LORD says: This shows how I will rot away the pride of Judah and Jerusalem. These wicked people refuse to listen to me. They stubbornly follow their own desires and worship other gods. Therefore, they will become like this loincloth—good for nothing! As a loincloth clings to a man's waist, so I created Judah and Israel to cling to me, says the LORD. They were to be my people, my pride, my glory—an honor to my name. But they would not listen to me.

"So tell them, 'This is what the LORD, the God of Israel, says: May all your jars be filled with wine.' And they will reply, 'Of course! Jars are made to be filled with wine!'

"Then tell them, 'No, this is what the LORD means: I will fill everyone in this land with drunkenness—from the king sitting on David's throne to the priests and the prophets, right down to the common people of Jerusalem. I will smash them against each other, even parents against children, says the LORD. I will not let my pity or mercy or compassion keep me from destroying them.'"

Listen and pay attention!
　　Do not be arrogant, for the LORD has spoken.
Give glory to the LORD your God
　　before it is too late.
Acknowledge him before he brings darkness upon you,
　　causing you to stumble and fall on the darkening mountains.
For then, when you look for light,
　　you will find only terrible darkness and gloom.
And if you still refuse to listen,
　　I will weep alone because of your pride.
My eyes will overflow with tears,
　　because the LORD's flock will be led away into exile.

Say to the king and his mother,
"Come down from your thrones
　　and sit in the dust,
for your glorious crowns
　　will soon be snatched from your heads."
The towns of the Negev will close their gates,
　　and no one will be able to open them.

The people of Judah will be taken away as captives.
　　All will be carried into exile.

Open up your eyes and see
　　the armies marching down from the north!
Where is your flock—
　　your beautiful flock—
　　that he gave you to care for?
What will you say when the LORD takes the allies you have cultivated
　　and appoints them as your rulers?
Pangs of anguish will grip you,
　　like those of a woman in labor!
You may ask yourself,
　　"Why is all this happening to me?"
　　It is because of your many sins!
That is why you have been stripped
　　and raped by invading armies.
Can an Ethiopian change the color of his skin?
　　Can a leopard take away its spots?
Neither can you start doing good,
　　for you have always done evil.

"I will scatter you like chaff
　　that is blown away by the desert winds.
This is your allotment,
　　the portion I have assigned to you,"
　　says the LORD,
"for you have forgotten me,
　　putting your trust in false gods.
I myself will strip you
　　and expose you to shame.
I have seen your adultery and lust,
　　and your disgusting idol worship out in the fields and on the hills.
What sorrow awaits you, Jerusalem!
　　How long before you are pure?"

+

This message came to Jeremiah from the LORD, explaining why he was holding back the rain:

"Judah wilts;
　　commerce at the city gates grinds to a halt.

All the people sit on the ground in mourning,
    and a great cry rises from Jerusalem.
The nobles send servants to get water,
    but all the wells are dry.
The servants return with empty pitchers,
    confused and desperate,
    covering their heads in grief.
The ground is parched
    and cracked for lack of rain.
The farmers are deeply troubled;
    they, too, cover their heads.
Even the doe abandons her newborn fawn
    because there is no grass in the field.
The wild donkeys stand on the bare hills
    panting like thirsty jackals.
They strain their eyes looking for grass,
    but there is none to be found."

The people say, "Our wickedness has caught up with us, LORD,
    but help us for the sake of your own reputation.
We have turned away from you
    and sinned against you again and again.
O Hope of Israel, our Savior in times of trouble,
    why are you like a stranger to us?
Why are you like a traveler passing through the land,
    stopping only for the night?
Are you also confused?
    Is our champion helpless to save us?
You are right here among us, LORD.
    We are known as your people.
    Please don't abandon us now!"

So this is what the LORD says to his people:
"You love to wander far from me
    and do not restrain yourselves.
Therefore, I will no longer accept you as my people.
    Now I will remember all your wickedness
    and will punish you for your sins."

Then the LORD said to me, "Do not pray for these people anymore. When they fast, I will pay no attention. When they present their burnt offerings and grain offerings to me, I will not accept them. Instead, I will devour them with war, famine, and disease."

Then I said, "O Sovereign LORD, their prophets are telling them, 'All is well—no war or famine will come. The LORD will surely send you peace.'"

Then the LORD said, "These prophets are telling lies in my name. I did not send them or tell them to speak. I did not give them any messages. They prophesy of visions and revelations they have never seen or heard. They speak foolishness made up in their own lying hearts. Therefore, this is what the LORD says: I will punish these lying prophets, for they have spoken in my name even though I never sent them. They say that no war or famine will come, but they themselves will die by war and famine! As for the people to whom they prophesy—their bodies will be thrown out into the streets of Jerusalem, victims of famine and war. There will be no one left to bury them. Husbands, wives, sons, and daughters—all will be gone. For I will pour out their own wickedness on them. Now, Jeremiah, say this to them:

"Night and day my eyes overflow with tears.
    I cannot stop weeping,
for my virgin daughter—my precious people—
    has been struck down
    and lies mortally wounded.
If I go out into the fields,
    I see the bodies of people slaughtered by the enemy.
If I walk the city streets,
    I see people who have died of starvation.
The prophets and priests continue with their work,
    but they don't know what they're doing."

LORD, have you completely rejected Judah?
    Do you really hate Jerusalem?
Why have you wounded us past all hope of healing?
    We hoped for peace, but no peace came.
    We hoped for a time of healing, but found only terror.
LORD, we confess our wickedness
    and that of our ancestors, too.
    We all have sinned against you.
For the sake of your reputation, LORD, do not
        abandon us.
    Do not disgrace your own glorious throne.
Please remember us,
    and do not break your covenant with us.

Can any of the worthless foreign gods send us rain?
    Does it fall from the sky by itself?

No, you are the one, O Lord our God!
Only you can do such things.
So we will wait for you to help us.

Then the Lord said to me, "Even if Moses and Samuel stood before me pleading for these people, I wouldn't help them. Away with them! Get them out of my sight! And if they say to you, 'But where can we go?' tell them, 'This is what the Lord says:

"'Those who are destined for death, to death;
   those who are destined for war, to war;
those who are destined for famine, to famine;
   those who are destined for captivity, to captivity.'

"I will send four kinds of destroyers against them," says the Lord. "I will send the sword to kill, the dogs to drag away, the vultures to devour, and the wild animals to finish up what is left. Because of the wicked things Manasseh son of Hezekiah, king of Judah, did in Jerusalem, I will make my people an object of horror to all the kingdoms of the earth.

"Who will feel sorry for you, Jerusalem?
   Who will weep for you?
   Who will even bother to ask how you are?
You have abandoned me
   and turned your back on me,"
   says the Lord.
"Therefore, I will raise my fist to destroy you.
   I am tired of always giving you another chance.
I will winnow you like grain at the gates of your cities
   and take away the children you hold dear.
I will destroy my own people,
   because they refuse to change their evil ways.
There will be more widows
   than the grains of sand on the seashore.
At noontime I will bring a destroyer
   against the mothers of young men.
I will cause anguish and terror
   to come upon them suddenly.
The mother of seven grows faint and gasps
      for breath;
   her sun has gone down while it is still day.
She sits childless now,
   disgraced and humiliated.
And I will hand over those who are left

> to be killed by the enemy.
> I, the LORD, have spoken!"

Then I said,

> "What sorrow is mine, my mother.
>   Oh, that I had died at birth!
>   I am hated everywhere I go.
> I am neither a lender who threatens to foreclose
>   nor a borrower who refuses to pay—
>   yet they all curse me."

The LORD replied,

> "I will take care of you, Jeremiah.
>   Your enemies will ask you to plead on their behalf
>   in times of trouble and distress.
> Can a man break a bar of iron from the north,
>   or a bar of bronze?
> At no cost to them,
>   I will hand over your wealth and treasures
> as plunder to your enemies,
>   for sin runs rampant in your land.
> I will tell your enemies to take you
>   as captives to a foreign land.
> For my anger blazes like a fire
>   that will burn forever."

Then I said,

> "LORD, you know what's happening to me.
>   Please step in and help me. Punish my persecutors!
> Please give me time; don't let me die young.
>   It's for your sake that I am suffering.
> When I discovered your words, I devoured them.
>   They are my joy and my heart's delight,
> for I bear your name,
>   O LORD God of Heaven's Armies.
> I never joined the people in their merry feasts.
>   I sat alone because your hand was on me.
>   I was filled with indignation at their sins.
> Why then does my suffering continue?
>   Why is my wound so incurable?
> Your help seems as uncertain as a seasonal brook,
>   like a spring that has gone dry."

This is how the LORD responds:

> "If you return to me, I will restore you
>   so you can continue to serve me.
> If you speak good words rather than worthless ones,
>   you will be my spokesman.
> You must influence them;
>   do not let them influence you!
> They will fight against you like an attacking army,
>   but I will make you as secure as a fortified wall of bronze.
> They will not conquer you,
>   for I am with you to protect and rescue you.
>   I, the LORD, have spoken!
> Yes, I will certainly keep you safe from these wicked men.
>   I will rescue you from their cruel hands."

+

The LORD gave me another message. He said, "Do not get married or have children in this place. For this is what the LORD says about the children born here in this city and about their mothers and fathers: They will die from terrible diseases. No one will mourn for them or bury them, and they will lie scattered on the ground like manure. They will die from war and famine, and their bodies will be food for the vultures and wild animals."

This is what the LORD says: "Do not go to funerals to mourn and show sympathy for these people, for I have removed my protection and peace from them. I have taken away my unfailing love and my mercy. Both the great and the lowly will die in this land. No one will bury them or mourn for them. Their friends will not cut themselves in sorrow or shave their heads in sadness. No one will offer a meal to comfort those who mourn for the dead—not even at the death of a mother or father. No one will send a cup of wine to console them.

"And do not go to their feasts and parties. Do not eat and drink with them at all. For this is what the LORD of Heaven's Armies, the God of Israel, says: In your own lifetime, before your very eyes, I will put an end to the happy singing and laughter in this land. The joyful voices of bridegrooms and brides will no longer be heard.

"When you tell the people all these things, they will ask, 'Why has the LORD decreed such terrible things against us? What have we done to deserve such treatment? What is our sin against the LORD our God?'

"Then you will give them the LORD's reply: 'It is because your ancestors were unfaithful to me. They worshiped other gods and served them. They abandoned me and did not obey my word. And you are even worse than your ancestors! You stubbornly follow your own evil desires and refuse to listen to me. So I will throw you out of this land and send you into a foreign land where you and your ancestors have never been. There you can worship idols day and night—and I will grant you no favors!'

"But the time is coming," says the LORD, "when people who are taking an oath will no longer say, 'As surely as the LORD lives, who rescued the people of Israel from the land of Egypt.' Instead, they will say, 'As surely as the LORD lives, who brought the people of Israel back to their own land from the land of the north and from all the countries to which he had exiled them.' For I will bring them back to this land that I gave their ancestors.

"But now I am sending for many fishermen who will catch them," says the LORD. "I am sending for hunters who will hunt them down in the mountains, hills, and caves. I am watching them closely, and I see every sin. They cannot hope to hide from me. I will double their punishment for all their sins, because they have defiled my land with lifeless images of their detestable gods and have filled my territory with their evil deeds."

> LORD, you are my strength and fortress,
>   my refuge in the day of trouble!
> Nations from around the world
>   will come to you and say,
> "Our ancestors left us a foolish heritage,
>   for they worshiped worthless idols.
> Can people make their own gods?
>   These are not real gods at all!"

> The LORD says,
> "Now I will show them my power;
>   now I will show them my might.
> At last they will know and understand
>   that I am the LORD.

> "The sin of Judah
>   is inscribed with an iron chisel—
> engraved with a diamond point on their stony hearts
>   and on the corners of their altars.
> Even their children go to worship
>   at their pagan altars and Asherah poles,
> beneath every green tree
>   and on every high hill.
> So I will hand over my holy mountain—

along with all your wealth and treasures
  and your pagan shrines—
as plunder to your enemies,
  for sin runs rampant in your land.
The wonderful possession I have reserved for you
  will slip from your hands.
I will tell your enemies to take you
  as captives to a foreign land.
For my anger blazes like a fire
  that will burn forever."

This is what the LORD says:
"Cursed are those who put their trust in mere humans,
  who rely on human strength
  and turn their hearts away from the LORD.
They are like stunted shrubs in the desert,
  with no hope for the future.
They will live in the barren wilderness,
  in an uninhabited salty land.

"But blessed are those who trust in the LORD
  and have made the LORD their hope and confidence.
They are like trees planted along a riverbank,
  with roots that reach deep into the water.
Such trees are not bothered by the heat
  or worried by long months of drought.
Their leaves stay green,
  and they never stop producing fruit.

"The human heart is the most deceitful of all things,
  and desperately wicked.
  Who really knows how bad it is?
But I, the LORD, search all hearts
  and examine secret motives.
I give all people their due rewards,
  according to what their actions deserve."

Like a partridge that hatches eggs she has not laid,
  so are those who get their wealth by unjust means.
At midlife they will lose their riches;
  in the end, they will become poor old fools.
But we worship at your throne—
  eternal, high, and glorious!
O LORD, the hope of Israel,

all who turn away from you will be disgraced.
They will be buried in the dust of the earth,
  for they have abandoned the LORD, the fountain of living water.

O LORD, if you heal me, I will be truly healed;
  if you save me, I will be truly saved.
  My praises are for you alone!
People scoff at me and say,
"What is this 'message from the LORD' you talk about?
  Why don't your predictions come true?"

LORD, I have not abandoned my job
  as a shepherd for your people.
I have not urged you to send disaster.
  You have heard everything I've said.
LORD, don't terrorize me!
  You alone are my hope in the day of disaster.
Bring shame and dismay on all who persecute me,
  but don't let me experience shame and dismay.
Bring a day of terror on them.
  Yes, bring double destruction upon them!

+

This is what the LORD said to me: "Go and stand in the gates of Jerusalem, first in the gate where the king goes in and out, and then in each of the other gates. Say to all the people, 'Listen to this message from the LORD, you kings of Judah and all you people of Judah and everyone living in Jerusalem. This is what the LORD says: Listen to my warning! Stop carrying on your trade at Jerusalem's gates on the Sabbath day. Do not do your work on the Sabbath, but make it a holy day. I gave this command to your ancestors, but they did not listen or obey. They stubbornly refused to pay attention or accept my discipline.

"'But if you obey me, says the LORD, and do not carry on your trade at the gates or work on the Sabbath day, and if you keep it holy, then kings and their officials will go in and out of these gates forever. There will always be a descendant of David sitting on the throne here in Jerusalem. Kings and their officials will always ride in and out among the people of Judah in chariots and on horses, and this city will remain forever. And from all around Jerusalem, from the towns of Judah and Benjamin, from the western foothills and the hill country and the Negev, the people will come with their burnt offerings and sacrifices. They will bring their grain offerings, frankincense, and thanksgiving offerings to the LORD's Temple.

"'But if you do not listen to me and refuse to keep the Sabbath holy, and if on the Sabbath day you bring loads of merchandise through the gates of Jerusalem just as on other days, then I will set fire to these gates. The fire will spread to the palaces, and no one will be able to put out the roaring flames.'"

+

The LORD gave another message to Jeremiah. He said, "Go down to the potter's shop, and I will speak to you there." So I did as he told me and found the potter working at his wheel. But the jar he was making did not turn out as he had hoped, so he crushed it into a lump of clay again and started over.

Then the LORD gave me this message: "O Israel, can I not do to you as this potter has done to his clay? As the clay is in the potter's hand, so are you in my hand. If I announce that a certain nation or kingdom is to be uprooted, torn down, and destroyed, but then that nation renounces its evil ways, I will not destroy it as I had planned. And if I announce that I will plant and build up a certain nation or kingdom, but then that nation turns to evil and refuses to obey me, I will not bless it as I said I would.

"Therefore, Jeremiah, go and warn all Judah and Jerusalem. Say to them, 'This is what the LORD says: I am planning disaster for you instead of good. So turn from your evil ways, each of you, and do what is right.'"

But the people replied, "Don't waste your breath. We will continue to live as we want to, stubbornly following our own evil desires."

So this is what the LORD says:

"Has anyone ever heard of such a thing,
    even among the pagan nations?
My virgin daughter Israel
    has done something terrible!
Does the snow ever disappear from the mountaintops of Lebanon?
    Do the cold streams flowing from those distant mountains ever
        run dry?
But my people are not so reliable, for they have deserted me;
    they burn incense to worthless idols.
They have stumbled off the ancient highways
    and walk in muddy paths.
Therefore, their land will become desolate,
    a monument to their stupidity.
All who pass by will be astonished
    and will shake their heads in amazement.
I will scatter my people before their enemies

as the east wind scatters dust.
And in all their trouble I will turn my back on them
and refuse to notice their distress."

Then the people said, "Come on, let's plot a way to stop Jeremiah. We have plenty of priests and wise men and prophets. We don't need him to teach the word and give us advice and prophecies. Let's spread rumors about him and ignore what he says."

LORD, hear me and help me!
Listen to what my enemies are saying.
Should they repay evil for good?
They have dug a pit to kill me,
though I pleaded for them
and tried to protect them from your anger.
So let their children starve!
Let them die by the sword!
Let their wives become childless widows.
Let their old men die in a plague,
and let their young men be killed in battle!
Let screaming be heard from their homes
as warriors come suddenly upon them.
For they have dug a pit for me
and have hidden traps along my path.
LORD, you know all about their murderous plots
against me.
Don't forgive their crimes and blot out their sins.
Let them die before you.
Deal with them in your anger.

This is what the LORD said to me: "Go and buy a clay jar. Then ask some of the leaders of the people and of the priests to follow you. Go out through the Gate of Broken Pots to the garbage dump in the valley of Ben-Hinnom, and give them this message. Say to them, 'Listen to this message from the LORD, you kings of Judah and citizens of Jerusalem! This is what the LORD of Heaven's Armies, the God of Israel, says: I will bring a terrible disaster on this place, and the ears of those who hear about it will ring!

"'For Israel has forsaken me and turned this valley into a place of wickedness. The people burn incense to foreign gods—idols never before acknowledged by this generation, by their ancestors, or by the kings of Judah. And they have filled this place with the blood of innocent children. They have built pagan shrines to Baal, and there they burn their sons as sacrifices to Baal. I have never commanded such a horrible deed;

it never even crossed my mind to command such a thing! So beware, for the time is coming, says the LORD, when this garbage dump will no longer be called Topheth or the valley of Ben-Hinnom, but the Valley of Slaughter.

"'For I will upset the careful plans of Judah and Jerusalem. I will allow the people to be slaughtered by invading armies, and I will leave their dead bodies as food for the vultures and wild animals. I will reduce Jerusalem to ruins, making it a monument to their stupidity. All who pass by will be astonished and will gasp at the destruction they see there. I will see to it that your enemies lay siege to the city until all the food is gone. Then those trapped inside will eat their own sons and daughters and friends. They will be driven to utter despair.'

"As these men watch you, Jeremiah, smash the jar you brought. Then say to them, 'This is what the LORD of Heaven's Armies says: As this jar lies shattered, so I will shatter the people of Judah and Jerusalem beyond all hope of repair. They will bury the bodies here in Topheth, the garbage dump, until there is no more room for them. This is what I will do to this place and its people, says the LORD. I will cause this city to become defiled like Topheth. Yes, all the houses in Jerusalem, including the palace of Judah's kings, will become like Topheth—all the houses where you burned incense on the rooftops to your star gods, and where liquid offerings were poured out to your idols.'"

Then Jeremiah returned from Topheth, the garbage dump where he had delivered this message, and he stopped in front of the Temple of the LORD. He said to the people there, "This is what the LORD of Heaven's Armies, the God of Israel, says: 'I will bring disaster upon this city and its surrounding towns as I promised, because you have stubbornly refused to listen to me.'"

Now Pashhur son of Immer, the priest in charge of the Temple of the LORD, heard what Jeremiah was prophesying. So he arrested Jeremiah the prophet and had him whipped and put in stocks at the Benjamin Gate of the LORD's Temple.

The next day, when Pashhur finally released him, Jeremiah said, "Pashhur, the LORD has changed your name. From now on you are to be called 'The Man Who Lives in Terror.' For this is what the LORD says: 'I will send terror upon you and all your friends, and you will watch as they are slaughtered by the swords of the enemy. I will hand the people of Judah over to the king of Babylon. He will take them captive to Babylon or run them through with the sword. And I will let your enemies plunder Jerusalem. All the famed treasures of the city—the precious jewels and gold and silver of your kings—will be carried off to Babylon. As for you, Pashhur, you and all your household will go as captives to Babylon. There you will die and be buried, you and all your friends to whom you prophesied that everything would be all right.'"

> O Lord, you misled me,
>   and I allowed myself to be misled.
> You are stronger than I am,
>   and you overpowered me.
> Now I am mocked every day;
>   everyone laughs at me.
> When I speak, the words burst out.
>   "Violence and destruction!" I shout.
> So these messages from the Lord
>   have made me a household joke.
> But if I say I'll never mention the Lord
>   or speak in his name,
> his word burns in my heart like a fire.
>   It's like a fire in my bones!
> I am worn out trying to hold it in!
>   I can't do it!
> I have heard the many rumors about me.
>   They call me "The Man Who Lives in Terror."
> They threaten, "If you say anything, we will report it."
>   Even my old friends are watching me,
>   waiting for a fatal slip.
> "He will trap himself," they say,
>   "and then we will get our revenge on him."
>
> But the Lord stands beside me like a great warrior.
>   Before him my persecutors will stumble.
>   They cannot defeat me.
> They will fail and be thoroughly humiliated.
>   Their dishonor will never be forgotten.
> O Lord of Heaven's Armies,
> you test those who are righteous,
>   and you examine the deepest thoughts and secrets.
> Let me see your vengeance against them,
>   for I have committed my cause to you.
> Sing to the Lord!
>   Praise the Lord!
> For though I was poor and needy,
>   he rescued me from my oppressors.

Yet I curse the day I was born!
  May no one celebrate the day of my birth.
I curse the messenger who told my father,
  "Good news—you have a son!"
Let him be destroyed like the cities of old
  that the LORD overthrew without mercy.
Terrify him all day long with battle shouts,
  because he did not kill me at birth.
Oh, that I had died in my mother's womb,
  that her body had been my grave!
Why was I ever born?
  My entire life has been filled
  with trouble, sorrow, and shame.

+

The LORD spoke through Jeremiah when King Zedekiah sent Pashhur son of Malkijah and Zephaniah son of Maaseiah, the priest, to speak with him. They begged Jeremiah, "Please speak to the LORD for us and ask him to help us. King Nebuchadnezzar of Babylon is attacking Judah. Perhaps the LORD will be gracious and do a mighty miracle as he has done in the past. Perhaps he will force Nebuchadnezzar to withdraw his armies."

Jeremiah replied, "Go back to King Zedekiah and tell him, 'This is what the LORD, the God of Israel, says: I will make your weapons useless against the king of Babylon and the Babylonians who are outside your walls attacking you. In fact, I will bring your enemies right into the heart of this city. I myself will fight against you with a strong hand and a powerful arm, for I am very angry. You have made me furious! I will send a terrible plague upon this city, and both people and animals will die. And after all that, says the LORD, I will hand over King Zedekiah, his staff, and everyone else in the city who survives the disease, war, and famine. I will hand them over to King Nebuchadnezzar of Babylon and to their other enemies. He will slaughter them and show them no mercy, pity, or compassion.'

"Tell all the people, 'This is what the LORD says: Take your choice of life or death! Everyone who stays in Jerusalem will die from war, famine, or disease, but those who go out and surrender to the Babylonians will live. Their reward will be life! For I have decided to bring disaster and not good upon this city, says the LORD. It will be handed over to the king of Babylon, and he will reduce it to ashes.'

"Say to the royal family of Judah, 'Listen to this message from the LORD! This is what the LORD says to the dynasty of David:

"'Give justice each morning to the people you judge!
    Help those who have been robbed;
    rescue them from their oppressors.
Otherwise, my anger will burn like an unquenchable fire
    because of all your sins.
I will personally fight against the people in Jerusalem,
    that mighty fortress—
the people who boast, "No one can touch us here.
    No one can break in here."
And I myself will punish you for your sinfulness,
    says the LORD.
I will light a fire in your forests
    that will burn up everything around you.'"

This is what the LORD said to me: "Go over and speak directly to the king of Judah. Say to him, 'Listen to this message from the LORD, you king of Judah, sitting on David's throne. Let your attendants and your people listen, too. This is what the LORD says: Be fair-minded and just. Do what is right! Help those who have been robbed; rescue them from their oppressors. Quit your evil deeds! Do not mistreat foreigners, orphans, and widows. Stop murdering the innocent! If you obey me, there will always be a descendant of David sitting on the throne here in Jerusalem. The king will ride through the palace gates in chariots and on horses, with his parade of attendants and subjects. But if you refuse to pay attention to this warning, I swear by my own name, says the LORD, that this palace will become a pile of rubble.'"

Now this is what the LORD says concerning Judah's royal palace:

"I love you as much as fruitful Gilead
    and the green forests of Lebanon.
But I will turn you into a desert,
    with no one living within your walls.
I will call for wreckers,
    who will bring out their tools to dismantle you.
They will tear out all your fine cedar beams
    and throw them on the fire.

"People from many nations will pass by the ruins of this city and say to one another, 'Why did the LORD destroy such a great city?' And the answer will be, 'Because they violated their covenant with the LORD their God by worshiping other gods.'"

Do not weep for the dead king or mourn his loss.
  Instead, weep for the captive king being led away!
  For he will never return to see his native land again.

For this is what the LORD says about Jehoahaz, who succeeded his father, King Josiah, and was taken away as a captive: "He will never return. He will die in a distant land and will never again see his own country."

And the LORD says, "What sorrow awaits Jehoiakim,
  who builds his palace with forced labor.
He builds injustice into its walls,
  for he makes his neighbors work for nothing.
  He does not pay them for their labor.
He says, 'I will build a magnificent palace
  with huge rooms and many windows.
I will panel it throughout with fragrant cedar
  and paint it a lovely red.'
But a beautiful cedar palace does not make a great king!
  Your father, Josiah, also had plenty to eat and drink.
But he was just and right in all his dealings.
  That is why God blessed him.
He gave justice and help to the poor and needy,
  and everything went well for him.
Isn't that what it means to know me?"
  says the LORD.
"But you! You have eyes only for greed and dishonesty!
  You murder the innocent,
  oppress the poor, and reign ruthlessly."

Therefore, this is what the LORD says about Jehoiakim, son of King Josiah:

"The people will not mourn for him, crying to one another,
  'Alas, my brother! Alas, my sister!'
His subjects will not mourn for him, crying,
  'Alas, our master is dead! Alas, his splendor is gone!'
He will be buried like a dead donkey—
  dragged out of Jerusalem and dumped outside the gates!
Weep for your allies in Lebanon.
  Shout for them in Bashan.
Search for them in the regions east of the river.
  See, they are all destroyed.
  Not one is left to help you.
I warned you when you were prosperous,
  but you replied, 'Don't bother me.'

You have been that way since childhood—
　you simply will not obey me!
And now the wind will blow away your allies.
　All your friends will be taken away as captives.
　Surely then you will see your wickedness and be ashamed.
It may be nice to live in a beautiful palace
　paneled with wood from the cedars of Lebanon,
but soon you will groan with pangs of anguish—
　anguish like that of a woman in labor.

"As surely as I live," says the LORD, "I will abandon you, Jehoiachin son of Jehoiakim, king of Judah. Even if you were the signet ring on my right hand, I would pull you off. I will hand you over to those who seek to kill you, those you so desperately fear—to King Nebuchadnezzar of Babylon and the mighty Babylonian army. I will expel you and your mother from this land, and you will die in a foreign country, not in your native land. You will never again return to the land you yearn for.

"Why is this man Jehoiachin like a discarded, broken jar?
　Why are he and his children to be exiled to a foreign land?
O earth, earth, earth!
　Listen to this message from the LORD!
This is what the LORD says:
'Let the record show that this man Jehoiachin was childless.
　He is a failure,
for none of his children will succeed him on the throne of David
　to rule over Judah.'

"What sorrow awaits the leaders of my people—the shepherds of my sheep—for they have destroyed and scattered the very ones they were expected to care for," says the LORD.

Therefore, this is what the LORD, the God of Israel, says to these shepherds: "Instead of caring for my flock and leading them to safety, you have deserted them and driven them to destruction. Now I will pour out judgment on you for the evil you have done to them. But I will gather together the remnant of my flock from the countries where I have driven them. I will bring them back to their own sheepfold, and they will be fruitful and increase in number. Then I will appoint responsible shepherds who will care for them, and they will never be afraid again. Not a single one will be lost or missing. I, the LORD, have spoken!

"For the time is coming,"
　says the LORD,

"when I will raise up a righteous descendant
    from King David's line.
He will be a King who rules with wisdom.
    He will do what is just and right throughout the land.
And this will be his name:
    'The LORD Is Our Righteousness.'
In that day Judah will be saved,
    and Israel will live in safety.

"In that day," says the LORD, "when people are taking an oath, they will
no longer say, 'As surely as the LORD lives, who rescued the people of Israel
from the land of Egypt.' Instead, they will say, 'As surely as the LORD lives,
who brought the people of Israel back to their own land from the land of
the north and from all the countries to which he had exiled them.' Then
they will live in their own land."

My heart is broken because of the false prophets,
    and my bones tremble.
I stagger like a drunkard,
    like someone overcome by wine,
because of the holy words
    the LORD has spoken against them.
For the land is full of adultery,
    and it lies under a curse.
The land itself is in mourning—
    its wilderness pastures are dried up.
For they all do evil
    and abuse what power they have.

"Even the priests and prophets
    are ungodly, wicked men.
I have seen their despicable acts
    right here in my own Temple,"
    says the LORD.
"Therefore, the paths they take
    will become slippery.
They will be chased through the dark,
    and there they will fall.
For I will bring disaster upon them
    at the time fixed for their punishment.
    I, the LORD, have spoken!

"I saw that the prophets of Samaria were terribly evil,
    for they prophesied in the name of Baal

and led my people of Israel into sin.
But now I see that the prophets of Jerusalem are even worse!
    They commit adultery and love dishonesty.
They encourage those who are doing evil
    so that no one turns away from their sins.
These prophets are as wicked
    as the people of Sodom and Gomorrah once were."

Therefore, this is what the LORD of Heaven's Armies says concerning the prophets:

"I will feed them with bitterness
    and give them poison to drink.
For it is because of Jerusalem's prophets
    that wickedness has filled this land."

This is what the LORD of Heaven's Armies says to his people:

"Do not listen to these prophets when they prophesy to you,
    filling you with futile hopes.
They are making up everything they say.
    They do not speak for the LORD!
They keep saying to those who despise my word,
    'Don't worry! The LORD says you will have peace!'
And to those who stubbornly follow their own desires,
    they say, 'No harm will come your way!'

"Have any of these prophets been in the LORD's presence
    to hear what he is really saying?
    Has even one of them cared enough to listen?
Look! The LORD's anger bursts out like a storm,
    a whirlwind that swirls down on the heads of the wicked.
The anger of the LORD will not diminish
    until it has finished all he has planned.
In the days to come
    you will understand all this very clearly.

"I have not sent these prophets,
    yet they run around claiming to speak for me.
I have given them no message,
    yet they go on prophesying.
If they had stood before me and listened to me,
    they would have spoken my words,
and they would have turned my people
    from their evil ways and deeds.

Am I a God who is only close at hand?" says the LORD.
"No, I am far away at the same time.
Can anyone hide from me in a secret place?
　Am I not everywhere in all the heavens and earth?"
　says the LORD.

"I have heard these prophets say, 'Listen to the dream I had from God last night.' And then they proceed to tell lies in my name. How long will this go on? If they are prophets, they are prophets of deceit, inventing everything they say. By telling these false dreams, they are trying to get my people to forget me, just as their ancestors did by worshiping the idols of Baal.

"Let these false prophets tell their dreams,
　but let my true messengers faithfully proclaim my every word.
　There is a difference between straw and grain!
Does not my word burn like fire?"
　says the LORD.
"Is it not like a mighty hammer
　that smashes a rock to pieces?"

"Therefore," says the LORD, "I am against these prophets who steal messages from each other and claim they are from me. I am against these smooth-tongued prophets who say, 'This prophecy is from the LORD!' I am against these false prophets. Their imaginary dreams are flagrant lies that lead my people into sin. I did not send or appoint them, and they have no message at all for my people. I, the LORD, have spoken!

"Suppose one of the people or one of the prophets or priests asks you, 'What prophecy has the LORD burdened you with now?' You must reply, 'You are the burden! The LORD says he will abandon you!'

"If any prophet, priest, or anyone else says, 'I have a prophecy from the LORD,' I will punish that person along with his entire family. You should keep asking each other, 'What is the LORD's answer?' or 'What is the LORD saying?' But stop using this phrase, 'prophecy from the LORD.' For people are using it to give authority to their own ideas, turning upside down the words of our God, the living God, the LORD of Heaven's Armies.

"This is what you should say to the prophets: 'What is the LORD's answer?' or 'What is the LORD saying?' But suppose they respond, 'This is a prophecy from the LORD!' Then you should say, 'This is what the LORD says: Because you have used this phrase, "prophecy from the LORD," even though I warned you not to use it, I will forget you completely. I will expel you from my presence, along with this city that I gave to you and your ancestors. And I will make you an object of ridicule, and your name will be infamous throughout the ages.'"

+

After King Nebuchadnezzar of Babylon exiled Jehoiachin son of Jehoiakim, king of Judah, to Babylon along with the officials of Judah and all the
craftsmen and artisans, the LORD gave me this vision. I saw two baskets
of figs placed in front of the LORD's Temple in Jerusalem. One basket was
filled with fresh, ripe figs, while the other was filled with bad figs that were
too rotten to eat.

Then the LORD said to me, "What do you see, Jeremiah?"

I replied, "Figs, some very good and some very bad, too rotten to eat."

Then the LORD gave me this message: "This is what the LORD, the God
of Israel, says: The good figs represent the exiles I sent from Judah to the
land of the Babylonians. I will watch over and care for them, and I will
bring them back here again. I will build them up and not tear them down. I
will plant them and not uproot them. I will give them hearts that recognize
me as the LORD. They will be my people, and I will be their God, for they
will return to me wholeheartedly.

"But the bad figs," the LORD said, "represent King Zedekiah of Judah, his
officials, all the people left in Jerusalem, and those who live in Egypt. I will
treat them like bad figs, too rotten to eat. I will make them an object of horror and a symbol of evil to every nation on earth. They will be disgraced
and mocked, taunted and cursed, wherever I scatter them. And I will send
war, famine, and disease until they have vanished from the land of Israel,
which I gave to them and their ancestors."

+

This message for all the people of Judah came to Jeremiah from the LORD
during the fourth year of Jehoiakim's reign over Judah. This was the year
when King Nebuchadnezzar of Babylon began his reign.

Jeremiah the prophet said to all the people in Judah and Jerusalem,
"For the past twenty-three years—from the thirteenth year of the reign of
Josiah son of Amon, king of Judah, until now—the LORD has been giving
me his messages. I have faithfully passed them on to you, but you have
not listened.

"Again and again the LORD has sent you his servants, the prophets, but
you have not listened or even paid attention. Each time the message was
this: 'Turn from the evil road you are traveling and from the evil things you
are doing. Only then will I let you live in this land that the LORD gave to
you and your ancestors forever. Do not provoke my anger by worshiping
idols you made with your own hands. Then I will not harm you.'

"But you would not listen to me," says the LORD. "You made me furious by worshiping idols you made with your own hands, bringing on your-selves all the disasters you now suffer. And now the LORD of Heaven's Armies says: Because you have not listened to me, I will gather together all the armies of the north under King Nebuchadnezzar of Babylon, whom I have appointed as my deputy. I will bring them all against this land and its people and against the surrounding nations. I will completely destroy you and make you an object of horror and contempt and a ruin forever. I will take away your happy singing and laughter. The joyful voices of bride-grooms and brides will no longer be heard. Your millstones will fall silent, and the lights in your homes will go out. This entire land will become a desolate wasteland. Israel and her neighboring lands will serve the king of Babylon for seventy years.

"Then, after the seventy years of captivity are over, I will punish the king of Babylon and his people for their sins," says the LORD. "I will make the country of the Babylonians a wasteland forever. I will bring upon them all the terrors I have promised in this book—all the penalties announced by Jeremiah against the nations. Many nations and great kings will enslave the Babylonians, just as they enslaved my people. I will punish them in proportion to the suffering they cause my people."

+ + +

This message came to Jeremiah from the LORD early in the reign of Jehoia-kim son of Josiah, king of Judah. "This is what the LORD says: Stand in the courtyard in front of the Temple of the LORD, and make an announcement to the people who have come there to worship from all over Judah. Give them my entire message; include every word. Perhaps they will listen and turn from their evil ways. Then I will change my mind about the disaster I am ready to pour out on them because of their sins.

"Say to them, 'This is what the LORD says: If you will not listen to me and obey my word I have given you, and if you will not listen to my ser-vants, the prophets—for I sent them again and again to warn you, but you would not listen to them—then I will destroy this Temple as I destroyed Shiloh, the place where the Tabernacle was located. And I will make Jeru-salem an object of cursing in every nation on earth.'"

The priests, the prophets, and all the people listened to Jeremiah as he spoke in front of the LORD's Temple. But when Jeremiah had finished his message, saying everything the LORD had told him to say, the priests and prophets and all the people at the Temple mobbed him. "Kill him!" they shouted. "What right do you have to prophesy in the LORD's name that this Temple will be destroyed like Shiloh? What do you mean, saying that

Jerusalem will be destroyed and left with no inhabitants?" And all the people threatened him as he stood in front of the Temple.

When the officials of Judah heard what was happening, they rushed over from the palace and sat down at the New Gate of the Temple to hold court. The priests and prophets presented their accusations to the officials and the people. "This man should die!" they said. "You have heard with your own ears what a traitor he is, for he has prophesied against this city."

Then Jeremiah spoke to the officials and the people in his own defense. "The LORD sent me to prophesy against this Temple and this city," he said. "The LORD gave me every word that I have spoken. But if you stop your sinning and begin to obey the LORD your God, he will change his mind about this disaster that he has announced against you. As for me, I am in your hands—do with me as you think best. But if you kill me, rest assured that you will be killing an innocent man! The responsibility for such a deed will lie on you, on this city, and on every person living in it. For it is absolutely true that the LORD sent me to speak every word you have heard."

Then the officials and the people said to the priests and prophets, "This man does not deserve the death sentence, for he has spoken to us in the name of the LORD our God."

Then some of the wise old men stood and spoke to all the people assembled there. They said, "Remember when Micah of Moresheth prophesied during the reign of King Hezekiah of Judah. He told the people of Judah,

'This is what the LORD of Heaven's Armies says:
Mount Zion will be plowed like an open field;
    Jerusalem will be reduced to ruins!
A thicket will grow on the heights
    where the Temple now stands.'

But did King Hezekiah and the people kill him for saying this? No, they turned from their sins and worshiped the LORD. They begged him for mercy. Then the LORD changed his mind about the terrible disaster he had pronounced against them. So we are about to do ourselves great harm."

At this time Uriah son of Shemaiah from Kiriath-jearim was also prophesying for the LORD. And he predicted the same terrible disaster against the city and nation as Jeremiah did. When King Jehoiakim and the army officers and officials heard what he was saying, the king sent someone to kill him. But Uriah heard about the plan and escaped in fear to Egypt. Then King Jehoiakim sent Elnathan son of Acbor to Egypt along with several other men to capture Uriah. They took him prisoner and brought him back to King Jehoiakim. The king then killed Uriah with a sword and had him buried in an unmarked grave.

Nevertheless, Ahikam son of Shaphan stood up for Jeremiah and persuaded the court not to turn him over to the mob to be killed.

+

This message came to Jeremiah from the LORD early in the reign of Zedekiah son of Josiah, king of Judah.

This is what the LORD said to me: "Make a yoke, and fasten it on your neck with leather straps. Then send messages to the kings of Edom, Moab, Ammon, Tyre, and Sidon through their ambassadors who have come to see King Zedekiah in Jerusalem. Give them this message for their masters: 'This is what the LORD of Heaven's Armies, the God of Israel, says: With my great strength and powerful arm I made the earth and all its people and every animal. I can give these things of mine to anyone I choose. Now I will give your countries to King Nebuchadnezzar of Babylon, who is my servant. I have put everything, even the wild animals, under his control. All the nations will serve him, his son, and his grandson until his time is up. Then many nations and great kings will conquer and rule over Babylon. So you must submit to Babylon's king and serve him; put your neck under Babylon's yoke! I will punish any nation that refuses to be his slave, says the LORD. I will send war, famine, and disease upon that nation until Babylon has conquered it.

"'Do not listen to your false prophets, fortune-tellers, interpreters of dreams, mediums, and sorcerers who say, "The king of Babylon will not conquer you." They are all liars, and their lies will lead to your being driven out of your land. I will drive you out and send you far away to die. But the people of any nation that submits to the king of Babylon will be allowed to stay in their own country to farm the land as usual. I, the LORD, have spoken!'"

Then I repeated this same message to King Zedekiah of Judah. "If you want to live, submit to the yoke of the king of Babylon and his people. Why do you insist on dying—you and your people? Why should you choose war, famine, and disease, which the LORD will bring against every nation that refuses to submit to Babylon's king? Do not listen to the false prophets who keep telling you, 'The king of Babylon will not conquer you.' They are liars. This is what the LORD says: 'I have not sent these prophets! They are telling you lies in my name, so I will drive you from this land. You will all die—you and all these prophets, too.'"

Then I spoke to the priests and the people and said, "This is what the LORD says: 'Do not listen to your prophets who claim that soon the gold articles taken from my Temple will be returned from Babylon. It is all a lie! Do not listen to them. Surrender to the king of Babylon, and you will live. Why should this whole city be destroyed? If they really are prophets and speak the LORD's messages, let them pray to the LORD of Heaven's Armies. Let them pray that the articles remaining in the LORD's Temple and in the king's palace and in the palaces of Jerusalem will not be carried away to Babylon!'

"For the LORD of Heaven's Armies has spoken about the pillars in front of the Temple, the great bronze basin called the Sea, the water carts, and all the other ceremonial articles. King Nebuchadnezzar of Babylon left them here when he exiled Jehoiachin son of Jehoiakim, king of Judah, to Babylon, along with all the other nobles of Judah and Jerusalem. Yes, this is what the LORD of Heaven's Armies, the God of Israel, says about the precious things still in the Temple, in the palace of Judah's king, and in Jerusalem: 'They will all be carried away to Babylon and will stay there until I send for them,' says the LORD. 'Then I will bring them back to Jerusalem again.'"

+

One day in late summer of that same year—the fourth year of the reign of Zedekiah, king of Judah—Hananiah son of Azzur, a prophet from Gibeon, addressed me publicly in the Temple while all the priests and people listened. He said, "This is what the LORD of Heaven's Armies, the God of Israel, says: 'I will remove the yoke of the king of Babylon from your necks. Within two years I will bring back all the Temple treasures that King Nebuchadnezzar carried off to Babylon. And I will bring back Jehoiachin son of Jehoiakim, king of Judah, and all the other captives that were taken to Babylon. I will surely break the yoke that the king of Babylon has put on your necks. I, the LORD, have spoken!'"

Jeremiah responded to Hananiah as they stood in front of all the priests and people at the Temple. He said, "Amen! May your prophecies come true! I hope the LORD does everything you say. I hope he does bring back from Babylon the treasures of this Temple and all the captives. But listen now to the solemn words I speak to you in the presence of all these people. The ancient prophets who preceded you and me spoke against many nations, always warning of war, disaster, and disease. So a prophet who predicts peace must show he is right. Only when his predictions come true can we know that he is really from the LORD."

Then Hananiah the prophet took the yoke off Jeremiah's neck and broke it in pieces. And Hananiah said again to the crowd that had gathered, "This is what the LORD says: 'Just as this yoke has been broken, within two years I will break the yoke of oppression from all the nations now subject to King Nebuchadnezzar of Babylon.'" With that, Jeremiah left the Temple area.

Soon after this confrontation with Hananiah, the LORD gave this message to Jeremiah: "Go and tell Hananiah, 'This is what the LORD says: You have broken a wooden yoke, but you have replaced it with a yoke of iron. The LORD of Heaven's Armies, the God of Israel, says: I have put a yoke of iron on the necks of all these nations, forcing them into slavery under King Nebuchadnezzar of Babylon. I have put everything, even the wild animals, under his control.'"

Then Jeremiah the prophet said to Hananiah, "Listen, Hananiah! The LORD has not sent you, but the people believe your lies. Therefore, this is what the LORD says: 'You must die. Your life will end this very year because you have rebelled against the LORD.'"

Two months later the prophet Hananiah died.

+

Jeremiah wrote a letter from Jerusalem to the elders, priests, prophets, and all the people who had been exiled to Babylon by King Nebuchadnezzar. This was after King Jehoiachin, the queen mother, the court officials, the other officials of Judah, and all the craftsmen and artisans had been deported from Jerusalem. He sent the letter with Elasah son of Shaphan and Gemariah son of Hilkiah when they went to Babylon as King Zedekiah's ambassadors to Nebuchadnezzar. This is what Jeremiah's letter said:

> This is what the LORD of Heaven's Armies, the God of Israel, says to all the captives he has exiled to Babylon from Jerusalem: "Build homes, and plan to stay. Plant gardens, and eat the food they produce. Marry and have children. Then find spouses for them so that you may have many grandchildren. Multiply! Do not dwindle away! And work for the peace and prosperity of the city where I sent you into exile. Pray to the LORD for it, for its welfare will determine your welfare."
>
> This is what the LORD of Heaven's Armies, the God of Israel, says: "Do not let your prophets and fortune-tellers who are with you in the land of Babylon trick you. Do not listen to their dreams, because they are telling you lies in my name. I have not sent them," says the LORD.
>
> This is what the LORD says: "You will be in Babylon for seventy years. But then I will come and do for you all the good things I have promised, and I will bring you home again. For I know the plans I have for you," says the LORD. "They are plans for good and not for disaster, to give you a future and a hope. In those days when you pray, I will listen. If you look for me wholeheartedly, you will find me. I will be found by you," says the LORD. "I will end your captivity and restore your fortunes. I will gather you out of the nations where I sent you and will bring you home again to your own land."

You claim that the LORD has raised up prophets for you in Babylon. But this is what the LORD says about the king who sits on David's throne and all those still living here in Jerusalem—your relatives who were not exiled to Babylon. This is what the LORD of Heaven's Armies says: "I will send war, famine, and disease upon them and make them like bad figs, too rotten to eat. Yes, I will pursue them with war, famine, and disease, and I will scatter them around the world. In every nation where I send them, I will make them an object of damnation, horror, contempt, and mockery. For they refuse to listen to me, though I have spoken to them repeatedly through the prophets I sent. And you who are in exile have not listened either," says the LORD.

Therefore, listen to this message from the LORD, all you captives there in Babylon. This is what the LORD of Heaven's Armies, the God of Israel, says about your prophets—Ahab son of Kolaiah and Zedekiah son of Maaseiah—who are telling you lies in my name: "I will turn them over to Nebuchadnezzar for execution before your eyes. Their terrible fate will become proverbial, so that the Judean exiles will curse someone by saying, 'May the LORD make you like Zedekiah and Ahab, whom the king of Babylon burned alive!' For these men have done terrible things among my people. They have committed adultery with their neighbors' wives and have lied in my name, saying things I did not command. I am a witness to this. I, the LORD, have spoken."

The LORD sent this message to Shemaiah the Nehelamite in Babylon: "This is what the LORD of Heaven's Armies, the God of Israel, says: You wrote a letter on your own authority to Zephaniah son of Maaseiah, the priest, and you sent copies to the other priests and people in Jerusalem. You wrote to Zephaniah,

"The LORD has appointed you to replace Jehoiada as the priest in charge of the house of the LORD. You are responsible to put into stocks and neck irons any crazy man who claims to be a prophet. So why have you done nothing to stop Jeremiah from Anathoth, who pretends to be a prophet among you? Jeremiah sent a letter here to Babylon, predicting that our captivity will be a long one. He said, 'Build homes, and plan to stay. Plant gardens, and eat the food they produce.'"

But when Zephaniah the priest received Shemaiah's letter, he took it to Jeremiah and read it to him. Then the LORD gave this message to Jeremiah: "Send an open letter to all the exiles in Babylon. Tell them, 'This is what the LORD says concerning Shemaiah the Nehelamite: Since he has prophesied to you when I did not send him and has tricked you into believing his lies, I will punish him and his family. None of his descendants will see the good things I will do for my people, for he has incited you to rebel against me. I, the LORD, have spoken!'"

+

The LORD gave another message to Jeremiah. He said, "This is what the LORD, the God of Israel, says: Write down for the record everything I have said to you, Jeremiah. For the time is coming when I will restore the fortunes of my people of Israel and Judah. I will bring them home to this land that I gave to their ancestors, and they will possess it again. I, the LORD, have spoken!"

This is the message the LORD gave concerning Israel and Judah. This is what the LORD says:

"I hear cries of fear;
    there is terror and no peace.
Now let me ask you a question:
    Do men give birth to babies?
Then why do they stand there, ashen-faced,
    hands pressed against their sides
    like a woman in labor?
In all history there has never been such a time of terror.
    It will be a time of trouble for my people Israel.
    Yet in the end they will be saved!
For in that day,"
    says the LORD of Heaven's Armies,
"I will break the yoke from their necks
    and snap their chains.
Foreigners will no longer be their masters.
    For my people will serve the LORD their God
and their king descended from David—
    the king I will raise up for them.

"So do not be afraid, Jacob, my servant;
    do not be dismayed, Israel,"
    says the LORD.
"For I will bring you home again from distant lands,
    and your children will return from their exile.
Israel will return to a life of peace and quiet,
    and no one will terrorize them.
For I am with you and will save you,"
    says the LORD.

"I will completely destroy the nations where I have scattered you,
   but I will not completely destroy you.
I will discipline you, but with justice;
   I cannot let you go unpunished."

This is what the LORD says:
"Your injury is incurable—
   a terrible wound.
There is no one to help you
   or to bind up your injury.
   No medicine can heal you.
All your lovers—your allies—have left you
   and do not care about you anymore.
I have wounded you cruelly,
   as though I were your enemy.
For your sins are many,
   and your guilt is great.
Why do you protest your punishment—
   this wound that has no cure?
I have had to punish you
   because your sins are many
   and your guilt is great.

"But all who devour you will be devoured,
   and all your enemies will be sent into exile.
All who plunder you will be plundered,
   and all who attack you will be attacked.
I will give you back your health
   and heal your wounds," says the LORD.
"For you are called an outcast—
   'Jerusalem for whom no one cares.'"

This is what the LORD says:
"When I bring Israel home again from captivity
   and restore their fortunes,
Jerusalem will be rebuilt on its ruins,
   and the palace reconstructed as before.
There will be joy and songs of thanksgiving,
   and I will multiply my people, not diminish them;
I will honor them, not despise them.
   Their children will prosper as they did long ago.
I will establish them as a nation before me,
   and I will punish anyone who hurts them.

They will have their own ruler again,
   and he will come from their own people.
I will invite him to approach me," says the LORD,
   "for who would dare to come unless invited?
You will be my people,
   and I will be your God."

Look! The LORD's anger bursts out like a storm,
   a driving wind that swirls down on the heads of the wicked.
The fierce anger of the LORD will not diminish
   until it has finished all he has planned.
In the days to come
   you will understand all this.

"In that day," says the LORD, "I will be the God of all the families of Israel, and they will be my people. This is what the LORD says:

"Those who survive the coming destruction
   will find blessings even in the barren land,
   for I will give rest to the people of Israel."

Long ago the LORD said to Israel:
"I have loved you, my people, with an everlasting love.
   With unfailing love I have drawn you to myself.
I will rebuild you, my virgin Israel.
   You will again be happy
   and dance merrily with your tambourines.
Again you will plant your vineyards on the mountains of Samaria
   and eat from your own gardens there.
The day will come when watchmen will shout
   from the hill country of Ephraim,
'Come, let us go up to Jerusalem
   to worship the LORD our God.'"

Now this is what the LORD says:
"Sing with joy for Israel.
   Shout for the greatest of nations!
Shout out with praise and joy:
'Save your people, O LORD,
   the remnant of Israel!'
For I will bring them from the north
   and from the distant corners of the earth.
I will not forget the blind and lame,
   the expectant mothers and women in labor.
   A great company will return!

Tears of joy will stream down their faces,
    and I will lead them home with great care.
They will walk beside quiet streams
    and on smooth paths where they will not stumble.
For I am Israel's father,
    and Ephraim is my oldest child.

"Listen to this message from the LORD,
    you nations of the world;
    proclaim it in distant coastlands:
The LORD, who scattered his people,
    will gather them and watch over them
    as a shepherd does his flock.
For the LORD has redeemed Israel
    from those too strong for them.
They will come home and sing songs of joy on the heights
      of Jerusalem.
    They will be radiant because of the LORD's good gifts—
the abundant crops of grain, new wine, and olive oil,
    and the healthy flocks and herds.
Their life will be like a watered garden,
    and all their sorrows will be gone.
The young women will dance for joy,
    and the men—old and young—will join in the celebration.
I will turn their mourning into joy.
    I will comfort them and exchange their sorrow for
      rejoicing.
The priests will enjoy abundance,
    and my people will feast on my good gifts.
    I, the LORD, have spoken!"

This is what the LORD says:

"A cry is heard in Ramah—
    deep anguish and bitter weeping.
Rachel weeps for her children,
    refusing to be comforted—
    for her children are gone."

But now this is what the LORD says:
"Do not weep any longer,
    for I will reward you," says the LORD.
"Your children will come back to you
    from the distant land of the enemy.

There is hope for your future," says the LORD.
      "Your children will come again to their own land.
I have heard Israel saying,
'You disciplined me severely,
      like a calf that needs training for the yoke.
Turn me again to you and restore me,
      for you alone are the LORD my God.
I turned away from God,
      but then I was sorry.
I kicked myself for my stupidity!
      I was thoroughly ashamed of all I did in my
            younger days.'

"Is not Israel still my son,
      my darling child?" says the LORD.
"I often have to punish him,
      but I still love him.
That's why I long for him
      and surely will have mercy on him.
Set up road signs;
      put up guideposts.
Mark well the path
      by which you came.
Come back again, my virgin Israel;
      return to your towns here.
How long will you wander,
      my wayward daughter?
For the LORD will cause something new to
            happen—
      Israel will embrace her God."

This is what the LORD of Heaven's Armies, the God of Israel, says: "When I bring them back from captivity, the people of Judah and its towns will again say, 'The LORD bless you, O righteous home, O holy mountain!' Townspeople and farmers and shepherds alike will live together in peace and happiness. For I have given rest to the weary and joy to the sorrowing."

At this, I woke up and looked around. My sleep had been very sweet.

"The day is coming," says the LORD, "when I will greatly increase the human population and the number of animals here in Israel and Judah. In the past I deliberately uprooted and tore down this nation. I overthrew it, destroyed it, and brought disaster upon it. But in the future I will just as deliberately plant it and build it up. I, the LORD, have spoken!

"The people will no longer quote this proverb:

'The parents have eaten sour grapes,
    but their children's mouths pucker at the taste.'

All people will die for their own sins—those who eat the sour grapes will be the ones whose mouths will pucker.

"The day is coming," says the LORD, "when I will make a new covenant with the people of Israel and Judah. This covenant will not be like the one I made with their ancestors when I took them by the hand and brought them out of the land of Egypt. They broke that covenant, though I loved them as a husband loves his wife," says the LORD.

"But this is the new covenant I will make with the people of Israel after those days," says the LORD. "I will put my instructions deep within them, and I will write them on their hearts. I will be their God, and they will be my people. And they will not need to teach their neighbors, nor will they need to teach their relatives, saying, 'You should know the LORD.' For everyone, from the least to the greatest, will know me already," says the LORD. "And I will forgive their wickedness, and I will never again remember their sins."

It is the LORD who provides the sun to light the day
    and the moon and stars to light the night,
    and who stirs the sea into roaring waves.
His name is the LORD of Heaven's Armies,
    and this is what he says:
"I am as likely to reject my people Israel
    as I am to abolish the laws of nature!"
This is what the LORD says:
"Just as the heavens cannot be measured
    and the foundations of the earth cannot
        be explored,
so I will not consider casting them away
    for the evil they have done.
    I, the LORD, have spoken!

"The day is coming," says the LORD, "when all Jerusalem will be rebuilt for me, from the Tower of Hananel to the Corner Gate. A measuring line will be stretched out over the hill of Gareb and across to Goah. And the entire area—including the graveyard and ash dump in the valley, and all the fields out to the Kidron Valley on the east as far as the Horse Gate—will be holy to the LORD. The city will never again be captured or destroyed."

+

The following message came to Jeremiah from the LORD in the tenth year of the reign of Zedekiah, king of Judah. This was also the eighteenth year of the reign of King Nebuchadnezzar. Jerusalem was then under siege from the Babylonian army, and Jeremiah was imprisoned in the courtyard of the guard in the royal palace. King Zedekiah had put him there, asking why he kept giving this prophecy: "This is what the LORD says: 'I am about to hand this city over to the king of Babylon, and he will take it. King Zedekiah will be captured by the Babylonians and taken to meet the king of Babylon face to face. He will take Zedekiah to Babylon, and I will deal with him there,' says the LORD. 'If you fight against the Babylonians, you will never succeed.'"

At that time the LORD sent me a message. He said, "Your cousin Hanamel son of Shallum will come and say to you, 'Buy my field at Anathoth. By law you have the right to buy it before it is offered to anyone else.'"

Then, just as the LORD had said he would, my cousin Hanamel came and visited me in the prison. He said, "Please buy my field at Anathoth in the land of Benjamin. By law you have the right to buy it before it is offered to anyone else, so buy it for yourself." Then I knew that the message I had heard was from the LORD.

So I bought the field at Anathoth, paying Hanamel seventeen pieces of silver for it. I signed and sealed the deed of purchase before witnesses, weighed out the silver, and paid him. Then I took the sealed deed and an unsealed copy of the deed, which contained the terms and conditions of the purchase, and I handed them to Baruch son of Neriah and grandson of Mahseiah. I did all this in the presence of my cousin Hanamel, the witnesses who had signed the deed, and all the men of Judah who were there in the courtyard of the guardhouse.

Then I said to Baruch as they all listened, "This is what the LORD of Heaven's Armies, the God of Israel, says: 'Take both this sealed deed and the unsealed copy, and put them into a pottery jar to preserve them for a long time.' For this is what the LORD of Heaven's Armies, the God of Israel, says: 'Someday people will again own property here in this land and will buy and sell houses and vineyards and fields.'"

Then after I had given the papers to Baruch, I prayed to the LORD:

"O Sovereign LORD! You made the heavens and earth by your strong hand and powerful arm. Nothing is too hard for you! You show unfailing love to thousands, but you also bring the consequences of one generation's sin upon the next. You are the great and powerful God, the LORD of Heaven's Armies. You have all wisdom and do great and mighty miracles. You see the conduct of all people, and you give them what they deserve. You performed miraculous signs and wonders in the land of Egypt—things still remembered to this day! And you have continued to do great miracles in Israel and all around the world. You have made your name famous to this day.

"You brought Israel out of Egypt with mighty signs and wonders, with a strong hand and powerful arm, and with overwhelming terror. You gave the people of Israel this land that you had promised their ancestors long before—a land flowing with milk and honey. Our ancestors came and conquered it and lived in it, but they refused to obey you or follow your word. They have not done anything you commanded. That is why you have sent this terrible disaster upon them.

"See how the siege ramps have been built against the city walls! Through war, famine, and disease, the city will be handed over to the Babylonians, who will conquer it. Everything has happened just as you said. And yet, O Sovereign LORD, you have told me to buy the field— paying good money for it before these witnesses—even though the city will soon be handed over to the Babylonians."

Then this message came to Jeremiah from the LORD: "I am the LORD, the God of all the peoples of the world. Is anything too hard for me? Therefore, this is what the LORD says: I will hand this city over to the Babylonians and to Nebuchadnezzar, king of Babylon, and he will capture it. The Babylonians outside the walls will come in and set fire to the city. They will burn down all these houses where the people provoked my anger by burning incense to Baal on the rooftops and by pouring out liquid offerings to other gods. Israel and Judah have done nothing but wrong since their earliest days. They have infuriated me with all their evil deeds," says the LORD. "From the time this city was built until now, it has done nothing but anger me, so I am determined to get rid of it.

"The sins of Israel and Judah—the sins of the people of Jerusalem, the kings, the officials, the priests, and the prophets—have stirred up my anger. My people have turned their backs on me and have refused to return. Even though I diligently taught them, they would not receive instruction or obey. They have set up their abominable idols right in my own Temple, defiling it. They have built pagan shrines to Baal in the valley of Ben-Hinnom, and there they sacrifice their sons and daughters to Molech. I have never commanded such a horrible deed; it never even crossed my mind to command such a thing. What an incredible evil, causing Judah to sin so greatly!

"Now I want to say something more about this city. You have been saying, 'It will fall to the king of Babylon through war, famine, and disease.'

But this is what the LORD, the God of Israel, says: I will certainly bring my people back again from all the countries where I will scatter them in my fury. I will bring them back to this very city and let them live in peace and safety. They will be my people, and I will be their God. And I will give them one heart and one purpose: to worship me forever, for their own good and for the good of all their descendants. And I will make an everlasting covenant with them: I will never stop doing good for them. I will put a desire in their hearts to worship me, and they will never leave me. I will find joy doing good for them and will faithfully and wholeheartedly replant them in this land.

"This is what the LORD says: Just as I have brought all these calamities on them, so I will do all the good I have promised them. Fields will again be bought and sold in this land about which you now say, 'It has been ravaged by the Babylonians, a desolate land where people and animals have all disappeared.' Yes, fields will once again be bought and sold—deeds signed and sealed and witnessed—in the land of Benjamin and here in Jerusalem, in the towns of Judah and in the hill country, in the foothills of Judah and in the Negev, too. For someday I will restore prosperity to them. I, the LORD, have spoken!"

+

While Jeremiah was still confined in the courtyard of the guard, the LORD gave him this second message: "This is what the LORD says—the LORD who made the earth, who formed and established it, whose name is the LORD: Ask me and I will tell you remarkable secrets you do not know about things to come. For this is what the LORD, the God of Israel, says: You have torn down the houses of this city and even the king's palace to get materials to strengthen the walls against the siege ramps and swords of the enemy. You expect to fight the Babylonians, but the men of this city are already as good as dead, for I have determined to destroy them in my terrible anger. I have abandoned them because of all their wickedness.

"Nevertheless, the time will come when I will heal Jerusalem's wounds and give it prosperity and true peace. I will restore the fortunes of Judah and Israel and rebuild their towns. I will cleanse them of their sins against me and forgive all their sins of rebellion. Then this city will bring me joy, glory, and honor before all the nations of the earth! The people of the world will see all the good I do for my people, and they will tremble with awe at the peace and prosperity I provide for them.

"This is what the LORD says: You have said, 'This is a desolate land where people and animals have all disappeared.' Yet in the empty streets of Jerusalem and Judah's other towns, there will be heard once more the sounds of joy and laughter. The joyful voices of bridegrooms and brides will be heard again, along with the joyous songs of people bringing thanksgiving offerings to the LORD. They will sing,

'Give thanks to the LORD of Heaven's Armies,
   for the LORD is good.
His faithful love endures forever!'

For I will restore the prosperity of this land to what it was in the past, says the LORD.

"This is what the LORD of Heaven's Armies says: This land—though it is now desolate and has no people and animals—will once more have pastures where shepherds can lead their flocks. Once again shepherds will count their flocks in the towns of the hill country, the foothills of Judah, the Negev, the land of Benjamin, the vicinity of Jerusalem, and all the towns of Judah. I, the LORD, have spoken!

"The day will come, says the LORD, when I will do for Israel and Judah all the good things I have promised them.

"In those days and at that time
   I will raise up a righteous descendant from King David's line.
   He will do what is just and right throughout the land.
In that day Judah will be saved,
   and Jerusalem will live in safety.
And this will be its name:
   'The LORD Is Our Righteousness.'

For this is what the LORD says: David will have a descendant sitting on the throne of Israel forever. And there will always be Levitical priests to offer burnt offerings and grain offerings and sacrifices to me."

Then this message came to Jeremiah from the LORD: "This is what the LORD says: If you can break my covenant with the day and the night so that one does not follow the other, only then will my covenant with my servant David be broken. Only then will he no longer have a descendant to reign on his throne. The same is true for my covenant with the Levitical priests who minister before me. And as the stars of the sky cannot be counted and the sand on the seashore cannot be measured, so I will multiply the descendants of my servant David and the Levites who minister before me."

The LORD gave another message to Jeremiah. He said, "Have you noticed what people are saying?—'The LORD chose Judah and Israel and then abandoned them!' They are sneering and saying that Israel is not worthy to be counted as a nation. But this is what the LORD says: I would no more reject my people than I would change my laws that govern night and day, earth and sky. I will never abandon the descendants of Jacob or

David, my servant, or change the plan that David's descendants will rule the descendants of Abraham, Isaac, and Jacob. Instead, I will restore them to their land and have mercy on them."

+

King Nebuchadnezzar of Babylon came with all the armies from the kingdoms he ruled, and he fought against Jerusalem and the towns of Judah. At that time this message came to Jeremiah from the LORD: "Go to King Zedekiah of Judah, and tell him, 'This is what the LORD, the God of Israel, says: I am about to hand this city over to the king of Babylon, and he will burn it down. You will not escape his grasp but will be captured and taken to meet the king of Babylon face to face. Then you will be exiled to Babylon.

"'But listen to this promise from the LORD, O Zedekiah, king of Judah. This is what the LORD says: You will not be killed in war but will die peacefully. People will burn incense in your memory, just as they did for your ancestors, the kings who preceded you. They will mourn for you, crying, "Alas, our master is dead!" This I have decreed, says the LORD.'"

So Jeremiah the prophet delivered the message to King Zedekiah of Judah. At this time the Babylonian army was besieging Jerusalem, Lachish, and Azekah—the only fortified cities of Judah not yet captured.

+

This message came to Jeremiah from the LORD after King Zedekiah made a covenant with the people, proclaiming freedom for the slaves. He had ordered all the people to free their Hebrew slaves—both men and women. No one was to keep a fellow Judean in bondage. The officials and all the people had obeyed the king's command, but later they changed their minds. They took back the men and women they had freed, forcing them to be slaves again.

So the LORD gave them this message through Jeremiah: "This is what the LORD, the God of Israel, says: I made a covenant with your ancestors long ago when I rescued them from their slavery in Egypt. I told them that every Hebrew slave must be freed after serving six years. But your ancestors paid no attention to me. Recently you repented and did what was right, following my command. You freed your slaves and made a solemn covenant with me in the Temple that bears my name. But now you have shrugged off your oath and defiled my name by taking back the men and women you had freed, forcing them to be slaves once again.

"Therefore, this is what the LORD says: Since you have not obeyed me by setting your countrymen free, I will set you free to be destroyed by war, disease, and famine. You will be an object of horror to all the nations of the earth. Because you have broken the terms of our covenant, I will cut you apart just as you cut apart the calf when you walked between its halves to solemnize your vows. Yes, I will cut you apart, whether you are officials of Judah or Jerusalem, court officials, priests, or common people—for you have broken your oath. I will give you to your enemies, and they will kill you. Your bodies will be food for the vultures and wild animals.

"I will hand over King Zedekiah of Judah and his officials to the army of the king of Babylon. And although they have left Jerusalem for a while, I will call the Babylonian armies back again. They will fight against this city and will capture it and burn it down. I will see to it that all the towns of Judah are destroyed, with no one living there."

+

This is the message the LORD gave Jeremiah when Jehoiakim son of Josiah was king of Judah: "Go to the settlement where the families of the Recabites live, and invite them to the LORD's Temple. Take them into one of the inner rooms, and offer them some wine."

So I went to see Jaazaniah son of Jeremiah and grandson of Habazziniah and all his brothers and sons—representing all the Recabite families. I took them to the Temple, and we went into the room assigned to the sons of Hanan son of Igdaliah, a man of God. This room was located next to the one used by the Temple officials, directly above the room of Maaseiah son of Shallum, the Temple gatekeeper.

I set cups and jugs of wine before them and invited them to have a drink, but they refused. "No," they said, "we don't drink wine, because our ancestor Jehonadab son of Recab gave us this command: 'You and your descendants must never drink wine. And do not build houses or plant crops or vineyards, but always live in tents. If you follow these commands, you will live long, good lives in the land.' So we have obeyed him in all these things. We have never had a drink of wine to this day, nor have our wives, our sons, or our daughters. We haven't built houses or owned vineyards or farms or planted crops. We have lived in tents and have fully obeyed all the commands of Jehonadab, our ancestor. But when King Nebuchadnezzar of Babylon attacked this country, we were afraid of the Babylonian and Syrian armies. So we decided to move to Jerusalem. That is why we are here."

Then the LORD gave this message to Jeremiah: "This is what the LORD of Heaven's Armies, the God of Israel, says: Go and say to the people in Judah and Jerusalem, 'Come and learn a lesson about how to obey me. The Recabites do not drink wine to this day because their ancestor Jehonadab told them not to. But I have spoken to you again and again, and you refuse to obey me. Time after time I sent you prophets, who told you, "Turn from your wicked ways, and start doing things right. Stop worshiping other gods so that you might live in peace here in the land I have given to you and your ancestors." But you would not listen to me or obey me. The descendants of Jehonadab son of Recab have obeyed their ancestor completely, but you have refused to listen to me.'

"Therefore, this is what the LORD God of Heaven's Armies, the God of Israel, says: 'Because you refuse to listen or answer when I call, I will send upon Judah and Jerusalem all the disasters I have threatened.'"

Then Jeremiah turned to the Recabites and said, "This is what the LORD of Heaven's Armies, the God of Israel, says: 'You have obeyed your ancestor Jehonadab in every respect, following all his instructions.' Therefore, this is what the LORD of Heaven's Armies, the God of Israel, says: 'Jehonadab son of Recab will always have descendants who serve me.'"

+

During the fourth year that Jehoiakim son of Josiah was king in Judah, the LORD gave this message to Jeremiah: "Get a scroll, and write down all my messages against Israel, Judah, and the other nations. Begin with the first message back in the days of Josiah, and write down every message, right up to the present time. Perhaps the people of Judah will repent when they hear again all the terrible things I have planned for them. Then I will be able to forgive their sins and wrongdoings."

So Jeremiah sent for Baruch son of Neriah, and as Jeremiah dictated all the prophecies that the LORD had given him, Baruch wrote them on a scroll. Then Jeremiah said to Baruch, "I am a prisoner here and unable to go to the Temple. So you go to the Temple on the next day of fasting, and read the messages from the LORD that I have had you write on this scroll. Read them so the people who are there from all over Judah will hear them. Perhaps even yet they will turn from their evil ways and ask the LORD's forgiveness before it is too late. For the LORD has threatened them with his terrible anger."

Baruch did as Jeremiah told him and read these messages from the LORD to the people at the Temple. He did this on a day of sacred fasting held in late autumn, during the fifth year of the reign of Jehoiakim son of Josiah. People from all over Judah had come to Jerusalem to attend the services at the Temple on that day. Baruch read Jeremiah's words on the scroll to all the people. He stood in front of the Temple room of Gemariah, son of Shaphan the secretary. This room was just off the upper courtyard of the Temple, near the New Gate entrance.

When Micaiah son of Gemariah and grandson of Shaphan heard the messages from the LORD, he went down to the secretary's room in the palace where the administrative officials were meeting. Elishama the secretary was there, along with Delaiah son of Shemaiah, Elnathan son of Acbor, Gemariah son of Shaphan, Zedekiah son of Hananiah, and all the other officials. When Micaiah told them about the messages Baruch was reading to the people, the officials sent Jehudi son of Nethaniah, grandson of Shelemiah and great-grandson of Cushi, to ask Baruch to come and read the messages to them, too. So Baruch took the scroll and went to them. "Sit down and read the scroll to us," the officials said, and Baruch did as they requested.

When they heard all the messages, they looked at one another in alarm. "We must tell the king what we have heard," they said to Baruch. "But first, tell us how you got these messages. Did they come directly from Jeremiah?"

So Baruch explained, "Jeremiah dictated them, and I wrote them down in ink, word for word, on this scroll."

"You and Jeremiah should both hide," the officials told Baruch. "Don't tell anyone where you are!" Then the officials left the scroll for safekeeping in the room of Elishama the secretary and went to tell the king what had happened.

The king sent Jehudi to get the scroll. Jehudi brought it from Elishama's room and read it to the king as all his officials stood by. It was late autumn, and the king was in a winterized part of the palace, sitting in front of a fire to keep warm. Each time Jehudi finished reading three or four columns, the king took a knife and cut off that section of the scroll. He then threw it into the fire, section by section, until the whole scroll was burned up. Neither the king nor his attendants showed any signs of fear or repentance at what they heard. Even when Elnathan, Delaiah, and Gemariah begged the king not to burn the scroll, he wouldn't listen.

Then the king commanded his son Jerahmeel, Seraiah son of Azriel, and Shelemiah son of Abdeel to arrest Baruch and Jeremiah. But the LORD had hidden them.

After the king had burned the scroll on which Baruch had written Jeremiah's words, the LORD gave Jeremiah another message. He said, "Get another scroll, and write everything again just as you did on the scroll King Jehoiakim burned. Then say to the king, 'This is what the LORD says: You burned the scroll because it said the king of Babylon would destroy this land and empty it of people and animals. Now this is what the LORD says about King Jehoiakim of Judah: He will have no heirs to sit on the throne of David. His dead body will be thrown out to lie unburied—exposed to the heat of the day and the frost of the night. I will punish him and his family and his attendants for their sins. I will pour out on them and on all the people of Jerusalem and Judah all the disasters I promised, for they would not listen to my warnings.'"

So Jeremiah took another scroll and dictated again to his secretary, Baruch. He wrote everything that had been on the scroll King Jehoiakim had burned in the fire. Only this time he added much more!

+ + +

Zedekiah son of Josiah succeeded Jehoiachin son of Jehoiakim as the king of Judah. He was appointed by King Nebuchadnezzar of Babylon. But neither King Zedekiah nor his attendants nor the people who were left in the land listened to what the LORD said through Jeremiah.

Nevertheless, King Zedekiah sent Jehucal son of Shelemiah, and Zephaniah the priest, son of Maaseiah, to ask Jeremiah, "Please pray to the LORD our God for us." Jeremiah had not yet been imprisoned, so he could come and go among the people as he pleased.

At this time the army of Pharaoh Hophra of Egypt appeared at the southern border of Judah. When the Babylonian army heard about it, they withdrew from their siege of Jerusalem.

Then the LORD gave this message to Jeremiah: "This is what the LORD, the God of Israel, says: The king of Judah sent you to ask me what is going to happen. Tell him, 'Pharaoh's army is about to return to Egypt, though he came here to help you. Then the Babylonians will come back and capture this city and burn it to the ground.'

"This is what the LORD says: Do not fool yourselves into thinking that the Babylonians are gone for good. They aren't! Even if you were to destroy the entire Babylonian army, leaving only a handful of wounded survivors, they would still stagger from their tents and burn this city to the ground!"

When the Babylonian army left Jerusalem because of Pharaoh's approaching army, Jeremiah started to leave the city on his way to the territory of Benjamin, to claim his share of the property among his relatives there. But as he was walking through the Benjamin Gate, a sentry arrested him and said, "You are defecting to the Babylonians!" The sentry making the arrest was Irijah son of Shelemiah, grandson of Hananiah.

"That's not true!" Jeremiah protested. "I had no intention of doing any such thing." But Irijah wouldn't listen, and he took Jeremiah before the officials. They were furious with Jeremiah and had him flogged and imprisoned in the house of Jonathan the secretary. Jonathan's house had been converted into a prison. Jeremiah was put into a dungeon cell, where he remained for many days.

Later King Zedekiah secretly requested that Jeremiah come to the palace, where the king asked him, "Do you have any messages from the LORD?"

"Yes, I do!" said Jeremiah. "You will be defeated by the king of Babylon."

Then Jeremiah asked the king, "What crime have I committed? What have I done against you, your attendants, or the people that I should be imprisoned like this? Where are your prophets now who told you the king of Babylon would not attack you or this land? Listen, my lord the king, I beg you. Don't send me back to the dungeon in the house of Jonathan the secretary, for I will die there."

So King Zedekiah commanded that Jeremiah not be returned to the dungeon. Instead, he was imprisoned in the courtyard of the guard in the royal palace. The king also commanded that Jeremiah be given a loaf of fresh bread every day as long as there was any left in the city. So Jeremiah was put in the palace prison.

Now Shephatiah son of Mattan, Gedaliah son of Pashhur, Jehucal son of Shelemiah, and Pashhur son of Malkijah heard what Jeremiah had been telling the people. He had been saying, "This is what the LORD says: 'Everyone who stays in Jerusalem will die from war, famine, or disease, but those who surrender to the Babylonians will live. Their reward will be life. They will live!' The LORD also says: 'The city of Jerusalem will certainly be handed over to the army of the king of Babylon, who will capture it.'"

So these officials went to the king and said, "Sir, this man must die! That kind of talk will undermine the morale of the few fighting men we have left, as well as that of all the people. This man is a traitor!"

King Zedekiah agreed. "All right," he said. "Do as you like. I can't stop you."

So the officials took Jeremiah from his cell and lowered him by ropes into an empty cistern in the prison yard. It belonged to Malkijah, a member of the royal family. There was no water in the cistern, but there was a thick layer of mud at the bottom, and Jeremiah sank down into it.

But Ebed-melech the Ethiopian, an important court official, heard that Jeremiah was in the cistern. At that time the king was holding court at the Benjamin Gate, so Ebed-melech rushed from the palace to speak with him. "My lord the king," he said, "these men have done a very evil thing in putting Jeremiah the prophet into the cistern. He will soon die of hunger, for almost all the bread in the city is gone."

So the king told Ebed-melech, "Take thirty of my men with you, and pull Jeremiah out of the cistern before he dies."

So Ebed-melech took the men with him and went to a room in the palace beneath the treasury, where he found some old rags and discarded clothing. He carried these to the cistern and lowered them to Jeremiah on a rope. Ebed-melech called down to Jeremiah, "Put these rags under your armpits to protect you from the ropes." Then when Jeremiah was ready, they pulled him out. So Jeremiah was returned to the courtyard of the guard—the palace prison—where he remained.

One day King Zedekiah sent for Jeremiah and had him brought to the third entrance of the LORD's Temple. "I want to ask you something," the king said. "And don't try to hide the truth."

Jeremiah said, "If I tell you the truth, you will kill me. And if I give you advice, you won't listen to me anyway."

So King Zedekiah secretly promised him, "As surely as the LORD our Creator lives, I will not kill you or hand you over to the men who want you dead."

Then Jeremiah said to Zedekiah, "This is what the LORD God of Heaven's Armies, the God of Israel, says: 'If you surrender to the Babylonian officers, you and your family will live, and the city will not be burned down. But if you refuse to surrender, you will not escape! This city will be handed over to the Babylonians, and they will burn it to the ground.'"

"But I am afraid to surrender," the king said, "for the Babylonians may hand me over to the Judeans who have defected to them. And who knows what they will do to me!"

Jeremiah replied, "You won't be handed over to them if you choose to obey the LORD. Your life will be spared, and all will go well for you. But if you refuse to surrender, this is what the LORD has revealed to me: All the women left in your palace will be brought out and given to the officers of the Babylonian army. Then the women will taunt you, saying,

'What fine friends you have!
    They have betrayed and misled you.
When your feet sank in the mud,
    they left you to your fate!'

All your wives and children will be led out to the Babylonians, and you will not escape. You will be seized by the king of Babylon, and this city will be burned down."

Then Zedekiah said to Jeremiah, "Don't tell anyone you told me this, or you will die! My officials may hear that I spoke to you, and they may say, 'Tell us what you and the king were talking about. If you don't tell us, we will kill you.' If this happens, just tell them you begged me not to send you back to Jonathan's dungeon, for fear you would die there."

Sure enough, it wasn't long before the king's officials came to Jeremiah and asked him why the king had called for him. But Jeremiah followed the king's instructions, and they left without finding out the truth. No one had overheard the conversation between Jeremiah and the king. And Jeremiah remained a prisoner in the courtyard of the guard until the day Jerusalem was captured.

In January of the ninth year of King Zedekiah's reign, King Nebuchadnezzar of Babylon came with his entire army to besiege Jerusalem. Two and a half years later, on July 18 in the eleventh year of Zedekiah's reign, a section of the city wall was broken down. All the officers of the Babylonian army came in and sat in triumph at the Middle Gate: Nergal-sharezer of Samgar, and Nebo-sarsekim, a chief officer, and Nergal-sharezer, the king's adviser, and all the other officers of the king of Babylon.

When King Zedekiah of Judah and all the soldiers saw that the Babylonians had broken into the city, they fled. They waited for nightfall and then slipped through the gate between the two walls behind the king's garden and headed toward the Jordan Valley.

But the Babylonian troops chased them and overtook Zedekiah on the plains of Jericho. They captured him and took him to King Nebuchadnezzar of Babylon, who was at Riblah in the land of Hamath. There the king of Babylon pronounced judgment upon Zedekiah. The king of Babylon made Zedekiah watch as he slaughtered his sons at Riblah. The king of Babylon also slaughtered all the nobles of Judah. Then he gouged out Zedekiah's eyes and bound him in bronze chains to lead him away to Babylon.

Meanwhile, the Babylonians burned Jerusalem, including the royal palace and the houses of the people, and they tore down the walls of the city. Then Nebuzaradan, the captain of the guard, took as exiles to Babylon the rest of the people who remained in the city, those who had defected to him, and everyone else who remained. But Nebuzaradan allowed some of the poorest people to stay behind in the land of Judah, and he assigned them to care for the vineyards and fields.

King Nebuchadnezzar had told Nebuzaradan, the captain of the guard, to find Jeremiah. "See that he isn't hurt," he said. "Look after him well, and give him anything he wants." So Nebuzaradan, the captain of the guard; Nebushazban, a chief officer; Nergal-sharezer, the king's adviser; and the other officers of Babylon's king sent messengers to bring Jeremiah out of the prison. They put him under the care of Gedaliah son of Ahikam and grandson of Shaphan, who took him back to his home. So Jeremiah stayed in Judah among his own people.

The Lord had given the following message to Jeremiah while he was still in prison: "Say to Ebed-melech the Ethiopian, 'This is what the Lord of Heaven's Armies, the God of Israel, says: I will do to this city everything I have threatened. I will send disaster, not prosperity. You will see its destruction, but I will rescue you from those you fear so much. Because you trusted me, I will give you your life as a reward. I will rescue you and keep you safe. I, the LORD, have spoken!'"

+

The LORD gave a message to Jeremiah after Nebuzaradan, the captain of the guard, had released him at Ramah. He had found Jeremiah bound in chains among all the other captives of Jerusalem and Judah who were being sent to exile in Babylon.

The captain of the guard called for Jeremiah and said, "The LORD your God has brought this disaster on this land, just as he said he would. For these people have sinned against the LORD and disobeyed him. That is why it happened. But I am going to take off your chains and let you go. If you want to come with me to Babylon, you are welcome. I will see that you are well cared for. But if you don't want to come, you may stay here. The whole land is before you—go wherever you like. If you decide to stay, then return to Gedaliah son of Ahikam and grandson of Shaphan. He has been appointed governor of Judah by the king of Babylon. Stay there with the people he rules. But it's up to you; go wherever you like."

Then Nebuzaradan, the captain of the guard, gave Jeremiah some food and money and let him go. So Jeremiah returned to Gedaliah son of Ahikam at Mizpah, and he lived in Judah with the few who were still left in the land.

+

The leaders of the Judean military groups in the countryside heard that the king of Babylon had appointed Gedaliah son of Ahikam as governor over the poor people who were left behind in Judah—the men, women, and children who hadn't been exiled to Babylon. So they went to see Gedaliah at Mizpah. These included: Ishmael son of Nethaniah, Johanan and Jonathan sons of Kareah, Seraiah son of Tanhumeth, the sons of Ephai the Netophathite, Jezaniah son of the Maacathite, and all their men.

Gedaliah vowed to them that the Babylonians meant them no harm. "Don't be afraid to serve them. Live in the land and serve the king of Babylon, and all will go well for you," he promised. "As for me, I will stay at Mizpah to represent you before the Babylonians who come to meet with us. Settle in the towns you have taken, and live off the land. Harvest the grapes and summer fruits and olives, and store them away."

When the Judeans in Moab, Ammon, Edom, and the other nearby countries heard that the king of Babylon had left a few people in Judah and that Gedaliah was the governor, they began to return to Judah from the places to which they had fled. They stopped at Mizpah to meet with Gedaliah and then went into the Judean countryside to gather a great harvest of grapes and other crops.

Soon after this, Johanan son of Kareah and the other military leaders came to Gedaliah at Mizpah. They said to him, "Did you know that Baalis, king of Ammon, has sent Ishmael son of Nethaniah to assassinate you?" But Gedaliah refused to believe them.

Later Johanan had a private conference with Gedaliah and volunteered to kill Ishmael secretly. "Why should we let him come and murder you?" Johanan asked. "What will happen then to the Judeans who have returned? Why should the few of us who are still left be scattered and lost?"

But Gedaliah said to Johanan, "I forbid you to do any such thing, for you are lying about Ishmael."

But in midautumn of that year, Ishmael son of Nethaniah and grandson of Elishama, who was a member of the royal family and had been one of the king's high officials, went to Mizpah with ten men to meet Gedaliah. While they were eating together, Ishmael and his ten men suddenly jumped up, drew their swords, and killed Gedaliah, whom the king of Babylon had appointed governor. Ishmael also killed all the Judeans and the Babylonian soldiers who were with Gedaliah at Mizpah.

The next day, before anyone had heard about Gedaliah's murder, eighty men arrived from Shechem, Shiloh, and Samaria to worship at the Temple of the LORD. They had shaved off their beards, torn their clothes, and cut themselves, and had brought along grain offerings and frankincense. Ishmael left Mizpah to meet them, weeping as he went. When he reached them, he said, "Oh, come and see what has happened to Gedaliah!"

But as soon as they were all inside the town, Ishmael and his men killed all but ten of them and threw their bodies into a cistern. The other ten had talked Ishmael into letting them go by promising to bring him their stores of wheat, barley, olive oil, and honey that they had hidden away. The cistern where Ishmael dumped the bodies of the men he murdered was the large one dug by King Asa when he fortified Mizpah to protect himself against King Baasha of Israel. Ishmael son of Nethaniah filled it with corpses.

Then Ishmael made captives of the king's daughters and the other people who had been left under Gedaliah's care in Mizpah by Nebuzaradan, the captain of the guard. Taking them with him, he started back toward the land of Ammon.

But when Johanan son of Kareah and the other military leaders heard about Ishmael's crimes, they took all their men and set out to stop him. They caught up with him at the large pool near Gibeon. The people

Ishmael had captured shouted for joy when they saw Johanan and the other military leaders. And all the captives from Mizpah escaped and began to help Johanan. Meanwhile, Ishmael and eight of his men escaped from Johanan into the land of Ammon.

Then Johanan son of Kareah and the other military leaders took all the people they had rescued in Gibeon—the soldiers, women, children, and court officials whom Ishmael had captured after he killed Gedaliah. They took them all to the village of Geruth-kimham near Bethlehem, where they prepared to leave for Egypt. They were afraid of what the Babylonians would do when they heard that Ishmael had killed Gedaliah, the governor appointed by the Babylonian king.

Then all the military leaders, including Johanan son of Kareah and Jezaniah son of Hoshaiah, and all the people, from the least to the greatest, approached Jeremiah the prophet. They said, "Please pray to the LORD your God for us. As you can see, we are only a tiny remnant compared to what we were before. Pray that the LORD your God will show us what to do and where to go."

"All right," Jeremiah replied. "I will pray to the LORD your God, as you have asked, and I will tell you everything he says. I will hide nothing from you."

Then they said to Jeremiah, "May the LORD your God be a faithful witness against us if we refuse to obey whatever he tells us to do! Whether we like it or not, we will obey the LORD our God to whom we are sending you with our plea. For if we obey him, everything will turn out well for us."

Ten days later the LORD gave his reply to Jeremiah. So he called for Johanan son of Kareah and the other military leaders, and for all the people, from the least to the greatest. He said to them, "You sent me to the LORD, the God of Israel, with your request, and this is his reply: 'Stay here in this land. If you do, I will build you up and not tear you down; I will plant you and not uproot you. For I am sorry about all the punishment I have had to bring upon you. Do not fear the king of Babylon anymore,' says the LORD. 'For I am with you and will save you and rescue you from his power. I will be merciful to you by making him kind, so he will let you stay here in your land.'

"But if you refuse to obey the LORD your God, and if you say, 'We will not stay here; instead, we will go to Egypt where we will be free from war, the call to arms, and hunger,' then hear the LORD's message to the remnant of Judah. This is what the LORD of Heaven's Armies, the God of Israel, says: 'If you are determined to go to Egypt and live there, the very war and famine you fear will catch up to you, and you will die there. That is the fate awaiting every one of you who insists on going to live in Egypt. Yes, you will die from war, famine, and disease. None of you will escape the disaster I will bring upon you there.'

"This is what the LORD of Heaven's Armies, the God of Israel, says: 'Just as my anger and fury have been poured out on the people of Jerusalem, so they will be poured out on you when you enter Egypt. You will be an object of damnation, horror, cursing, and mockery. And you will never see your homeland again.'

"Listen, you remnant of Judah. The LORD has told you: 'Do not go to Egypt!' Don't forget this warning I have given you today. For you were not being honest when you sent me to pray to the LORD your God for you. You said, 'Just tell us what the LORD our God says, and we will do it!' And today I have told you exactly what he said, but you will not obey the LORD your God any better now than you have in the past. So you can be sure that you will die from war, famine, and disease in Egypt, where you insist on going."

When Jeremiah had finished giving this message from the LORD their God to all the people, Azariah son of Hoshaiah and Johanan son of Kareah and all the other proud men said to Jeremiah, "You lie! The LORD our God hasn't forbidden us to go to Egypt! Baruch son of Neriah has convinced you to say this, because he wants us to stay here and be killed by the Babylonians or be carried off into exile."

So Johanan and the other military leaders and all the people refused to obey the LORD's command to stay in Judah. Johanan and the other leaders took with them all the people who had returned from the nearby countries to which they had fled. In the crowd were men, women, and children, the king's daughters, and all those whom Nebuzaradan, the captain of the guard, had left with Gedaliah. The prophet Jeremiah and Baruch were also included. The people refused to obey the voice of the LORD and went to Egypt, going as far as the city of Tahpanhes.

+

Then at Tahpanhes, the LORD gave another message to Jeremiah. He said, "While the people of Judah are watching, take some large rocks and bury them under the pavement stones at the entrance of Pharaoh's palace here in Tahpanhes. Then say to the people of Judah, 'This is what the LORD of Heaven's Armies, the God of Israel, says: I will certainly bring my servant Nebuchadnezzar, king of Babylon, here to Egypt. I will set his throne over these stones that I have hidden. He will spread his royal canopy over them. And when he comes, he will destroy the land of Egypt. He will bring death to those destined for death, captivity to those destined for captivity, and war to those destined for war. He will set fire to the temples of Egypt's gods; he will burn the temples and carry the idols away as plunder. He will pick clean the land of Egypt as a shepherd picks fleas from his cloak. And he himself will leave unharmed. He will break down the sacred pillars standing in the temple of the sun in Egypt, and he will burn down the temples of Egypt's gods.'"

+

This is the message Jeremiah received concerning the Judeans living in northern Egypt in the cities of Migdol, Tahpanhes, and Memphis, and in southern Egypt as well: "This is what the LORD of Heaven's Armies, the God of Israel, says: You saw the calamity I brought on Jerusalem and all the towns of Judah. They now lie deserted and in ruins. They provoked my anger with all their wickedness. They burned incense and worshiped other gods—gods that neither they nor you nor any of your ancestors had ever even known.

"Again and again I sent my servants, the prophets, to plead with them, 'Don't do these horrible things that I hate so much.' But my people would not listen or turn back from their wicked ways. They kept on burning incense to these gods. And so my fury boiled over and fell like fire on the towns of Judah and into the streets of Jerusalem, and they are still a desolate ruin today.

"And now the LORD God of Heaven's Armies, the God of Israel, asks you: Why are you destroying yourselves? For not one of you will survive—not a man, woman, or child among you who has come here from Judah, not even the babies in your arms. Why provoke my anger by burning incense to the idols you have made here in Egypt? You will only destroy yourselves and make yourselves an object of cursing and mockery for all the nations of the earth. Have you forgotten the sins of your ancestors, the sins of the kings and queens of Judah, and the sins you and your wives committed in Judah and Jerusalem? To this very hour you have shown no remorse or reverence. No one has chosen to follow my word and the decrees I gave to you and your ancestors before you.

"Therefore, this is what the LORD of Heaven's Armies, the God of Israel, says: I am determined to destroy every one of you! I will take this remnant of Judah—those who were determined to come here and live in Egypt—and I will consume them. They will fall here in Egypt, killed by war and famine. All will die, from the least to the greatest. They will be an object of damnation, horror, cursing, and mockery. I will punish them in Egypt just as I punished them in Jerusalem, by war, famine, and disease. Of that remnant who fled to Egypt, hoping someday to return to Judah, there will be no survivors. Even though they long to return home, only a handful will do so."

Then all the women present and all the men who knew that their wives had burned incense to idols—a great crowd of all the Judeans living in northern Egypt and southern Egypt—answered Jeremiah, "We will not listen to your messages from the LORD! We will do whatever we want. We will burn incense and pour out liquid offerings to the Queen of Heaven just as much as we like—just as we, and our ancestors, and our kings and officials have always done in the towns of Judah and in the streets of Jerusalem. For in those days we had plenty to eat, and we were well off and had no troubles! But ever since we quit burning incense to the Queen of Heaven and stopped worshiping her with liquid offerings, we have been in great trouble and have been dying from war and famine."

"Besides," the women added, "do you suppose that we were burning incense and pouring out liquid offerings to the Queen of Heaven, and making cakes marked with her image, without our husbands knowing it and helping us? Of course not!"

Then Jeremiah said to all of them, men and women alike, who had given him that answer, "Do you think the LORD did not know that you and your ancestors, your kings and officials, and all the people were burning incense to idols in the towns of Judah and in the streets of Jerusalem? It was because the LORD could no longer bear all the disgusting things you were doing that he made your land an object of cursing—a desolate ruin without inhabitants—as it is today. All these terrible things happened to you because you have burned incense to idols and sinned against the LORD. You have refused to obey him and have not followed his instructions, his decrees, and his laws."

Then Jeremiah said to them all, including the women, "Listen to this message from the LORD, all you citizens of Judah who live in Egypt. This is what the LORD of Heaven's Armies, the God of Israel, says: 'You and your wives have said, "We will keep our promises to burn incense and pour out liquid offerings to the Queen of Heaven," and you have proved by your actions that you meant it. So go ahead and carry out your promises and vows to her!'

"But listen to this message from the LORD, all you Judeans now living in Egypt: 'I have sworn by my great name,' says the LORD, 'that my name will no longer be spoken by any of the Judeans in the land of Egypt. None of you may invoke my name or use this oath: "As surely as the Sovereign LORD lives." For I will watch over you to bring you disaster and not good. Everyone from Judah who is now living in Egypt will suffer war and famine until all of you are dead. Only a small number will escape death and return to Judah from Egypt. Then all those who came to Egypt will find out whose words are true—mine or theirs!

"'And this is the proof I give you,' says the LORD, 'that all I have threatened will happen to you and that I will punish you here.' This is what the

LORD says: 'I will turn Pharaoh Hophra, king of Egypt, over to his enemies who want to kill him, just as I turned King Zedekiah of Judah over to King Nebuchadnezzar of Babylon.'"

+

The prophet Jeremiah gave a message to Baruch son of Neriah in the fourth year of the reign of Jehoiakim son of Josiah, after Baruch had written down everything Jeremiah had dictated to him. He said, "This is what the LORD, the God of Israel, says to you, Baruch: You have said, 'I am overwhelmed with trouble! Haven't I had enough pain already? And now the LORD has added more! I am worn out from sighing and can find no rest.'

"Baruch, this is what the LORD says: 'I will destroy this nation that I built. I will uproot what I planted. Are you seeking great things for yourself? Don't do it! I will bring great disaster upon all these people; but I will give you your life as a reward wherever you go. I, the LORD, have spoken!'"

+ + +

This is what the LORD, the God of Israel, said to me: "Take from my hand this cup filled to the brim with my anger, and make all the nations to whom I send you drink from it. When they drink from it, they will stagger, crazed by the warfare I will send against them."

So I took the cup of anger from the LORD and made all the nations drink from it—every nation to which the LORD sent me. I went to Jerusalem and the other towns of Judah, and their kings and officials drank from the cup. From that day until this, they have been a desolate ruin, an object of horror, contempt, and cursing. I gave the cup to Pharaoh, king of Egypt, his attendants, his officials, and all his people, along with all the foreigners living in that land. I also gave it to all the kings of the land of Uz and the kings of the Philistine cities of Ashkelon, Gaza, Ekron, and what remains of Ashdod. Then I gave the cup to the nations of Edom, Moab, and Ammon, and the kings of Tyre and Sidon, and the kings of the regions across the sea. I gave it to Dedan, Tema, and Buz, and to the people who live in distant places. I gave it to the kings of Arabia, the kings of the nomadic tribes of the desert, and to the kings of Zimri, Elam, and Media. And I gave it to the kings of the northern countries, far and near, one after the other—all the kingdoms of the world. And finally, the king of Babylon himself drank from the cup of the LORD's anger.

Then the LORD said to me, "Now tell them, 'This is what the LORD of Heaven's Armies, the God of Israel, says: Drink from this cup of my anger. Get drunk and vomit; fall to rise no more, for I am sending terrible wars against you.' And if they refuse to accept the cup, tell them, 'The LORD of Heaven's Armies says: You have no choice but to drink from it. I have begun to punish Jerusalem, the city that bears my name. Now should I let you go unpunished? No, you will not escape disaster. I will call for war against all the nations of the earth. I, the LORD of Heaven's Armies, have spoken!'

"Now prophesy all these things, and say to them,

> "'The LORD will roar against his own land
> from his holy dwelling in heaven.
> He will shout like those who tread grapes;
> he will shout against everyone on earth.
> His cry of judgment will reach the ends of the earth,
> for the LORD will bring his case against all the nations.
> He will judge all the people of the earth,
> slaughtering the wicked with the sword.
> I, the LORD, have spoken!'"

> This is what the LORD of Heaven's Armies says:
> "Look! Disaster will fall upon nation after nation!
> A great whirlwind of fury is rising
> from the most distant corners of the earth!"

In that day those the LORD has slaughtered will fill the earth from one end to the other. No one will mourn for them or gather up their bodies to bury them. They will be scattered on the ground like manure.

> Weep and moan, you evil shepherds!
> Roll in the dust, you leaders of the flock!
> The time of your slaughter has arrived;
> you will fall and shatter like a fragile vase.
> You will find no place to hide;
> there will be no way to escape.
> Listen to the frantic cries of the shepherds.
> The leaders of the flock are wailing in despair,
> for the LORD is ruining their pastures.
> Peaceful meadows will be turned into a wasteland
> by the LORD's fierce anger.
> He has left his den like a strong lion seeking its prey,
> and their land will be made desolate
> by the sword of the enemy
> and the LORD's fierce anger.

The following messages were given to Jeremiah the prophet from the LORD concerning foreign nations.

+

This message concerning Egypt was given in the fourth year of the reign of Jehoiakim son of Josiah, the king of Judah, on the occasion of the battle of Carchemish when Pharaoh Neco, king of Egypt, and his army were defeated beside the Euphrates River by King Nebuchadnezzar of Babylon.

"Prepare your shields,
    and advance into battle!
Harness the horses,
    and mount the stallions.
Take your positions.
    Put on your helmets.
Sharpen your spears,
    and prepare your armor.
But what do I see?
    The Egyptian army flees in terror.
The bravest of its fighting men run
    without a backward glance.
They are terrorized at every turn,"
    says the LORD.
"The swiftest runners cannot flee;
    the mightiest warriors cannot escape.
By the Euphrates River to the north,
    they stumble and fall.

"Who is this, rising like the Nile at floodtime,
    overflowing all the land?
It is the Egyptian army,
    overflowing all the land,
boasting that it will cover the earth like a flood,
    destroying cities and their people.
Charge, you horses and chariots;
    attack, you mighty warriors of Egypt!
Come, all you allies from Ethiopia, Libya, and Lydia
    who are skilled with the shield and bow!
For this is the day of the Lord, the LORD of Heaven's Armies,
    a day of vengeance on his enemies.
The sword will devour until it is satisfied,
    yes, until it is drunk with your blood!
The Lord, the LORD of Heaven's Armies, will receive a sacrifice today
    in the north country beside the Euphrates River.

"Go up to Gilead to get medicine,
  O virgin daughter of Egypt!
But your many treatments
  will bring you no healing.
The nations have heard of your shame.
  The earth is filled with your cries of despair.
Your mightiest warriors will run into each other
  and fall down together."

Then the LORD gave the prophet Jeremiah this message about King Nebuchadnezzar's plans to attack Egypt.

"Shout it out in Egypt!
  Publish it in the cities of Migdol, Memphis, and Tahpanhes!
Mobilize for battle,
  for the sword will devour everyone around you.
Why have your warriors fallen?
  They cannot stand, for the LORD has knocked
    them down.
They stumble and fall over each other
  and say among themselves,
'Come, let's go back to our people,
  to the land of our birth.
  Let's get away from the sword of the enemy!'
There they will say,
  'Pharaoh, the king of Egypt, is a loudmouth
  who missed his opportunity!'

"As surely as I live," says the King,
  whose name is the LORD of Heaven's Armies,
"one is coming against Egypt
  who is as tall as Mount Tabor,
  or as Mount Carmel by the sea!
Pack up! Get ready to leave for exile,
  you citizens of Egypt!
The city of Memphis will be destroyed,
  without a single inhabitant.
Egypt is as sleek as a beautiful heifer,
  but a horsefly from the north is on its way!
Egypt's mercenaries have become like fattened calves.
  They, too, will turn and run,
for it is a day of great disaster for Egypt,
  a time of great punishment.

Egypt flees, silent as a serpent gliding away.
　　The invading army marches in;
　　they come against her with axes like woodsmen.
They will cut down her people like trees," says the LORD,
　　"for they are more numerous than locusts.
Egypt will be humiliated;
　　she will be handed over to people from the north."

The LORD of Heaven's Armies, the God of Israel, says: "I will punish Amon, the god of Thebes, and all the other gods of Egypt. I will punish its rulers and Pharaoh, too, and all who trust in him. I will hand them over to those who want them killed—to King Nebuchadnezzar of Babylon and his army. But afterward the land will recover from the ravages of war. I, the LORD, have spoken!

"But do not be afraid, Jacob, my servant;
　　do not be dismayed, Israel.
For I will bring you home again from distant lands,
　　and your children will return from their exile.
Israel will return to a life of peace and quiet,
　　and no one will terrorize them.
Do not be afraid, Jacob, my servant,
　　for I am with you," says the LORD.
"I will completely destroy the nations to which I have exiled you,
　　but I will not completely destroy you.
I will discipline you, but with justice;
　　I cannot let you go unpunished."

+

This is the LORD's message to the prophet Jeremiah concerning the Philistines of Gaza, before it was captured by the Egyptian army. This is what the LORD says:

"A flood is coming from the north
　　to overflow the land.
It will destroy the land and everything in it—
　　cities and people alike.
People will scream in terror,
　　and everyone in the land will wail.
Hear the clatter of stallions' hooves
　　and the rumble of wheels as the chariots rush by.
Terrified fathers run madly,
　　without a backward glance at their helpless children.

"The time has come for the Philistines to be destroyed,
　along with their allies from Tyre and Sidon.
Yes, the LORD is destroying the remnant of the Philistines,
　those colonists from the island of Crete.
Gaza will be humiliated, its head shaved bald;
　Ashkelon will lie silent.
You remnant from the Mediterranean coast,
　how long will you cut yourselves in mourning?

"Now, O sword of the LORD,
　when will you be at rest again?
Go back into your sheath;
　rest and be still.

"But how can it be still
　when the LORD has sent it on a mission?
For the city of Ashkelon
　and the people living along the sea
　must be destroyed."

+

This message was given concerning Moab. This is what the LORD of Heaven's Armies, the God of Israel, says:

"What sorrow awaits the city of Nebo;
　it will soon lie in ruins.
The city of Kiriathaim will be humiliated and captured;
　the fortress will be humiliated and broken down.
No one will ever brag about Moab again,
　for in Heshbon there is a plot to destroy her.
'Come,' they say, 'we will cut her off from being a nation.'
　The town of Madmen, too, will be silenced;
　the sword will follow you there.
Listen to the cries from Horonaim,
　cries of devastation and great destruction.
All Moab is destroyed.
　Her little ones will cry out.
Her refugees weep bitterly,
　climbing the slope to Luhith.
They cry out in terror,
　descending the slope to Horonaim.
Flee for your lives!
　Hide in the wilderness!

Because you have trusted in your wealth and skill,
  you will be taken captive.
Your god Chemosh, with his priests and officials,
  will be hauled off to distant lands!

"All the towns will be destroyed,
  and no one will escape—
either on the plateaus or in the valleys,
  for the LORD has spoken.
Oh, that Moab had wings
  so she could fly away,
for her towns will be left empty,
  with no one living in them.
Cursed are those who refuse to do the LORD's work,
  who hold back their swords from shedding blood!

"From his earliest history, Moab has lived in peace,
  never going into exile.
He is like wine that has been allowed to settle.
  He has not been poured from flask to flask,
  and he is now fragrant and smooth.
But the time is coming soon," says the LORD,
  "when I will send men to pour him from his jar.
They will pour him out,
  then shatter the jar!
At last Moab will be ashamed of his idol Chemosh,
  as the people of Israel were ashamed of their gold calf at Bethel.

"You used to boast, 'We are heroes,
  mighty men of war.'
But now Moab and his towns will be destroyed.
  His most promising youth are doomed to slaughter,"
  says the King, whose name is the LORD of Heaven's Armies.
"Destruction is coming fast for Moab;
  calamity threatens ominously.
You friends of Moab,
  weep for him and cry!
See how the strong scepter is broken,
  how the beautiful staff is shattered!

"Come down from your glory
  and sit in the dust, you people of Dibon,
for those who destroy Moab will shatter Dibon, too.
  They will tear down all your towers.

You people of Aroer,
    stand beside the road and watch.
Shout to those who flee from Moab,
    'What has happened there?'

"And the reply comes back,
'Moab lies in ruins, disgraced;
    weep and wail!
Tell it by the banks of the Arnon River:
    Moab has been destroyed!'
Judgment has been poured out on the towns
      of the plateau—
    on Holon and Jahaz and Mephaath,
on Dibon and Nebo and Beth-diblathaim,
    on Kiriathaim and Beth-gamul and Beth-meon,
on Kerioth and Bozrah—
    all the towns of Moab, far and near.

"The strength of Moab has ended.
    His arm has been broken," says the LORD.
"Let him stagger and fall like a drunkard,
    for he has rebelled against the LORD.
Moab will wallow in his own vomit,
    ridiculed by all.
Did you not ridicule the people of Israel?
    Were they caught in the company of thieves
    that you should despise them as you do?

"You people of Moab,
    flee from your towns and live in the caves.
Hide like doves that nest
    in the clefts of the rocks.
We have all heard of the pride of Moab,
    for his pride is very great.
We know of his lofty pride,
    his arrogance, and his haughty heart.
I know about his insolence,"
    says the LORD,
"but his boasts are empty—
    as empty as his deeds.
So now I wail for Moab;
    yes, I will mourn for Moab.
    My heart is broken for the men of Kir-hareseth.

"You people of Sibmah, rich in vineyards,
　　I will weep for you even more than I did for Jazer.
Your spreading vines once reached as far as the Dead Sea,
　　but the destroyer has stripped you bare!
　　He has harvested your grapes and summer fruits.
Joy and gladness are gone from fruitful Moab.
　　The presses yield no wine.
No one treads the grapes with shouts of joy.
　　There is shouting, yes, but not of joy.

"Instead, their awful cries of terror can be heard from Heshbon clear across to Elealeh and Jahaz; from Zoar all the way to Horonaim and Eglath-shelishiyah. Even the waters of Nimrim are dried up now.

"I will put an end to Moab," says the LORD, "for the people offer sacrifices at the pagan shrines and burn incense to their false gods. My heart moans like a flute for Moab and Kir-hareseth, for all their wealth has disappeared. The people shave their heads and beards in mourning. They slash their hands and put on clothes made of burlap. There is crying and sorrow in every Moabite home and on every street. For I have smashed Moab like an old, unwanted jar. How it is shattered! Hear the wailing! See the shame of Moab! It has become an object of ridicule, an example of ruin to all its neighbors."

This is what the LORD says:

"Look! The enemy swoops down like an eagle,
　　spreading his wings over Moab.
Its cities will fall,
　　and its strongholds will be seized.
Even the mightiest warriors will be in anguish
　　like a woman in labor.
Moab will no longer be a nation,
　　for it has boasted against the LORD.

"Terror and traps and snares will be your lot,
　　O Moab," says the LORD.
"Those who flee in terror will fall into a trap,
　　and those who escape the trap will step into a snare.
I will see to it that you do not get away,
　　for the time of your judgment has come,"
　　says the LORD.
"The people flee as far as Heshbon
　　but are unable to go on.
For a fire comes from Heshbon,
　　King Sihon's ancient home,

> to devour the entire land
>> with all its rebellious people.

> "What sorrow awaits you, O people of Moab!
>> The people of the god Chemosh are destroyed!
> Your sons and your daughters
>> have been taken away as captives.
> But I will restore the fortunes of Moab
>> in days to come.
>> I, the LORD, have spoken!"

This is the end of Jeremiah's prophecy concerning Moab.

+

This message was given concerning the Ammonites. This is what the LORD says:

> "Are there no descendants of Israel
>> to inherit the land of Gad?
> Why are you, who worship Molech,
>> living in its towns?
> In the days to come," says the LORD,
>> "I will sound the battle cry against your city of Rabbah.
> It will become a desolate heap of ruins,
>> and the neighboring towns will be burned.
> Then Israel will take back the land
>> you took from her," says the LORD.

> "Cry out, O Heshbon,
>> for the town of Ai is destroyed.
> Weep, O people of Rabbah!
>> Put on your clothes of mourning.
> Weep and wail, hiding in the hedges,
>> for your god Molech, with his priests and officials,
>>> will be hauled off to distant lands.
> You are proud of your fertile valleys,
>> but they will soon be ruined.
> You trusted in your wealth,
>> you rebellious daughter,
>> and thought no one could ever harm you.
> But look! I will bring terror upon you,"
>> says the Lord, the LORD of Heaven's Armies.

"Your neighbors will chase you from your land,
   and no one will help your exiles as they flee.
But I will restore the fortunes of the Ammonites
   in days to come.
   I, the LORD, have spoken."

+

This message was given concerning Edom. This is what the LORD of Heaven's Armies says:

"Is there no wisdom in Teman?
   Is no one left to give wise counsel?
Turn and flee!
   Hide in deep caves, you people of Dedan!
For when I bring disaster on Edom,
   I will punish you, too!
Those who harvest grapes
   always leave a few for the poor.
If thieves came at night,
   they would not take everything.
But I will strip bare the land of Edom,
   and there will be no place left to hide.
Its children, its brothers, and its neighbors
   will all be destroyed,
   and Edom itself will be no more.
But I will protect the orphans who remain among you.
   Your widows, too, can depend on me for help."

And this is what the LORD says: "If the innocent must suffer, how much more must you! You will not go unpunished! You must drink this cup of judgment! For I have sworn by my own name," says the LORD, "that Bozrah will become an object of horror and a heap of ruins; it will be mocked and cursed. All its towns and villages will be desolate forever."

I have heard a message from the LORD
   that an ambassador was sent to the nations to say,
"Form a coalition against Edom,
   and prepare for battle!"

The LORD says to Edom,
"I will cut you down to size among the nations.
   You will be despised by all.
You have been deceived

by the fear you inspire in others
and by your own pride.
You live in a rock fortress
and control the mountain heights.
But even if you make your nest among the peaks with the eagles,
I will bring you crashing down,"
says the LORD.

"Edom will be an object of horror.
All who pass by will be appalled
and will gasp at the destruction they see there.
It will be like the destruction of Sodom and Gomorrah
and their neighboring towns," says the LORD.
"No one will live there;
no one will inhabit it.
I will come like a lion from the thickets of the Jordan,
leaping on the sheep in the pasture.
I will chase Edom from its land,
and I will appoint the leader of my choice.
For who is like me, and who can challenge me?
What ruler can oppose my will?"

Listen to the LORD's plans against Edom
and the people of Teman.
Even the little children will be dragged off like sheep,
and their homes will be destroyed.
The earth will shake with the noise of Edom's fall,
and its cry of despair will be heard all the way to the Red Sea.
Look! The enemy swoops down like an eagle,
spreading his wings over Bozrah.
Even the mightiest warriors will be in anguish
like a woman in labor.

+

This message was given concerning Damascus. This is what the LORD says:

"The towns of Hamath and Arpad are struck with fear,
for they have heard the news of their destruction.
Their hearts are troubled
like a wild sea in a raging storm.
Damascus has become feeble,
and all her people turn to flee.
Fear, anguish, and pain have gripped her
as they grip a woman in labor.

That famous city, a city of joy,
  will be forsaken!
Her young men will fall in the streets and die.
  Her soldiers will all be killed,"
    says the LORD of Heaven's Armies.
"And I will set fire to the walls of Damascus
  that will burn up the palaces of Ben-hadad."

+

This message was given concerning Kedar and the kingdoms of Hazor, which were attacked by King Nebuchadnezzar of Babylon. This is what the LORD says:

"Advance against Kedar!
  Destroy the warriors from the East!
Their flocks and tents will be captured,
  and their household goods and camels will be taken away.
Everywhere shouts of panic will be heard:
  'We are terrorized at every turn!'
Run for your lives," says the LORD.
  "Hide yourselves in deep caves, you people of Hazor,
for King Nebuchadnezzar of Babylon has plotted against you
  and is preparing to destroy you.

"Go up and attack that complacent nation,"
  says the LORD.
"Its people live alone in the desert
  without walls or gates.
Their camels and other livestock will all be yours.
  I will scatter to the winds these people
  who live in remote places.
I will bring calamity upon them
  from every direction," says the LORD.
"Hazor will be inhabited by jackals,
  and it will be desolate forever.
No one will live there;
  no one will inhabit it."

+

This message concerning Elam came to the prophet Jeremiah from the LORD at the beginning of the reign of King Zedekiah of Judah. This is what the LORD of Heaven's Armies says:

"I will destroy the archers of Elam—
　　the best of their forces.
I will bring enemies from all directions,
　　and I will scatter the people of Elam to the four winds.
　　They will be exiled to countries around the world.
I myself will go with Elam's enemies to shatter it.
　　In my fierce anger, I will bring great disaster
　　upon the people of Elam," says the LORD.
"Their enemies will chase them with the sword
　　until I have destroyed them completely.
I will set my throne in Elam," says the LORD,
　　"and I will destroy its king and officials.
But I will restore the fortunes of Elam
　　in days to come.
　　I, the LORD, have spoken!"

✝

The LORD gave Jeremiah the prophet this message concerning Babylon and the land of the Babylonians. This is what the LORD says:

"Tell the whole world,
　　and keep nothing back.
Raise a signal flag
　　to tell everyone that Babylon will fall!
Her images and idols will be shattered.
　　Her gods Bel and Marduk will be utterly disgraced.
For a nation will attack her from the north
　　and bring such destruction that no one will live there again.
Everything will be gone;
　　both people and animals will flee.

"In those coming days,"
　　says the LORD,
"the people of Israel will return home
　　together with the people of Judah.
They will come weeping
　　and seeking the LORD their God.
They will ask the way to Jerusalem
　　and will start back home again.
They will bind themselves to the LORD
　　with an eternal covenant that will never be forgotten.

"My people have been lost sheep.
   Their shepherds have led them astray
   and turned them loose in the mountains.
They have lost their way
   and can't remember how to get back to the sheepfold.
All who found them devoured them.
   Their enemies said,
'We did nothing wrong in attacking them,
   for they sinned against the LORD,
their true place of rest,
   and the hope of their ancestors.'

"But now, flee from Babylon!
   Leave the land of the Babylonians.
Like male goats at the head of the flock,
   lead my people home again.
For I am raising up an army
   of great nations from the north.
They will join forces to attack Babylon,
   and she will be captured.
The enemies' arrows will go straight to the mark;
   they will not miss!
Babylonia will be looted
   until the attackers are glutted with loot.
   I, the LORD, have spoken!

"You rejoice and are glad,
   you who plundered my chosen people.
You frisk about like a calf in a meadow
   and neigh like a stallion.
But your homeland will be overwhelmed
   with shame and disgrace.
You will become the least of nations—
   a wilderness, a dry and desolate land.
Because of the LORD's anger,
   Babylon will become a deserted wasteland.
All who pass by will be horrified
   and will gasp at the destruction they see there.

"Yes, prepare to attack Babylon,
   all you surrounding nations.
Let your archers shoot at her; spare no arrows.
   For she has sinned against the LORD.

Shout war cries against her from every side.
  Look! She surrenders!
  Her walls have fallen.
It is the LORD's vengeance,
  so take vengeance on her.
  Do to her as she has done to others!
Take from Babylon all those who plant crops;
  send all the harvesters away.
Because of the sword of the enemy,
  everyone will run away and rush back to their own lands.

"The Israelites are like sheep
  that have been scattered by lions.
First the king of Assyria ate them up.
  Then King Nebuchadnezzar of Babylon cracked
    their bones."
Therefore, this is what the LORD of Heaven's Armies,
  the God of Israel, says:
"Now I will punish the king of Babylon and his land,
  just as I punished the king of Assyria.
And I will bring Israel home again to its own land,
  to feed in the fields of Carmel and Bashan,
and to be satisfied once more
  in the hill country of Ephraim and Gilead.
In those days," says the LORD,
  "no sin will be found in Israel or in Judah,
  for I will forgive the remnant I preserve.

"Go up, my warriors, against the land of Merathaim
  and against the people of Pekod.
Pursue, kill, and completely destroy them,
  as I have commanded you," says the LORD.
"Let the battle cry be heard in the land,
  a shout of great destruction.
Babylon, the mightiest hammer in all the earth,
  lies broken and shattered.
  Babylon is desolate among the nations!
Listen, Babylon, for I have set a trap for you.
  You are caught, for you have fought against the LORD.
The LORD has opened his armory
  and brought out weapons to vent his fury.
The terror that falls upon the Babylonians
  will be the work of the Sovereign LORD of Heaven's Armies.

Yes, come against her from distant lands.
　　Break open her granaries.
Crush her walls and houses into heaps of rubble.
　　Destroy her completely, and leave nothing!
Destroy even her young bulls—
　　it will be terrible for them, too!
Slaughter them all!
　　For Babylon's day of reckoning has come.
Listen to the people who have escaped from Babylon,
　　as they tell in Jerusalem
how the LORD our God has taken vengeance
　　against those who destroyed his Temple.

"Send out a call for archers to come to Babylon.
　　Surround the city so none can escape.
Do to her as she has done to others,
　　for she has defied the LORD, the Holy One of Israel.
Her young men will fall in the streets and die.
　　Her soldiers will all be killed,"
　　says the LORD.

"See, I am your enemy, you arrogant people,"
　　says the Lord, the LORD of Heaven's Armies.
"Your day of reckoning has arrived—
　　the day when I will punish you.
O land of arrogance, you will stumble and fall,
　　and no one will raise you up.
For I will light a fire in the cities of Babylon
　　that will burn up everything around them."

This is what the LORD of Heaven's Armies says:
"The people of Israel and Judah have been wronged.
　　Their captors hold them and refuse to let them go.
But the one who redeems them is strong.
　　His name is the LORD of Heaven's Armies.
He will defend them
　　and give them rest again in Israel.
But for the people of Babylon
　　there will be no rest!

"The sword of destruction will strike the Babylonians,"
　　says the LORD.
"It will strike the people of Babylon—
　　her officials and wise men, too.

The sword will strike her wise counselors,
   and they will become fools.
The sword will strike her mightiest warriors,
   and panic will seize them.
The sword will strike her horses and chariots
   and her allies from other lands,
   and they will all become like women.
The sword will strike her treasures,
   and they all will be plundered.
A drought will strike her water supply,
   causing it to dry up.
And why? Because the whole land is filled with idols,
   and the people are madly in love with them.

"Soon Babylon will be inhabited by desert animals and hyenas.
   It will be a home for owls.
Never again will people live there;
   it will lie desolate forever.
I will destroy it as I destroyed Sodom and Gomorrah
   and their neighboring towns," says the LORD.
"No one will live there;
   no one will inhabit it.

"Look! A great army is coming from the north.
   A great nation and many kings
   are rising against you from far-off lands.
They are armed with bows and spears.
   They are cruel and show no mercy.
As they ride forward on horses,
   they sound like a roaring sea.
They are coming in battle formation,
   planning to destroy you, Babylon.
The king of Babylon has heard reports about the enemy,
   and he is weak with fright.
Pangs of anguish have gripped him,
   like those of a woman in labor.

"I will come like a lion from the thickets of the Jordan,
   leaping on the sheep in the pasture.
I will chase Babylon from its land,
   and I will appoint the leader of my choice.
For who is like me, and who can challenge me?
   What ruler can oppose my will?"

Listen to the LORD's plans against Babylon
    and the land of the Babylonians.
Even the little children will be dragged off like sheep,
    and their homes will be destroyed.
The earth will shake with the shout, "Babylon has been taken!"
    and its cry of despair will be heard around the world.

This is what the LORD says:
"I will stir up a destroyer against Babylon
    and the people of Babylonia.
Foreigners will come and winnow her,
    blowing her away as chaff.
They will come from every side
    to rise against her in her day of trouble.
Don't let the archers put on their armor
    or draw their bows.
Don't spare even her best soldiers!
    Let her army be completely destroyed.
They will fall dead in the land of the Babylonians,
    slashed to death in her streets.
For the LORD of Heaven's Armies
    has not abandoned Israel and Judah.
He is still their God,
    even though their land was filled with sin
    against the Holy One of Israel."

Flee from Babylon! Save yourselves!
    Don't get trapped in her punishment!
It is the LORD's time for vengeance;
    he will repay her in full.
Babylon has been a gold cup in the LORD's hands,
    a cup that made the whole earth drunk.
The nations drank Babylon's wine,
    and it drove them all mad.
But suddenly Babylon, too, has fallen.
    Weep for her.
Give her medicine.
    Perhaps she can yet be healed.
We would have helped her if we could,
    but nothing can save her now.
Let her go; abandon her.
    Return now to your own land.
For her punishment reaches to the heavens;

it is so great it cannot be measured.
The LORD has vindicated us.
　　Come, let us announce in Jerusalem
　　everything the LORD our God has done.

Sharpen the arrows!
　　Lift up the shields!
For the LORD has inspired the kings of the Medes
　　to march against Babylon and destroy her.
This is his vengeance against those
　　who desecrated his Temple.
Raise the battle flag against Babylon!
　　Reinforce the guard and station the watchmen.
Prepare an ambush,
　　for the LORD will fulfill all his plans against Babylon.
You are a city by a great river,
　　a great center of commerce,
but your end has come.
　　The thread of your life is cut.
The LORD of Heaven's Armies has taken this vow
　　and has sworn to it by his own name:
"Your cities will be filled with enemies,
　　like fields swarming with locusts,
　　and they will shout in triumph over you."

The LORD made the earth by his power,
　　and he preserves it by his wisdom.
With his own understanding
　　he stretched out the heavens.
When he speaks in the thunder,
　　the heavens roar with rain.
He causes the clouds to rise over the earth.
　　He sends the lightning with the rain
　　and releases the wind from his storehouses.

The whole human race is foolish and has no knowledge!
　　The craftsmen are disgraced by the idols they make,
for their carefully shaped works are a fraud.
　　These idols have no breath or power.
Idols are worthless; they are ridiculous lies!
　　On the day of reckoning they will all be destroyed.
But the God of Israel is no idol!
　　He is the Creator of everything that exists,

including his people, his own special possession.
   The LORD of Heaven's Armies is his name!

"You are my battle-ax and sword,"
   says the LORD.
"With you I will shatter nations
   and destroy many kingdoms.
With you I will shatter armies—
   destroying the horse and rider,
   the chariot and charioteer.
With you I will shatter men and women,
   old people and children,
   young men and young women.
With you I will shatter shepherds and flocks,
   farmers and oxen,
   captains and officers.

"I will repay Babylon
   and the people of Babylonia
for all the wrong they have done
   to my people in Jerusalem," says the LORD.

"Look, O mighty mountain, destroyer of the earth!
   I am your enemy," says the LORD.
"I will raise my fist against you,
   to knock you down from the heights.
When I am finished,
   you will be nothing but a heap of burnt rubble.
You will be desolate forever.
   Even your stones will never again be used
     for building.
You will be completely wiped out,"
   says the LORD.

Raise a signal flag to the nations.
   Sound the battle cry!
Mobilize them all against Babylon.
   Prepare them to fight against her!
Bring out the armies of Ararat, Minni, and Ashkenaz.
   Appoint a commander,
   and bring a multitude of horses like swarming locusts!
Bring against her the armies of the nations—
   led by the kings of the Medes
   and all their captains and officers.

The earth trembles and writhes in pain,
   for everything the LORD has planned against Babylon stands
     unchanged.
Babylon will be left desolate without a single inhabitant.
   Her mightiest warriors no longer fight.
They stay in their barracks, their courage gone.
   They have become like women.
The invaders have burned the houses
   and broken down the city gates.
The news is passed from one runner to the next
   as the messengers hurry to tell the king
   that his city has been captured.
All the escape routes are blocked.
   The marshes have been set aflame,
   and the army is in a panic.

This is what the LORD of Heaven's Armies,
   the God of Israel, says:
"Babylon is like wheat on a threshing floor,
   about to be trampled.
In just a little while
   her harvest will begin."

"King Nebuchadnezzar of Babylon has eaten and crushed us
   and drained us of strength.
He has swallowed us like a great monster
   and filled his belly with our riches.
   He has thrown us out of our own country.
Make Babylon suffer as she made us suffer,"
   say the people of Zion.
"Make the people of Babylonia pay for spilling our blood,"
   says Jerusalem.

This is what the LORD says to Jerusalem:

"I will be your lawyer to plead your case,
   and I will avenge you.
I will dry up her river,
   as well as her springs,
and Babylon will become a heap of ruins,
   haunted by jackals.
She will be an object of horror and contempt,
   a place where no one lives.
Her people will roar together like strong lions.

They will growl like lion cubs.
And while they lie inflamed with all their wine,
   I will prepare a different kind of feast for them.
I will make them drink until they fall asleep,
   and they will never wake up again,"
   says the LORD.
"I will bring them down
   like lambs to the slaughter,
   like rams and goats to be sacrificed.

"How Babylon is fallen—
   great Babylon, praised throughout the earth!
Now she has become an object of horror
   among the nations.
The sea has risen over Babylon;
   she is covered by its crashing waves.
Her cities now lie in ruins;
   she is a dry wasteland
   where no one lives or even passes by.
And I will punish Bel, the god of Babylon,
   and make him vomit up all he has eaten.
The nations will no longer come and worship him.
   The wall of Babylon has fallen!

"Come out, my people, flee from Babylon.
   Save yourselves! Run from the LORD's fierce anger.
But do not panic; don't be afraid
   when you hear the first rumor of approaching forces.
   For rumors will keep coming year by year.
Violence will erupt in the land
   as the leaders fight against each other.
For the time is surely coming
   when I will punish this great city and all her idols.
Her whole land will be disgraced,
   and her dead will lie in the streets.
Then the heavens and earth will rejoice,
   for out of the north will come destroying armies
   against Babylon," says the LORD.
"Just as Babylon killed the people of Israel
   and others throughout the world,
   so must her people be killed.
Get out, all you who have escaped the sword!
   Do not stand and watch—flee while you can!

Remember the LORD, though you are in a far-off land,
    and think about your home in Jerusalem."

"We are ashamed," the people say.
    "We are insulted and disgraced
because the LORD's Temple
    has been defiled by foreigners."

"Yes," says the LORD, "but the time is coming
    when I will destroy Babylon's idols.
The groans of her wounded people
    will be heard throughout the land.
Though Babylon reaches as high as the heavens
    and makes her fortifications incredibly strong,
I will still send enemies to plunder her.
    I, the LORD, have spoken!

"Listen! Hear the cry of Babylon,
    the sound of great destruction from the land of the Babylonians.
For the LORD is destroying Babylon.
    He will silence her loud voice.
Waves of enemies pound against her;
    the noise of battle rings through the city.
Destroying armies come against Babylon.
    Her mighty men are captured,
    and their weapons break in their hands.
For the LORD is a God who gives just punishment;
    he always repays in full.
I will make her officials and wise men drunk,
    along with her captains, officers, and warriors.
They will fall asleep
    and never wake up again!"
says the King, whose name is
    the LORD of Heaven's Armies.

This is what the LORD of Heaven's Armies says:
"The thick walls of Babylon will be leveled to the ground,
    and her massive gates will be burned.
The builders from many lands have worked in vain,
    for their work will be destroyed by fire!"

The prophet Jeremiah gave this message to Seraiah son of Neriah and grandson of Mahseiah, a staff officer, when Seraiah went to Babylon with King Zedekiah of Judah. This was during the fourth year of Zedekiah's reign. Jeremiah had recorded on a scroll all the terrible disasters that would soon come upon Babylon—all the words written here. He said to Seraiah, "When you get to Babylon, read aloud everything on this scroll. Then say, 'LORD, you have said that you will destroy Babylon so that neither people nor animals will remain here. She will lie empty and abandoned forever.' When you have finished reading the scroll, tie it to a stone and throw it into the Euphrates River. Then say, 'In this same way Babylon and her people will sink, never again to rise, because of the disasters I will bring upon her.'"

This is the end of Jeremiah's messages.

+ + +

Zedekiah was twenty-one years old when he became king, and he reigned in Jerusalem eleven years. His mother was Hamutal, the daughter of Jeremiah from Libnah. But Zedekiah did what was evil in the LORD's sight, just as Jehoiakim had done. These things happened because of the LORD's anger against the people of Jerusalem and Judah, until he finally banished them from his presence and sent them into exile.

Zedekiah rebelled against the king of Babylon. So on January 15, during the ninth year of Zedekiah's reign, King Nebuchadnezzar of Babylon led his entire army against Jerusalem. They surrounded the city and built siege ramps against its walls. Jerusalem was kept under siege until the eleventh year of King Zedekiah's reign.

By July 18 in the eleventh year of Zedekiah's reign, the famine in the city had become very severe, and the last of the food was entirely gone. Then a section of the city wall was broken down, and all the soldiers fled. Since the city was surrounded by the Babylonians, they waited for nightfall. Then they slipped through the gate between the two walls behind the king's garden and headed toward the Jordan Valley.

But the Babylonian troops chased King Zedekiah and overtook him on the plains of Jericho, for his men had all deserted him and scattered. They captured the king and took him to the king of Babylon at Riblah in the land of Hamath. There the king of Babylon pronounced judgment upon Zedekiah. The king of Babylon made Zedekiah watch as he slaughtered his sons. He also slaughtered all the officials of Judah at Riblah. Then he gouged out Zedekiah's eyes and bound him in bronze chains, and the king of Babylon led him away to Babylon. Zedekiah remained there in prison until the day of his death.

On August 17 of that year, which was the nineteenth year of King Nebuchadnezzar's reign, Nebuzaradan, the captain of the guard and an official of the Babylonian king, arrived in Jerusalem. He burned down the Temple of the LORD, the royal palace, and all the houses of Jerusalem.

He destroyed all the important buildings in the city. Then he supervised the entire Babylonian army as they tore down the walls of Jerusalem on every side. Then Nebuzaradan, the captain of the guard, took as exiles some of the poorest of the people, the rest of the people who remained in the city, the defectors who had declared their allegiance to the king of Babylon, and the rest of the craftsmen. But Nebuzaradan allowed some of the poorest people to stay behind to care for the vineyards and fields.

The Babylonians broke up the bronze pillars in front of the LORD's Temple, the bronze water carts, and the great bronze basin called the Sea, and they carried all the bronze away to Babylon. They also took all the ash buckets, shovels, lamp snuffers, basins, dishes, and all the other bronze articles used for making sacrifices at the Temple. The captain of the guard also took the small bowls, incense burners, basins, pots, lampstands, ladles, bowls used for liquid offerings, and all the other articles made of pure gold or silver.

The weight of the bronze from the two pillars, the Sea with the twelve bronze oxen beneath it, and the water carts was too great to be measured. These things had been made for the LORD's Temple in the days of King Solomon. Each of the pillars was 27 feet tall and 18 feet in circumference. They were hollow, with walls 3 inches thick. The bronze capital on top of each pillar was 7½ feet high and was decorated with a network of bronze pomegranates all the way around. There were 96 pomegranates on the sides, and a total of 100 pomegranates on the network around the top.

Nebuzaradan, the captain of the guard, took with him as prisoners Seraiah the high priest, Zephaniah the priest of the second rank, and the three chief gatekeepers. And from among the people still hiding in the city, he took an officer who had been in charge of the Judean army; seven of the king's personal advisers; the army commander's chief secretary, who was in charge of recruitment; and sixty other citizens. Nebuzaradan, the captain of the guard, took them all to the king of Babylon at Riblah. And there at Riblah, in the land of Hamath, the king of Babylon had them all put to death. So the people of Judah were sent into exile from their land.

The number of captives taken to Babylon in the seventh year of Nebuchadnezzar's reign was 3,023. Then in Nebuchadnezzar's eighteenth year he took 832 more. In Nebuchadnezzar's twenty-third year he sent Nebuzaradan, the captain of the guard, who took 745 more—a total of 4,600 captives in all.

In the thirty-seventh year of the exile of King Jehoiachin of Judah, Evil-merodach ascended to the Babylonian throne. He was kind to Jehoiachin and released him from prison on March 31 of that year. He spoke kindly to Jehoiachin and gave him a higher place than all the other exiled kings in Babylon. He supplied Jehoiachin with new clothes to replace his prison garb and allowed him to dine in the king's presence for the rest of his life. So the Babylonian king gave him a regular food allowance as long as he lived. This continued until the day of his death.

THE PEOPLE OF EDOM were neighbors to the people of Judah. They lived in the rocky, mountainous region south of the Dead Sea, a place scarcely accessible to attacking armies. This made the Edomites complacent about their safety and security, confident and proud that no one could harm them.

When the Babylonians besieged Jerusalem, the Edomites joined in the attack. After the city fell, they pillaged it. They even captured people from Judah who were fleeing and either killed them or sold them into slavery.

Two of the LORD's prophets warned the Edomites in very similar terms that because they had done this, they also would be conquered and devastated. One of these prophets was Jeremiah, who included a denunciation of Edom in his oracles against the nations. The other prophet was a man named Obadiah. We know nothing about Obadiah other than the fact that he, too, delivered an oracle against Edom.

Speaking for the LORD, Obadiah told the Edomites, "You have been deceived by your own pride because you live in a rock fortress and make your home high in the mountains. 'Who can ever reach us way up here?' you ask boastfully. But even if you soar as high as eagles and build your nest among the stars, I will bring you crashing down."

And that is just what happened. After accepting the Edomites' help in their campaign against Jerusalem, the Babylonians turned against them and devastated them so thoroughly that they ceased to be a nation. And so Obadiah's words were fulfilled: "If thieves came at night and robbed you . . . they would not take everything. Those who harvest grapes always leave a few for the poor. But your enemies will wipe you out completely!"

The first half of Obadiah's oracle against Edom is very similar to the first half of Jeremiah's, though the material in Obadiah is longer and in a slightly different order. Toward the end, the focus of the oracle shifts to Jerusalem and a promise about its future. The exiles of Israel will return and reclaim their ancient inheritance. God himself will come to rule from Mount Zion.

This brief book sends a clear and emphatic message, presenting us with the theological core of Israel's prophetic message: The LORD is sovereign over all nations, and he will surely act to restore justice and to protect and renew his people.

OBADIAH

✛

This is the vision that the Sovereign LORD revealed to Obadiah concerning the land of Edom.

We have heard a message from the LORD
    that an ambassador was sent to the nations to say,
"Get ready, everyone!
    Let's assemble our armies and attack Edom!"

The LORD says to Edom,
"I will cut you down to size among the nations;
    you will be greatly despised.
You have been deceived by your own pride
    because you live in a rock fortress
    and make your home high in the mountains.
'Who can ever reach us way up here?'
    you ask boastfully.
But even if you soar as high as eagles
    and build your nest among the stars,
I will bring you crashing down,"
    says the LORD.

"If thieves came at night and robbed you
    (what a disaster awaits you!),
    they would not take everything.
Those who harvest grapes
    always leave a few for the poor.
    But your enemies will wipe you out completely!
Every nook and cranny of Edom
    will be searched and looted.
    Every treasure will be found and taken.

"All your allies will turn against you.
    They will help to chase you from your land.

They will promise you peace
  while plotting to deceive and destroy you.
Your trusted friends will set traps for you,
  and you won't even know about it.
At that time not a single wise person
  will be left in the whole land of Edom,"
  says the LORD.
"For on the mountains of Edom
  I will destroy everyone who has understanding.
The mightiest warriors of Teman
  will be terrified,
and everyone on the mountains of Edom
  will be cut down in the slaughter.

"Because of the violence you did
  to your close relatives in Israel,
you will be filled with shame
  and destroyed forever.
When they were invaded,
  you stood aloof, refusing to help them.
Foreign invaders carried off their wealth
  and cast lots to divide up Jerusalem,
  but you acted like one of Israel's enemies.

"You should not have gloated
  when they exiled your relatives to distant lands.
You should not have rejoiced
  when the people of Judah suffered such misfortune.
You should not have spoken arrogantly
  in that terrible time of trouble.
You should not have plundered the land of Israel
  when they were suffering such calamity.
You should not have gloated over their destruction
  when they were suffering such calamity.
You should not have seized their wealth
  when they were suffering such calamity.
You should not have stood at the crossroads,
  killing those who tried to escape.
You should not have captured the survivors
  and handed them over in their terrible time of trouble.

"The day is near when I, the LORD,
  will judge all godless nations!

As you have done to Israel,
  so it will be done to you.
All your evil deeds
  will fall back on your own heads.
Just as you swallowed up my people
  on my holy mountain,
so you and the surrounding nations
  will swallow the punishment I pour out on you.
Yes, all you nations will drink and stagger
  and disappear from history.

"But Jerusalem will become a refuge for those who escape;
  it will be a holy place.
And the people of Israel will come back
  to reclaim their inheritance.
The people of Israel will be a raging fire,
  and Edom a field of dry stubble.
The descendants of Joseph will be a flame
  roaring across the field, devouring everything.
There will be no survivors in Edom.
  I, the LORD, have spoken!

"Then my people living in the Negev
  will occupy the mountains of Edom.
Those living in the foothills of Judah
  will possess the Philistine plains
  and take over the fields of Ephraim and Samaria.
And the people of Benjamin
  will occupy the land of Gilead.
The exiles of Israel will return to their land
  and occupy the Phoenician coast as far north as Zarephath.
The captives from Jerusalem exiled in the north
  will return home and resettle the towns of the Negev.
Those who have been rescued will go up to Mount Zion in Jerusalem
  to rule over the mountains of Edom.
And the LORD himself will be king!"

THE PROPHECIES OF EZEKIEL, like those of Jeremiah, revolve around the Babylonian threat to Judah, which culminated in the destruction of Jerusalem. But unlike Jeremiah, Ezekiel was not in Jerusalem. Instead, as he tells us, he was in the land of Babylonia, living in a "colony of Judean exiles in Tel-abib, beside the Kebar River."

In 597 BC, the Babylonians forced Judah to become a vassal state. They took King Jehoiachin and many of the nation's elites into exile as hostages. Ezekiel was from a priestly family, so he was among these earlier exiles. Because he saw the world through the eyes of a priest associated with the Temple, he was concerned with issues of purity and holiness and especially with God's presence or absence.

The people of Judah wrongly assumed that the exiles wouldn't stay in Babylon for very long. So God sent messages to the residents of Judah and Jerusalem through Jeremiah and to the exiles in Babylonia through Ezekiel. The messages of both prophets make it clear that this time of judgment is the one God had long promised was coming.

Ezekiel confirms that God was going to continue to judge Judah for its idolatry and oppression of the powerless. These practices were corrupting the kingdom from top to bottom: Everyone—from the political and religious leaders to the common people—was ignoring God's instructions. Ezekiel is particularly emphatic about the failure of Israel's leaders to guide the people in keeping God's covenant. As a result, Israel is unclean, and God is going to remove his presence from the land.

God used some extraordinary means to demonstrate that he was speaking through Ezekiel. For example, just before the destruction of Jerusalem, he took away Ezekiel's ability to speak except on occasions when he received a message from God. But then, just before news of the city's destruction reached the exiles, Ezekiel was able to speak freely once again.

Ezekiel sometimes engaged in symbolic actions to illustrate what his prophecies meant. For example, God told him to dig a hole through a wall and go through it with a pack, showing how King Zedekiah would soon try to flee from Jerusalem. God also gave Ezekiel remarkable powers of literary expression. His prophecies contain parables—stories with a symbolic meaning—and memorable poetic images such as a vine, an eagle, a lion, and two sisters.

Despite all this, the Judeans in exile wouldn't listen to Ezekiel any more than those in Jerusalem listened to Jeremiah. But the time had come for all the prophecies against Judah to be fulfilled. One of Ezekiel's most desolate visions was of the LORD's glory and presence leaving the Temple. This provides further confirmation of what Jeremiah was saying: No longer could anyone promise safety in Jerusalem simply because the LORD's Temple was there. God had left, and there was no more protection against the invasion. This judgment was disorienting for God's people. But it was a necessary first step toward the bigger goal: the reorientation of the people to a new future with God.

Overall, the book of Ezekiel follows the same threefold pattern as the earlier and much shorter book of Zephaniah: oracles of judgment against Israel (pp. 319-355), oracles of judgment against other nations (pp. 355-371), and promises of Israel's restoration (pp. 371-396).

Again like Jeremiah, Ezekiel was granted visions of the restoration of God's people. His visions of Israel's coming renewal are some of the most memorable in the prophets. Since Israel's shepherds (leaders) have destroyed their own people, God himself will come and be their good Shepherd—leading, protecting, and feeding them. The LORD also makes the amazing promise that he will transform his people from the inside out: "I will give you a new heart, and I will put a new spirit in you. . . . I will put my Spirit in you so that you will follow my decrees and be careful to obey my regulations."

While in exile, Israel is like a valley of old, dry bones. But the creator of life will revive his people and bring them back home. The book closes with a lengthy vision of a new Temple in a restored Jerusalem. A river will flow from this Temple, like the rivers in the Garden of Eden, and life will flourish wherever it goes. When all things—leaders, people, hearts, and land—are healed, then God himself will once again come to live there among them.

EZEKIEL

———— ✦ ————

On July 31 of my thirtieth year, while I was with the Judean exiles beside the Kebar River in Babylon, the heavens were opened and I saw visions of God. This happened during the fifth year of King Jehoiachin's captivity. (The LORD gave this message to Ezekiel son of Buzi, a priest, beside the Kebar River in the land of the Babylonians, and he felt the hand of the LORD take hold of him.)

As I looked, I saw a great storm coming from the north, driving before it a huge cloud that flashed with lightning and shone with brilliant light. There was fire inside the cloud, and in the middle of the fire glowed something like gleaming amber. From the center of the cloud came four living beings that looked human, except that each had four faces and four wings. Their legs were straight, and their feet had hooves like those of a calf and shone like burnished bronze. Under each of their four wings I could see human hands. So each of the four beings had four faces and four wings. The wings of each living being touched the wings of the beings beside it. Each one moved straight forward in any direction without turning around.

Each had a human face in the front, the face of a lion on the right side, the face of an ox on the left side, and the face of an eagle at the back. Each had two pairs of outstretched wings—one pair stretched out to touch the wings of the living beings on either side of it, and the other pair covered its body. They went in whatever direction the spirit chose, and they moved straight forward in any direction without turning around.

The living beings looked like bright coals of fire or brilliant torches, and lightning seemed to flash back and forth among them. And the living beings darted to and fro like flashes of lightning.

As I looked at these beings, I saw four wheels touching the ground beside them, one wheel belonging to each. The wheels sparkled as if made of beryl. All four wheels looked alike and were made the same; each wheel had a second wheel turning crosswise within it. The beings could move in any of the four directions they faced, without turning as they moved. The rims of the four wheels were tall and frightening, and they were covered with eyes all around.

When the living beings moved, the wheels moved with them. When they flew upward, the wheels went up, too. The spirit of the living beings was in the wheels. So wherever the spirit went, the wheels and the living beings also went. When the beings moved, the wheels moved. When the beings stopped, the wheels stopped. When the beings flew upward, the wheels rose up, for the spirit of the living beings was in the wheels.

Spread out above them was a surface like the sky, glittering like crystal. Beneath this surface the wings of each living being stretched out to touch the others' wings, and each had two wings covering its body. As they flew, their wings sounded to me like waves crashing against the shore or like the voice of the Almighty or like the shouting of a mighty army. When they stopped, they let down their wings. As they stood with wings lowered, a voice spoke from beyond the crystal surface above them.

Above this surface was something that looked like a throne made of blue lapis lazuli. And on this throne high above was a figure whose appearance resembled a man. From what appeared to be his waist up, he looked like gleaming amber, flickering like a fire. And from his waist down, he looked like a burning flame, shining with splendor. All around him was a glowing halo, like a rainbow shining in the clouds on a rainy day. This is what the glory of the LORD looked like to me. When I saw it, I fell face down on the ground, and I heard someone's voice speaking to me.

"Stand up, son of man," said the voice. "I want to speak with you." The Spirit came into me as he spoke, and he set me on my feet. I listened carefully to his words. "Son of man," he said, "I am sending you to the nation of Israel, a rebellious nation that has rebelled against me. They and their ancestors have been rebelling against me to this very day. They are a stubborn and hard-hearted people. But I am sending you to say to them, 'This is what the Sovereign LORD says!' And whether they listen or refuse to listen—for remember, they are rebels—at least they will know they have had a prophet among them.

"Son of man, do not fear them or their words. Don't be afraid even though their threats surround you like nettles and briers and stinging scorpions. Do not be dismayed by their dark scowls, even though they are rebels. You must give them my messages whether they listen or not. But they won't listen, for they are completely rebellious! Son of man, listen to what I say to you. Do not join them in their rebellion. Open your mouth, and eat what I give you."

Then I looked and saw a hand reaching out to me. It held a scroll, which he unrolled. And I saw that both sides were covered with funeral songs, words of sorrow, and pronouncements of doom.

The voice said to me, "Son of man, eat what I am giving you—eat this scroll! Then go and give its message to the people of Israel." So I opened my mouth, and he fed me the scroll. "Fill your stomach with this," he said. And when I ate it, it tasted as sweet as honey in my mouth.

Then he said, "Son of man, go to the people of Israel and give them my messages. I am not sending you to a foreign people whose language you cannot understand. No, I am not sending you to people with strange and difficult speech. If I did, they would listen! But the people of Israel won't listen to you any more than they listen to me! For the whole lot of them are hard-hearted and stubborn. But look, I have made you as obstinate and hard-hearted as they are. I have made your forehead as hard as the hardest rock! So don't be afraid of them or fear their angry looks, even though they are rebels."

Then he added, "Son of man, let all my words sink deep into your own heart first. Listen to them carefully for yourself. Then go to your people in exile and say to them, 'This is what the Sovereign LORD says!' Do this whether they listen to you or not."

Then the Spirit lifted me up, and I heard a loud rumbling sound behind me. (May the glory of the LORD be praised in his place!) It was the sound of the wings of the living beings as they brushed against each other and the rumbling of their wheels beneath them.

The Spirit lifted me up and took me away. I went in bitterness and turmoil, but the LORD's hold on me was strong. Then I came to the colony of Judean exiles in Tel-abib, beside the Kebar River. I was overwhelmed and sat among them for seven days.

+

After seven days the LORD gave me a message. He said, "Son of man, I have appointed you as a watchman for Israel. Whenever you receive a message from me, warn people immediately. If I warn the wicked, saying, 'You are under the penalty of death,' but you fail to deliver the warning, they will die in their sins. And I will hold you responsible for their deaths. If you warn them and they refuse to repent and keep on sinning, they will die in their sins. But you will have saved yourself because you obeyed me.

"If righteous people turn away from their righteous behavior and ignore the obstacles I put in their way, they will die. And if you do not warn them, they will die in their sins. None of their righteous acts will be remembered, and I will hold you responsible for their deaths. But if you warn righteous people not to sin and they listen to you and do not sin, they will live, and you will have saved yourself, too."

Then the LORD took hold of me and said, "Get up and go out into the valley, and I will speak to you there." So I got up and went, and there I saw the glory of the LORD, just as I had seen in my first vision by the Kebar River. And I fell face down on the ground.

Then the Spirit came into me and set me on my feet. He spoke to me and said, "Go to your house and shut yourself in. There, son of man, you will be tied with ropes so you cannot go out among the people. And I will make your tongue stick to the roof of your mouth so that you will be speechless and unable to rebuke them, for they are rebels. But when I give you a message, I will loosen your tongue and let you speak. Then you will say to them, 'This is what the Sovereign LORD says!' Those who choose to listen will listen, but those who refuse will refuse, for they are rebels.

"And now, son of man, take a large clay brick and set it down in front of you. Then draw a map of the city of Jerusalem on it. Show the city under siege. Build a wall around it so no one can escape. Set up the enemy camp, and surround the city with siege ramps and battering rams. Then take an iron griddle and place it between you and the city. Turn toward the city and demonstrate how harsh the siege will be against Jerusalem. This will be a warning to the people of Israel.

"Now lie on your left side and place the sins of Israel on yourself. You are to bear their sins for the number of days you lie there on your side. I am requiring you to bear Israel's sins for 390 days—one day for each year of their sin. After that, turn over and lie on your right side for 40 days—one day for each year of Judah's sin.

"Meanwhile, keep staring at the siege of Jerusalem. Lie there with your arm bared and prophesy her destruction. I will tie you up with ropes so you won't be able to turn from side to side until the days of your siege have been completed.

"Now go and get some wheat, barley, beans, lentils, millet, and emmer wheat, and mix them together in a storage jar. Use them to make bread for yourself during the 390 days you will be lying on your side. Ration this out to yourself, eight ounces of food for each day, and eat it at set times. Then measure out a jar of water for each day, and drink it at set times. Prepare and eat this food as you would barley cakes. While all the people are watching, bake it over a fire using dried human dung as fuel and then eat the bread." Then the LORD said, "This is how Israel will eat defiled bread in the Gentile lands to which I will banish them!"

Then I said, "O Sovereign LORD, must I be defiled by using human dung? For I have never been defiled before. From the time I was a child until now I have never eaten any animal that died of sickness or was killed by other animals. I have never eaten any meat forbidden by the law."

"All right," the LORD said. "You may bake your bread with cow dung instead of human dung." Then he told me, "Son of man, I will make food very scarce in Jerusalem. It will be weighed out with great care and eaten fearfully. The water will be rationed out drop by drop, and the people will drink it with dismay. Lacking food and water, people will look at one another in terror, and they will waste away under their punishment.

"Son of man, take a sharp sword and use it as a razor to shave your head and beard. Use a scale to weigh the hair into three equal parts. Place a third of it at the center of your map of Jerusalem. After acting out the siege, burn it there. Scatter another third across your map and chop it with a sword. Scatter the last third to the wind, for I will scatter my people with the sword. Keep just a bit of the hair and tie it up in your robe. Then take some of these hairs out and throw them into the fire, burning them up. A fire will then spread from this remnant and destroy all of Israel.

"This is what the Sovereign Lord says: This is an illustration of what will happen to Jerusalem. I placed her at the center of the nations, but she has rebelled against my regulations and decrees and has been even more wicked than the surrounding nations. She has refused to obey the regulations and decrees I gave her to follow.

"Therefore, this is what the Sovereign Lord says: You people have behaved worse than your neighbors and have refused to obey my decrees and regulations. You have not even lived up to the standards of the nations around you. Therefore, I myself, the Sovereign Lord, am now your enemy. I will punish you publicly while all the nations watch. Because of your detestable idols, I will punish you like I have never punished anyone before or ever will again. Parents will eat their own children, and children will eat their parents. I will punish you and scatter to the winds the few who survive.

"As surely as I live, says the Sovereign Lord, I will cut you off completely. I will show you no pity at all because you have defiled my Temple with your vile images and detestable sins. A third of your people will die in the city from disease and famine. A third of them will be slaughtered by the enemy outside the city walls. And I will scatter a third to the winds, chasing them with my sword. Then at last my anger will be spent, and I will be satisfied. And when my fury against them has subsided, all Israel will know that I, the Lord, have spoken to them in my jealous anger.

"So I will turn you into a ruin, a mockery in the eyes of the surrounding nations and to all who pass by. You will become an object of mockery and taunting and horror. You will be a warning to all the nations around you. They will see what happens when the Lord punishes a nation in anger and rebukes it, says the Lord.

"I will shower you with the deadly arrows of famine to destroy you. The famine will become more and more severe until every crumb of food is gone. And along with the famine, wild animals will attack you and rob you of your children. Disease and war will stalk your land, and I will bring the sword of the enemy against you. I, the LORD, have spoken!"

✦

Again a message came to me from the LORD: "Son of man, turn and face the mountains of Israel and prophesy against them. Proclaim this message from the Sovereign LORD against the mountains of Israel. This is what the Sovereign LORD says to the mountains and hills and to the ravines and valleys: I am about to bring war upon you, and I will smash your pagan shrines. All your altars will be demolished, and your places of worship will be destroyed. I will kill your people in front of your idols. I will lay your corpses in front of your idols and scatter your bones around your altars. Wherever you live there will be desolation, and I will destroy your pagan shrines. Your altars will be demolished, your idols will be smashed, your places of worship will be torn down, and all the religious objects you have made will be destroyed. The place will be littered with corpses, and you will know that I alone am the LORD.

"But I will let a few of my people escape destruction, and they will be scattered among the nations of the world. Then when they are exiled among the nations, they will remember me. They will recognize how hurt I am by their unfaithful hearts and lustful eyes that long for their idols. Then at last they will hate themselves for all their detestable sins. They will know that I alone am the LORD and that I was serious when I said I would bring this calamity on them.

"This is what the Sovereign LORD says: Clap your hands in horror, and stamp your feet. Cry out because of all the detestable sins the people of Israel have committed. Now they are going to die from war and famine and disease. Disease will strike down those who are far away in exile. War will destroy those who are nearby. And anyone who survives will be killed by famine. So at last I will spend my fury on them. They will know that I am the LORD when their dead lie scattered among their idols and altars on every hill and mountain and under every green tree and every great shade tree—the places where they offered sacrifices to their idols. I will crush them and make their cities desolate from the wilderness in the south to Riblah in the north. Then they will know that I am the LORD."

✦

Then this message came to me from the LORD: "Son of man, this is what the Sovereign LORD says to Israel:

"The end is here!
> Wherever you look—
east, west, north, or south—
> your land is finished.
No hope remains,
> for I will unleash my anger against you.
I will call you to account
> for all your detestable sins.
I will turn my eyes away and show no pity.
> I will repay you for all your detestable sins.
Then you will know that I am the LORD.

"This is what the Sovereign LORD says:
Disaster after disaster
> is coming your way!
The end has come.
> It has finally arrived.
> Your final doom is waiting!
O people of Israel, the day of your destruction is dawning.
> The time has come; the day of trouble is near.
Shouts of anguish will be heard on the mountains,
> not shouts of joy.
Soon I will pour out my fury on you
> and unleash my anger against you.
I will call you to account
> for all your detestable sins.
I will turn my eyes away and show no pity.
> I will repay you for all your detestable sins.
Then you will know that it is I, the LORD,
> who is striking the blow.

"The day of judgment is here;
> your destruction awaits!
The people's wickedness and pride
> have blossomed to full flower.
Their violence has grown into a rod
> that will beat them for their wickedness.
None of these proud and wicked people will survive.
> All their wealth and prestige will be swept away.
Yes, the time has come;
> the day is here!
Buyers should not rejoice over bargains,
> nor sellers grieve over losses,

for all of them will fall
   under my terrible anger.
Even if the merchants survive,
   they will never return to their business.
For what God has said applies to everyone—
   it will not be changed!
Not one person whose life is twisted by sin
   will ever recover.

"The trumpet calls Israel's army to mobilize,
   but no one listens,
   for my fury is against them all.
There is war outside the city
   and disease and famine within.
Those outside the city walls
   will be killed by enemy swords.
Those inside the city
   will die of famine and disease.
The survivors who escape to the mountains
   will moan like doves, weeping for their sins.
Their hands will hang limp,
   their knees will be weak as water.
They will dress themselves in burlap;
   horror and shame will cover them.
They will shave their heads
   in sorrow and remorse.

"They will throw their money in the streets,
   tossing it out like worthless trash.
Their silver and gold won't save them
   on that day of the LORD's anger.
It will neither satisfy nor feed them,
   for their greed can only trip them up.
They were proud of their beautiful jewelry
   and used it to make detestable idols and vile images.
Therefore, I will make all their wealth
   disgusting to them.
I will give it as plunder to foreigners,
   to the most wicked of nations,
   and they will defile it.
I will turn my eyes from them
   as these robbers invade and defile my treasured land.

"Prepare chains for my people,
   for the land is bloodied by terrible crimes.
   Jerusalem is filled with violence.
I will bring the most ruthless of nations
   to occupy their homes.
I will break down their proud fortresses
   and defile their sanctuaries.
Terror and trembling will overcome my people.
   They will look for peace but not find it.
Calamity will follow calamity;
   rumor will follow rumor.
They will look in vain
   for a vision from the prophets.
They will receive no teaching from the priests
   and no counsel from the leaders.
The king and the prince will stand helpless,
   weeping in despair,
and the people's hands
   will tremble with fear.
I will bring on them
   the evil they have done to others,
and they will receive the punishment
   they so richly deserve.
Then they will know that I am the LORD."

+

Then on September 17, during the sixth year of King Jehoiachin's captivity, while the leaders of Judah were in my home, the Sovereign LORD took hold of me. I saw a figure that appeared to be a man. From what appeared to be his waist down, he looked like a burning flame. From the waist up he looked like gleaming amber. He reached out what seemed to be a hand and took me by the hair. Then the Spirit lifted me up into the sky and transported me to Jerusalem in a vision from God. I was taken to the north gate of the inner courtyard of the Temple, where there is a large idol that has made the LORD very jealous. Suddenly, the glory of the God of Israel was there, just as I had seen it before in the valley.

Then the LORD said to me, "Son of man, look toward the north." So I looked, and there to the north, beside the entrance to the gate near the altar, stood the idol that had made the LORD so jealous.

"Son of man," he said, "do you see what they are doing? Do you see the detestable sins the people of Israel are committing to drive me from my

Temple? But come, and you will see even more detestable sins than these!" Then he brought me to the door of the Temple courtyard, where I could see a hole in the wall. He said to me, "Now, son of man, dig into the wall." So I dug into the wall and found a hidden doorway.

"Go in," he said, "and see the wicked and detestable sins they are committing in there!" So I went in and saw the walls covered with engravings of all kinds of crawling animals and detestable creatures. I also saw the various idols worshiped by the people of Israel. Seventy leaders of Israel were standing there with Jaazaniah son of Shaphan in the center. Each of them held an incense burner, from which a cloud of incense rose above their heads.

Then the LORD said to me, "Son of man, have you seen what the leaders of Israel are doing with their idols in dark rooms? They are saying, 'The LORD doesn't see us; he has deserted our land!'" Then the LORD added, "Come, and I will show you even more detestable sins than these!"

He brought me to the north gate of the LORD's Temple, and some women were sitting there, weeping for the god Tammuz. "Have you seen this?" he asked. "But I will show you even more detestable sins than these!"

Then he brought me into the inner courtyard of the LORD's Temple. At the entrance to the sanctuary, between the entry room and the bronze altar, there were about twenty-five men with their backs to the sanctuary of the LORD. They were facing east, bowing low to the ground, worshiping the sun!

"Have you seen this, son of man?" he asked. "Is it nothing to the people of Judah that they commit these detestable sins, leading the whole nation into violence, thumbing their noses at me, and provoking my anger? Therefore, I will respond in fury. I will neither pity nor spare them. And though they cry for mercy, I will not listen."

Then the LORD thundered, "Bring on the men appointed to punish the city! Tell them to bring their weapons with them!" Six men soon appeared from the upper gate that faces north, each carrying a deadly weapon in his hand. With them was a man dressed in linen, who carried a writer's case at his side. They all went into the Temple courtyard and stood beside the bronze altar.

Then the glory of the God of Israel rose up from between the cherubim, where it had rested, and moved to the entrance of the Temple. And the LORD called to the man dressed in linen who was carrying the writer's case. He said to him, "Walk through the streets of Jerusalem and put a mark on the foreheads of all who weep and sigh because of the detestable sins being committed in their city."

Then I heard the LORD say to the other men, "Follow him through the city and kill everyone whose forehead is not marked. Show no mercy; have no pity! Kill them all—old and young, girls and women and little children. But do not touch anyone with the mark. Begin right here at the Temple." So they began by killing the seventy leaders.

"Defile the Temple!" the LORD commanded. "Fill its courtyards with corpses. Go!" So they went and began killing throughout the city.

While they were out killing, I was all alone. I fell face down on the ground and cried out, "O Sovereign LORD! Will your fury against Jerusalem wipe out everyone left in Israel?"

Then he said to me, "The sins of the people of Israel and Judah are very, very great. The entire land is full of murder; the city is filled with injustice. They are saying, 'The LORD doesn't see it! The LORD has abandoned the land!' So I will not spare them or have any pity on them. I will fully repay them for all they have done."

Then the man in linen clothing, who carried the writer's case, reported back and said, "I have done as you commanded."

In my vision I saw what appeared to be a throne of blue lapis lazuli above the crystal surface over the heads of the cherubim. Then the LORD spoke to the man in linen clothing and said, "Go between the whirling wheels beneath the cherubim, and take a handful of burning coals and scatter them over the city." He did this as I watched.

The cherubim were standing at the south end of the Temple when the man went in, and the cloud of glory filled the inner courtyard. Then the glory of the LORD rose up from above the cherubim and went over to the entrance of the Temple. The Temple was filled with this cloud of glory, and the courtyard glowed brightly with the glory of the LORD. The moving wings of the cherubim sounded like the voice of God Almighty and could be heard even in the outer courtyard.

The LORD said to the man in linen clothing, "Go between the cherubim and take some burning coals from between the wheels." So the man went in and stood beside one of the wheels. Then one of the cherubim reached out his hand and took some live coals from the fire burning among them. He put the coals into the hands of the man in linen clothing, and the man took them and went out. (All the cherubim had what looked like human hands under their wings.)

I looked, and each of the four cherubim had a wheel beside him, and the wheels sparkled like beryl. All four wheels looked alike and were made the same; each wheel had a second wheel turning crosswise within it. The cherubim could move in any of the four directions they faced, without turning as they moved. They went straight in the direction they faced, never turning aside. Both the cherubim and the wheels were covered with eyes. The cherubim had eyes all over their bodies, including their hands, their backs, and their wings. I heard someone refer to the wheels as "the whirling wheels." Each of the four cherubim had four faces: the first was the face of an ox, the second was a human face, the third was the face of a lion, and the fourth was the face of an eagle.

Then the cherubim rose upward. These were the same living beings I had seen beside the Kebar River. When the cherubim moved, the wheels moved with them. When they lifted their wings to fly, the wheels stayed beside them. When the cherubim stopped, the wheels stopped. When they flew upward, the wheels rose up, for the spirit of the living beings was in the wheels.

Then the glory of the LORD moved out from the entrance of the Temple and hovered above the cherubim. And as I watched, the cherubim flew with their wheels to the east gate of the LORD's Temple. And the glory of the God of Israel hovered above them.

These were the same living beings I had seen beneath the God of Israel when I was by the Kebar River. I knew they were cherubim, for each had four faces and four wings and what looked like human hands under their wings. And their faces were just like the faces of the beings I had seen at the Kebar, and they traveled straight ahead, just as the others had.

Then the Spirit lifted me and brought me to the east gateway of the LORD's Temple, where I saw twenty-five prominent men of the city. Among them were Jaazaniah son of Azzur and Pelatiah son of Benaiah, who were leaders among the people.

The Spirit said to me, "Son of man, these are the men who are planning evil and giving wicked counsel in this city. They say to the people, 'Is it not a good time to build houses? This city is like an iron pot. We are safe inside it like meat in a pot.' Therefore, son of man, prophesy against them loudly and clearly."

Then the Spirit of the LORD came upon me, and he told me to say, "This is what the LORD says to the people of Israel: I know what you are saying, for I know every thought that comes into your minds. You have murdered many in this city and filled its streets with the dead.

"Therefore, this is what the Sovereign LORD says: This city is an iron pot all right, but the pieces of meat are the victims of your injustice. As for you, I will soon drag you from this pot. I will bring on you the sword of war you so greatly fear, says the Sovereign LORD. I will drive you out of Jerusalem and hand you over to foreigners, who will carry out my judgments against you. You will be slaughtered all the way to the borders of Israel. I will execute judgment on you, and you will know that I am the LORD. No, this city will not be an iron pot for you, and you will not be like meat safe inside it. I will judge you even to the borders of Israel, and you will know that I am the LORD. For you have refused to obey my decrees and regulations; instead, you have copied the standards of the nations around you."

While I was still prophesying, Pelatiah son of Benaiah suddenly died. Then I fell face down on the ground and cried out, "O Sovereign LORD, are you going to kill everyone in Israel?"

Then this message came to me from the LORD: "Son of man, the people still left in Jerusalem are talking about you and your relatives and all the people of Israel who are in exile. They are saying, 'Those people are far away from the LORD, so now he has given their land to us!'

"Therefore, tell the exiles, 'This is what the Sovereign LORD says: Although I have scattered you in the countries of the world, I will be a sanctuary to you during your time in exile. I, the Sovereign LORD, will gather you back from the nations where you have been scattered, and I will give you the land of Israel once again.'

"When the people return to their homeland, they will remove every trace of their vile images and detestable idols. And I will give them singleness of heart and put a new spirit within them. I will take away their stony, stubborn heart and give them a tender, responsive heart, so they will obey my decrees and regulations. Then they will truly be my people, and I will be their God. But as for those who long for vile images and detestable idols, I will repay them fully for their sins. I, the Sovereign LORD, have spoken!"

Then the cherubim lifted their wings and rose into the air with their wheels beside them, and the glory of the God of Israel hovered above them. Then the glory of the LORD went up from the city and stopped above the mountain to the east.

Afterward the Spirit of God carried me back again to Babylonia, to the people in exile there. And so ended the vision of my visit to Jerusalem. And I told the exiles everything the LORD had shown me.

+

Again a message came to me from the LORD: "Son of man, you live among rebels who have eyes but refuse to see. They have ears but refuse to hear. For they are a rebellious people.

"So now, son of man, pretend you are being sent into exile. Pack the few items an exile could carry, and leave your home to go somewhere else. Do this right in front of the people so they can see you. For perhaps they will pay attention to this, even though they are such rebels. Bring your baggage outside during the day so they can watch you. Then in the evening, as they are watching, leave your house as captives do when they begin a long march to distant lands. Dig a hole through the wall while they are watching and go out through it. As they watch, lift your pack to your shoulders and walk away into the night. Cover your face so you cannot see the land you are leaving. For I have made you a sign for the people of Israel."

So I did as I was told. In broad daylight I brought my pack outside, filled with the things I might carry into exile. Then in the evening while the people looked on, I dug through the wall with my hands and went out into the night with my pack on my shoulder.

The next morning this message came to me from the LORD: "Son of man, these rebels, the people of Israel, have asked you what all this means. Say to them, 'This is what the Sovereign LORD says: These actions contain a message for King Zedekiah in Jerusalem and for all the people of Israel.' Explain that your actions are a sign to show what will soon happen to them, for they will be driven into exile as captives.

"Even Zedekiah will leave Jerusalem at night through a hole in the wall, taking only what he can carry with him. He will cover his face, and his eyes will not see the land he is leaving. Then I will throw my net over him and capture him in my snare. I will bring him to Babylon, the land of the Babylonians, though he will never see it, and he will die there. I will scatter his servants and warriors to the four winds and send the sword after them. And when I scatter them among the nations, they will know that I am the LORD. But I will spare a few of them from death by war, famine, or disease, so they can confess all their detestable sins to their captors. Then they will know that I am the LORD."

+

Then this message came to me from the LORD: "Son of man, tremble as you eat your food. Shake with fear as you drink your water. Tell the people, 'This is what the Sovereign LORD says concerning those living in Israel and Jerusalem: They will eat their food with trembling and sip their water in despair, for their land will be stripped bare because of their violence. The cities will be destroyed and the farmland made desolate. Then you will know that I am the LORD.'"

+

Again a message came to me from the LORD: "Son of man, you've heard that proverb they quote in Israel: 'Time passes, and prophecies come to nothing.' Tell the people, 'This is what the Sovereign LORD says: I will put an end to this proverb, and you will soon stop quoting it.' Now give them this new proverb to replace the old one: 'The time has come for every prophecy to be fulfilled!'

"There will be no more false visions and flattering predictions in Israel. For I am the LORD! If I say it, it will happen. There will be no more delays, you rebels of Israel. I will fulfill my threat of destruction in your own lifetime. I, the Sovereign LORD, have spoken!"

✛

Then this message came to me from the LORD: "Son of man, the people of Israel are saying, 'He's talking about the distant future. His visions won't come true for a long, long time.' Therefore, tell them, 'This is what the Sovereign LORD says: No more delay! I will now do everything I have threatened. I, the Sovereign LORD, have spoken!'"

✛

Then this message came to me from the LORD: "Son of man, prophesy against the false prophets of Israel who are inventing their own prophecies. Say to them, 'Listen to the word of the LORD. This is what the Sovereign LORD says: What sorrow awaits the false prophets who are following their own imaginations and have seen nothing at all!'

"O people of Israel, these prophets of yours are like jackals digging in the ruins. They have done nothing to repair the breaks in the walls around the nation. They have not helped it to stand firm in battle on the day of the LORD. Instead, they have told lies and made false predictions. They say, 'This message is from the LORD,' even though the LORD never sent them. And yet they expect him to fulfill their prophecies! Can your visions be anything but false if you claim, 'This message is from the LORD,' when I have not even spoken to you?

"Therefore, this is what the Sovereign LORD says: Because what you say is false and your visions are a lie, I will stand against you, says the Sovereign LORD. I will raise my fist against all the prophets who see false visions and make lying predictions, and they will be banished from the community of Israel. I will blot their names from Israel's record books, and they will never again set foot in their own land. Then you will know that I am the Sovereign LORD.

"This will happen because these evil prophets deceive my people by saying, 'All is peaceful' when there is no peace at all! It's as if the people have built a flimsy wall, and these prophets are trying to reinforce it by covering it with whitewash! Tell these whitewashers that their wall will soon fall down. A heavy rainstorm will undermine it; great hailstones and mighty winds will knock it down. And when the wall falls, the people will cry out, 'What happened to your whitewash?'

"Therefore, this is what the Sovereign LORD says: I will sweep away your whitewashed wall with a storm of indignation, with a great flood of anger, and with hailstones of fury. I will break down your wall right to its foundation, and when it falls, it will crush you. Then you will know that I am the LORD. At last my anger against the wall and those who covered it with whitewash will be satisfied. Then I will say to you: 'The wall and those who whitewashed it are both gone. They were lying prophets who claimed peace would come to Jerusalem when there was no peace. I, the Sovereign LORD, have spoken!'

"Now, son of man, speak out against the women who prophesy from their own imaginations. This is what the Sovereign LORD says: What sorrow awaits you women who are ensnaring the souls of my people, young and old alike. You tie magic charms on their wrists and furnish them with magic veils. Do you think you can trap others without bringing destruction on yourselves? You bring shame on me among my people for a few handfuls of barley or a piece of bread. By lying to my people who love to listen to lies, you kill those who should not die, and you promise life to those who should not live.

"This is what the Sovereign LORD says: I am against all your magic charms, which you use to ensnare my people like birds. I will tear them from your arms, setting my people free like birds set free from a cage. I will tear off the magic veils and save my people from your grasp. They will no longer be your victims. Then you will know that I am the LORD. You have discouraged the righteous with your lies, but I didn't want them to be sad. And you have encouraged the wicked by promising them life, even though they continue in their sins. Because of all this, you will no longer talk of seeing visions that you never saw, nor will you make predictions. For I will rescue my people from your grasp. Then you will know that I am the LORD."

+

Then some of the leaders of Israel visited me, and while they were sitting with me, this message came to me from the LORD: "Son of man, these leaders have set up idols in their hearts. They have embraced things that will make them fall into sin. Why should I listen to their requests? Tell them, 'This is what the Sovereign LORD says: The people of Israel have set up idols in their hearts and fallen into sin, and then they go to a prophet asking for a message. So I, the LORD, will give them the kind of answer their great idolatry deserves. I will do this to capture the minds and hearts of all my people who have turned from me to worship their detestable idols.'

"Therefore, tell the people of Israel, 'This is what the Sovereign LORD says: Repent and turn away from your idols, and stop all your detestable sins. I, the LORD, will answer all those, both Israelites and foreigners, who reject me and set up idols in their hearts and so fall into sin, and who then come to a prophet asking for my advice. I will turn against such people and make a terrible example of them, eliminating them from among my people. Then you will know that I am the LORD.

"'And if a prophet is deceived into giving a message, it is because I, the LORD, have deceived that prophet. I will lift my fist against such prophets and cut them off from the community of Israel. False prophets and those who seek their guidance will all be punished for their sins. In this way, the people of Israel will learn not to stray from me, polluting themselves with sin. They will be my people, and I will be their God. I, the Sovereign LORD, have spoken!'"

+

Then this message came to me from the LORD: "Son of man, suppose the people of a country were to sin against me, and I lifted my fist to crush them, cutting off their food supply and sending a famine to destroy both people and animals. Even if Noah, Daniel, and Job were there, their righteousness would save no one but themselves, says the Sovereign LORD.

"Or suppose I were to send wild animals to invade the country, kill the people, and make the land too desolate and dangerous to pass through. As surely as I live, says the Sovereign LORD, even if those three men were there, they wouldn't be able to save their own sons or daughters. They alone would be saved, but the land would be made desolate.

"Or suppose I were to bring war against the land, and I sent enemy armies to destroy both people and animals. As surely as I live, says the Sovereign LORD, even if those three men were there, they wouldn't be able to save their own sons or daughters. They alone would be saved.

"Or suppose I were to pour out my fury by sending an epidemic into the land, and the disease killed people and animals alike. As surely as I live, says the Sovereign LORD, even if Noah, Daniel, and Job were there, they wouldn't be able to save their own sons or daughters. They alone would be saved by their righteousness.

"Now this is what the Sovereign LORD says: How terrible it will be when all four of these dreadful punishments fall upon Jerusalem—war, famine, wild animals, and disease—destroying all her people and animals. Yet there will be survivors, and they will come here to join you as exiles in Babylon. You will see with your own eyes how wicked they are, and then you will feel better about what I have done to Jerusalem. When you meet them and see their behavior, you will understand that these things are not being done to Israel without cause. I, the Sovereign LORD, have spoken!"

+

Then this message came to me from the LORD: "Son of man, how does a grapevine compare to a tree? Is a vine's wood as useful as the wood of a tree? Can its wood be used for making things, like pegs to hang up pots and pans? No, it can only be used for fuel, and even as fuel, it burns too quickly. Vines are useless both before and after being put into the fire!

"And this is what the Sovereign LORD says: The people of Jerusalem are like grapevines growing among the trees of the forest. Since they are useless, I have thrown them on the fire to be burned. And I will see to it that if they escape from one fire, they will fall into another. When I turn against them, you will know that I am the LORD. And I will make the land desolate because my people have been unfaithful to me. I, the Sovereign LORD, have spoken!"

+

Then another message came to me from the LORD: "Son of man, confront Jerusalem with her detestable sins. Give her this message from the Sovereign LORD: You are nothing but a Canaanite! Your father was an Amorite and your mother a Hittite. On the day you were born, no one cared about you. Your umbilical cord was not cut, and you were never washed, rubbed with salt, and wrapped in cloth. No one had the slightest interest in you; no one pitied you or cared for you. On the day you were born, you were unwanted, dumped in a field and left to die.

"But I came by and saw you there, helplessly kicking about in your own blood. As you lay there, I said, 'Live!' And I helped you to thrive like a plant in the field. You grew up and became a beautiful jewel. Your breasts became full, and your body hair grew, but you were still naked. And when I passed by again, I saw that you were old enough for love. So I wrapped my cloak around you to cover your nakedness and declared my marriage vows. I made a covenant with you, says the Sovereign LORD, and you became mine.

"Then I bathed you and washed off your blood, and I rubbed fragrant oils into your skin. I gave you expensive clothing of fine linen and silk, beautifully embroidered, and sandals made of fine goatskin leather. I gave you lovely jewelry, bracelets, beautiful necklaces, a ring for your nose, earrings for your ears, and a lovely crown for your head. And so you were adorned with gold and silver. Your clothes were made of fine linen and costly fabric and were beautifully embroidered. You ate the finest foods— choice flour, honey, and olive oil—and became more beautiful than ever. You looked like a queen, and so you were! Your fame soon spread throughout the world because of your beauty. I dressed you in my splendor and perfected your beauty, says the Sovereign LORD.

"But you thought your fame and beauty were your own. So you gave yourself as a prostitute to every man who came along. Your beauty was theirs for the asking. You used the lovely things I gave you to make shrines for idols, where you played the prostitute. Unbelievable! How could such a thing ever happen? You took the very jewels and gold and silver ornaments I had given you and made statues of men and worshiped them. This is adultery against me! You used the beautifully embroidered clothes I gave you to dress your idols. Then you used my special oil and my incense to worship them. Imagine it! You set before them as a sacrifice the choice flour, olive oil, and honey I had given you, says the Sovereign LORD.

"Then you took your sons and daughters—the children you had borne to me—and sacrificed them to your gods. Was your prostitution not enough? Must you also slaughter my children by sacrificing them to idols? In all your years of adultery and detestable sin, you have not once remembered the days long ago when you lay naked in a field, kicking about in your own blood.

"What sorrow awaits you, says the Sovereign LORD. In addition to all your other wickedness, you built a pagan shrine and put altars to idols in every town square. On every street corner you defiled your beauty, offering your body to every passerby in an endless stream of prostitution. Then you added lustful Egypt to your lovers, provoking my anger with your increasing promiscuity. That is why I struck you with my fist and reduced your boundaries. I handed you over to your enemies, the Philistines, and even they were shocked by your lewd conduct. You have prostituted yourself with the Assyrians, too. It seems you can never find enough new lovers! And after your prostitution there, you still were not satisfied. You added to your lovers by embracing Babylonia, the land of merchants, but you still weren't satisfied.

"What a sick heart you have, says the Sovereign LORD, to do such things as these, acting like a shameless prostitute. You build your pagan shrines on every street corner and your altars to idols in every square. In fact, you have been worse than a prostitute, so eager for sin that you have not even demanded payment. Yes, you are an adulterous wife who takes in strangers instead of her own husband. Prostitutes charge for their services—but not you! You give gifts to your lovers, bribing them to come and have sex with you. So you are the opposite of other prostitutes. You pay your lovers instead of their paying you!

"Therefore, you prostitute, listen to this message from the LORD! This is what the Sovereign LORD says: Because you have poured out your lust and exposed yourself in prostitution to all your lovers, and because you have worshiped detestable idols, and because you have slaughtered your children as sacrifices to your gods, this is what I am going to do. I will gather together all your allies—the lovers with whom you have sinned, both those you loved and those you hated—and I will strip you naked in front of them so they can stare at you. I will punish you for your murder and adultery. I will cover you with blood in my jealous fury. Then I will give you to these many nations who are your lovers, and they will destroy you. They will knock down your pagan shrines and the altars to your idols. They will strip you and take your beautiful jewels, leaving you stark naked. They will band together in a mob to stone you and cut you up with swords. They will burn your homes and punish you in front of many women. I will stop your prostitution and end your payments to your many lovers.

"Then at last my fury against you will be spent, and my jealous anger will subside. I will be calm and will not be angry with you anymore. But first, because you have not remembered your youth but have angered me by doing all these evil things, I will fully repay you for all of your sins, says the Sovereign Lord. For you have added lewd acts to all your detestable sins. Everyone who makes up proverbs will say of you, 'Like mother, like daughter.' For your mother loathed her husband and her children, and so do you. And you are exactly like your sisters, for they despised their husbands and their children. Truly your mother was a Hittite and your father an Amorite.

"Your older sister was Samaria, who lived with her daughters in the north. Your younger sister was Sodom, who lived with her daughters in the south. But you have not merely sinned as they did. You quickly surpassed them in corruption. As surely as I live, says the Sovereign Lord, Sodom and her daughters were never as wicked as you and your daughters. Sodom's sins were pride, gluttony, and laziness, while the poor and needy suffered outside her door. She was proud and committed detestable sins, so I wiped her out, as you have seen.

"Even Samaria did not commit half your sins. You have done far more detestable things than your sisters ever did. They seem righteous compared to you. Shame on you! Your sins are so terrible that you make your sisters seem righteous, even virtuous.

"But someday I will restore the fortunes of Sodom and Samaria, and I will restore you, too. Then you will be truly ashamed of everything you have done, for your sins make them feel good in comparison. Yes, your sisters, Sodom and Samaria, and all their people will be restored, and at that time you also will be restored. In your proud days you held Sodom in contempt. But now your greater wickedness has been exposed to all the world, and you are the one who is scorned—by Edom and all her neighbors and by Philistia. This is your punishment for all your lewdness and detestable sins, says the Lord.

"Now this is what the Sovereign LORD says: I will give you what you deserve, for you have taken your solemn vows lightly by breaking your covenant. Yet I will remember the covenant I made with you when you were young, and I will establish an everlasting covenant with you. Then you will remember with shame all the evil you have done. I will make your sisters, Samaria and Sodom, to be your daughters, even though they are not part of our covenant. And I will reaffirm my covenant with you, and you will know that I am the LORD. You will remember your sins and cover your mouth in silent shame when I forgive you of all that you have done. I, the Sovereign LORD, have spoken!"

+

Then this message came to me from the LORD: "Son of man, give this riddle, and tell this story to the people of Israel. Give them this message from the Sovereign LORD:

"A great eagle with broad wings and long feathers,
    covered with many-colored plumage,
    came to Lebanon.
He seized the top of a cedar tree
    and plucked off its highest branch.
He carried it away to a city filled with merchants.
    He planted it in a city of traders.
He also took a seedling from the land
    and planted it in fertile soil.
He placed it beside a broad river,
    where it could grow like a willow tree.
It took root there and
    grew into a low, spreading vine.
Its branches turned up toward the eagle,
    and its roots grew down into the ground.
It produced strong branches
    and put out shoots.
But then another great eagle came
    with broad wings and full plumage.
So the vine now sent its roots and branches
    toward him for water,
even though it was already planted in good soil
    and had plenty of water
so it could grow into a splendid vine
    and produce rich leaves and luscious fruit.

"So now the Sovereign LORD asks:
Will this vine grow and prosper?
     No! I will pull it up, roots and all!
I will cut off its fruit
     and let its leaves wither and die.
I will pull it up easily
     without a strong arm or a large army.
But when the vine is transplanted,
     will it thrive?
No, it will wither away
     when the east wind blows against it.
It will die in the same good soil
     where it had grown so well."

Then this message came to me from the LORD: "Say to these rebels of Israel: Don't you understand the meaning of this riddle of the eagles? The king of Babylon came to Jerusalem, took away her king and princes, and brought them to Babylon. He made a treaty with a member of the royal family and forced him to take an oath of loyalty. He also exiled Israel's most influential leaders, so Israel would not become strong again and revolt. Only by keeping her treaty with Babylon could Israel survive.

"Nevertheless, this man of Israel's royal family rebelled against Babylon, sending ambassadors to Egypt to request a great army and many horses. Can Israel break her sworn treaties like that and get away with it? No! For as surely as I live, says the Sovereign LORD, the king of Israel will die in Babylon, the land of the king who put him in power and whose treaty he disregarded and broke. Pharaoh and all his mighty army will fail to help Israel when the king of Babylon lays siege to Jerusalem again and destroys many lives. For the king of Israel disregarded his treaty and broke it after swearing to obey; therefore, he will not escape.

"So this is what the Sovereign LORD says: As surely as I live, I will punish him for breaking my covenant and disregarding the solemn oath he made in my name. I will throw my net over him and capture him in my snare. I will bring him to Babylon and put him on trial for this treason against me. And all his best warriors will be killed in battle, and those who survive will be scattered to the four winds. Then you will know that I, the LORD, have spoken.

"This is what the Sovereign LORD says: I will take a branch from the top of a tall cedar, and I will plant it on the top of Israel's highest mountain. It will become a majestic cedar, sending forth its branches and producing seed. Birds of every sort will nest in it, finding shelter in the shade of its branches. And all the trees will know that it is I, the LORD, who cuts the tall tree down and makes the short tree grow tall. It is I who makes the green tree wither and gives the dead tree new life. I, the LORD, have spoken, and I will do what I said!"

+

Then another message came to me from the LORD: "Why do you quote this proverb concerning the land of Israel: 'The parents have eaten sour grapes, but their children's mouths pucker at the taste'? As surely as I live, says the Sovereign LORD, you will not quote this proverb anymore in Israel. For all people are mine to judge—both parents and children alike. And this is my rule: The person who sins is the one who will die.

"Suppose a certain man is righteous and does what is just and right. He does not feast in the mountains before Israel's idols or worship them. He does not commit adultery or have intercourse with a woman during her menstrual period. He is a merciful creditor, not keeping the items given as security by poor debtors. He does not rob the poor but instead gives food to the hungry and provides clothes for the needy. He grants loans without interest, stays away from injustice, is honest and fair when judging others, and faithfully obeys my decrees and regulations. Anyone who does these things is just and will surely live, says the Sovereign LORD.

"But suppose that man has a son who grows up to be a robber or murderer and refuses to do what is right. And that son does all the evil things his father would never do—he worships idols on the mountains, commits adultery, oppresses the poor and helpless, steals from debtors by refusing to let them redeem their security, worships idols, commits detestable sins, and lends money at excessive interest. Should such a sinful person live? No! He must die and must take full blame.

"But suppose that sinful son, in turn, has a son who sees his father's wickedness and decides against that kind of life. This son refuses to worship idols on the mountains and does not commit adultery. He does not exploit the poor, but instead is fair to debtors and does not rob them. He gives food to the hungry and provides clothes for the needy. He helps the poor, does not lend money at interest, and obeys all my regulations and decrees. Such a person will not die because of his father's sins; he will surely live. But the father will die for his many sins—for being cruel, robbing people, and doing what was clearly wrong among his people.

"'What?' you ask. 'Doesn't the child pay for the parent's sins?' No! For if the child does what is just and right and keeps my decrees, that child will surely live. The person who sins is the one who will die. The child will not be punished for the parent's sins, and the parent will not be punished for the child's sins. Righteous people will be rewarded for their own righteous behavior, and wicked people will be punished for their own wickedness.

But if wicked people turn away from all their sins and begin to obey my decrees and do what is just and right, they will surely live and not die. All their past sins will be forgotten, and they will live because of the righteous things they have done.

"Do you think that I like to see wicked people die? says the Sovereign Lord. Of course not! I want them to turn from their wicked ways and live. However, if righteous people turn from their righteous behavior and start doing sinful things and act like other sinners, should they be allowed to live? No, of course not! All their righteous acts will be forgotten, and they will die for their sins.

"Yet you say, 'The Lord isn't doing what's right!' Listen to me, O people of Israel. Am I the one not doing what's right, or is it you? When righteous people turn from their righteous behavior and start doing sinful things, they will die for it. Yes, they will die because of their sinful deeds. And if wicked people turn from their wickedness, obey the law, and do what is just and right, they will save their lives. They will live because they thought it over and decided to turn from their sins. Such people will not die. And yet the people of Israel keep saying, 'The Lord isn't doing what's right!' O people of Israel, it is you who are not doing what's right, not I.

"Therefore, I will judge each of you, O people of Israel, according to your actions, says the Sovereign Lord. Repent, and turn from your sins. Don't let them destroy you! Put all your rebellion behind you, and find yourselves a new heart and a new spirit. For why should you die, O people of Israel? I don't want you to die, says the Sovereign Lord. Turn back and live!

"Sing this funeral song for the princes of Israel:

"What is your mother?
    A lioness among lions!
She lay down among the young lions
    and reared her cubs.
She raised one of her cubs
    to become a strong young lion.
He learned to hunt and devour prey,
    and he became a man-eater.
Then the nations heard about him,
    and he was trapped in their pit.
They led him away with hooks
    to the land of Egypt.

"When the lioness saw
    that her hopes for him were gone,

she took another of her cubs
　　and taught him to be a strong young lion.
He prowled among the other lions
　　and stood out among them in his strength.
He learned to hunt and devour prey,
　　and he, too, became a man-eater.
He demolished fortresses
　　and destroyed their towns and cities.
Their farms were desolated,
　　and their crops were destroyed.
The land and its people trembled in fear
　　when they heard him roar.
Then the armies of the nations attacked him,
　　surrounding him from every direction.
They threw a net over him
　　and captured him in their pit.
With hooks, they dragged him into a cage
　　and brought him before the king of Babylon.
They held him in captivity,
　　so his voice could never again be heard
　　on the mountains of Israel.

"Your mother was like a vine
　　planted by the water's edge.
It had lush, green foliage
　　because of the abundant water.
Its branches became strong—
　　strong enough to be a ruler's scepter.
It grew very tall,
　　towering above all others.
It stood out because of its height
　　and its many lush branches.
But the vine was uprooted in fury
　　and thrown down to the ground.
The desert wind dried up its fruit
　　and tore off its strong branches,
so that it withered
　　and was destroyed by fire.
Now the vine is transplanted to the wilderness,
　　where the ground is hard and dry.
A fire has burst out from its branches
　　and devoured its fruit.

Its remaining limbs are not
    strong enough to be a ruler's scepter.

"This is a funeral song, and it will be used in a funeral."

+

On August 14, during the seventh year of King Jehoiachin's captivity, some of the leaders of Israel came to request a message from the LORD. They sat down in front of me to wait for his reply. Then this message came to me from the LORD: "Son of man, tell the leaders of Israel, 'This is what the Sovereign LORD says: How dare you come to ask me for a message? As surely as I live, says the Sovereign LORD, I will tell you nothing!'

"Son of man, bring charges against them and condemn them. Make them realize how detestable the sins of their ancestors really were. Give them this message from the Sovereign LORD: When I chose Israel—when I revealed myself to the descendants of Jacob in Egypt—I took a solemn oath that I, the LORD, would be their God. I took a solemn oath that day that I would bring them out of Egypt to a land I had discovered and explored for them—a good land, a land flowing with milk and honey, the best of all lands anywhere. Then I said to them, 'Each of you, get rid of the vile images you are so obsessed with. Do not defile yourselves with the idols of Egypt, for I am the LORD your God.'

"But they rebelled against me and would not listen. They did not get rid of the vile images they were obsessed with, or forsake the idols of Egypt. Then I threatened to pour out my fury on them to satisfy my anger while they were still in Egypt. But I didn't do it, for I acted to protect the honor of my name. I would not allow shame to be brought on my name among the surrounding nations who saw me reveal myself by bringing the Israelites out of Egypt. So I brought them out of Egypt and led them into the wilderness. There I gave them my decrees and regulations so they could find life by keeping them. And I gave them my Sabbath days of rest as a sign between them and me. It was to remind them that I am the LORD, who had set them apart to be holy.

"But the people of Israel rebelled against me, and they refused to obey my decrees there in the wilderness. They wouldn't obey my regulations even though obedience would have given them life. They also violated my Sabbath days. So I threatened to pour out my fury on them, and I made plans to utterly consume them in the wilderness. But again I held back in order to protect the honor of my name before the nations who had seen my power in bringing Israel out of Egypt. But I took a solemn oath against them in the wilderness. I swore I would not bring them into the land I had given them, a land flowing with milk and honey, the most beautiful place on earth. For they had rejected my regulations, refused to follow my decrees, and violated my Sabbath days. Their hearts were given to their idols. Nevertheless, I took pity on them and held back from destroying them in the wilderness.

"Then I warned their children not to follow in their parents' footsteps, defiling themselves with their idols. 'I am the LORD your God,' I told them. 'Follow my decrees, pay attention to my regulations, and keep my Sabbath days holy, for they are a sign to remind you that I am the LORD your God.'

"But their children, too, rebelled against me. They refused to keep my decrees and follow my regulations, even though obedience would have given them life. And they also violated my Sabbath days. So again I threatened to pour out my fury on them in the wilderness. Nevertheless, I withdrew my judgment against them to protect the honor of my name before the nations that had seen my power in bringing them out of Egypt. But I took a solemn oath against them in the wilderness. I swore I would scatter them among all the nations because they did not obey my regulations. They scorned my decrees by violating my Sabbath days and longing for the idols of their ancestors. I gave them over to worthless decrees and regulations that would not lead to life. I let them pollute themselves with the very gifts I had given them, and I allowed them to give their firstborn children as offerings to their gods—so I might devastate them and remind them that I alone am the LORD.

"Therefore, son of man, give the people of Israel this message from the Sovereign LORD: Your ancestors continued to blaspheme and betray me, for when I brought them into the land I had promised them, they offered sacrifices on every high hill and under every green tree they saw! They roused my fury as they offered up sacrifices to their gods. They brought their perfumes and incense and poured out their liquid offerings to them. I said to them, 'What is this high place where you are going?' (This kind of pagan shrine has been called Bamah—'high place'—ever since.)

"Therefore, give the people of Israel this message from the Sovereign LORD: Do you plan to pollute yourselves just as your ancestors did? Do you intend to keep prostituting yourselves by worshiping vile images? For when you offer gifts to them and give your little children to be burned as sacrifices, you continue to pollute yourselves with idols to this day. Should I allow you to ask for a message from me, O people of Israel? As surely as I live, says the Sovereign LORD, I will tell you nothing.

"You say, 'We want to be like the nations all around us, who serve idols of wood and stone.' But what you have in mind will never happen. As surely as I live, says the Sovereign LORD, I will rule over you with an iron fist in great anger and with awesome power. And in anger I will reach out with my strong hand and powerful arm, and I will bring you back from the lands where you are scattered. I will bring you into the wilderness of the nations, and there I will judge you face to face. I will judge you there just as I did your ancestors in the wilderness after bringing them out of Egypt, says the Sovereign LORD. I will examine you carefully and hold you to the terms of the covenant. I will purge you of all those who rebel and revolt against me. I will bring them out of the countries where they are in exile, but they will never enter the land of Israel. Then you will know that I am the LORD.

"As for you, O people of Israel, this is what the Sovereign LORD says: Go right ahead and worship your idols, but sooner or later you will obey me and will stop bringing shame on my holy name by worshiping idols. For on my holy mountain, the great mountain of Israel, says the Sovereign LORD, the people of Israel will someday worship me, and I will accept them. There I will require that you bring me all your offerings and choice gifts and sacrifices. When I bring you home from exile, you will be like a pleasing sacrifice to me. And I will display my holiness through you as all the nations watch. Then when I have brought you home to the land I promised with a solemn oath to give to your ancestors, you will know that I am the LORD. You will look back on all the ways you defiled yourselves and will hate yourselves because of the evil you have done. You will know that I am the LORD, O people of Israel, when I have honored my name by treating you mercifully in spite of your wickedness. I, the Sovereign LORD, have spoken!"

✦

Then this message came to me from the LORD: "Son of man, turn and face the south and speak out against it; prophesy against the brushlands of the Negev. Tell the southern wilderness, 'This is what the Sovereign LORD says: Hear the word of the LORD! I will set you on fire, and every tree, both green and dry, will be burned. The terrible flames will not be quenched and will scorch everything from south to north. And everyone in the world will see that I, the LORD, have set this fire. It will not be put out.'"

Then I said, "O Sovereign LORD, they are saying of me, 'He only talks in riddles!'"

✦

Then this message came to me from the LORD: "Son of man, turn and face Jerusalem and prophesy against Israel and her sanctuaries. Tell her, 'This is what the LORD says: I am your enemy, O Israel, and I am about to unsheath my sword to destroy your people—the righteous and the wicked alike. Yes, I will cut off both the righteous and the wicked! I will draw my sword against everyone in the land from south to north. Everyone in the world will know that I am the LORD. My sword is in my hand, and it will not return to its sheath until its work is finished.'

"Son of man, groan before the people! Groan before them with bitter anguish and a broken heart. When they ask why you are groaning, tell them, 'I groan because of the terrifying news I have heard. When it comes true, the boldest heart will melt with fear; all strength will disappear. Every spirit will faint; strong knees will become as weak as water. And the Sovereign LORD says: It is coming! It's on its way!'"

✝

Then the LORD said to me, "Son of man, give the people this message from the Lord:

"A sword, a sword
　　is being sharpened and polished.
It is sharpened for terrible slaughter
　　and polished to flash like lightning!
Now will you laugh?
　　Those far stronger than you have fallen beneath its power!
Yes, the sword is now being sharpened and polished;
　　it is being prepared for the executioner.

"Son of man, cry out and wail;
　　pound your thighs in anguish,
for that sword will slaughter my people and their leaders—
　　everyone will die!
It will put them all to the test.
　　What chance do they have?
　　says the Sovereign LORD.

"Son of man, prophesy to them
　　and clap your hands.
Then take the sword and brandish it twice,
　　even three times,
to symbolize the great massacre,
　　the great massacre facing them on every side.
Let their hearts melt with terror,
　　for the sword glitters at every gate.
It flashes like lightning
　　and is polished for slaughter!
O sword, slash to the right,
　　then slash to the left,

wherever you will,
  wherever you want.
I, too, will clap my hands,
  and I will satisfy my fury.
  I, the LORD, have spoken!"

+

Then this message came to me from the LORD: "Son of man, make a map and trace two routes on it for the sword of Babylon's king to follow. Put a signpost on the road that comes out of Babylon where the road forks into two—one road going to Ammon and its capital, Rabbah, and the other to Judah and fortified Jerusalem. The king of Babylon now stands at the fork, uncertain whether to attack Jerusalem or Rabbah. He calls his magicians to look for omens. They cast lots by shaking arrows from the quiver. They inspect the livers of animal sacrifices. The omen in his right hand says, 'Jerusalem!' With battering rams his soldiers will go against the gates, shouting for the kill. They will put up siege towers and build ramps against the walls. The people of Jerusalem will think it is a false omen, because of their treaty with the Babylonians. But the king of Babylon will remind the people of their rebellion. Then he will attack and capture them.

"Therefore, this is what the Sovereign LORD says: Again and again you remind me of your sin and your guilt. You don't even try to hide it! In everything you do, your sins are obvious for all to see. So now the time of your punishment has come!

"O you corrupt and wicked prince of Israel, your final day of reckoning is here! This is what the Sovereign LORD says:

"Take off your jeweled crown,
  for the old order changes.
Now the lowly will be exalted,
  and the mighty will be brought down.
Destruction! Destruction!
  I will surely destroy the kingdom.
And it will not be restored until the one appears
  who has the right to judge it.
Then I will hand it over to him.

"And now, son of man, prophesy concerning the Ammonites and their mockery. Give them this message from the Sovereign LORD:

"A sword, a sword
  is drawn for your slaughter.

It is polished to destroy,
   flashing like lightning!
Your prophets have given false visions,
   and your fortune-tellers have told lies.
The sword will fall on the necks of the wicked
   for whom the day of final reckoning has come.

"Now return the sword to its sheath,
   for in your own country,
the land of your birth,
   I will pass judgment upon you.
I will pour out my fury on you
   and blow on you with the fire of my anger.
I will hand you over to cruel men
   who are skilled in destruction.
You will be fuel for the fire,
   and your blood will be spilled in your own land.
You will be utterly wiped out,
   your memory lost to history,
   for I, the LORD, have spoken!"

＋

Now this message came to me from the LORD: "Son of man, are you ready to judge Jerusalem? Are you ready to judge this city of murderers? Publicly denounce her detestable sins, and give her this message from the Sovereign LORD: O city of murderers, doomed and damned—city of idols, filthy and foul—you are guilty because of the blood you have shed. You are defiled because of the idols you have made. Your day of destruction has come! You have reached the end of your years. I will make you an object of mockery throughout the world. O infamous city, filled with confusion, you will be mocked by people far and near.

"Every leader in Israel who lives within your walls is bent on murder. Fathers and mothers are treated with contempt. Foreigners are forced to pay for protection. Orphans and widows are wronged and oppressed among you. You despise my holy things and violate my Sabbath days of rest. People accuse others falsely and send them to their death. You are filled with idol worshipers and people who do obscene things. Men sleep with their fathers' wives and force themselves on women who are menstruating. Within your walls live men who commit adultery with their neighbors' wives, who defile their daughters-in-law, or who rape their own sisters. There are hired murderers, loan racketeers, and extortioners everywhere. They never even think of me and my commands, says the Sovereign LORD.

"But now I clap my hands in indignation over your dishonest gain and bloodshed. How strong and courageous will you be in my day of reckoning? I, the LORD, have spoken, and I will do what I said. I will scatter you among the nations and purge you of your wickedness. And when I have been dishonored among the nations because of you, you will know that I am the LORD."

+

Then this message came to me from the LORD: "Son of man, the people of Israel are the worthless slag that remains after silver is smelted. They are the dross that is left over—a useless mixture of copper, tin, iron, and lead. So tell them, 'This is what the Sovereign LORD says: Because you are all worthless slag, I will bring you to my crucible in Jerusalem. Just as silver, copper, iron, lead, and tin are melted down in a furnace, I will melt you down in the heat of my fury. I will gather you together and blow the fire of my anger upon you, and you will melt like silver in fierce heat. Then you will know that I, the LORD, have poured out my fury on you.'"

+

Again a message came to me from the LORD: "Son of man, give the people of Israel this message: In the day of my indignation, you will be like a polluted land, a land without rain. Your princes plot conspiracies just as lions stalk their prey. They devour innocent people, seizing treasures and extorting wealth. They make many widows in the land. Your priests have violated my instructions and defiled my holy things. They make no distinction between what is holy and what is not. And they do not teach my people the difference between what is ceremonially clean and unclean. They disregard my Sabbath days so that I am dishonored among them. Your leaders are like wolves who tear apart their victims. They actually destroy people's lives for money! And your prophets cover up for them by announcing false visions and making lying predictions. They say, 'My message is from the Sovereign LORD,' when the LORD hasn't spoken a single word to them. Even common people oppress the poor, rob the needy, and deprive foreigners of justice.

"I looked for someone who might rebuild the wall of righteousness that guards the land. I searched for someone to stand in the gap in the wall so I wouldn't have to destroy the land, but I found no one. So now I will pour out my fury on them, consuming them with the fire of my anger. I will heap on their heads the full penalty for all their sins. I, the Sovereign LORD, have spoken!"

✛

This message came to me from the LORD: "Son of man, once there were two sisters who were daughters of the same mother. They became prostitutes in Egypt. Even as young girls, they allowed men to fondle their breasts. The older girl was named Oholah, and her sister was Oholibah. I married them, and they bore me sons and daughters. I am speaking of Samaria and Jerusalem, for Oholah is Samaria and Oholibah is Jerusalem.

"Then Oholah lusted after other lovers instead of me, and she gave her love to the Assyrian officers. They were all attractive young men, captains and commanders dressed in handsome blue, charioteers driving their horses. And so she prostituted herself with the most desirable men of Assyria, worshiping their idols and defiling herself. For when she left Egypt, she did not leave her spirit of prostitution behind. She was still as lewd as in her youth, when the Egyptians slept with her, fondled her breasts, and used her as a prostitute.

"And so I handed her over to her Assyrian lovers, whom she desired so much. They stripped her, took away her children as their slaves, and then killed her. After she received her punishment, her reputation was known to every woman in the land.

"Yet even though Oholibah saw what had happened to Oholah, her sister, she followed right in her footsteps. And she was even more depraved, abandoning herself to her lust and prostitution. She fawned over all the Assyrian officers—those captains and commanders in handsome uniforms, those charioteers driving their horses—all of them attractive young men. I saw the way she was going, defiling herself just like her older sister.

"Then she carried her prostitution even further. She fell in love with pictures that were painted on a wall—pictures of Babylonian military officers, outfitted in striking red uniforms. Handsome belts encircled their waists, and flowing turbans crowned their heads. They were dressed like chariot officers from the land of Babylonia. When she saw these paintings, she longed to give herself to them, so she sent messengers to Babylonia to invite them to come to her. So they came and committed adultery with her, defiling her in the bed of love. After being defiled, however, she rejected them in disgust.

"In the same way, I became disgusted with Oholibah and rejected her, just as I had rejected her sister, because she flaunted herself before them and gave herself to satisfy their lusts. Yet she turned to even greater prostitution, remembering her youth when she was a prostitute in Egypt. She lusted after lovers with genitals as large as a donkey's and emissions like those of a horse. And so, Oholibah, you relived your former days as a young girl in Egypt, when you first allowed your breasts to be fondled.

"Therefore, Oholibah, this is what the Sovereign LORD says: I will send your lovers against you from every direction—those very nations from which you turned away in disgust. For the Babylonians will come with all the Chaldeans from Pekod and Shoa and Koa. And all the Assyrians will come with them—handsome young captains, commanders, chariot officers, and other high-ranking officers, all riding their horses. They will all come against you from the north with chariots, wagons, and a great army prepared for attack. They will take up positions on every side, surrounding you with men armed with shields and helmets. And I will hand you over to them for punishment so they can do with you as they please. I will turn my jealous anger against you, and they will deal harshly with you. They will cut off your nose and ears, and any survivors will then be slaughtered by the sword. Your children will be taken away as captives, and everything that is left will be burned. They will strip you of your beautiful clothes and jewels. In this way, I will put a stop to the lewdness and prostitution you brought from Egypt. You will never again cast longing eyes on those things or fondly remember your time in Egypt.

"For this is what the Sovereign LORD says: I will surely hand you over to your enemies, to those you loathe, those you rejected. They will treat you with hatred and rob you of all you own, leaving you stark naked. The shame of your prostitution will be exposed to all the world. You brought all this on yourself by prostituting yourself to other nations, defiling yourself with all their idols. Because you have followed in your sister's footsteps, I will force you to drink the same cup of terror she drank.

"Yes, this is what the Sovereign LORD says:

"You will drink from your sister's cup of terror,
    a cup that is large and deep.
It is filled to the brim
    with scorn and derision.
Drunkenness and anguish will fill you,
    for your cup is filled to the brim with distress
        and desolation,
    the same cup your sister Samaria drank.
You will drain that cup of terror
    to the very bottom.
Then you will smash it to pieces
    and beat your breast in anguish.
    I, the Sovereign LORD, have spoken!

"And because you have forgotten me and turned your back on me, this is what the Sovereign LORD says: You must bear the consequences of all your lewdness and prostitution."

The LORD said to me, "Son of man, you must accuse Oholah and Oholibah of all their detestable sins. They have committed both adultery and murder—adultery by worshiping idols and murder by burning as sacrifices the children they bore to me. Furthermore, they have defiled my Temple and violated my Sabbath day! On the very day that they sacrificed their children to their idols, they boldly came into my Temple to worship! They came in and defiled my house.

"You sisters sent messengers to distant lands to get men. Then when they arrived, you bathed yourselves, painted your eyelids, and put on your finest jewels for them. You sat with them on a beautifully embroidered couch and put my incense and my special oil on a table that was spread before you. From your room came the sound of many men carousing. They were lustful men and drunkards from the wilderness, who put bracelets on your wrists and beautiful crowns on your heads. Then I said, 'If they really want to have sex with old worn-out prostitutes like these, let them!' And that is what they did. They had sex with Oholah and Oholibah, these shameless prostitutes. But righteous people will judge these sister cities for what they really are—adulterers and murderers.

"Now this is what the Sovereign LORD says: Bring an army against them and hand them over to be terrorized and plundered. For their enemies will stone them and kill them with swords. They will butcher their sons and daughters and burn their homes. In this way, I will put an end to lewdness and idolatry in the land, and my judgment will be a warning to all women not to follow your wicked example. You will be fully repaid for all your prostitution—your worship of idols. Yes, you will suffer the full penalty. Then you will know that I am the Sovereign LORD."

+

On January 15, during the ninth year of King Jehoiachin's captivity, this message came to me from the LORD: "Son of man, write down today's date, because on this very day the king of Babylon is beginning his attack against Jerusalem. Then give these rebels an illustration with this message from the Sovereign LORD:

"Put a pot on the fire,
    and pour in some water.
Fill it with choice pieces of meat—
    the rump and the shoulder
    and all the most tender cuts.
Use only the best sheep from the flock,
    and heap fuel on the fire beneath the pot.

Bring the pot to a boil,
  and cook the bones along with the meat.

"Now this is what the Sovereign LORD says:
What sorrow awaits Jerusalem,
  the city of murderers!
She is a cooking pot
  whose corruption can't be cleaned out.
Take the meat out in random order,
  for no piece is better than another.
For the blood of her murders
  is splashed on the rocks.
It isn't even spilled on the ground,
  where the dust could cover it!
So I will splash her blood on a rock
  for all to see,
an expression of my anger
  and vengeance against her.

"This is what the Sovereign LORD says:
What sorrow awaits Jerusalem,
  the city of murderers!
  I myself will pile up the fuel beneath her.
Yes, heap on the wood!
  Let the fire roar to make the pot boil.
Cook the meat with many spices,
  and afterward burn the bones.
Now set the empty pot on the coals.
  Heat it red hot!
  Burn away the filth and corruption.
But it's hopeless;
  the corruption can't be cleaned out.
  So throw it into the fire.
Your impurity is your lewdness
  and the corruption of your idolatry.
I tried to cleanse you,
  but you refused.
So now you will remain in your filth
  until my fury against you has been satisfied.

"I, the LORD, have spoken! The time has come, and I won't hold back. I will not change my mind, and I will have no pity on you. You will be judged on the basis of all your wicked actions, says the Sovereign LORD."

+

Then this message came to me from the LORD: "Son of man, with one blow I will take away your dearest treasure. Yet you must not show any sorrow at her death. Do not weep; let there be no tears. Groan silently, but let there be no wailing at her grave. Do not uncover your head or take off your sandals. Do not perform the usual rituals of mourning or accept any food brought to you by consoling friends."

So I proclaimed this to the people the next morning, and in the evening my wife died. The next morning I did everything I had been told to do. Then the people asked, "What does all this mean? What are you trying to tell us?"

So I said to them, "A message came to me from the LORD, and I was told to give this message to the people of Israel. This is what the Sovereign LORD says: I will defile my Temple, the source of your security and pride, the place your heart delights in. Your sons and daughters whom you left behind in Judah will be slaughtered by the sword. Then you will do as Ezekiel has done. You will not mourn in public or console yourselves by eating the food brought by friends. Your heads will remain covered, and your sandals will not be taken off. You will not mourn or weep, but you will waste away because of your sins. You will groan among yourselves for all the evil you have done. Ezekiel is an example for you; you will do just as he has done. And when that time comes, you will know that I am the Sovereign LORD."

Then the LORD said to me, "Son of man, on the day I take away their stronghold—their joy and glory, their heart's desire, their dearest treasure—I will also take away their sons and daughters. And on that day a survivor from Jerusalem will come to you in Babylon and tell you what has happened. And when he arrives, your voice will suddenly return so you can talk to him, and you will be a symbol for these people. Then they will know that I am the LORD."

+ + +

Then this message came to me from the LORD: "Son of man, turn and face the land of Ammon and prophesy against its people. Give the Ammonites this message from the Sovereign LORD: Hear the word of the Sovereign LORD! Because you cheered when my Temple was defiled, mocked Israel in her desolation, and laughed at Judah as she went away into exile, I will allow nomads from the eastern deserts to overrun your country. They will set up their camps among you and pitch their tents on your land. They will harvest all your fruit and drink the milk from your livestock. And I will turn the city of Rabbah into a pasture for camels, and all the land of the Ammonites into a resting place for sheep and goats. Then you will know that I am the LORD.

"This is what the Sovereign LORD says: Because you clapped and danced and cheered with glee at the destruction of my people, I will raise my fist of judgment against you. I will give you as plunder to many nations. I will cut you off from being a nation and destroy you completely. Then you will know that I am the LORD.

"This is what the Sovereign LORD says: Because the people of Moab have said that Judah is just like all the other nations, I will open up their eastern flank and wipe out their glorious frontier towns—Beth-jeshimoth, Baal-meon, and Kiriathaim. And I will hand Moab over to nomads from the eastern deserts, just as I handed over Ammon. Yes, the Ammonites will no longer be counted among the nations. In the same way, I will bring my judgment down on the Moabites. Then they will know that I am the LORD.

"This is what the Sovereign LORD says: The people of Edom have sinned greatly by avenging themselves against the people of Judah. Therefore, says the Sovereign LORD, I will raise my fist of judgment against Edom. I will wipe out its people and animals with the sword. I will make a wasteland of everything from Teman to Dedan. I will accomplish this by the hand of my people of Israel. They will carry out my vengeance with anger, and Edom will know that this vengeance is from me. I, the Sovereign LORD, have spoken!

"This is what the Sovereign LORD says: The people of Philistia have acted against Judah out of bitter revenge and long-standing contempt. Therefore, this is what the Sovereign LORD says: I will raise my fist of judgment against the land of the Philistines. I will wipe out the Kerethites and utterly destroy the people who live by the sea. I will execute terrible vengeance against them to punish them for what they have done. And when I have inflicted my revenge, they will know that I am the LORD."

+

On February 3, during the twelfth year of King Jehoiachin's captivity, this message came to me from the LORD: "Son of man, Tyre has rejoiced over the fall of Jerusalem, saying, 'Ha! She who was the gateway to the rich trade routes to the east has been broken, and I am the heir! Because she has been made desolate, I will become wealthy!'

"Therefore, this is what the Sovereign LORD says: I am your enemy,

O Tyre, and I will bring many nations against you, like the waves of the sea crashing against your shoreline. They will destroy the walls of Tyre and tear down its towers. I will scrape away its soil and make it a bare rock! It will be just a rock in the sea, a place for fishermen to spread their nets, for I have spoken, says the Sovereign LORD. Tyre will become the prey of many nations, and its mainland villages will be destroyed by the sword. Then they will know that I am the LORD.

"This is what the Sovereign LORD says: From the north I will bring King Nebuchadnezzar of Babylon against Tyre. He is king of kings and brings his horses, chariots, charioteers, and great army. First he will destroy your mainland villages. Then he will attack you by building a siege wall, constructing a ramp, and raising a roof of shields against you. He will pound your walls with battering rams and demolish your towers with sledgehammers. The hooves of his horses will choke the city with dust, and the noise of the charioteers and chariot wheels will shake your walls as they storm through your broken gates. His horsemen will trample through every street in the city. They will butcher your people, and your strong pillars will topple.

"They will plunder all your riches and merchandise and break down your walls. They will destroy your lovely homes and dump your stones and timbers and even your dust into the sea. I will stop the music of your songs. No more will the sound of harps be heard among your people. I will make your island a bare rock, a place for fishermen to spread their nets. You will never be rebuilt, for I, the LORD, have spoken. Yes, the Sovereign LORD has spoken!

"This is what the Sovereign LORD says to Tyre: The whole coastline will tremble at the sound of your fall, as the screams of the wounded echo in the continuing slaughter. All the seaport rulers will step down from their thrones and take off their royal robes and beautiful clothing. They will sit on the ground trembling with horror at your destruction. Then they will wail for you, singing this funeral song:

"O famous island city,
    once ruler of the sea,
    how you have been destroyed!
Your people, with their naval power,
    once spread fear around the world.
Now the coastlands tremble at your fall.
    The islands are dismayed as you disappear.

"This is what the Sovereign LORD says: I will make Tyre an uninhabited ruin, like many others. I will bury you beneath the terrible waves of enemy attack. Great seas will swallow you. I will send you to the pit to join those who descended there long ago. Your city will lie in ruins, buried beneath the earth, like those in the pit who have entered the world of the dead. You will have no place of respect here in the land of the living. I will bring you to a terrible end, and you will exist no more. You will be looked for, but you will never again be found. I, the Sovereign LORD, have spoken!"

+

Then this message came to me from the LORD: "Son of man, sing a funeral song for Tyre, that mighty gateway to the sea, the trading center of the world. Give Tyre this message from the Sovereign LORD:

"You boasted, O Tyre,
　'My beauty is perfect!'
You extended your boundaries into the sea.
　Your builders made your beauty perfect.
You were like a great ship
　built of the finest cypress from Senir.
They took a cedar from Lebanon
　to make a mast for you.
They carved your oars
　from the oaks of Bashan.
Your deck of pine from the coasts of Cyprus
　was inlaid with ivory.
Your sails were made of Egypt's finest linen,
　and they flew as a banner above you.
You stood beneath blue and purple awnings
　made bright with dyes from the coasts of Elishah.
Your oarsmen came from Sidon and Arvad;
　your helmsmen were skilled men from Tyre itself.
Wise old craftsmen from Gebal did the caulking.
　Ships from every land came with goods to barter for your trade.

"Men from distant Persia, Lydia, and Libya served in your great army. They hung their shields and helmets on your walls, giving you great honor. Men from Arvad and Helech stood on your walls. Your towers were manned by men from Gammad. Their shields hung on your walls, completing your beauty.

"Tarshish sent merchants to buy your wares in exchange for silver, iron, tin, and lead. Merchants from Greece, Tubal, and Meshech brought slaves and articles of bronze to trade with you.

"From Beth-togarmah came riding horses, chariot horses, and mules, all in exchange for your goods. Merchants came to you from Dedan.

Numerous coastlands were your captive markets; they brought payment in ivory tusks and ebony wood.

"Syria sent merchants to buy your rich variety of goods. They traded turquoise, purple dyes, embroidery, fine linen, and jewelry of coral and rubies. Judah and Israel traded for your wares, offering wheat from Minnith, figs, honey, olive oil, and balm.

"Damascus sent merchants to buy your rich variety of goods, bringing wine from Helbon and white wool from Zahar. Greeks from Uzal came to trade for your merchandise. Wrought iron, cassia, and fragrant calamus were bartered for your wares.

"Dedan sent merchants to trade their expensive saddle blankets with you. The Arabians and the princes of Kedar sent merchants to trade lambs and rams and male goats in exchange for your goods. The merchants of Sheba and Raamah came with all kinds of spices, jewels, and gold in exchange for your wares.

"Haran, Canneh, Eden, Sheba, Asshur, and Kilmad came with their merchandise, too. They brought choice fabrics to trade—blue cloth, embroidery, and multicolored carpets rolled up and bound with cords. The ships of Tarshish were your ocean caravans. Your island warehouse was filled to the brim!

"But look! Your oarsmen
    have taken you into stormy seas!
A mighty eastern gale
    has wrecked you in the heart of the sea!
Everything is lost—
    your riches and wares,
your sailors and pilots,
    your ship builders, merchants, and warriors.
On the day of your ruin,
    everyone on board sinks into the depths of the sea.
Your cities by the sea tremble
    as your pilots cry out in terror.
All the oarsmen abandon their ships;
    the sailors and pilots stand on the shore.
They cry aloud over you
    and weep bitterly.
They throw dust on their heads
    and roll in ashes.
They shave their heads in grief for you
    and dress themselves in burlap.
They weep for you with bitter anguish

and deep mourning.
As they wail and mourn over you,
   they sing this sad funeral song:
'Was there ever such a city as Tyre,
   now silent at the bottom of the sea?
The merchandise you traded
   satisfied the desires of many nations.
Kings at the ends of the earth
   were enriched by your trade.
Now you are a wrecked ship,
   broken at the bottom of the sea.
All your merchandise and crew
   have gone down with you.
All who live along the coastlands
   are appalled at your terrible fate.
Their kings are filled with horror
   and look on with twisted faces.
The merchants among the nations
   shake their heads at the sight of you,
for you have come to a horrible end
   and will exist no more.'"

+

Then this message came to me from the LORD: "Son of man, give the prince of Tyre this message from the Sovereign LORD:

"In your great pride you claim, 'I am a god!
   I sit on a divine throne in the heart of the sea.'
But you are only a man and not a god,
   though you boast that you are a god.
You regard yourself as wiser than Daniel
   and think no secret is hidden from you.
With your wisdom and understanding you have amassed great
     wealth—
   gold and silver for your treasuries.
Yes, your wisdom has made you very rich,
   and your riches have made you very proud.

"Therefore, this is what the Sovereign LORD says:
Because you think you are as wise as a god,
   I will now bring against you a foreign army,
   the terror of the nations.

They will draw their swords against your marvelous wisdom
    and defile your splendor!
They will bring you down to the pit,
    and you will die in the heart of the sea,
    pierced with many wounds.
Will you then boast, 'I am a god!'
    to those who kill you?
To them you will be no god
    but merely a man!
You will die like an outcast
    at the hands of foreigners.
    I, the Sovereign LORD, have spoken!"

✢

Then this further message came to me from the LORD: "Son of man, sing this funeral song for the king of Tyre. Give him this message from the Sovereign LORD:

"You were the model of perfection,
    full of wisdom and exquisite in beauty.
You were in Eden,
    the garden of God.
Your clothing was adorned with every precious stone—
    red carnelian, pale-green peridot, white moonstone,
    blue-green beryl, onyx, green jasper,
    blue lapis lazuli, turquoise, and emerald—
all beautifully crafted for you
    and set in the finest gold.
They were given to you
    on the day you were created.
I ordained and anointed you
    as the mighty angelic guardian.
You had access to the holy mountain of God
    and walked among the stones of fire.

"You were blameless in all you did
    from the day you were created
    until the day evil was found in you.
Your rich commerce led you to violence,
    and you sinned.
So I banished you in disgrace
    from the mountain of God.

I expelled you, O mighty guardian,
  from your place among the stones of fire.
Your heart was filled with pride
  because of all your beauty.
Your wisdom was corrupted
  by your love of splendor.
So I threw you to the ground
  and exposed you to the curious gaze of kings.
You defiled your sanctuaries
  with your many sins and your dishonest trade.
So I brought fire out from within you,
  and it consumed you.
I reduced you to ashes on the ground
  in the sight of all who were watching.
All who knew you are appalled at your fate.
  You have come to a terrible end,
  and you will exist no more."

+

Then another message came to me from the LORD: "Son of man, turn and face the city of Sidon and prophesy against it. Give the people of Sidon this message from the Sovereign LORD:

"I am your enemy, O Sidon,
  and I will reveal my glory by what I do to you.
When I bring judgment against you
  and reveal my holiness among you,
everyone watching will know
  that I am the LORD.
I will send a plague against you,
  and blood will be spilled in your streets.
The attack will come from every direction,
  and your people will lie slaughtered within your walls.
Then everyone will know
  that I am the LORD.
No longer will Israel's scornful neighbors
  prick and tear at her like briers and thorns.
For then they will know
  that I am the Sovereign LORD.

"This is what the Sovereign LORD says: The people of Israel will again live in their own land, the land I gave my servant Jacob. For I will gather them from the distant lands where I have scattered them. I will reveal to the nations of the world my holiness among my people. They will live safely in Israel and build homes and plant vineyards. And when I punish the neighboring nations that treated them with contempt, they will know that I am the LORD their God."

+

On January 7, during the tenth year of King Jehoiachin's captivity, this message came to me from the LORD: "Son of man, turn and face Egypt and prophesy against Pharaoh the king and all the people of Egypt. Give them this message from the Sovereign LORD:

"I am your enemy, O Pharaoh, king of Egypt—
    you great monster, lurking in the streams of the Nile.
For you have said, 'The Nile River is mine;
    I made it for myself.'
I will put hooks in your jaws
    and drag you out on the land
    with fish sticking to your scales.
I will leave you and all your fish
    stranded in the wilderness to die.
You will lie unburied on the open ground,
    for I have given you as food to the wild animals and birds.
All the people of Egypt will know that I am the LORD,
    for to Israel you were just a staff made of reeds.
When Israel leaned on you,
    you splintered and broke
    and stabbed her in the armpit.
When she put her weight on you,
    you collapsed, and her legs gave way.

"Therefore, this is what the Sovereign LORD says: I will bring an army against you, O Egypt, and destroy both people and animals. The land of Egypt will become a desolate wasteland, and the Egyptians will know that I am the LORD.

"Because you said, 'The Nile River is mine; I made it,' I am now the enemy of both you and your river. I will make the land of Egypt a totally desolate wasteland, from Migdol to Aswan, as far south as the border of Ethiopia. For forty years not a soul will pass that way, neither people nor animals. It will be completely uninhabited. I will make Egypt desolate, and it will be surrounded by other desolate nations. Its cities will be empty and desolate for forty years, surrounded by other ruined cities. I will scatter the Egyptians to distant lands.

"But this is what the Sovereign LORD also says: At the end of the forty years I will bring the Egyptians home again from the nations to which they have been scattered. I will restore the prosperity of Egypt and bring its people back to the land of Pathros in southern Egypt from which they came. But Egypt will remain an unimportant, minor kingdom. It will be the lowliest of all the nations, never again great enough to rise above its neighbors.

"Then Israel will no longer be tempted to trust in Egypt for help. Egypt's shattered condition will remind Israel of how sinful she was to trust Egypt in earlier days. Then Israel will know that I am the Sovereign LORD."

On April 26, the first day of the new year, during the twenty-seventh year of King Jehoiachin's captivity, this message came to me from the LORD: "Son of man, the army of King Nebuchadnezzar of Babylon fought so hard against Tyre that the warriors' heads were rubbed bare and their shoulders were raw and blistered. Yet Nebuchadnezzar and his army won no plunder to compensate them for all their work. Therefore, this is what the Sovereign LORD says: I will give the land of Egypt to Nebuchadnezzar, king of Babylon. He will carry off its wealth, plundering everything it has so he can pay his army. Yes, I have given him the land of Egypt as a reward for his work, says the Sovereign LORD, because he was working for me when he destroyed Tyre.

"And the day will come when I will cause the ancient glory of Israel to revive, and then, Ezekiel, your words will be respected. Then they will know that I am the LORD."

+

This is another message that came to me from the LORD: "Son of man, prophesy and give this message from the Sovereign LORD:

"Weep and wail
    for that day,
for the terrible day is almost here—
    the day of the LORD!
It is a day of clouds and gloom,
    a day of despair for the nations.
A sword will come against Egypt,
    and those who are slaughtered will cover the ground.
Its wealth will be carried away
    and its foundations destroyed.

The land of Ethiopia will be ravished.
   Ethiopia, Libya, Lydia, all Arabia,
and all their other allies
   will be destroyed in that war.

"For this is what the LORD says:
All of Egypt's allies will fall,
   and the pride of her power will end.
From Migdol to Aswan
   they will be slaughtered by the sword,
      says the Sovereign LORD.
Egypt will be desolate,
   surrounded by desolate nations,
and its cities will be in ruins,
   surrounded by other ruined cities.
And the people of Egypt will know that I am
      the LORD
   when I have set Egypt on fire
   and destroyed all their allies.
At that time I will send swift messengers in ships
   to terrify the complacent Ethiopians.
Great panic will come upon them
   on that day of Egypt's certain destruction.
Watch for it!
   It is sure to come!

"For this is what the Sovereign LORD says:
By the power of King Nebuchadnezzar of
      Babylon,
   I will destroy the hordes of Egypt.
He and his armies—the most ruthless of all—
   will be sent to demolish the land.
They will make war against Egypt
   until slaughtered Egyptians cover the ground.
I will dry up the Nile River
   and sell the land to wicked men.
I will destroy the land of Egypt and everything in it
   by the hands of foreigners.
   I, the LORD, have spoken!

"This is what the Sovereign LORD says:
I will smash the idols of Egypt
   and the images at Memphis.

There will be no rulers left in Egypt;
   terror will sweep the land.
I will destroy southern Egypt,
   set fire to Zoan,
   and bring judgment against Thebes.
I will pour out my fury on Pelusium,
   the strongest fortress of Egypt,
and I will stamp out
   the hordes of Thebes.
Yes, I will set fire to all Egypt!
   Pelusium will be racked with pain;
Thebes will be torn apart;
   Memphis will live in constant terror.
The young men of Heliopolis and Bubastis will die
     in battle,
   and the women will be taken away as slaves.
When I come to break the proud strength of Egypt,
   it will be a dark day for Tahpanhes, too.
A dark cloud will cover Tahpanhes,
   and its daughters will be led away as captives.
And so I will greatly punish Egypt,
   and they will know that I am the Lord."

+

On April 29, during the eleventh year of King Jehoiachin's captivity, this message came to me from the Lord: "Son of man, I have broken the arm of Pharaoh, the king of Egypt. His arm has not been put in a cast so that it may heal. Neither has it been bound up with a splint to make it strong enough to hold a sword. Therefore, this is what the Sovereign Lord says: I am the enemy of Pharaoh, the king of Egypt! I will break both of his arms—the good arm along with the broken one—and I will make his sword clatter to the ground. I will scatter the Egyptians to many lands throughout the world. I will strengthen the arms of Babylon's king and put my sword in his hand. But I will break the arms of Pharaoh, king of Egypt, and he will lie there mortally wounded, groaning in pain. I will strengthen the arms of the king of Babylon, while the arms of Pharaoh fall useless to his sides. And when I put my sword in the hand of Babylon's king and he brings it against the land of Egypt, Egypt will know that I am the Lord. I will scatter the Egyptians among the nations, dispersing them throughout the earth. Then they will know that I am the Lord."

+

On June 21, during the eleventh year of King Jehoiachin's captivity, this
message came to me from the LORD: "Son of man, give this message to
Pharaoh, king of Egypt, and all his hordes:

"To whom would you compare your greatness?
You are like mighty Assyria,
    which was once like a cedar of Lebanon,
with beautiful branches that cast deep forest shade
    and with its top high among the clouds.
Deep springs watered it
    and helped it to grow tall and luxuriant.
The water flowed around it like a river,
    streaming to all the trees nearby.
This great tree towered high,
    higher than all the other trees around it.
It prospered and grew long thick branches
    because of all the water at its roots.
The birds nested in its branches,
    and in its shade all the wild animals gave birth.
All the great nations of the world
    lived in its shadow.
It was strong and beautiful,
    with wide-spreading branches,
for its roots went deep
    into abundant water.
No other cedar in the garden of God
    could rival it.
No cypress had branches to equal it;
    no plane tree had boughs to compare.
No tree in the garden of God
    came close to it in beauty.
Because I made this tree so beautiful,
    and gave it such magnificent foliage,
it was the envy of all the other trees of Eden,
    the garden of God.

"Therefore, this is what the Sovereign LORD says: Because Egypt became proud and arrogant, and because it set itself so high above the others,
with its top reaching to the clouds, I will hand it over to a mighty nation
that will destroy it as its wickedness deserves. I have already discarded it. A
foreign army—the terror of the nations—has cut it down and left it fallen

on the ground. Its branches are scattered across the mountains and valleys and ravines of the land. All those who lived in its shadow have gone away and left it lying there.

> "The birds roost on its fallen trunk,
>   and the wild animals lie among its branches.
> Let the tree of no other nation
>   proudly exult in its own prosperity,
> though it be higher than the clouds
>   and it be watered from the depths.
> For all are doomed to die,
>   to go down to the depths of the earth.
> They will land in the pit
>   along with everyone else on earth.

"This is what the Sovereign LORD says: When Assyria went down to the grave, I made the deep springs mourn. I stopped its rivers and dried up its abundant water. I clothed Lebanon in black and caused the trees of the field to wilt. I made the nations shake with fear at the sound of its fall, for I sent it down to the grave with all the others who descend to the pit. And all the other proud trees of Eden, the most beautiful and the best of Lebanon, the ones whose roots went deep into the water, took comfort to find it there with them in the depths of the earth. Its allies, too, were all destroyed and had passed away. They had gone down to the grave—all those nations that had lived in its shade.

"O Egypt, to which of the trees of Eden will you compare your strength and glory? You, too, will be brought down to the depths with all these other nations. You will lie there among the outcasts who have died by the sword. This will be the fate of Pharaoh and all his hordes. I, the Sovereign LORD, have spoken!"

+

On March 3, during the twelfth year of King Jehoiachin's captivity, this message came to me from the LORD: "Son of man, mourn for Pharaoh, king of Egypt, and give him this message:

> "You think of yourself as a strong young lion among the nations,
>   but you are really just a sea monster,
> heaving around in your own rivers,
>   stirring up mud with your feet.
> Therefore, this is what the Sovereign LORD says:
> I will send many people
>   to catch you in my net
>   and haul you out of the water.

I will leave you stranded on the land to die.
    All the birds of the heavens will land on you,
and the wild animals of the whole earth
    will gorge themselves on you.
I will scatter your flesh on the hills
    and fill the valleys with your bones.
I will drench the earth with your gushing blood
    all the way to the mountains,
    filling the ravines to the brim.
When I blot you out,
    I will veil the heavens and darken the stars.
I will cover the sun with a cloud,
    and the moon will not give you its light.
I will darken the bright stars overhead
    and cover your land in darkness.
    I, the Sovereign LORD, have spoken!

"I will disturb many hearts when I bring news of your downfall to distant nations you have never seen. Yes, I will shock many lands, and their kings will be terrified at your fate. They will shudder in fear for their lives as I brandish my sword before them on the day of your fall. For this is what the Sovereign LORD says:

"The sword of the king of Babylon
    will come against you.
I will destroy your hordes with the swords of mighty
      warriors—
    the terror of the nations.
They will shatter the pride of Egypt,
    and all its hordes will be destroyed.
I will destroy all your flocks and herds
    that graze beside the streams.
Never again will people or animals
    muddy those waters with their feet.
Then I will let the waters of Egypt become calm again,
    and they will flow as smoothly as olive oil,
    says the Sovereign LORD.
And when I destroy Egypt
    and strip you of everything you own
and strike down all your people,
    then you will know that I am the LORD.
Yes, this is the funeral song
    they will sing for Egypt.

Let all the nations mourn.
> Let them mourn for Egypt and its hordes.
> I, the Sovereign LORD, have spoken!"

+

On March 17, during the twelfth year, another message came to me from the LORD: "Son of man, weep for the hordes of Egypt and for the other mighty nations. For I will send them down to the world below in company with those who descend to the pit. Say to them,

> 'O Egypt, are you lovelier than the other nations?
> No! So go down to the pit and lie there among the outcasts.'

The Egyptians will fall with the many who have died by the sword, for the sword is drawn against them. Egypt and its hordes will be dragged away to their judgment. Down in the grave mighty leaders will mockingly welcome Egypt and its allies, saying, 'They have come down; they lie among the outcasts, hordes slaughtered by the sword.'

"Assyria lies there surrounded by the graves of its army, those who were slaughtered by the sword. Their graves are in the depths of the pit, and they are surrounded by their allies. They struck terror in the hearts of people everywhere, but now they have been slaughtered by the sword.

"Elam lies there surrounded by the graves of all its hordes, those who were slaughtered by the sword. They struck terror in the hearts of people everywhere, but now they have descended as outcasts to the world below. Now they lie in the pit and share the shame of those who have gone before them. They have a resting place among the slaughtered, surrounded by the graves of all their hordes. Yes, they terrorized the nations while they lived, but now they lie in shame with others in the pit, all of them outcasts, slaughtered by the sword.

"Meshech and Tubal are there, surrounded by the graves of all their hordes. They once struck terror in the hearts of people everywhere. But now they are outcasts, all slaughtered by the sword. They are not buried in honor like their fallen heroes, who went down to the grave with their weapons—their shields covering their bodies and their swords beneath their heads. Their guilt rests upon them because they brought terror to everyone while they were still alive.

"You too, Egypt, will lie crushed and broken among the outcasts, all slaughtered by the sword.

"Edom is there with its kings and princes. Mighty as they were, they also lie among those slaughtered by the sword, with the outcasts who have gone down to the pit.

"All the princes of the north and the Sidonians are there with others who have died. Once a terror, they have been put to shame. They lie there as outcasts with others who were slaughtered by the sword. They share the shame of all who have descended to the pit.

"When Pharaoh and his entire army arrive, he will take comfort that he is not alone in having his hordes killed, says the Sovereign LORD. Although I have caused his terror to fall upon all the living, Pharaoh and his hordes will lie there among the outcasts who were slaughtered by the sword. I, the Sovereign LORD, have spoken!"

✝ ✝ ✝

Once again a message came to me from the LORD: "Son of man, give your people this message: 'When I bring an army against a country, the people of that land choose one of their own to be a watchman. When the watchman sees the enemy coming, he sounds the alarm to warn the people. Then if those who hear the alarm refuse to take action, it is their own fault if they die. They heard the alarm but ignored it, so the responsibility is theirs. If they had listened to the warning, they could have saved their lives. But if the watchman sees the enemy coming and doesn't sound the alarm to warn the people, he is responsible for their captivity. They will die in their sins, but I will hold the watchman responsible for their deaths.'

"Now, son of man, I am making you a watchman for the people of Israel. Therefore, listen to what I say and warn them for me. If I announce that some wicked people are sure to die and you fail to tell them to change their ways, then they will die in their sins, and I will hold you responsible for their deaths. But if you warn them to repent and they don't repent, they will die in their sins, but you will have saved yourself.

"Son of man, give the people of Israel this message: You are saying, 'Our sins are heavy upon us; we are wasting away! How can we survive?' As surely as I live, says the Sovereign LORD, I take no pleasure in the death of wicked people. I only want them to turn from their wicked ways so they can live. Turn! Turn from your wickedness, O people of Israel! Why should you die?

"Son of man, give your people this message: The righteous behavior of righteous people will not save them if they turn to sin, nor will the wicked behavior of wicked people destroy them if they repent and turn from their sins. When I tell righteous people that they will live, but then they sin, expecting their past righteousness to save them, then none of their righteous acts will be remembered. I will destroy them for their sins. And suppose I tell some wicked people that they will surely die, but then they turn from their sins and do what is just and right. For instance, they might give back a debtor's security, return what they have stolen, and obey my life-giving laws, no longer doing what is evil. If they do this, then they will surely live and not die. None of their past sins will be brought up again, for they have done what is just and right, and they will surely live.

"Your people are saying, 'The Lord isn't doing what's right,' but it is they who are not doing what's right. For again I say, when righteous people turn away from their righteous behavior and turn to evil, they will die. But if wicked people turn from their wickedness and do what is just and right, they will live. O people of Israel, you are saying, 'The Lord isn't doing what's right.' But I judge each of you according to your deeds."

+

On January 8, during the twelfth year of our captivity, a survivor from Jerusalem came to me and said, "The city has fallen!" The previous evening the LORD had taken hold of me and given me back my voice. So I was able to speak when this man arrived the next morning.

Then this message came to me from the LORD: "Son of man, the scattered remnants of Israel living among the ruined cities keep saying, 'Abraham was only one man, yet he gained possession of the entire land. We are many; surely the land has been given to us as a possession.' So tell these people, 'This is what the Sovereign LORD says: You eat meat with blood in it, you worship idols, and you murder the innocent. Do you really think the land should be yours? Murderers! Idolaters! Adulterers! Should the land belong to you?'

"Say to them, 'This is what the Sovereign LORD says: As surely as I live, those living in the ruins will die by the sword. And I will send wild animals to eat those living in the open fields. Those hiding in the forts and caves will die of disease. I will completely destroy the land and demolish her pride. Her arrogant power will come to an end. The mountains of Israel will be so desolate that no one will even travel through them. When I have completely destroyed the land because of their detestable sins, then they will know that I am the LORD.'

"Son of man, your people talk about you in their houses and whisper about you at the doors. They say to each other, 'Come on, let's go hear the prophet tell us what the LORD is saying!' So my people come pretending to be sincere and sit before you. They listen to your words, but they have no intention of doing what you say. Their mouths are full of lustful words, and their hearts seek only after money. You are very entertaining to them, like someone who sings love songs with a beautiful voice or plays fine music on an instrument. They hear what you say, but they don't act on it! But when all these terrible things happen to them—as they certainly will—then they will know a prophet has been among them."

+

Then this message came to me from the LORD: "Son of man, prophesy against the shepherds, the leaders of Israel. Give them this message from the Sovereign LORD: What sorrow awaits you shepherds who feed your-selves instead of your flocks. Shouldn't shepherds feed their sheep? You drink the milk, wear the wool, and butcher the best animals, but you let your flocks starve. You have not taken care of the weak. You have not tended the sick or bound up the injured. You have not gone looking for those who have wandered away and are lost. Instead, you have ruled them with harshness and cruelty. So my sheep have been scattered without a shepherd, and they are easy prey for any wild animal. They have wandered through all the mountains and all the hills, across the face of the earth, yet no one has gone to search for them.

"Therefore, you shepherds, hear the word of the LORD: As surely as I live, says the Sovereign LORD, you abandoned my flock and left them to be attacked by every wild animal. And though you were my shepherds, you didn't search for my sheep when they were lost. You took care of your-selves and left the sheep to starve. Therefore, you shepherds, hear the word of the LORD. This is what the Sovereign LORD says: I now consider these shepherds my enemies, and I will hold them responsible for what has happened to my flock. I will take away their right to feed the flock, and I will stop them from feeding themselves. I will rescue my flock from their mouths; the sheep will no longer be their prey.

"For this is what the Sovereign LORD says: I myself will search and find my sheep. I will be like a shepherd looking for his scattered flock. I will find my sheep and rescue them from all the places where they were scattered on that dark and cloudy day. I will bring them back home to their own land of Israel from among the peoples and nations. I will feed them on the moun-tains of Israel and by the rivers and in all the places where people live. Yes, I will give them good pastureland on the high hills of Israel. There they will lie down in pleasant places and feed in the lush pastures of the hills. I myself will tend my sheep and give them a place to lie down in peace, says the Sovereign LORD. I will search for my lost ones who strayed away, and I will bring them safely home again. I will bandage the injured and strengthen the weak. But I will destroy those who are fat and powerful. I will feed them, yes—feed them justice!

"And as for you, my flock, this is what the Sovereign LORD says to his people: I will judge between one animal of the flock and another, separating the sheep from the goats. Isn't it enough for you to keep the best of the pastures for yourselves? Must you also trample down the rest? Isn't it enough for you to drink clear water for yourselves? Must you also muddy the rest with your feet? Why must my flock eat what you have trampled down and drink water you have fouled?

"Therefore, this is what the Sovereign LORD says: I will surely judge between the fat sheep and the scrawny sheep. For you fat sheep pushed and butted and crowded my sick and hungry flock until you scattered them to distant lands. So I will rescue my flock, and they will no longer be abused. I will judge between one animal of the flock and another. And I will set over them one shepherd, my servant David. He will feed them and be a shepherd to them. And I, the LORD, will be their God, and my servant David will be a prince among my people. I, the LORD, have spoken!

"I will make a covenant of peace with my people and drive away the dangerous animals from the land. Then they will be able to camp safely in the wildest places and sleep in the woods without fear. I will bless my people and their homes around my holy hill. And in the proper season I will send the showers they need. There will be showers of blessing. The orchards and fields of my people will yield bumper crops, and everyone will live in safety. When I have broken their chains of slavery and rescued them from those who enslaved them, then they will know that I am the LORD. They will no longer be prey for other nations, and wild animals will no longer devour them. They will live in safety, and no one will frighten them.

"And I will make their land famous for its crops, so my people will never again suffer from famines or the insults of foreign nations. In this way, they will know that I, the LORD their God, am with them. And they will know that they, the people of Israel, are my people, says the Sovereign LORD. You are my flock, the sheep of my pasture. You are my people, and I am your God. I, the Sovereign LORD, have spoken!"

+

Again a message came to me from the LORD: "Son of man, turn and face Mount Seir, and prophesy against its people. Give them this message from the Sovereign LORD:

"I am your enemy, O Mount Seir,
    and I will raise my fist against you
    to destroy you completely.
I will demolish your cities
    and make you desolate.
Then you will know that I am the LORD.

"Your eternal hatred for the people of Israel led you to butcher them when they were helpless, when I had already punished them for all their sins. As surely as I live, says the Sovereign LORD, since you show no distaste for blood, I will give you a bloodbath of your own. Your turn has come! I will make Mount Seir utterly desolate, killing off all who try to escape and any who return. I will fill your mountains with the dead. Your hills, your valleys, and your ravines will be filled with people slaughtered by the sword. I will make you desolate forever. Your cities will never be rebuilt. Then you will know that I am the LORD.

"For you said, 'The lands of Israel and Judah will be ours. We will take possession of them. What do we care that the LORD is there!' Therefore, as surely as I live, says the Sovereign LORD, I will pay back your angry deeds with my own. I will punish you for all your acts of anger, envy, and hatred. And I will make myself known to Israel by what I do to you. Then you will know that I, the LORD, have heard every contemptuous word you spoke against the mountains of Israel. For you said, 'They are desolate; they have been given to us as food to eat!' In saying that, you boasted proudly against me, and I have heard it all!

"This is what the Sovereign LORD says: The whole world will rejoice when I make you desolate. You rejoiced at the desolation of Israel's territory. Now I will rejoice at yours! You will be wiped out, you people of Mount Seir and all who live in Edom! Then you will know that I am the LORD.

+

"Son of man, prophesy to Israel's mountains. Give them this message: O mountains of Israel, hear the word of the LORD! This is what the Sovereign LORD says: Your enemies have taunted you, saying, 'Aha! Now the ancient heights belong to us!' Therefore, son of man, give the mountains of Israel this message from the Sovereign LORD: Your enemies have attacked you from all directions, making you the property of many nations and the object of much mocking and slander. Therefore, O mountains of Israel, hear the word of the Sovereign LORD. He speaks to the hills and mountains, ravines and valleys, and to ruined wastes and long-deserted cities that have been destroyed and mocked by the surrounding nations. This is what the Sovereign LORD says: My jealous anger burns against these nations, especially Edom, because they have shown utter contempt for me by gleefully taking my land for themselves as plunder.

"Therefore, prophesy to the hills and mountains, the ravines and valleys of Israel. This is what the Sovereign LORD says: I am furious that you have suffered shame before the surrounding nations. Therefore, this is what the

Sovereign Lord says: I have taken a solemn oath that those nations will soon have their own shame to endure.

"But the mountains of Israel will produce heavy crops of fruit for my people—for they will be coming home again soon! See, I care about you, and I will pay attention to you. Your ground will be plowed and your crops planted. I will greatly increase the population of Israel, and the ruined cities will be rebuilt and filled with people. I will increase not only the people, but also your animals. O mountains of Israel, I will bring people to live on you once again. I will make you even more prosperous than you were before. Then you will know that I am the Lord. I will cause my people to walk on you once again, and you will be their territory. You will never again rob them of their children.

"This is what the Sovereign Lord says: The other nations taunt you, saying, 'Israel is a land that devours its own people and robs them of their children!' But you will never again devour your people or rob them of their children, says the Sovereign Lord. I will not let you hear those other nations insult you, and you will no longer be mocked by them. You will not be a land that causes its nation to fall, says the Sovereign Lord."

+

Then this further message came to me from the Lord: "Son of man, when the people of Israel were living in their own land, they defiled it by the evil way they lived. To me their conduct was as unclean as a woman's menstrual cloth. They polluted the land with murder and the worship of idols, so I poured out my fury on them. I scattered them to many lands to punish them for the evil way they had lived. But when they were scattered among the nations, they brought shame on my holy name. For the nations said, 'These are the people of the Lord, but he couldn't keep them safe in his own land!' Then I was concerned for my holy name, on which my people brought shame among the nations.

"Therefore, give the people of Israel this message from the Sovereign Lord: I am bringing you back, but not because you deserve it. I am doing it to protect my holy name, on which you brought shame while you were scattered among the nations. I will show how holy my great name is—the name on which you brought shame among the nations. And when I reveal my holiness through you before their very eyes, says the Sovereign Lord, then the nations will know that I am the Lord. For I will gather you up from all the nations and bring you home again to your land.

"Then I will sprinkle clean water on you, and you will be clean. Your filth will be washed away, and you will no longer worship idols. And I will give you a new heart, and I will put a new spirit in you. I will take out your stony, stubborn heart and give you a tender, responsive heart. And I will put my Spirit in you so that you will follow my decrees and be careful to obey my regulations.

"And you will live in Israel, the land I gave your ancestors long ago. You will be my people, and I will be your God. I will cleanse you of your filthy behavior. I will give you good crops of grain, and I will send no more famines on the land. I will give you great harvests from your fruit trees and fields, and never again will the surrounding nations be able to scoff at your land for its famines. Then you will remember your past sins and despise yourselves for all the detestable things you did. But remember, says the Sovereign LORD, I am not doing this because you deserve it. O my people of Israel, you should be utterly ashamed of all you have done!

"This is what the Sovereign LORD says: When I cleanse you from your sins, I will repopulate your cities, and the ruins will be rebuilt. The fields that used to lie empty and desolate in plain view of everyone will again be farmed. And when I bring you back, people will say, 'This former wasteland is now like the Garden of Eden! The abandoned and ruined cities now have strong walls and are filled with people!' Then the surrounding nations that survive will know that I, the LORD, have rebuilt the ruins and replanted the wasteland. For I, the LORD, have spoken, and I will do what I say.

"This is what the Sovereign LORD says: I am ready to hear Israel's prayers and to increase their numbers like a flock. They will be as numerous as the sacred flocks that fill Jerusalem's streets at the time of her festivals. The ruined cities will be crowded with people once more, and everyone will know that I am the LORD."

+

The LORD took hold of me, and I was carried away by the Spirit of the LORD to a valley filled with bones. He led me all around among the bones that covered the valley floor. They were scattered everywhere across the ground and were completely dried out. Then he asked me, "Son of man, can these bones become living people again?"

"O Sovereign LORD," I replied, "you alone know the answer to that."

Then he said to me, "Speak a prophetic message to these bones and say, 'Dry bones, listen to the word of the LORD! This is what the Sovereign LORD says: Look! I am going to put breath into you and make you live again! I will put flesh and muscles on you and cover you with skin. I will put breath into you, and you will come to life. Then you will know that I am the LORD.'"

So I spoke this message, just as he told me. Suddenly as I spoke, there was a rattling noise all across the valley. The bones of each body came together and attached themselves as complete skeletons. Then as I watched, muscles and flesh formed over the bones. Then skin formed to cover their bodies, but they still had no breath in them.

Then he said to me, "Speak a prophetic message to the winds, son of man. Speak a prophetic message and say, 'This is what the Sovereign LORD says: Come, O breath, from the four winds! Breathe into these dead bodies so they may live again.'"

So I spoke the message as he commanded me, and breath came into their bodies. They all came to life and stood up on their feet—a great army.

Then he said to me, "Son of man, these bones represent the people of Israel. They are saying, 'We have become old, dry bones—all hope is gone. Our nation is finished.' Therefore, prophesy to them and say, 'This is what the Sovereign LORD says: O my people, I will open your graves of exile and cause you to rise again. Then I will bring you back to the land of Israel. When this happens, O my people, you will know that I am the LORD. I will put my Spirit in you, and you will live again and return home to your own land. Then you will know that I, the LORD, have spoken, and I have done what I said. Yes, the LORD has spoken!'"

+

Again a message came to me from the LORD: "Son of man, take a piece of wood and carve on it these words: 'This represents Judah and its allied tribes.' Then take another piece and carve these words on it: 'This represents Ephraim and the northern tribes of Israel.' Now hold them together in your hand as if they were one piece of wood. When your people ask you what your actions mean, say to them, 'This is what the Sovereign LORD says: I will take Ephraim and the northern tribes and join them to Judah. I will make them one piece of wood in my hand.'

"Then hold out the pieces of wood you have inscribed, so the people can see them. And give them this message from the Sovereign LORD: I will gather the people of Israel from among the nations. I will bring them home to their own land from the places where they have been scattered. I will unify them into one nation on the mountains of Israel. One king will rule them all; no longer will they be divided into two nations or into two kingdoms. They will never again pollute themselves with their idols and vile images and rebellion, for I will save them from their sinful apostasy. I will cleanse them. Then they will truly be my people, and I will be their God.

"My servant David will be their king, and they will have only one shepherd. They will obey my regulations and be careful to keep my decrees. They will live in the land I gave my servant Jacob, the land where their ancestors lived. They and their children and their grandchildren after them will live there forever, generation after generation. And my servant David will be their prince forever. And I will make a covenant of peace with them, an everlasting covenant. I will give them their land and increase their numbers, and I will put my Temple among them forever. I will make my home among them. I will be their God, and they will be my people. And when my Temple is among them forever, the nations will know that I am the LORD, who makes Israel holy."

✢

This is another message that came to me from the LORD: "Son of man, turn and face Gog of the land of Magog, the prince who rules over the nations of Meshech and Tubal, and prophesy against him. Give him this message from the Sovereign LORD: Gog, I am your enemy! I will turn you around and put hooks in your jaws to lead you out with your whole army—your horses and charioteers in full armor and a great horde armed with shields and swords. Persia, Ethiopia, and Libya will join you, too, with all their weapons. Gomer and all its armies will also join you, along with the armies of Beth-togarmah from the distant north, and many others.

"Get ready; be prepared! Keep all the armies around you mobilized, and take command of them. A long time from now you will be called into action. In the distant future you will swoop down on the land of Israel, which will be enjoying peace after recovering from war and after its people have returned from many lands to the mountains of Israel. You and all your allies—a vast and awesome army—will roll down on them like a storm and cover the land like a cloud.

"This is what the Sovereign LORD says: At that time evil thoughts will come to your mind, and you will devise a wicked scheme. You will say, 'Israel is an unprotected land filled with unwalled villages! I will march against her and destroy these people who live in such confidence! I will go to those formerly desolate cities that are now filled with people who have returned from exile in many nations. I will capture vast amounts of plunder, for the people are rich with livestock and other possessions now. They think the whole world revolves around them!' But Sheba and Dedan and the merchants of Tarshish will ask, 'Do you really think the armies you have gathered can rob them of silver and gold? Do you think you can drive away their livestock and seize their goods and carry off plunder?'

"Therefore, son of man, prophesy against Gog. Give him this message from the Sovereign LORD: When my people are living in peace in their land, then you will rouse yourself. You will come from your homeland in the distant north with your vast cavalry and your mighty army, and you will attack my people Israel, covering their land like a cloud. At that time in the distant future, I will bring you against my land as everyone watches, and my holiness will be displayed by what happens to you, Gog. Then all the nations will know that I am the LORD.

"This is what the Sovereign LORD asks: Are you the one I was talking about long ago, when I announced through Israel's prophets that in the future I would bring you against my people? But this is what the Sovereign LORD says: When Gog invades the land of Israel, my fury will boil over! In my jealousy and blazing anger, I promise a mighty shaking in the land of Israel on that day. All living things—the fish in the sea, the birds of the sky, the animals of the field, the small animals that scurry along the ground, and all the people on earth—will quake in terror at my presence. Mountains will be thrown down; cliffs will crumble; walls will fall to the earth. I will summon the sword against you on all the hills of Israel, says the Sovereign LORD. Your men will turn their swords against each other. I will punish you and your armies with disease and bloodshed; I will send torrential rain, hailstones, fire, and burning sulfur! In this way, I will show my greatness and holiness, and I will make myself known to all the nations of the world. Then they will know that I am the LORD.

"Son of man, prophesy against Gog. Give him this message from the Sovereign LORD: I am your enemy, O Gog, ruler of the nations of Meshech and Tubal. I will turn you around and drive you toward the mountains of Israel, bringing you from the distant north. I will knock the bow from your left hand and the arrows from your right hand, and I will leave you helpless. You and your army and your allies will all die on the mountains. I will feed you to the vultures and wild animals. You will fall in the open fields, for I have spoken, says the Sovereign LORD. And I will rain down fire on Magog and on all your allies who live safely on the coasts. Then they will know that I am the LORD.

"In this way, I will make known my holy name among my people of Israel. I will not let anyone bring shame on it. And the nations, too, will know that I am the LORD, the Holy One of Israel. That day of judgment will come, says the Sovereign LORD. Everything will happen just as I have declared it.

"Then the people in the towns of Israel will go out and pick up your small and large shields, bows and arrows, javelins and spears, and they will use them for fuel. There will be enough to last them seven years! They won't need to cut wood from the fields or forests, for these weapons will give them all the fuel they need. They will plunder those who planned to plunder them, and they will rob those who planned to rob them, says the Sovereign LORD.

"And I will make a vast graveyard for Gog and his hordes in the Valley of the Travelers, east of the Dead Sea. It will block the way of those who travel there, and they will change the name of the place to the Valley of

Gog's Hordes. It will take seven months for the people of Israel to bury the bodies and cleanse the land. Everyone in Israel will help, for it will be a glorious victory for Israel when I demonstrate my glory on that day, says the Sovereign LORD.

"After seven months, teams of men will be appointed to search the land for skeletons to bury, so the land will be made clean again. Whenever bones are found, a marker will be set up so the burial crews will take them to be buried in the Valley of Gog's Hordes. (There will be a town there named Hamonah, which means 'horde.') And so the land will finally be cleansed.

"And now, son of man, this is what the Sovereign LORD says: Call all the birds and wild animals. Say to them: Gather together for my great sacrificial feast. Come from far and near to the mountains of Israel, and there eat flesh and drink blood! Eat the flesh of mighty men and drink the blood of princes as though they were rams, lambs, goats, and bulls—all fattened animals from Bashan! Gorge yourselves with flesh until you are glutted; drink blood until you are drunk. This is the sacrificial feast I have prepared for you. Feast at my banquet table—feast on horses and charioteers, on mighty men and all kinds of valiant warriors, says the Sovereign LORD.

"In this way, I will demonstrate my glory to the nations. Everyone will see the punishment I have inflicted on them and the power of my fist when I strike. And from that time on the people of Israel will know that I am the LORD their God. The nations will then know why Israel was sent away to exile—it was punishment for sin, for they were unfaithful to their God. Therefore, I turned away from them and let their enemies destroy them. I turned my face away and punished them because of their defilement and their sins.

"So now, this is what the Sovereign LORD says: I will end the captivity of my people; I will have mercy on all Israel, for I jealously guard my holy reputation! They will accept responsibility for their past shame and unfaithfulness after they come home to live in peace in their own land, with no one to bother them. When I bring them home from the lands of their enemies, I will display my holiness among them for all the nations to see. Then my people will know that I am the LORD their God, because I sent them away to exile and brought them home again. I will leave none of my people behind. And I will never again turn my face from them, for I will pour out my Spirit upon the people of Israel. I, the Sovereign LORD, have spoken!"

+

On April 28, during the twenty-fifth year of our captivity—fourteen years after the fall of Jerusalem—the LORD took hold of me. In a vision from

God he took me to the land of Israel and set me down on a very high mountain. From there I could see toward the south what appeared to be a city. As he brought me nearer, I saw a man whose face shone like bronze standing beside a gateway entrance. He was holding in his hand a linen measuring cord and a measuring rod.

He said to me, "Son of man, watch and listen. Pay close attention to everything I show you. You have been brought here so I can show you many things. Then you will return to the people of Israel and tell them everything you have seen."

I could see a wall completely surrounding the Temple area. The man took a measuring rod that was 10½ feet long and measured the wall, and the wall was 10½ feet thick and 10½ feet high.

Then he went over to the eastern gateway. He climbed the steps and measured the threshold of the gateway; it was 10½ feet front to back. There were guard alcoves on each side built into the gateway passage. Each of these alcoves was 10½ feet square, with a distance between them of 8¾ feet along the passage wall. The gateway's inner threshold, which led to the entry room at the inner end of the gateway passage, was 10½ feet front to back. He also measured the entry room of the gateway. It was 14 feet across, with supporting columns 3½ feet thick. This entry room was at the inner end of the gateway structure, facing toward the Temple.

There were three guard alcoves on each side of the gateway passage. Each had the same measurements, and the dividing walls separating them were also identical. The man measured the gateway entrance, which was 17½ feet wide at the opening and 22¾ feet wide in the gateway passage. In front of each of the guard alcoves was a 21-inch curb. The alcoves themselves were 10½ feet on each side.

Then he measured the entire width of the gateway, measuring the distance between the back walls of facing guard alcoves; this distance was 43¾ feet. He measured the dividing walls all along the inside of the gateway up to the entry room of the gateway; this distance was 105 feet. The full length of the gateway passage was 87½ feet from one end to the other. There were recessed windows that narrowed inward through the walls of the guard alcoves and their dividing walls. There were also windows in the entry room. The surfaces of the dividing walls were decorated with carved palm trees.

Then the man brought me through the gateway into the outer courtyard of the Temple. A stone pavement ran along the walls of the courtyard, and thirty rooms were built against the walls, opening onto the pavement. This pavement flanked the gates and extended out from the walls into the courtyard the same distance as the gateway entrance. This was the lower pavement. Then the man measured across the Temple's outer courtyard between the outer and inner gateways; the distance was 175 feet.

The man measured the gateway on the north just like the one on the east. Here, too, there were three guard alcoves on each side, with dividing walls and an entry room. All the measurements matched those of the east gateway. The gateway passage was 87½ feet long and 43¾ feet wide between the back walls of facing guard alcoves. The windows, the entry room, and the palm tree decorations were identical to those in the east gateway. There were seven steps leading up to the gateway entrance, and the entry room was at the inner end of the gateway passage. Here on the north side, just as on the east, there was another gateway leading to the Temple's inner courtyard directly opposite this outer gateway. The distance between the two gateways was 175 feet.

Then the man took me around to the south gateway and measured its various parts, and they were exactly the same as in the others. It had windows along the walls as the others did, and there was an entry room where the gateway passage opened into the outer courtyard. And like the others, the gateway passage was 87½ feet long and 43¾ feet wide between the back walls of facing guard alcoves. This gateway also had a stairway of seven steps leading up to it, and an entry room at the inner end, and palm tree decorations along the dividing walls. And here again, directly opposite the outer gateway, was another gateway that led into the inner courtyard. The distance between the two gateways was 175 feet.

Then the man took me to the south gateway leading into the inner courtyard. He measured it, and it had the same measurements as the other gateways. Its guard alcoves, dividing walls, and entry room were the same size as those in the others. It also had windows along its walls and in the entry room. And like the others, the gateway passage was 87½ feet long and 43¾ feet wide. (The entry rooms of the gateways leading into the inner courtyard were 14 feet across and 43¾ feet wide.) The entry room to the south gateway faced into the outer courtyard. It had palm tree decorations on its columns, and there were eight steps leading to its entrance.

Then he took me to the east gateway leading to the inner courtyard. He measured it, and it had the same measurements as the other gateways. Its guard alcoves, dividing walls, and entry room were the same size as those of the others, and there were windows along the walls and in the entry room. The gateway passage measured 87½ feet long and 43¾ feet wide. Its entry room faced into the outer courtyard. It had palm tree decorations on its columns, and there were eight steps leading to its entrance.

Then he took me around to the north gateway leading to the inner courtyard. He measured it, and it had the same measurements as the other gateways. The guard alcoves, dividing walls, and entry room of this gateway had the same measurements as in the others and the same window arrangements. The gateway passage measured 87½ feet long and 43¾ feet wide. Its entry room faced into the outer courtyard, and it had palm tree decorations on the columns. There were eight steps leading to its entrance.

A door led from the entry room of one of the inner gateways into a side room, where the meat for sacrifices was washed. On each side of this entry room were two tables, where the sacrificial animals were slaughtered for the burnt offerings, sin offerings, and guilt offerings. Outside the entry room, on each side of the stairs going up to the north entrance, were two more tables. So there were eight tables in all—four inside and four outside—where the sacrifices were cut up and prepared. There were also four tables of finished stone for preparation of the burnt offerings, each 31½ inches square and 21 inches high. On these tables were placed the butchering knives and other implements for slaughtering the sacrificial animals. There were hooks, each 3 inches long, fastened all around the foyer walls. The sacrificial meat was laid on the tables.

Inside the inner courtyard were two rooms, one beside the north gateway, facing south, and the other beside the south gateway, facing north. And the man said to me, "The room beside the north inner gate is for the priests who supervise the Temple maintenance. The room beside the south inner gate is for the priests in charge of the altar—the descendants of Zadok—for they alone of all the Levites may approach the LORD to minister to him."

Then the man measured the inner courtyard, and it was a square, 175 feet wide and 175 feet across. The altar stood in the courtyard in front of the Temple. Then he brought me to the entry room of the Temple. He measured the walls on either side of the opening to the entry room, and they were 8¾ feet thick. The entrance itself was 24½ feet wide, and the walls on each side of the entrance were an additional 5¼ feet long. The entry room was 35 feet wide and 21 feet deep. There were ten steps leading up to it, with a column on each side.

After that, the man brought me into the sanctuary of the Temple. He measured the walls on either side of its doorway, and they were 10½ feet thick. The doorway was 17½ feet wide, and the walls on each side of it were 8¾ feet long. The sanctuary itself was 70 feet long and 35 feet wide.

Then he went beyond the sanctuary into the inner room. He measured the walls on either side of its entrance, and they were 3½ feet thick. The entrance was 10½ feet wide, and the walls on each side of the entrance were 12¼ feet long. The inner room of the sanctuary was 35 feet long and 35 feet wide. "This," he told me, "is the Most Holy Place."

Then he measured the wall of the Temple, and it was 10½ feet thick. There was a row of rooms along the outside wall; each room was 7 feet wide. These side rooms were built in three levels, one above the other, with thirty rooms on each level. The supports for these side rooms rested on exterior ledges on the Temple wall; they did not extend into the wall. Each level was wider than the one below it, corresponding to the narrowing of the Temple wall as it rose higher. A stairway led up from the bottom level through the middle level to the top level.

I saw that the Temple was built on a terrace, which provided a foundation for the side rooms. This terrace was 10½ feet high. The outer wall of the Temple's side rooms was 8¾ feet thick. This left an open area between these side rooms and the row of rooms along the outer wall of the inner courtyard. This open area was 35 feet wide, and it went all the way around the Temple. Two doors opened from the side rooms into the terrace yard, which was 8¾ feet wide. One door faced north and the other south.

A large building stood on the west, facing the Temple courtyard. It was 122½ feet wide and 157½ feet long, and its walls were 8¾ feet thick. Then the man measured the Temple, and it was 175 feet long. The courtyard around the building, including its walls, was an additional 175 feet in length. The inner courtyard to the east of the Temple was also 175 feet wide. The building to the west, including its two walls, was also 175 feet wide.

The sanctuary, the inner room, and the entry room of the Temple were all paneled with wood, as were the frames of the recessed windows. The inner walls of the Temple were paneled with wood above and below the windows. The space above the door leading into the inner room, and its walls inside and out, were also paneled. All the walls were decorated with carvings of cherubim, each with two faces, and there was a carving of a palm tree between each of the cherubim. One face—that of a man—looked toward the palm tree on one side. The other face—that of a young lion—looked toward the palm tree on the other side. The figures were carved all along the inside of the Temple, from the floor to the top of the walls, including the outer wall of the sanctuary.

There were square columns at the entrance to the sanctuary, and the ones at the entrance of the Most Holy Place were similar. There was an altar made of wood, 5¼ feet high and 3½ feet across. Its corners, base, and sides were all made of wood. "This," the man told me, "is the table that stands in the Lord's presence."

Both the sanctuary and the Most Holy Place had double doorways, each with two swinging doors. The doors leading into the sanctuary were decorated with carved cherubim and palm trees, just as on the walls. And there was a wooden roof at the front of the entry room to the Temple. On both sides of the entry room were recessed windows decorated with carved palm trees. The side rooms along the outside wall also had roofs.

Then the man led me out of the Temple courtyard by way of the north gateway. We entered the outer courtyard and came to a group of rooms against the north wall of the inner courtyard. This structure, whose entrance opened toward the north, was 175 feet long and 87½ feet wide. One block of rooms overlooked the 35-foot width of the inner courtyard. Another block of rooms looked out onto the pavement of the outer courtyard. The two blocks were built three levels high and stood across from each other. Between the two blocks of rooms ran a walkway 17½ feet wide. It extended the entire 175 feet of the complex, and all the doors faced north. Each of the two upper levels of rooms was narrower than the one beneath it because the upper levels had to allow space for walkways in front of them. Since there were three levels and they did not have supporting columns as in the courtyards, each of the upper levels was set back from the level beneath it. There was an outer wall that separated the rooms from the outer courtyard; it was 87½ feet long. This wall added length to the outer block of rooms, which extended for only 87½ feet, while the inner block—the rooms toward the Temple—extended for 175 feet. There was an eastern entrance from the outer courtyard to these rooms.

On the south side of the Temple there were two blocks of rooms just south of the inner courtyard between the Temple and the outer courtyard. These rooms were arranged just like the rooms on the north. There was a walkway between the two blocks of rooms just like the complex on the north side of the Temple. This complex of rooms was the same length and width as the other one, and it had the same entrances and doors. The dimensions of each were identical. So there was an entrance in the wall facing the doors of the inner block of rooms, and another on the east at the end of the interior walkway.

Then the man told me, "These rooms that overlook the Temple from the north and south are holy. Here the priests who offer sacrifices to the LORD will eat the most holy offerings. And because these rooms are holy, they will be used to store the sacred offerings—the grain offerings, sin offerings, and guilt offerings. When the priests leave the sanctuary, they must not go directly to the outer courtyard. They must first take off the clothes they wore while ministering, because these clothes are holy. They must put on other clothes before entering the parts of the building complex open to the public."

When the man had finished measuring the inside of the Temple area, he led me out through the east gateway to measure the entire perimeter. He measured the east side with his measuring rod, and it was 875 feet long. Then he measured the north side, and it was also 875 feet. The south side was also 875 feet, and the west side was also 875 feet. So the area was

875 feet on each side with a wall all around it to separate what was holy from what was common.

After this, the man brought me back around to the east gateway. Suddenly, the glory of the God of Israel appeared from the east. The sound of his coming was like the roar of rushing waters, and the whole landscape shone with his glory. This vision was just like the others I had seen, first by the Kebar River and then when he came to destroy Jerusalem. I fell face down on the ground. And the glory of the LORD came into the Temple through the east gateway.

Then the Spirit took me up and brought me into the inner courtyard, and the glory of the LORD filled the Temple. And I heard someone speaking to me from within the Temple, while the man who had been measuring stood beside me. The LORD said to me, "Son of man, this is the place of my throne and the place where I will rest my feet. I will live here forever among the people of Israel. They and their kings will not defile my holy name any longer by their adulterous worship of other gods or by honoring the relics of their kings who have died. They put their idol altars right next to mine with only a wall between them and me. They defiled my holy name by such detestable sin, so I consumed them in my anger. Now let them stop worshiping other gods and honoring the relics of their kings, and I will live among them forever.

"Son of man, describe to the people of Israel the Temple I have shown you, so they will be ashamed of all their sins. Let them study its plan, and they will be ashamed of what they have done. Describe to them all the specifications of the Temple—including its entrances and exits—and everything else about it. Tell them about its decrees and laws. Write down all these specifications and decrees as they watch so they will be sure to remember and follow them. And this is the basic law of the Temple: absolute holiness! The entire top of the mountain where the Temple is built is holy. Yes, this is the basic law of the Temple.

"These are the measurements of the altar: There is a gutter all around the altar 21 inches deep and 21 inches wide, with a curb 9 inches wide around its edge. And this is the height of the altar: From the gutter the altar rises 3½ feet to a lower ledge that surrounds the altar and is 21 inches wide. From the lower ledge the altar rises 7 feet to the upper ledge that is also 21 inches wide. The top of the altar, the hearth, rises another 7 feet higher, with a horn rising up from each of the four corners. The top of the altar is square, measuring 21 feet by 21 feet. The upper ledge also forms a square, measuring 24½ feet by 24½ feet, with a 21-inch gutter and a 10½-inch curb all around the edge. There are steps going up the east side of the altar."

Then he said to me, "Son of man, this is what the Sovereign LORD says: These will be the regulations for the burning of offerings and the sprinkling of blood when the altar is built. At that time, the Levitical priests of the family of Zadok, who minister before me, are to be given a young bull for a sin offering, says the Sovereign LORD. You will take some of its blood and smear it on the four horns of the altar, the four corners of the upper ledge, and the curb that runs around that ledge. This will cleanse and make atonement for the altar. Then take the young bull for the sin offering and burn it at the appointed place outside the Temple area.

"On the second day, sacrifice as a sin offering a young male goat that has no physical defects. Then cleanse and make atonement for the altar again, just as you did with the young bull. When you have finished the cleansing ceremony, offer another young bull that has no defects and a perfect ram from the flock. You are to present them to the LORD, and the priests are to sprinkle salt on them and offer them as a burnt offering to the LORD.

"Every day for seven days a male goat, a young bull, and a ram from the flock will be sacrificed as a sin offering. None of these animals may have physical defects of any kind. Do this each day for seven days to cleanse and make atonement for the altar, thus setting it apart for holy use. On the eighth day, and on each day afterward, the priests will sacrifice on the altar the burnt offerings and peace offerings of the people. Then I will accept you. I, the Sovereign LORD, have spoken!"

Then the man brought me back to the east gateway in the outer wall of the Temple area, but it was closed. And the LORD said to me, "This gate must remain closed; it will never again be opened. No one will ever open it and pass through, for the LORD, the God of Israel, has entered here. Therefore, it must always remain shut. Only the prince himself may sit inside this gateway to feast in the LORD's presence. But he may come and go only through the entry room of the gateway."

Then the man brought me through the north gateway to the front of the Temple. I looked and saw that the glory of the LORD filled the Temple of the LORD, and I fell face down on the ground.

And the LORD said to me, "Son of man, take careful notice. Use your eyes and ears, and listen to everything I tell you about the regulations concerning the LORD's Temple. Take careful note of the procedures for using the Temple's entrances and exits. And give these rebels, the people of Israel, this message from the Sovereign LORD: O people of Israel, enough of your detestable sins! You have brought uncircumcised foreigners into my sanctuary—people who have no heart for God. In this way, you defiled my Temple even as you offered me my food, the fat and blood of sacrifices. In addition to all your other detestable sins, you have broken my covenant.

Instead of safeguarding my sacred rituals, you have hired foreigners to take charge of my sanctuary.

"So this is what the Sovereign LORD says: No foreigners, including those who live among the people of Israel, will enter my sanctuary if they have not been circumcised and have not surrendered themselves to the LORD. And the men of the tribe of Levi who abandoned me when Israel strayed away from me to worship idols must bear the consequences of their unfaithfulness. They may still be Temple guards and gatekeepers, and they may slaughter the animals brought for burnt offerings and be present to help the people. But they encouraged my people to worship idols, causing Israel to fall into deep sin. So I have taken a solemn oath that they must bear the consequences for their sins, says the Sovereign LORD. They may not approach me to minister as priests. They may not touch any of my holy things or the holy offerings, for they must bear the shame of all the detestable sins they have committed. They are to serve as the Temple caretakers, taking charge of the maintenance work and performing general duties.

"However, the Levitical priests of the family of Zadok continued to minister faithfully in the Temple when Israel abandoned me for idols. These men will serve as my ministers. They will stand in my presence and offer the fat and blood of the sacrifices, says the Sovereign LORD. They alone will enter my sanctuary and approach my table to serve me. They will fulfill all my requirements.

"When they enter the gateway to the inner courtyard, they must wear only linen clothing. They must wear no wool while on duty in the inner courtyard or in the Temple itself. They must wear linen turbans and linen undergarments. They must not wear anything that would cause them to perspire. When they return to the outer courtyard where the people are, they must take off the clothes they wear while ministering to me. They must leave them in the sacred rooms and put on other clothes so they do not endanger anyone by transmitting holiness to them through this clothing.

"They must neither shave their heads nor let their hair grow too long. Instead, they must trim it regularly. The priests must not drink wine before entering the inner courtyard. They may choose their wives only from among the virgins of Israel or the widows of the priests. They may not marry other widows or divorced women. They will teach my people the difference between what is holy and what is common, what is ceremonially clean and unclean.

"They will serve as judges to resolve any disagreements among my people. Their decisions must be based on my regulations. And the priests themselves must obey my instructions and decrees at all the sacred festivals, and see to it that the Sabbaths are set apart as holy days.

"A priest must not defile himself by being in the presence of a dead person unless it is his father, mother, child, brother, or unmarried sister. In such cases it is permitted. Even then, he can return to his Temple duties only after being ceremonially cleansed and then waiting for seven days. The first day he returns to work and enters the inner courtyard and the sanctuary, he must offer a sin offering for himself, says the Sovereign LORD.

"The priests will not have any property or possession of land, for I alone am their special possession. Their food will come from the gifts and sacrifices brought to the Temple by the people—the grain offerings, the sin offerings, and the guilt offerings. Whatever anyone sets apart for the LORD will belong to the priests. The first of the ripe fruits and all the gifts brought to the LORD will go to the priests. The first batch of dough must also be given to the priests so the LORD will bless your homes. The priests may not eat meat from any bird or animal that dies a natural death or that dies after being attacked by another animal.

"When you divide the land among the tribes of Israel, you must set aside a section for the LORD as his holy portion. This piece of land will be 8⅓ miles long and 6⅔ miles wide. The entire area will be holy. A section of this land, measuring 875 feet by 875 feet, will be set aside for the Temple. An additional strip of land 87½ feet wide is to be left empty all around it. Within the larger sacred area, measure out a portion of land 8⅓ miles long and 3⅓ miles wide. Within it the sanctuary of the Most Holy Place will be located. This area will be holy, set aside for the priests who minister to the LORD in the sanctuary. They will use it for their homes, and my Temple will be located within it. The strip of sacred land next to it, also 8⅓ miles long and 3⅓ miles wide, will be a living area for the Levites who work at the Temple. It will be their possession and a place for their towns.

"Adjacent to the larger sacred area will be a section of land 8⅓ miles long and 1⅔ miles wide. This will be set aside for a city where anyone in Israel can live.

"Two special sections of land will be set apart for the prince. One section will share a border with the east side of the sacred lands and city, and the second section will share a border on the west side. Then the far eastern and western borders of the prince's lands will line up with the eastern and western boundaries of the tribal areas. These sections of land will be the prince's allotment. Then my princes will no longer oppress and rob my people; they will assign the rest of the land to the people, giving an allotment to each tribe.

"For this is what the Sovereign LORD says: Enough, you princes of Israel! Stop your violence and oppression and do what is just and right. Quit robbing and cheating my people out of their land. Stop expelling them from their homes, says the Sovereign LORD. Use only honest weights and scales and honest measures, both dry and liquid. The homer will be your standard unit for measuring volume. The ephah and the bath will each measure one-tenth of a homer. The standard unit for weight will be the silver shekel. One shekel will consist of twenty gerahs, and sixty shekels will be equal to one mina.

"You must give this tax to the prince: one bushel of wheat or barley for every 60 you harvest, one percent of your olive oil, and one sheep or goat for every 200 in your flocks in Israel. These will be the grain offerings, burnt offerings, and peace offerings that will make atonement for the people who bring them, says the Sovereign LORD. All the people of Israel must join in bringing these offerings to the prince. The prince will be required to provide offerings that are given at the religious festivals, the new moon celebrations, the Sabbath days, and all other similar occasions. He will provide the sin offerings, burnt offerings, grain offerings, liquid offerings, and peace offerings to purify the people of Israel, making them right with the LORD.

"This is what the Sovereign LORD says: In early spring, on the first day of each new year, sacrifice a young bull with no defects to purify the Temple. The priest will take blood from this sin offering and put it on the doorposts of the Temple, the four corners of the upper ledge of the altar, and the gateposts at the entrance to the inner courtyard. Do this also on the seventh day of the new year for anyone who has sinned through error or ignorance. In this way, you will purify the Temple.

"On the fourteenth day of the first month, you must celebrate the Passover. This festival will last for seven days. The bread you eat during that time must be made without yeast. On the day of Passover the prince will provide a young bull as a sin offering for himself and the people of Israel. On each of the seven days of the feast he will prepare a burnt offering to the LORD, consisting of seven young bulls and seven rams without defects. A male goat will also be given each day for a sin offering. The prince will provide a basket of flour as a grain offering and a gallon of olive oil with each young bull and ram.

"During the seven days of the Festival of Shelters, which occurs every year in early autumn, the prince will provide these same sacrifices for the sin offering, the burnt offering, and the grain offering, along with the required olive oil.

"This is what the Sovereign LORD says: The east gateway of the inner courtyard will be closed during the six workdays each week, but it will be open on Sabbath days and the days of new moon celebrations. The prince will enter the entry room of the gateway from the outside. Then he will stand by the gatepost while the priest offers his burnt offering and peace offering. He will bow down in worship inside the gateway passage and then go back out the way he came. The gateway will not be closed until evening. The common people will bow down and worship the LORD in front of this gateway on Sabbath days and the days of new moon celebrations.

"Each Sabbath day the prince will present to the LORD a burnt offering of six lambs and one ram, all with no defects. He will present a grain offering of a basket of choice flour to go with the ram and whatever amount of flour he chooses to go with each lamb, and he is to offer one gallon of olive oil for each basket of flour. At the new moon celebrations, he will bring one young bull, six lambs, and one ram, all with no defects. With the young bull he must bring a basket of choice flour for a grain offering. With the ram he must bring another basket of flour. And with each lamb he is to bring whatever amount of flour he chooses to give. With each basket of flour he must offer one gallon of olive oil.

"The prince must enter the gateway through the entry room, and he must leave the same way. But when the people come in through the north gateway to worship the LORD during the religious festivals, they must leave by the south gateway. And those who entered through the south gateway must leave by the north gateway. They must never leave by the same gateway they came in, but must always use the opposite gateway. The prince will enter and leave with the people on these occasions.

"So at the special feasts and sacred festivals, the grain offering will be a basket of choice flour with each young bull, another basket of flour with each ram, and as much flour as the worshiper chooses to give with each lamb. Give one gallon of olive oil with each basket of flour. When the prince offers a voluntary burnt offering or peace offering to the LORD, the east gateway to the inner courtyard will be opened for him, and he will offer his sacrifices as he does on Sabbath days. Then he will leave, and the gateway will be shut behind him.

"Each morning you must sacrifice a one-year-old lamb with no defects as a burnt offering to the LORD. With the lamb, a grain offering must also be given to the LORD—about three quarts of flour with a third of a gallon of olive oil to moisten the choice flour. This will be a permanent law for you. The lamb, the grain offering, and the olive oil must be given as a daily sacrifice every morning without fail.

"This is what the Sovereign LORD says: If the prince gives a gift of land to one of his sons as his inheritance, it will belong to him and his descendants forever. But if the prince gives a gift of land from his inheritance to one of his servants, the servant may keep it only until the Year of Jubilee, which comes every fiftieth year. At that time the land will return to the prince. But when the prince gives gifts to his sons, those gifts will be permanent. And the prince may never take anyone's property by force. If he gives property to his sons, it must be from his own land, for I do not want any of my people unjustly evicted from their property."

In my vision, the man brought me through the entrance beside the gateway and led me to the sacred rooms assigned to the priests, which faced toward the north. He showed me a place at the extreme west end of these rooms. He explained, "This is where the priests will cook the meat from the guilt offerings and sin offerings and bake the flour from the grain offerings into bread. They will do it here to avoid carrying the sacrifices through the outer courtyard and endangering the people by transmitting holiness to them."

Then he brought me back to the outer courtyard and led me to each of its four corners. In each corner I saw an enclosure. Each of these enclosures was 70 feet long and 52½ feet wide, surrounded by walls. Along the inside of these walls was a ledge of stone with fireplaces under the ledge all the way around. The man said to me, "These are the kitchens to be used by the Temple assistants to boil the sacrifices offered by the people."

In my vision, the man brought me back to the entrance of the Temple. There I saw a stream flowing east from beneath the door of the Temple and passing to the right of the altar on its south side. The man brought me outside the wall through the north gateway and led me around to the eastern entrance. There I could see the water flowing out through the south side of the east gateway.

Measuring as he went, he took me along the stream for 1,750 feet and then led me across. The water was up to my ankles. He measured off another 1,750 feet and led me across again. This time the water was up to my knees. After another 1,750 feet, it was up to my waist. Then he measured another 1,750 feet, and the river was too deep to walk across. It was deep enough to swim in, but too deep to walk through.

He asked me, "Have you been watching, son of man?" Then he led me back along the riverbank. When I returned, I was surprised by the sight of many trees growing on both sides of the river. Then he said to me, "This river flows east through the desert into the valley of the Dead Sea. The waters of this stream will make the salty waters of the Dead Sea fresh and pure. There will be swarms of living things wherever the water of this river flows. Fish will abound in the Dead Sea, for its waters will become fresh. Life will flourish wherever this water flows. Fishermen will stand along the shores of the Dead Sea. All the way from En-gedi to En-eglaim, the shores will be covered with nets drying in the sun. Fish of every kind will fill the Dead Sea, just as they fill the Mediterranean. But the marshes and swamps will not be purified; they will still be salty. Fruit trees of all kinds will grow along both sides of the river. The leaves of these trees will never turn brown and fall, and there will always be fruit on their branches. There will be a new crop every month, for they are watered by the river flowing from the Temple. The fruit will be for food and the leaves for healing."

This is what the Sovereign LORD says: "Divide the land in this way for the twelve tribes of Israel: The descendants of Joseph will be given two shares of land. Otherwise each tribe will receive an equal share. I took a solemn oath and swore that I would give this land to your ancestors, and it will now come to you as your possession.

"These are the boundaries of the land: The northern border will run from the Mediterranean toward Hethlon, then on through Lebo-hamath to Zedad; then it will run to Berothah and Sibraim, which are on the border between Damascus and Hamath, and finally to Hazer-hatticon, on the border of Hauran. So the northern border will run from the Mediterranean to Hazar-enan, on the border between Hamath to the north and Damascus to the south.

"The eastern border starts at a point between Hauran and Damascus and runs south along the Jordan River between Israel and Gilead, past the Dead Sea and as far south as Tamar. This will be the eastern border.

"The southern border will go west from Tamar to the waters of Meribah at Kadesh and then follow the course of the Brook of Egypt to the Mediterranean. This will be the southern border.

"On the west side, the Mediterranean itself will be your border from the southern border to the point where the northern border begins, opposite Lebo-hamath.

"Divide the land within these boundaries among the tribes of Israel. Distribute the land as an allotment for yourselves and for the foreigners who have joined you and are raising their families among you. They will be like native-born Israelites to you and will receive an allotment among the tribes. These foreigners are to be given land within the territory of the tribe with whom they now live. I, the Sovereign LORD, have spoken!

"Here is the list of the tribes of Israel and the territory each is to receive. The territory of Dan is in the extreme north. Its boundary line follows the Hethlon road to Lebo-hamath and then runs on to Hazar-enan on the border of Damascus, with Hamath to the north. Dan's territory extends all the way across the land of Israel from east to west.

"Asher's territory lies south of Dan's and also extends from east to west. Naphtali's land lies south of Asher's, also extending from east to west. Then comes Manasseh south of Naphtali, and its territory also extends from east to west. South of Manasseh is Ephraim, and then Reuben, and then Judah, all of whose boundaries extend from east to west.

"South of Judah is the land set aside for a special purpose. It will be 8⅓ miles wide and will extend as far east and west as the tribal territories, with the Temple at the center.

"The area set aside for the LORD's Temple will be 8⅓ miles long and 6⅔ miles wide. For the priests there will be a strip of land measuring 8⅓ miles long by 3⅓ miles wide, with the LORD's Temple at the center. This area is set aside for the ordained priests, the descendants of Zadok who served me faithfully and did not go astray with the people of Israel and the rest of the Levites. It will be their special portion when the land is distributed, the most sacred land of all. Next to the priests' territory will lie the land where the other Levites will live.

"The land allotted to the Levites will be the same size and shape as that belonging to the priests—8⅓ miles long and 3⅓ miles wide. Together these portions of land will measure 8⅓ miles long by 6⅔ miles wide. None of this special land may ever be sold or traded or used by others, for it belongs to the LORD; it is set apart as holy.

"An additional strip of land 8⅓ miles long by 1⅔ miles wide, south of the sacred Temple area, will be allotted for public use—homes, pasture-lands, and common lands, with a city at the center. The city will measure 1½ miles on each side—north, south, east, and west. Open lands will surround the city for 150 yards in every direction. Outside the city there will be a farming area that stretches 3⅓ miles to the east and 3⅓ miles to the west along the border of the sacred area. This farmland will produce food for the people working in the city. Those who come from the various tribes to work in the city may farm it. This entire area—including the sacred lands and the city—is a square that measures 8⅓ miles on each side.

"The areas that remain, to the east and to the west of the sacred lands and the city, will belong to the prince. Each of these areas will be 8⅓ miles wide, extending in opposite directions to the eastern and western borders of Israel, with the sacred lands and the sanctuary of the Temple in the center. So the prince's land will include everything between the territories allotted to Judah and Benjamin, except for the areas set aside for the sacred lands and the city.

"These are the territories allotted to the rest of the tribes. Benjamin's territory lies just south of the prince's lands, and it extends across the entire land of Israel from east to west. South of Benjamin's territory lies that of Simeon, also extending across the land from east to west. Next is the territory of Issachar with the same eastern and western boundaries.

"Then comes the territory of Zebulun, which also extends across the land from east to west. The territory of Gad is just south of Zebulun with the same borders to the east and west. The southern border of Gad runs from Tamar to the waters of Meribah at Kadesh and then follows the Brook of Egypt to the Mediterranean.

"These are the allotments that will be set aside for each tribe's exclusive possession. I, the Sovereign LORD, have spoken!

"These will be the exits to the city: On the north wall, which is 1½ miles long, there will be three gates, each one named after a tribe of Israel. The first will be named for Reuben, the second for Judah, and the third for Levi. On the east wall, also 1½ miles long, the gates will be named for Joseph, Benjamin, and Dan. The south wall, also 1½ miles long, will have gates named for Simeon, Issachar, and Zebulun. And on the west wall, also 1½ miles long, the gates will be named for Gad, Asher, and Naphtali.

"The distance around the entire city will be 6 miles. And from that day the name of the city will be 'The LORD Is There.'"

IMMERSED IN HAGGAI

THE YEAR WAS 520 BC. The exiles had returned to Judea nearly twenty years earlier and had enthusiastically begun the work of rebuilding the Temple. However, they had been forced to stop construction after the Temple foundation was completed because their opponents complained to the ruler of the Persian Empire. But now there was a new ruler, Darius, and his policies allowed the rebuilding to continue.

Still, the people claimed, "The time has not yet come to rebuild the house of the LORD." They had become so involved in building their own luxurious homes that they were neglecting the LORD's house.

So God sent the prophet Haggai to deliver a series of messages to the exiles. Haggai explained to the people that since they were so interested in material things, God had been trying to get their attention through drought, blight, mildew, and hail. "You hoped for rich harvests, but they were poor. . . . Why? Because my house lies in ruins, says the LORD."

Challenged and inspired by Haggai's words, Zerubbabel (the governor) and Jeshua (the high priest) led the people to resume reconstruction of the Temple. In words that echo God's encouragement to Joshua when ancient Israel was about to enter the Promised Land, Zerubbabel and Jeshua are told to be strong and to complete the task. Israel is being renewed and God's Spirit is with them, just like when the LORD brought the people out of Egypt. Over the next few months, God gave Haggai three more messages to encourage them in this project.

Even though the rebuilt Temple would be very modest compared to the one Solomon had commissioned, God promises that "the future glory of this Temple will be greater than its past glory." For Israel, the Temple was the focal point of God's special presence among them. They knew that, ultimately, blessings and peace could come to them only when he lived among them.

In Israel's story, monarchy and Temple always belong together. So God also sent one more reassuring message through Haggai, keeping his promise of a lasting dynasty through King David. This assurance seemed to be in jeopardy when Jeremiah, at the height of the people's resistance to his warnings, said that King Jehoiachin would never return from exile and that "none of his children will succeed him on the throne of David." God even told Jehoiachin, "Even if you were the signet ring on my right hand, I would pull you off." But now God tells Jehoiachin's grandson Zerubbabel, "I will make you like a signet ring on my finger . . . for I have chosen you." God has not forgotten his covenant, and the promised restoration of a Davidic king will surely come.

Haggai is a prophet for both the present and the future. The people must rebuild God's house now. But the book ends with a vision of a time when God will "shake the heavens and the earth" and overthrow all those who oppose his rule.

HAGGAI

✙

On August 29 of the second year of King Darius's reign, the LORD gave a message through the prophet Haggai to Zerubbabel son of Shealtiel, governor of Judah, and to Jeshua son of Jehozadak, the high priest.

"This is what the LORD of Heaven's Armies says: The people are saying, 'The time has not yet come to rebuild the house of the LORD.'"

Then the LORD sent this message through the prophet Haggai: "Why are you living in luxurious houses while my house lies in ruins? This is what the LORD of Heaven's Armies says: Look at what's happening to you! You have planted much but harvest little. You eat but are not satisfied. You drink but are still thirsty. You put on clothes but cannot keep warm. Your wages disappear as though you were putting them in pockets filled with holes!

"This is what the LORD of Heaven's Armies says: Look at what's happening to you! Now go up into the hills, bring down timber, and rebuild my house. Then I will take pleasure in it and be honored, says the LORD. You hoped for rich harvests, but they were poor. And when you brought your harvest home, I blew it away. Why? Because my house lies in ruins, says the LORD of Heaven's Armies, while all of you are busy building your own fine houses. It's because of you that the heavens withhold the dew and the earth produces no crops. I have called for a drought on your fields and hills—a drought to wither the grain and grapes and olive trees and all your other crops, a drought to starve you and your livestock and to ruin everything you have worked so hard to get."

Then Zerubbabel son of Shealtiel, and Jeshua son of Jehozadak, the high priest, and the whole remnant of God's people began to obey the message from the LORD their God. When they heard the words of the prophet Haggai, whom the LORD their God had sent, the people feared the LORD. Then Haggai, the LORD's messenger, gave the people this message from the LORD: "I am with you, says the LORD!"

So the LORD sparked the enthusiasm of Zerubbabel son of Shealtiel, governor of Judah, and the enthusiasm of Jeshua son of Jehozadak, the high priest, and the enthusiasm of the whole remnant of God's people. They began to work on the house of their God, the LORD of Heaven's Armies, on September 21 of the second year of King Darius's reign.

+

Then on October 17 of that same year, the LORD sent another message through the prophet Haggai. "Say this to Zerubbabel son of Shealtiel, governor of Judah, and to Jeshua son of Jehozadak, the high priest, and to the remnant of God's people there in the land: 'Does anyone remember this house—this Temple—in its former splendor? How, in comparison, does it look to you now? It must seem like nothing at all! But now the LORD says: Be strong, Zerubbabel. Be strong, Jeshua son of Jehozadak, the high priest. Be strong, all you people still left in the land. And now get to work, for I am with you, says the LORD of Heaven's Armies. My Spirit remains among you, just as I promised when you came out of Egypt. So do not be afraid.'

"For this is what the LORD of Heaven's Armies says: In just a little while I will again shake the heavens and the earth, the oceans and the dry land. I will shake all the nations, and the treasures of all the nations will be brought to this Temple. I will fill this place with glory, says the LORD of Heaven's Armies. The silver is mine, and the gold is mine, says the LORD of Heaven's Armies. The future glory of this Temple will be greater than its past glory, says the LORD of Heaven's Armies. And in this place I will bring peace. I, the LORD of Heaven's Armies, have spoken!"

+

On December 18 of the second year of King Darius's reign, the LORD sent this message to the prophet Haggai: "This is what the LORD of Heaven's Armies says. Ask the priests this question about the law: 'If one of you is carrying some meat from a holy sacrifice in his robes and his robe happens to brush against some bread or stew, wine or olive oil, or any other kind of food, will it also become holy?'"

The priests replied, "No."

Then Haggai asked, "If someone becomes ceremonially unclean by touching a dead person and then touches any of these foods, will the food be defiled?"

And the priests answered, "Yes."

Then Haggai responded, "That is how it is with this people and this nation, says the LORD. Everything they do and everything they offer is defiled by their sin. Look at what was happening to you before you began to lay the foundation of the LORD's Temple. When you hoped for a twenty-bushel crop, you harvested only ten. When you expected to draw fifty gallons from the winepress, you found only twenty. I sent blight and mildew and hail to destroy everything you worked so hard to produce. Even so, you refused to return to me, says the LORD.

"Think about this eighteenth day of December, the day when the foundation of the LORD's Temple was laid. Think carefully. I am giving you a promise now while the seed is still in the barn. You have not yet harvested your grain, and your grapevines, fig trees, pomegranates, and olive trees have not yet produced their crops. But from this day onward I will bless you."

+

On that same day, December 18, the LORD sent this second message to Haggai: "Tell Zerubbabel, the governor of Judah, that I am about to shake the heavens and the earth. I will overthrow royal thrones and destroy the power of foreign kingdoms. I will overturn their chariots and riders. The horses will fall, and their riders will kill each other.

"But when this happens, says the LORD of Heaven's Armies, I will honor you, Zerubbabel son of Shealtiel, my servant. I will make you like a signet ring on my finger, says the LORD, for I have chosen you. I, the LORD of Heaven's Armies, have spoken!"

IMMERSED IN ZECHARIAH

AFTER GETTING PERMISSION FROM THE PERSIANS, the new power in the region, a remnant of Judah's exiled people had returned to their homeland to rebuild the Temple. But nearly twenty years after King Cyrus's decree, the Temple still lay in ruins. New questions arise for God's people: Will they still be able to rebuild the Temple after all this delay? Is God still with them? Does God still have a plan to use them to bring about his purposes for the world?

In response, the book of Zechariah sets forth a series of visions and prophecies revealing that God is still concerned about Jerusalem and the Temple and that he will continue to work to bring his worldwide reign of justice and peace through his people, Israel. God punished his people and has now rescued them. But what's next for them? Zechariah was a member of a priestly family, so it was natural for him to be concerned for the Temple. His prophecies emphasize that it's time for the people to finish rebuilding the Temple and to move forward with their God-given mission to be a light to the world.

The strange visions and vivid prophecies of both judgment and promise that we find in Zechariah make it one of the more challenging books in the Bible to understand. But it provides a crucial link between the story of Israel in the First Testament and God's vision for his people that will unfold in the future.

The book has two main parts, each using a different kind of writing. The first part focuses on the immediate task in front of the people: to finish rebuilding the Temple and to reinstitute true worship of God. It consists of two series of messages, each presented in a highly structured way, one of which contains a set of symbolic vision reports. The second main part of the book is about an indefinite future, revealing how God will use judgment and restoration to bring his saving purposes for Israel and the world to glorious fulfillment. In this section, the message is conveyed through oracles that are structured in the classic parallel lines of Hebrew poetry.

The two sets of visions in the first part of the book each fit into an intricate pattern called a chiasm, a literary device found in many other places in the Hebrew Bible. In this structure, the first and last elements are paired, as are the second and next-to-last elements, and so forth. Typically, whatever is found at the center of a chiasm is the key point of emphasis.

Here's how the first set of messages, containing eight symbolic visions, is structured:

A Riders on four differently colored horses patrol the earth.
   B Four horns are knocked down by four blacksmiths.
   B Jerusalem is measured, and people who were scattered to the four winds return to the city.
      C The high priest is given new garments and a jewel with seven facets.
      C' A lampstand with seven lamps appears between two olive trees.
   B' A scroll flies through the air.
   B' Two women fly through the air and carry away a basket.
A' Riders on four chariots drawn by differently colored horses patrol the earth.

The visions reveal that the conditions are now right for Israel to recommit to finishing the new Temple: The earth is at peace, Israel's sins have been dealt with, and new leadership is in place.

The second set of six messages is also structured as a chiasm. But this time they are straightforward messages about Israel's religious fasts and issues of justice and mercy. Zechariah says it is time to end the fasts and begin a new season filled with festivals of joy and celebration.

While the first part of the book addresses a present historical moment in Israel's life, the second part looks ahead to a time when God will intervene to remove wrongdoing and establish his reign in Jerusalem for the sake of the world. Israel's story has not ended. A new Shepherd and King is coming to fulfill God's purposes. Even though there will be a dark time of suffering and loss, the end result will be the long-awaited establishment of God's peaceful rule and the arrival of his promised restoration.

ZECHARIAH

✝

In November of the second year of King Darius's reign, the Lord gave this message to the prophet Zechariah son of Berekiah and grandson of Iddo:

"I, the Lord, was very angry with your ancestors. Therefore, say to the people, 'This is what the Lord of Heaven's Armies says: Return to me, and I will return to you, says the Lord of Heaven's Armies.' Don't be like your ancestors who would not listen or pay attention when the earlier prophets said to them, 'This is what the Lord of Heaven's Armies says: Turn from your evil ways, and stop all your evil practices.'

"Where are your ancestors now? They and the prophets are long dead. But everything I said through my servants the prophets happened to your ancestors, just as I said. As a result, they repented and said, 'We have received what we deserved from the Lord of Heaven's Armies. He has done what he said he would do.'"

✝

Three months later, on February 15, the Lord sent another message to the prophet Zechariah son of Berekiah and grandson of Iddo.

In a vision during the night, I saw a man sitting on a red horse that was standing among some myrtle trees in a small valley. Behind him were riders on red, brown, and white horses. I asked the angel who was talking with me, "My lord, what do these horses mean?"

"I will show you," the angel replied.

The rider standing among the myrtle trees then explained, "They are the ones the Lord has sent out to patrol the earth."

Then the other riders reported to the angel of the Lord, who was standing among the myrtle trees, "We have been patrolling the earth, and the whole earth is at peace."

Upon hearing this, the angel of the Lord prayed this prayer: "O Lord of Heaven's Armies, for seventy years now you have been angry with Jerusalem and the towns of Judah. How long until you again show mercy to them?" And the LORD spoke kind and comforting words to the angel who talked with me.

Then the angel said to me, "Shout this message for all to hear: 'This is what the LORD of Heaven's Armies says: My love for Jerusalem and Mount Zion is passionate and strong. But I am very angry with the other nations that are now enjoying peace and security. I was only a little angry with my people, but the nations inflicted harm on them far beyond my intentions.

"'Therefore, this is what the LORD says: I have returned to show mercy to Jerusalem. My Temple will be rebuilt, says the LORD of Heaven's Armies, and measurements will be taken for the reconstruction of Jerusalem.'

"Say this also: 'This is what the LORD of Heaven's Armies says: The towns of Israel will again overflow with prosperity, and the LORD will again comfort Zion and choose Jerusalem as his own.'"

Then I looked up and saw four animal horns. "What are these?" I asked the angel who was talking with me.

He replied, "These horns represent the nations that scattered Judah, Israel, and Jerusalem."

Then the LORD showed me four blacksmiths. "What are these men coming to do?" I asked.

The angel replied, "These four horns—these nations—scattered and humbled Judah. Now these blacksmiths have come to terrify those nations and throw them down and destroy them."

When I looked again, I saw a man with a measuring line in his hand. "Where are you going?" I asked.

He replied, "I am going to measure Jerusalem, to see how wide and how long it is."

Then the angel who was with me went to meet a second angel who was coming toward him. The other angel said, "Hurry, and say to that young man, 'Jerusalem will someday be so full of people and livestock that there won't be room enough for everyone! Many will live outside the city walls. Then I, myself, will be a protective wall of fire around Jerusalem, says the LORD. And I will be the glory inside the city!'"

The LORD says, "Come away! Flee from Babylon in the land of the north, for I have scattered you to the four winds. Come away, people of Zion, you who are exiled in Babylon!"

After a period of glory, the LORD of Heaven's Armies sent me against the nations who plundered you. For he said, "Anyone who harms you harms my most precious possession. I will raise my fist to crush them, and their own slaves will plunder them." Then you will know that the LORD of Heaven's Armies has sent me.

The LORD says, "Shout and rejoice, O beautiful Jerusalem, for I am coming to live among you. Many nations will join themselves to the LORD on that day, and they, too, will be my people. I will live among you, and you will know that the LORD of Heaven's Armies sent me to you. The land of Judah will be the LORD's special possession in the holy land, and he will once again choose Jerusalem to be his own city. Be silent before the LORD, all humanity, for he is springing into action from his holy dwelling."

Then the angel showed me Jeshua the high priest standing before the angel of the LORD. The Accuser, Satan, was there at the angel's right hand, making accusations against Jeshua. And the LORD said to Satan, "I, the LORD, reject your accusations, Satan. Yes, the LORD, who has chosen Jerusalem, rebukes you. This man is like a burning stick that has been snatched from the fire."

Jeshua's clothing was filthy as he stood there before the angel. So the angel said to the others standing there, "Take off his filthy clothes." And turning to Jeshua he said, "See, I have taken away your sins, and now I am giving you these fine new clothes."

Then I said, "They should also place a clean turban on his head." So they put a clean priestly turban on his head and dressed him in new clothes while the angel of the LORD stood by.

Then the angel of the LORD spoke very solemnly to Jeshua and said, "This is what the LORD of Heaven's Armies says: If you follow my ways and carefully serve me, then you will be given authority over my Temple and its courtyards. I will let you walk among these others standing here.

"Listen to me, O Jeshua the high priest, and all you other priests. You are symbols of things to come. Soon I am going to bring my servant, the Branch. Now look at the jewel I have set before Jeshua, a single stone with seven facets. I will engrave an inscription on it, says the LORD of Heaven's Armies, and I will remove the sins of this land in a single day.

"And on that day, says the LORD of Heaven's Armies, each of you will invite your neighbor to sit with you peacefully under your own grapevine and fig tree."

Then the angel who had been talking with me returned and woke me, as though I had been asleep. "What do you see now?" he asked.

I answered, "I see a solid gold lampstand with a bowl of oil on top of it. Around the bowl are seven lamps, each having seven spouts with wicks. And I see two olive trees, one on each side of the bowl." Then I asked the angel, "What are these, my lord? What do they mean?"

"Don't you know?" the angel asked.

"No, my lord," I replied.

Then he said to me, "This is what the LORD says to Zerubbabel: It is not by force nor by strength, but by my Spirit, says the LORD of Heaven's Armies. Nothing, not even a mighty mountain, will stand in Zerubbabel's way; it will become a level plain before him! And when Zerubbabel sets the final stone of the Temple in place, the people will shout: 'May God bless it! May God bless it!'"

Then another message came to me from the LORD: "Zerubbabel is the one who laid the foundation of this Temple, and he will complete it. Then you will know that the LORD of Heaven's Armies has sent me. Do not despise these small beginnings, for the LORD rejoices to see the work begin, to see the plumb line in Zerubbabel's hand."

(The seven lamps represent the eyes of the LORD that search all around the world.)

Then I asked the angel, "What are these two olive trees on each side of the lampstand, and what are the two olive branches that pour out golden oil through two gold tubes?"

"Don't you know?" he asked.

"No, my lord," I replied.

Then he said to me, "They represent the two anointed ones who stand in the court of the Lord of all the earth."

I looked up again and saw a scroll flying through the air.

"What do you see?" the angel asked.

"I see a flying scroll," I replied. "It appears to be about 30 feet long and 15 feet wide."

Then he said to me, "This scroll contains the curse that is going out over the entire land. One side of the scroll says that those who steal will be banished from the land; the other side says that those who swear falsely will be banished from the land. And this is what the LORD of Heaven's Armies says: I am sending this curse into the house of every thief and into the house of everyone who swears falsely using my name. And my curse will remain in that house and completely destroy it—even its timbers and stones."

Then the angel who was talking with me came forward and said, "Look up and see what's coming."

"What is it?" I asked.

He replied, "It is a basket for measuring grain, and it's filled with the sins of everyone throughout the land."

Then the heavy lead cover was lifted off the basket, and there was a woman sitting inside it. The angel said, "The woman's name is Wickedness," and he pushed her back into the basket and closed the heavy lid again.

Then I looked up and saw two women flying toward us, gliding on the wind. They had wings like a stork, and they picked up the basket and flew into the sky.

"Where are they taking the basket?" I asked the angel.

He replied, "To the land of Babylonia, where they will build a temple for the basket. And when the temple is ready, they will set the basket there on its pedestal."

Then I looked up again and saw four chariots coming from between two bronze mountains. The first chariot was pulled by red horses, the second by black horses, the third by white horses, and the fourth by powerful dappled-gray horses. "And what are these, my lord?" I asked the angel who was talking with me.

The angel replied, "These are the four spirits of heaven who stand before the Lord of all the earth. They are going out to do his work. The chariot with black horses is going north, the chariot with white horses is going west, and the chariot with dappled-gray horses is going south."

The powerful horses were eager to set out to patrol the earth. And the LORD said, "Go and patrol the earth!" So they left at once on their patrol.

Then the LORD summoned me and said, "Look, those who went north have vented the anger of my Spirit there in the land of the north."

+

Then I received another message from the LORD: "Heldai, Tobijah, and Jedaiah will bring gifts of silver and gold from the Jews exiled in Babylon. As soon as they arrive, meet them at the home of Josiah son of Zephaniah. Accept their gifts, and make a crown from the silver and gold. Then put the crown on the head of Jeshua son of Jehozadak, the high priest. Tell him, 'This is what the LORD of Heaven's Armies says: Here is the man called the Branch. He will branch out from where he is and build the Temple of the LORD. Yes, he will build the Temple of the LORD. Then he will receive royal honor and will rule as king from his throne. He will also serve as priest from his throne, and there will be perfect harmony between his two roles.'

"The crown will be a memorial in the Temple of the LORD to honor those who gave it—Heldai, Tobijah, Jedaiah, and Josiah son of Zephaniah."

People will come from distant lands to rebuild the Temple of the LORD. And when this happens, you will know that my messages have been from the LORD of Heaven's Armies. All this will happen if you carefully obey what the LORD your God says.

+

On December 7 of the fourth year of King Darius's reign, another message came to Zechariah from the LORD. The people of Bethel had sent Sharezer and Regemmelech, along with their attendants, to seek the LORD's favor. They were to ask this question of the prophets and the priests at the Temple of the LORD of Heaven's Armies: "Should we continue to mourn and fast each summer on the anniversary of the Temple's destruction, as we have done for so many years?"

The LORD of Heaven's Armies sent me this message in reply: "Say to all your people and your priests, 'During these seventy years of exile, when you fasted and mourned in the summer and in early autumn, was it really for me that you were fasting? And even now in your holy festivals, aren't you eating and drinking just to please yourselves? Isn't this the same message the LORD proclaimed through the prophets in years past when Jerusalem and the towns of Judah were bustling with people, and the Negev and the foothills of Judah were well populated?'"

Then this message came to Zechariah from the LORD: "This is what the LORD of Heaven's Armies says: Judge fairly, and show mercy and kindness to one another. Do not oppress widows, orphans, foreigners, and the poor. And do not scheme against each other.

"Your ancestors refused to listen to this message. They stubbornly turned away and put their fingers in their ears to keep from hearing. They made their hearts as hard as stone, so they could not hear the instructions or the messages that the LORD of Heaven's Armies had sent them by his Spirit through the earlier prophets. That is why the LORD of Heaven's Armies was so angry with them.

"Since they refused to listen when I called to them, I would not listen when they called to me, says the LORD of Heaven's Armies. As with a whirlwind, I scattered them among the distant nations, where they lived as strangers. Their land became so desolate that no one even traveled through it. They turned their pleasant land into a desert."

Then another message came to me from the LORD of Heaven's Armies: "This is what the LORD of Heaven's Armies says: My love for Mount Zion is passionate and strong; I am consumed with passion for Jerusalem!

"And now the LORD says: I am returning to Mount Zion, and I will live in Jerusalem. Then Jerusalem will be called the Faithful City; the mountain of the LORD of Heaven's Armies will be called the Holy Mountain.

"This is what the LORD of Heaven's Armies says: Once again old men and women will walk Jerusalem's streets with their canes and will sit together in the city squares. And the streets of the city will be filled with boys and girls at play.

"This is what the LORD of Heaven's Armies says: All this may seem impossible to you now, a small remnant of God's people. But is it impossible for me? says the LORD of Heaven's Armies.

"This is what the LORD of Heaven's Armies says: You can be sure that I will rescue my people from the east and from the west. I will bring them home again to live safely in Jerusalem. They will be my people, and I will be faithful and just toward them as their God.

"This is what the LORD of Heaven's Armies says: Be strong and finish the task! Ever since the laying of the foundation of the Temple of the LORD of Heaven's Armies, you have heard what the prophets have been saying about completing the building. Before the work on the Temple began, there were no jobs and no money to hire people or animals. No traveler was safe from the enemy, for there were enemies on all sides. I had turned everyone against each other.

"But now I will not treat the remnant of my people as I treated them before, says the LORD of Heaven's Armies. For I am planting seeds of peace and prosperity among you. The grapevines will be heavy with fruit. The earth will produce its crops, and the heavens will release the dew. Once more I will cause the remnant in Judah and Israel to inherit these blessings. Among the other nations, Judah and Israel became symbols of a cursed nation. But no longer! Now I will rescue you and make you both a symbol and a source of blessing. So don't be afraid. Be strong, and get on with rebuilding the Temple!

"For this is what the LORD of Heaven's Armies says: I was determined to punish you when your ancestors angered me, and I did not change my mind, says the LORD of Heaven's Armies. But now I am determined to bless Jerusalem and the people of Judah. So don't be afraid. But this is what you must do: Tell the truth to each other. Render verdicts in your courts that are just and that lead to peace. Don't scheme against each other. Stop your love of telling lies that you swear are the truth. I hate all these things, says the LORD."

Here is another message that came to me from the LORD of Heaven's Armies. "This is what the LORD of Heaven's Armies says: The traditional fasts and times of mourning you have kept in early summer, midsummer, autumn, and winter are now ended. They will become festivals of joy and celebration for the people of Judah. So love truth and peace.

"This is what the LORD of Heaven's Armies says: People from nations and cities around the world will travel to Jerusalem. The people of one city will say to the people of another, 'Come with us to Jerusalem to ask the LORD to bless us. Let's worship the LORD of Heaven's Armies. I'm determined to go.' Many peoples and powerful nations will come to Jerusalem to seek the LORD of Heaven's Armies and to ask for his blessing.

"This is what the LORD of Heaven's Armies says: In those days ten men from different nations and languages of the world will clutch at the sleeve of one Jew. And they will say, 'Please let us walk with you, for we have heard that God is with you.'"

+ + +

This is the message from the LORD against the land of Aram and the city of Damascus, for the eyes of humanity, including all the tribes of Israel, are on the LORD.

Doom is certain for Hamath,
    near Damascus,
and for the cities of Tyre and Sidon,
    though they are so clever.
Tyre has built a strong fortress
    and has made silver and gold
    as plentiful as dust in the streets!
But now the Lord will strip away Tyre's possessions
    and hurl its fortifications into the sea,
    and it will be burned to the ground.
The city of Ashkelon will see Tyre fall
    and will be filled with fear.
Gaza will shake with terror,
    as will Ekron, for their hopes will be dashed.
Gaza's king will be killed,
    and Ashkelon will be deserted.
Foreigners will occupy the city of Ashdod.
    I will destroy the pride of the Philistines.
I will grab the bloody meat from their mouths
    and snatch the detestable sacrifices from their teeth.
Then the surviving Philistines will worship our God
    and become like a clan in Judah.
The Philistines of Ekron will join my people,
    as the ancient Jebusites once did.
I will guard my Temple
    and protect it from invading armies.

I am watching closely to ensure
   that no more foreign oppressors overrun my people's land.

Rejoice, O people of Zion!
   Shout in triumph, O people of Jerusalem!
Look, your king is coming to you.
   He is righteous and victorious,
yet he is humble, riding on a donkey—
   riding on a donkey's colt.
I will remove the battle chariots from Israel
   and the warhorses from Jerusalem.
I will destroy all the weapons used in battle,
   and your king will bring peace to the nations.
His realm will stretch from sea to sea
   and from the Euphrates River to the ends of the earth.
Because of the covenant I made with you,
   sealed with blood,
I will free your prisoners
   from death in a waterless dungeon.
Come back to the place of safety,
   all you prisoners who still have hope!
I promise this very day
   that I will repay two blessings for each of your troubles.
Judah is my bow,
   and Israel is my arrow.
Jerusalem is my sword,
   and like a warrior, I will brandish it against the Greeks.

The LORD will appear above his people;
   his arrows will fly like lightning!
The Sovereign LORD will sound the ram's horn
   and attack like a whirlwind from the southern desert.
The LORD of Heaven's Armies will protect his people,
   and they will defeat their enemies by hurling great stones.
They will shout in battle as though drunk with wine.
   They will be filled with blood like a bowl,
   drenched with blood like the corners of the altar.
On that day the LORD their God will rescue his people,
   just as a shepherd rescues his sheep.
They will sparkle in his land
   like jewels in a crown.
How wonderful and beautiful they will be!

The young men will thrive on abundant grain,
and the young women will flourish on new wine.

Ask the LORD for rain in the spring,
for he makes the storm clouds.
And he will send showers of rain
so every field becomes a lush pasture.
Household gods give worthless advice,
fortune-tellers predict only lies,
and interpreters of dreams pronounce
falsehoods that give no comfort.
So my people are wandering like lost sheep;
they are attacked because they have no shepherd.

"My anger burns against your shepherds,
and I will punish these leaders.
For the LORD of Heaven's Armies has arrived
to look after Judah, his flock.
He will make them strong and glorious,
like a proud warhorse in battle.
From Judah will come the cornerstone,
the tent peg,
the bow for battle,
and all the rulers.
They will be like mighty warriors in battle,
trampling their enemies in the mud under their feet.
Since the LORD is with them as they fight,
they will overthrow even the enemy's horsemen.

"I will strengthen Judah and save Israel;
I will restore them because of my compassion.
It will be as though I had never rejected them,
for I am the LORD their God, who will hear their cries.
The people of Israel will become like mighty warriors,
and their hearts will be made happy as if by wine.
Their children, too, will see it and be glad;
their hearts will rejoice in the LORD.
When I whistle to them, they will come running,
for I have redeemed them.
From the few who are left,
they will grow as numerous as they were before.
Though I have scattered them like seeds among the nations,
they will still remember me in distant lands.

They and their children will survive
    and return again to Israel.
I will bring them back from Egypt
    and gather them from Assyria.
I will resettle them in Gilead and Lebanon
    until there is no more room for them all.
They will pass safely through the sea of distress,
    for the waves of the sea will be held back,
    and the waters of the Nile will dry up.
The pride of Assyria will be crushed,
    and the rule of Egypt will end.
By my power I will make my people strong,
    and by my authority they will go wherever they wish.
    I, the LORD, have spoken!"

Open your doors, Lebanon,
    so that fire may devour your cedar forests.
Weep, you cypress trees, for all the ruined cedars;
    the most majestic ones have fallen.
Weep, you oaks of Bashan,
    for the thick forests have been cut down.
Listen to the wailing of the shepherds,
    for their rich pastures are destroyed.
Hear the young lions roaring,
    for their thickets in the Jordan Valley are ruined.

This is what the LORD my God says: "Go and care for the flock that is intended for slaughter. The buyers slaughter their sheep without remorse. The sellers say, 'Praise the LORD! Now I'm rich!' Even the shepherds have no compassion for them. Likewise, I will no longer have pity on the people of the land," says the LORD. "I will let them fall into each other's hands and into the hands of their king. They will turn the land into a wilderness, and I will not rescue them."

So I cared for the flock intended for slaughter—the flock that was oppressed. Then I took two shepherd's staffs and named one Favor and the other Union. I got rid of their three evil shepherds in a single month.

But I became impatient with these sheep, and they hated me, too. So I told them, "I won't be your shepherd any longer. If you die, you die. If you are killed, you are killed. And let those who remain devour each other!"

Then I took my staff called Favor and cut it in two, showing that I had revoked the covenant I had made with all the nations. That was the end of my covenant with them. The suffering flock was watching me, and they knew that the LORD was speaking through my actions.

And I said to them, "If you like, give me my wages, whatever I am worth; but only if you want to." So they counted out for my wages thirty pieces of silver.

And the LORD said to me, "Throw it to the potter"—this magnificent sum at which they valued me! So I took the thirty coins and threw them to the potter in the Temple of the LORD.

Then I took my other staff, Union, and cut it in two, showing that the bond of unity between Judah and Israel was broken.

Then the LORD said to me, "Go again and play the part of a worthless shepherd. This illustrates how I will give this nation a shepherd who will not care for those who are dying, nor look after the young, nor heal the injured, nor feed the healthy. Instead, this shepherd will eat the meat of the fattest sheep and tear off their hooves.

"What sorrow awaits this worthless shepherd
    who abandons the flock!
The sword will cut his arm
    and pierce his right eye.
His arm will become useless,
    and his right eye completely blind."

+

This message concerning the fate of Israel came from the LORD: "This message is from the LORD, who stretched out the heavens, laid the foundations of the earth, and formed the human spirit. I will make Jerusalem like an intoxicating drink that makes the nearby nations stagger when they send their armies to besiege Jerusalem and Judah. On that day I will make Jerusalem an immovable rock. All the nations will gather against it to try to move it, but they will only hurt themselves.

"On that day," says the LORD, "I will cause every horse to panic and every rider to lose his nerve. I will watch over the people of Judah, but I will blind all the horses of their enemies. And the clans of Judah will say to themselves, 'The people of Jerusalem have found strength in the LORD of Heaven's Armies, their God.'

"On that day I will make the clans of Judah like a flame that sets a woodpile ablaze or like a burning torch among sheaves of grain. They will burn up all the neighboring nations right and left, while the people living in Jerusalem remain secure.

"The LORD will give victory to the rest of Judah first, before Jerusalem, so that the people of Jerusalem and the royal line of David will not have greater honor than the rest of Judah. On that day the LORD will defend the people of Jerusalem; the weakest among them will be as mighty as King David! And the royal descendants will be like God, like the angel of the LORD who goes before them! For on that day I will begin to destroy all the nations that come against Jerusalem.

"Then I will pour out a spirit of grace and prayer on the family of David and on the people of Jerusalem. They will look on me whom they have pierced and mourn for him as for an only son. They will grieve bitterly for him as for a firstborn son who has died. The sorrow and mourning in Jerusalem on that day will be like the great mourning for Hadad-rimmon in the valley of Megiddo.

"All Israel will mourn, each clan by itself, and with the husbands separate from their wives. The clan of David will mourn alone, as will the clan of Nathan, the clan of Levi, and the clan of Shimei. Each of the surviving clans from Judah will mourn separately, and with the husbands separate from their wives.

"On that day a fountain will be opened for the dynasty of David and for the people of Jerusalem, a fountain to cleanse them from all their sins and impurity.

"And on that day," says the LORD of Heaven's Armies, "I will erase idol worship throughout the land, so that even the names of the idols will be forgotten. I will remove from the land both the false prophets and the spirit of impurity that came with them. If anyone continues to prophesy, his own father and mother will tell him, 'You must die, for you have prophesied lies in the name of the LORD.' And as he prophesies, his own father and mother will stab him.

"On that day people will be ashamed to claim the prophetic gift. No one will pretend to be a prophet by wearing prophet's clothes. He will say, 'I'm no prophet; I'm a farmer. I began working for a farmer as a boy.' And if someone asks, 'Then what about those wounds on your chest?' he will say, 'I was wounded at my friends' house!'

"Awake, O sword, against my shepherd,
   the man who is my partner,"
   says the LORD of Heaven's Armies.
"Strike down the shepherd,
   and the sheep will be scattered,
   and I will turn against the lambs.
Two-thirds of the people in the land
   will be cut off and die," says the LORD.
   "But one-third will be left in the land.

I will bring that group through the fire
  and make them pure.
I will refine them like silver
  and purify them like gold.
They will call on my name,
  and I will answer them.
I will say, 'These are my people,'
  and they will say, 'The LORD is our God.'"

Watch, for the day of the LORD is coming when your possessions will be plundered right in front of you! I will gather all the nations to fight against Jerusalem. The city will be taken, the houses looted, and the women raped. Half the population will be taken into captivity, and the rest will be left among the ruins of the city.

Then the LORD will go out to fight against those nations, as he has fought in times past. On that day his feet will stand on the Mount of Olives, east of Jerusalem. And the Mount of Olives will split apart, making a wide valley running from east to west. Half the mountain will move toward the north and half toward the south. You will flee through this valley, for it will reach across to Azal. Yes, you will flee as you did from the earthquake in the days of King Uzziah of Judah. Then the LORD my God will come, and all his holy ones with him.

On that day the sources of light will no longer shine, yet there will be continuous day! Only the LORD knows how this could happen. There will be no normal day and night, for at evening time it will still be light.

On that day life-giving waters will flow out from Jerusalem, half toward the Dead Sea and half toward the Mediterranean, flowing continuously in both summer and winter.

And the LORD will be king over all the earth. On that day there will be one LORD—his name alone will be worshiped.

All the land from Geba, north of Judah, to Rimmon, south of Jerusalem, will become one vast plain. But Jerusalem will be raised up in its original place and will be inhabited all the way from the Benjamin Gate over to the site of the old gate, then to the Corner Gate, and from the Tower of Hananel to the king's winepresses. And Jerusalem will be filled, safe at last, never again to be cursed and destroyed.

And the LORD will send a plague on all the nations that fought against Jerusalem. Their people will become like walking corpses, their flesh rotting away. Their eyes will rot in their sockets, and their tongues will rot in their mouths. On that day they will be terrified, stricken by the LORD with great panic. They will fight their neighbors hand to hand. Judah, too, will be fighting at Jerusalem. The wealth of all the neighboring nations will be captured—great quantities of gold and silver and fine clothing. This same plague will strike the horses, mules, camels, donkeys, and all the other animals in the enemy camps.

In the end, the enemies of Jerusalem who survive the plague will go up to Jerusalem each year to worship the King, the LORD of Heaven's Armies, and to celebrate the Festival of Shelters. Any nation in the world that refuses to come to Jerusalem to worship the King, the LORD of Heaven's Armies, will have no rain. If the people of Egypt refuse to attend the festival, the LORD will punish them with the same plague that he sends on the other nations who refuse to go. Egypt and the other nations will all be punished if they don't go to celebrate the Festival of Shelters.

On that day even the harness bells of the horses will be inscribed with these words: HOLY TO THE LORD. And the cooking pots in the Temple of the LORD will be as sacred as the basins used beside the altar. In fact, every cooking pot in Jerusalem and Judah will be holy to the LORD of Heaven's Armies. All who come to worship will be free to use any of these pots to boil their sacrifices. And on that day there will no longer be traders in the Temple of the LORD of Heaven's Armies.

IMMERSED IN MALACHI

SOMETIME AFTER THE TEMPLE had been rebuilt through the encouragement of the prophets Haggai and Zechariah, God sent another prophet
to urge the people to worship him properly there. This message came
from the LORD through the prophet we know as Malachi. Since the
prophet's name in Hebrew means "my messenger," it is possible that
we don't know his real name and that he was simply a messenger
of God.

Malachi took a distinctive approach in bringing God's word to the
people who had returned from exile. To draw their attention to issues
that needed correcting, he would make a provocative claim, antici-
pate their defensive response, and then answer their objections. For
example, speaking as God's messenger, he says, "Should people cheat
God? Yet you have cheated me!" He envisions the people responding,
"What do you mean? When did we ever cheat you?" Then he explains,
"You have cheated me of the tithes and offerings due to me."

The book of Malachi includes six such exchanges with the people,
arranged in a chiasm:

    A Evildoers will not prosper: Edom will not be rebuilt.
      B The people are not bringing the right offerings: defective
        animals.
        C Concern for justice: Men are divorcing and abandoning
          their wives.
        C' Concern for justice: People are complaining, "Where is
          God's justice?"
      B' The people are not bringing the right offerings: no tithes.
    A' Evildoers will not prosper: The people are saying that evildoers
      go unpunished.

There's also a special word of correction to the priests after the second
exchange and a series of hopeful promises at the end of the book for
those who take Malachi's corrections to heart and choose to live in a
way that honors God.

Ever since the destruction of Israel's first Temple and the nation's
exile to Babylon, the twin questions of God's presence with his people

and the possibility of a new Temple have been prominent. Malachi continues this twofold emphasis by focusing on Israel's proper worship practices in the rebuilt Temple. God will be present with his people, but he will contend with them so they will become the nation he called for a purpose.

"The great and dreadful day of the LORD" is coming, when God will set the whole world right. But first he will provide an opportunity for reconciliation, promising to raise up a new prophet, a new Elijah: "His preaching will turn the hearts of fathers to their children, and the hearts of children to their fathers."

A dual message of obedience and hope closes the book. Israel is called to remember and obey God's ancient instructions in the *Torah*, and there are consequences for those who ignore his teaching. But towering over it all is the promise of freedom and healing after the destruction of those who do wrong. Surely the LORD will return to his people, and "the Sun of Righteousness will rise with healing in his wings."

MALACHI

—————— ✛ ——————

This is the message that the LORD gave to Israel through the prophet
Malachi.

✛

"I have always loved you," says the LORD.

But you retort, "Really? How have you loved us?"

And the LORD replies, "This is how I showed my love for you: I loved
your ancestor Jacob, but I rejected his brother, Esau, and devastated his hill
country. I turned Esau's inheritance into a desert for jackals."

Esau's descendants in Edom may say, "We have been shattered, but we
will rebuild the ruins."

But the LORD of Heaven's Armies replies, "They may try to rebuild,
but I will demolish them again. Their country will be known as 'The
Land of Wickedness,' and their people will be called 'The People with
Whom the LORD Is Forever Angry.' When you see the destruction for
yourselves, you will say, 'Truly, the LORD's greatness reaches far beyond
Israel's borders!'"

✛

The LORD of Heaven's Armies says to the priests: "A son honors his father, and a servant respects his master. If I am your father and master,
where are the honor and respect I deserve? You have shown contempt
for my name!

"But you ask, 'How have we ever shown contempt for your name?'

"You have shown contempt by offering defiled sacrifices on my altar.

"Then you ask, 'How have we defiled the sacrifices?'

"You defile them by saying the altar of the LORD deserves no respect.
When you give blind animals as sacrifices, isn't that wrong? And isn't it
wrong to offer animals that are crippled and diseased? Try giving gifts
like that to your governor, and see how pleased he is!" says the LORD of
Heaven's Armies.

"Go ahead, beg God to be merciful to you! But when you bring that kind of offering, why should he show you any favor at all?" asks the LORD of Heaven's Armies.

"How I wish one of you would shut the Temple doors so that these worthless sacrifices could not be offered! I am not pleased with you," says the LORD of Heaven's Armies, "and I will not accept your offerings. But my name is honored by people of other nations from morning till night. All around the world they offer sweet incense and pure offerings in honor of my name. For my name is great among the nations," says the LORD of Heaven's Armies.

"But you dishonor my name with your actions. By bringing contemptible food, you are saying it's all right to defile the Lord's table. You say, 'It's too hard to serve the LORD,' and you turn up your noses at my commands," says the LORD of Heaven's Armies. "Think of it! Animals that are stolen and crippled and sick are being presented as offerings! Should I accept from you such offerings as these?" asks the LORD.

"Cursed is the cheat who promises to give a fine ram from his flock but then sacrifices a defective one to the Lord. For I am a great king," says the LORD of Heaven's Armies, "and my name is feared among the nations!

"Listen, you priests—this command is for you! Listen to me and make up your minds to honor my name," says the LORD of Heaven's Armies, "or I will bring a terrible curse against you. I will curse even the blessings you receive. Indeed, I have already cursed them, because you have not taken my warning to heart. I will punish your descendants and splatter your faces with the manure from your festival sacrifices, and I will throw you on the manure pile. Then at last you will know it was I who sent you this warning so that my covenant with the Levites can continue," says the LORD of Heaven's Armies.

"The purpose of my covenant with the Levites was to bring life and peace, and that is what I gave them. This required reverence from them, and they greatly revered me and stood in awe of my name. They passed on to the people the truth of the instructions they received from me. They did not lie or cheat; they walked with me, living good and righteous lives, and they turned many from lives of sin.

"The words of a priest's lips should preserve knowledge of God, and people should go to him for instruction, for the priest is the messenger of the LORD of Heaven's Armies. But you priests have left God's paths. Your instructions have caused many to stumble into sin. You have corrupted the covenant I made with the Levites," says the LORD of Heaven's Armies. "So I have made you despised and humiliated in the eyes of all the people. For you have not obeyed me but have shown favoritism in the way you carry out my instructions."

+

Are we not all children of the same Father? Are we not all created by the same God? Then why do we betray each other, violating the covenant of our ancestors?

Judah has been unfaithful, and a detestable thing has been done in Israel and in Jerusalem. The men of Judah have defiled the LORD's beloved sanctuary by marrying women who worship idols. May the LORD cut off from the nation of Israel every last man who has done this and yet brings an offering to the LORD of Heaven's Armies.

Here is another thing you do. You cover the LORD's altar with tears, weeping and groaning because he pays no attention to your offerings and doesn't accept them with pleasure. You cry out, "Why doesn't the LORD accept my worship?" I'll tell you why! Because the LORD witnessed the vows you and your wife made when you were young. But you have been unfaithful to her, though she remained your faithful partner, the wife of your marriage vows.

Didn't the LORD make you one with your wife? In body and spirit you are his. And what does he want? Godly children from your union. So guard your heart; remain loyal to the wife of your youth. "For I hate divorce!" says the LORD, the God of Israel. "To divorce your wife is to overwhelm her with cruelty," says the LORD of Heaven's Armies. "So guard your heart; do not be unfaithful to your wife."

+

You have wearied the LORD with your words.

"How have we wearied him?" you ask.

You have wearied him by saying that all who do evil are good in the LORD's sight, and he is pleased with them. You have wearied him by asking, "Where is the God of justice?"

"Look! I am sending my messenger, and he will prepare the way before me. Then the Lord you are seeking will suddenly come to his Temple. The messenger of the covenant, whom you look for so eagerly, is surely coming," says the LORD of Heaven's Armies.

"But who will be able to endure it when he comes? Who will be able to stand and face him when he appears? For he will be like a blazing fire that refines metal, or like a strong soap that bleaches clothes. He will sit like a refiner of silver, burning away the dross. He will purify the Levites, refining them like gold and silver, so that they may once again offer acceptable sacrifices to the LORD. Then once more the LORD will accept the offerings brought to him by the people of Judah and Jerusalem, as he did in the past.

"At that time I will put you on trial. I am eager to witness against all sorcerers and adulterers and liars. I will speak against those who cheat employees of their wages, who oppress widows and orphans, or who deprive the foreigners living among you of justice, for these people do not fear me," says the LORD of Heaven's Armies.

+

"I am the LORD, and I do not change. That is why you descendants of Jacob are not already destroyed. Ever since the days of your ancestors, you have scorned my decrees and failed to obey them. Now return to me, and I will return to you," says the LORD of Heaven's Armies.

"But you ask, 'How can we return when we have never gone away?'

"Should people cheat God? Yet you have cheated me!

"But you ask, 'What do you mean? When did we ever cheat you?'

"You have cheated me of the tithes and offerings due to me. You are under a curse, for your whole nation has been cheating me. Bring all the tithes into the storehouse so there will be enough food in my Temple. If you do," says the LORD of Heaven's Armies, "I will open the windows of heaven for you. I will pour out a blessing so great you won't have enough room to take it in! Try it! Put me to the test! Your crops will be abundant, for I will guard them from insects and disease. Your grapes will not fall from the vine before they are ripe," says the LORD of Heaven's Armies. "Then all nations will call you blessed, for your land will be such a delight," says the LORD of Heaven's Armies.

+

"You have said terrible things about me," says the LORD.

"But you say, 'What do you mean? What have we said against you?'

"You have said, 'What's the use of serving God? What have we gained by obeying his commands or by trying to show the LORD of Heaven's Armies that we are sorry for our sins? From now on we will call the arrogant blessed. For those who do evil get rich, and those who dare God to punish them suffer no harm.'"

+

Then those who feared the LORD spoke with each other, and the LORD listened to what they said. In his presence, a scroll of remembrance was written to record the names of those who feared him and always thought about the honor of his name.

"They will be my people," says the LORD of Heaven's Armies. "On the day when I act in judgment, they will be my own special treasure. I will spare them as a father spares an obedient child. Then you will again see the difference between the righteous and the wicked, between those who serve God and those who do not."

The LORD of Heaven's Armies says, "The day of judgment is coming, burning like a furnace. On that day the arrogant and the wicked will be burned up like straw. They will be consumed—roots, branches, and all.

"But for you who fear my name, the Sun of Righteousness will rise with healing in his wings. And you will go free, leaping with joy like calves let out to pasture. On the day when I act, you will tread upon the wicked as if they were dust under your feet," says the LORD of Heaven's Armies.

"Remember to obey the Law of Moses, my servant—all the decrees and regulations that I gave him on Mount Sinai for all Israel.

"Look, I am sending you the prophet Elijah before the great and dreadful day of the LORD arrives. His preaching will turn the hearts of fathers to their children, and the hearts of children to their fathers. Otherwise I will come and strike the land with a curse."

IT'S NOT CLEAR when Joel lived and prophesied, and we know very little
about him. However, there are some good reasons to believe that he
was one of the latest prophets. This is suggested by several elements
in his prophecies. For example, he makes reference to the Greeks,
whose influence did not reach the land of Judah until after the return
from exile. He also appears to make allusions to many earlier prophets.
He frequently echoes their phrases, probably to show that the whole
prophetic tradition stands behind his message.

For example, in a combined allusion, Joel echoes both Ezekiel's fre-
quent statement, "Then you will know that I am the LORD," and Isaiah's
repeated insistence, "I am the LORD, and there is no other." Sometimes
Joel ironically reverses the images found in earlier prophets' oracles.
Micah and Isaiah share an oracle that says, "They will hammer their
swords into plowshares and their spears into pruning hooks." But Joel
says, "Hammer your plowshares into swords and your pruning hooks
into spears." Such reversals are effective, of course, only if the image is
already known in its original form.

A standard feature of God's covenant with Israel was that the people's
response to God would determine whether they experienced blessings
or curses in the land God had given them. This element can clearly be
seen in the presentations of God's instructions in books like Deuteronomy and Leviticus. Israel's prophets assume this structure in Israel's
covenant relationship with God, announcing the consequences both for
the people's loyalty and for their unfaithfulness.

The prophets frequently follow a certain order in their writings. First,
they address the wrongdoings of God's covenant people, including
promises of just punishment. Next they typically present oracles against
other nations, followed by hope-filled visions of ultimate restoration
and renewal. Joel's oracles begin in the usual way, describing judgment
against Israel. But then he changes the common pattern, speaking of
Israel's restoration before turning to announce judgment against other
nations.

Joel identifies the judgment as "the day of the LORD," coming in the
form of a devastating locust attack: "Ahead of them the land lies as

beautiful as the Garden of Eden. Behind them is nothing but desolation; not one thing escapes." God calls the people to respond to this
plague with repentance. Then, in a stunning oracle revealing God's
longing to bless the land and make it flourish again, Joel presents an
extended vision of renewal and life:

> Surely the LORD has done great things!
>   Don't be afraid, O land.
> Be glad now and rejoice,
>   for the LORD has done great things.
> Don't be afraid, you animals of the field,
>   for the wilderness pastures will soon be green.
> The trees will again be filled with fruit;
>   fig trees and grapevines will be loaded down once more.

Like many of the other prophets, Joel looks forward to an era when
God will do brand-new things in his dealings with humanity. Just as
Jeremiah foresaw a "new covenant" and Ezekiel envisioned a people
with "a new heart and . . . a new spirit," God says through Joel: "I will
pour out my Spirit upon all people" and "everyone who calls on the
name of the LORD will be saved." The prophets served as God's covenant messengers to the people of Israel in their own day, but Joel
reveals that God's purpose has always been to extend his covenant of
love to all nations.

JOEL

✛

The LORD gave this message to Joel son of Pethuel.

Hear this, you leaders of the people.
    Listen, all who live in the land.
In all your history,
    has anything like this happened before?
Tell your children about it in the years to come,
    and let your children tell their children.
    Pass the story down from generation to generation.
After the cutting locusts finished eating the crops,
    the swarming locusts took what was left!
After them came the hopping locusts,
    and then the stripping locusts, too!

Wake up, you drunkards, and weep!
    Wail, all you wine-drinkers!
All the grapes are ruined,
    and all your sweet wine is gone.
A vast army of locusts has invaded my land,
    a terrible army too numerous to count.
Its teeth are like lions' teeth,
    its fangs like those of a lioness.
It has destroyed my grapevines
    and ruined my fig trees,
stripping their bark and destroying it,
    leaving the branches white and bare.

Weep like a bride dressed in black,
    mourning the death of her husband.
For there is no grain or wine
    to offer at the Temple of the LORD.
So the priests are in mourning.
    The ministers of the LORD are weeping.

The fields are ruined,
   the land is stripped bare.
The grain is destroyed,
   the grapes have shriveled,
   and the olive oil is gone.

Despair, all you farmers!
   Wail, all you vine growers!
Weep, because the wheat and barley—
   all the crops of the field—are ruined.
The grapevines have dried up,
   and the fig trees have withered.
The pomegranate trees, palm trees, and apple trees—
   all the fruit trees—have dried up.
   And the people's joy has dried up with them.

Dress yourselves in burlap and weep, you priests!
   Wail, you who serve before the altar!
Come, spend the night in burlap,
   you ministers of my God.
For there is no grain or wine
   to offer at the Temple of your God.
Announce a time of fasting;
   call the people together for a solemn meeting.
Bring the leaders
   and all the people of the land
into the Temple of the LORD your God,
   and cry out to him there.
The day of the LORD is near,
   the day when destruction comes from the Almighty.
   How terrible that day will be!

Our food disappears before our very eyes.
   No joyful celebrations are held in the house
     of our God.
The seeds die in the parched ground,
   and the grain crops fail.
The barns stand empty,
   and granaries are abandoned.
How the animals moan with hunger!
   The herds of cattle wander about confused,
because they have no pasture.
   The flocks of sheep and goats bleat in misery.

LORD, help us!
The fire has consumed the wilderness pastures,
   and flames have burned up all the trees.
Even the wild animals cry out to you
   because the streams have dried up,
   and fire has consumed the wilderness pastures.

Sound the trumpet in Jerusalem!
   Raise the alarm on my holy mountain!
Let everyone tremble in fear
   because the day of the LORD is upon us.
It is a day of darkness and gloom,
   a day of thick clouds and deep blackness.
Suddenly, like dawn spreading across the mountains,
   a great and mighty army appears.
Nothing like it has been seen before
   or will ever be seen again.

Fire burns in front of them,
   and flames follow after them.
Ahead of them the land lies
   as beautiful as the Garden of Eden.
Behind them is nothing but desolation;
   not one thing escapes.
They look like horses;
   they charge forward like warhorses.
Look at them as they leap along the mountaintops.
   Listen to the noise they make—like the rumbling of chariots,
like the roar of fire sweeping across a field of stubble,
   or like a mighty army moving into battle.

Fear grips all the people;
   every face grows pale with terror.
The attackers march like warriors
   and scale city walls like soldiers.
Straight forward they march,
   never breaking rank.
They never jostle each other;
   each moves in exactly the right position.
They break through defenses
   without missing a step.
They swarm over the city
   and run along its walls.

They enter all the houses,
    climbing like thieves through the windows.
The earth quakes as they advance,
    and the heavens tremble.
The sun and moon grow dark,
    and the stars no longer shine.

The Lord is at the head of the column.
    He leads them with a shout.
This is his mighty army,
    and they follow his orders.
The day of the Lord is an awesome, terrible thing.
    Who can possibly survive?

That is why the Lord says,
    "Turn to me now, while there is time.
Give me your hearts.
    Come with fasting, weeping, and mourning.
Don't tear your clothing in your grief,
    but tear your hearts instead."
Return to the Lord your God,
    for he is merciful and compassionate,
slow to get angry and filled with unfailing love.
    He is eager to relent and not punish.
Who knows? Perhaps he will give you a reprieve,
    sending you a blessing instead of this curse.
Perhaps you will be able to offer grain and wine
    to the Lord your God as before.

Blow the ram's horn in Jerusalem!
    Announce a time of fasting;
call the people together
    for a solemn meeting.
Gather all the people—
    the elders, the children, and even the babies.
Call the bridegroom from his quarters
    and the bride from her private room.
Let the priests, who minister in the Lord's presence,
    stand and weep between the entry room to the Temple and the altar.
Let them pray, "Spare your people, Lord!
    Don't let your special possession become an object of mockery.
Don't let them become a joke for unbelieving foreigners who say,
    'Has the God of Israel left them?'"

Then the LORD will pity his people
    and jealously guard the honor of his land.
The LORD will reply,
"Look! I am sending you grain and new wine and olive oil,
    enough to satisfy your needs.
You will no longer be an object of mockery
    among the surrounding nations.
I will drive away these armies from the north.
    I will send them into the parched wastelands.
Those in the front will be driven into the Dead Sea,
    and those at the rear into the Mediterranean.
The stench of their rotting bodies will rise over the land."

Surely the LORD has done great things!
    Don't be afraid, O land.
Be glad now and rejoice,
    for the LORD has done great things.
Don't be afraid, you animals of the field,
    for the wilderness pastures will soon be green.
The trees will again be filled with fruit;
    fig trees and grapevines will be loaded down once more.
Rejoice, you people of Jerusalem!
    Rejoice in the LORD your God!
For the rain he sends demonstrates his faithfulness.
    Once more the autumn rains will come,
    as well as the rains of spring.
The threshing floors will again be piled high with grain,
    and the presses will overflow with new wine and olive oil.

The LORD says, "I will give you back what you lost
    to the swarming locusts, the hopping locusts,
the stripping locusts, and the cutting locusts.
    It was I who sent this great destroying army against you.
Once again you will have all the food you want,
    and you will praise the LORD your God,
who does these miracles for you.
    Never again will my people be disgraced.
Then you will know that I am among my people Israel,
    that I am the LORD your God, and there is no other.
    Never again will my people be disgraced.

"Then, after doing all those things,
    I will pour out my Spirit upon all people.

Your sons and daughters will prophesy.
  Your old men will dream dreams,
  and your young men will see visions.
In those days I will pour out my Spirit
  even on servants—men and women alike.
And I will cause wonders in the heavens and on the earth—
  blood and fire and columns of smoke.
The sun will become dark,
  and the moon will turn blood red
  before that great and terrible day of the LORD arrives.
But everyone who calls on the name of the LORD
  will be saved,
for some on Mount Zion in Jerusalem will escape,
  just as the LORD has said.
These will be among the survivors
  whom the LORD has called.

"At the time of those events," says the LORD,
  "when I restore the prosperity of Judah and Jerusalem,
I will gather the armies of the world
  into the valley of Jehoshaphat.
There I will judge them
  for harming my people, my special possession,
for scattering my people among the nations,
  and for dividing up my land.
They threw dice to decide which of my people
  would be their slaves.
They traded boys to obtain prostitutes
  and sold girls for enough wine to get drunk.

"What do you have against me, Tyre and Sidon and you cities of Philistia? Are you trying to take revenge on me? If you are, then watch out! I will strike swiftly and pay you back for everything you have done. You have taken my silver and gold and all my precious treasures, and have carried them off to your pagan temples. You have sold the people of Judah and Jerusalem to the Greeks, so they could take them far from their homeland.

"But I will bring them back from all the places to which you sold them, and I will pay you back for everything you have done. I will sell your sons and daughters to the people of Judah, and they will sell them to the people of Arabia, a nation far away. I, the LORD, have spoken!"

Say to the nations far and wide:
  "Get ready for war!

Call out your best warriors.
  Let all your fighting men advance for the attack.
Hammer your plowshares into swords
  and your pruning hooks into spears.
  Train even your weaklings to be warriors.
Come quickly, all you nations everywhere.
  Gather together in the valley."

And now, O Lord, call out your warriors!

"Let the nations be called to arms.
  Let them march to the valley of Jehoshaphat.
There I, the Lord, will sit
  to pronounce judgment on them all.
Swing the sickle,
  for the harvest is ripe.
Come, tread the grapes,
  for the winepress is full.
The storage vats are overflowing
  with the wickedness of these people."

Thousands upon thousands are waiting in the valley of decision.
  There the day of the Lord will soon arrive.
The sun and moon will grow dark,
  and the stars will no longer shine.
The Lord's voice will roar from Zion
  and thunder from Jerusalem,
  and the heavens and the earth will shake.
But the Lord will be a refuge for his people,
  a strong fortress for the people of Israel.

"Then you will know that I, the Lord your God,
  live in Zion, my holy mountain.
Jerusalem will be holy forever,
  and foreign armies will never conquer her again.
In that day the mountains will drip with sweet wine,
  and the hills will flow with milk.
Water will fill the streambeds of Judah,
  and a fountain will burst forth from the Lord's Temple,
  watering the arid valley of acacias.
But Egypt will become a wasteland
  and Edom will become a wilderness,
because they attacked the people of Judah
  and killed innocent people in their land.

"But Judah will be filled with people forever,
    and Jerusalem will endure through all generations.
I will pardon my people's crimes,
    which I have not yet pardoned;
and I, the LORD, will make my home
    in Jerusalem with my people."

IMMERSED IN JONAH

JONAH WAS A PROPHET, but the book of Jonah is not a book of prophecy. Instead, it is a book about the prophet himself. Unlike the other books in this volume, it doesn't present a collection of oracles that Jonah spoke. Rather, with great literary skill, it tells a story about him. And it appears to do so from a later vantage point, not like the messages of other prophets, which were recorded during or just after their lifetimes.

According to Samuel–Kings, the prophet Jonah lived in the northern kingdom of Israel during the reign of Jeroboam II, that is, in the first half of the eighth century BC. It is hard to be certain, but there is evidence that the book of Jonah may have been written after the return from exile in order to bring a particular message to God's people in that day.

In the story, Jonah is sent to announce God's message to the city of Nineveh, the capital of the powerful Assyrian Empire. God is going to destroy Nineveh because of its wickedness. But Jonah has a problem with this assignment, and he tries to run from God. What's the problem? He is afraid that Israel's enemies, the Assyrians, will actually repent of their wrongdoing and that God will not punish them after all. As Jonah says later in the story, "I knew that you are a merciful and compassionate God, slow to get angry and filled with unfailing love. You are eager to turn back from destroying people."

Jonah's description is exactly the language God used to describe himself to Moses after he rescued Israel at the time of the Exodus. But Jonah believes God's compassion should only be for Israel. He doesn't share God's concern for the other nations of the world. So, through an unusual series of events, God gets Jonah back on his mission. Jonah is thrown overboard during a storm at sea, swallowed by a great fish, and then spit out on the land. Ironically, Jonah sings a song thanking God for rescuing him from great personal danger while he is trying to make sure God doesn't rescue the people of Nineveh.

Jonah finally gets to Nineveh and delivers a one-sentence warning to them: "Forty days from now Nineveh will be destroyed!" And sure enough, as Jonah feared, the king of Nineveh responds by telling his people, "Everyone must pray earnestly to God. They must turn from their evil ways and stop all their violence. Who can tell? Perhaps even

yet God will change his mind and hold back his fierce anger from destroying us." The people of Nineveh do repent, and the LORD does
indeed relent, his grace triumphing over judgment.

Jonah protests unhappily that his enemies are spared and that he saw
this coming all along. In the closing scene, Jonah struggles with God's
mercy while God defends his greater interest in creating and preserving
life in the world.

The literary structure of Jonah shows that this short story has been built
with artistry and care. Its two main narrative parts are separated by a
psalm of thanksgiving, which is set right in the middle. Both narrative
sections begin with God commanding Jonah to "Go to the great city
of Nineveh" and deliver God's message. The two parts of the story also
mirror each other through the repetition of key Hebrew terms at the
beginning, middle, and end.

Jonah's experiences also seem to mirror the experiences of the nation of Israel. His leaving the land, being swallowed by a great fish, and
being deposited back on the land appear to symbolize Israel's exile
and return. The challenge that Jonah faces—to accept that God might
have good purposes for Israel's enemies—is also a challenge for the
returned exiles. Is Jonah the only one God wants to save from chaos
and destruction? Are psalms of thanksgiving for God's great acts of
rescue only for Israel to sing?

Reading the book of Jonah at the end of all the prophetic books
helps prepare us for where Israel's story is going. The Bible's narrative is
moving toward the time when God's larger vision to bring his salvation
to all the earth—including people, great cities, and even the animals—
will be realized in a new creation.

JONAH

✝

The LORD gave this message to Jonah son of Amittai: "Get up and go to the great city of Nineveh. Announce my judgment against it because I have seen how wicked its people are."

But Jonah got up and went in the opposite direction to get away from the LORD. He went down to the port of Joppa, where he found a ship leaving for Tarshish. He bought a ticket and went on board, hoping to escape from the LORD by sailing to Tarshish.

But the LORD hurled a powerful wind over the sea, causing a violent storm that threatened to break the ship apart. Fearing for their lives, the desperate sailors shouted to their gods for help and threw the cargo overboard to lighten the ship.

But all this time Jonah was sound asleep down in the hold. So the captain went down after him. "How can you sleep at a time like this?" he shouted. "Get up and pray to your god! Maybe he will pay attention to us and spare our lives."

Then the crew cast lots to see which of them had offended the gods and caused the terrible storm. When they did this, the lots identified Jonah as the culprit. "Why has this awful storm come down on us?" they demanded. "Who are you? What is your line of work? What country are you from? What is your nationality?"

Jonah answered, "I am a Hebrew, and I worship the LORD, the God of heaven, who made the sea and the land."

The sailors were terrified when they heard this, for he had already told them he was running away from the LORD. "Oh, why did you do it?" they groaned. And since the storm was getting worse all the time, they asked him, "What should we do to you to stop this storm?"

"Throw me into the sea," Jonah said, "and it will become calm again. I know that this terrible storm is all my fault."

Instead, the sailors rowed even harder to get the ship to the land. But the stormy sea was too violent for them, and they couldn't make it. Then they cried out to the LORD, Jonah's God. "O LORD," they pleaded, "don't make us die for this man's sin. And don't hold us responsible for his death. O LORD, you have sent this storm upon him for your own good reasons."

Then the sailors picked Jonah up and threw him into the raging sea, and the storm stopped at once! The sailors were awestruck by the LORD's great power, and they offered him a sacrifice and vowed to serve him.

Now the LORD had arranged for a great fish to swallow Jonah. And Jonah was inside the fish for three days and three nights.

+

Then Jonah prayed to the LORD his God from inside the fish. He said,

> "I cried out to the LORD in my great trouble,
>   and he answered me.
> I called to you from the land of the dead,
>   and LORD, you heard me!
> You threw me into the ocean depths,
>   and I sank down to the heart of the sea.
> The mighty waters engulfed me;
>   I was buried beneath your wild and stormy waves.
> Then I said, 'O LORD, you have driven me from your
>   presence.
>   Yet I will look once more toward your holy Temple.'
>
> "I sank beneath the waves,
>   and the waters closed over me.
>   Seaweed wrapped itself around my head.
> I sank down to the very roots of the mountains.
>   I was imprisoned in the earth,
>   whose gates lock shut forever.
> But you, O LORD my God,
>   snatched me from the jaws of death!
> As my life was slipping away,
>   I remembered the LORD.
> And my earnest prayer went out to you
>   in your holy Temple.
> Those who worship false gods
>   turn their backs on all God's mercies.
> But I will offer sacrifices to you with songs of praise,
>   and I will fulfill all my vows.
>   For my salvation comes from the LORD alone."

Then the LORD ordered the fish to spit Jonah out onto the beach.

✢

Then the LORD spoke to Jonah a second time: "Get up and go to the great city of Nineveh, and deliver the message I have given you."

This time Jonah obeyed the LORD's command and went to Nineveh, a city so large that it took three days to see it all. On the day Jonah entered the city, he shouted to the crowds: "Forty days from now Nineveh will be destroyed!" The people of Nineveh believed God's message, and from the greatest to the least, they declared a fast and put on burlap to show their sorrow.

When the king of Nineveh heard what Jonah was saying, he stepped down from his throne and took off his royal robes. He dressed himself in burlap and sat on a heap of ashes. Then the king and his nobles sent this decree throughout the city:

"No one, not even the animals from your herds and flocks, may eat or drink anything at all. People and animals alike must wear garments of mourning, and everyone must pray earnestly to God. They must turn from their evil ways and stop all their violence. Who can tell? Perhaps even yet God will change his mind and hold back his fierce anger from destroying us."

When God saw what they had done and how they had put a stop to their evil ways, he changed his mind and did not carry out the destruction he had threatened.

This change of plans greatly upset Jonah, and he became very angry. So he complained to the LORD about it: "Didn't I say before I left home that you would do this, LORD? That is why I ran away to Tarshish! I knew that you are a merciful and compassionate God, slow to get angry and filled with unfailing love. You are eager to turn back from destroying people. Just kill me now, LORD! I'd rather be dead than alive if what I predicted will not happen."

The LORD replied, "Is it right for you to be angry about this?"

Then Jonah went out to the east side of the city and made a shelter to sit under as he waited to see what would happen to the city. And the LORD God arranged for a leafy plant to grow there, and soon it spread its broad leaves over Jonah's head, shading him from the sun. This eased his discomfort, and Jonah was very grateful for the plant.

But God also arranged for a worm! The next morning at dawn the worm ate through the stem of the plant so that it withered away. And as the sun grew hot, God arranged for a scorching east wind to blow on Jonah. The sun beat down on his head until he grew faint and wished to die. "Death is certainly better than living like this!" he exclaimed.

Then God said to Jonah, "Is it right for you to be angry because the plant died?"

"Yes," Jonah retorted, "even angry enough to die!"

Then the LORD said, "You feel sorry about the plant, though you did nothing to put it there. It came quickly and died quickly. But Nineveh has more than 120,000 people living in spiritual darkness, not to mention all the animals. Shouldn't I feel sorry for such a great city?"

THE STORIES AND THE STORY
——————— *How the Bible Works* ———————

The Bible is a gift. The Creator of all things has entered into our human story, and he has spoken. Working through all the authors of the Bible's various writings, God brings wisdom into our lives and light to our path. But his biggest intention for the Bible is to invite us into its Story. What God wants from us, more than anything else, is to make the Bible's great drama of restoration and new life the story of our lives too.

The appropriate way to receive a gift like this is to come to know the Bible deeply, to lose ourselves in it precisely so that we can find ourselves in it. In other words, the best thing we can do with the Bible is to immerse ourselves in it.

The first step on this journey of immersion is to become intimately familiar with the Bible's individual books—the songs and stories, the visions and letters. These books reflect different kinds of writing, and each book with its various parts must first be read and understood on its own terms. Your *Immerse Bible* is designed to help you easily see what kind of writing is found in each book. This will foster a better reading experience that leads to reading more and to reading in context.

But there is an even bigger goal than understanding the individual books. At its heart, the Bible is God's grand narrative of the world and his intentions for it. By reading whole books and then reading them as a collection of writings, we discover how the Bible presents God's big story—*the* Story. The true destination of Bible reading is for us to inhabit the Story. All the smaller parts of the Bible—Gospels and histories, proverbs and prophecies—take their rightful places in revealing the saving drama of God.

As we begin our journey deep into the heart of the Bible, we come across many stories. The plots and subplots of these stories fit together to tell the Bible's big Story. All the characters, communities, and covenants play a part in bringing the overall Story to its fitting conclusion. That is, they are related to each other and work together to reveal God's bigger purposes for the world.

But how are they related?

The following overview of the main stories that make up the Story will help you understand the overall flow of the Bible. It will reveal how the major stories in the Bible are really subplots of the big Story. As each new subplot is introduced, we will see how it serves the bigger narrative, particularly the story that immediately precedes it.

The Bible is a connected, multi-layered story, and Jesus the Messiah is directly at the center of it all. Sent by the Father and empowered by the Spirit, he is the One who ultimately brings resolution to all the stories. He is the thread—the beginning and the end—that ties the Scriptures together. Jesus the Messiah makes the Story's good ending possible, enabling the completion of God's one, big, saving purpose for all things.

1. The Story of God and His World

In the beginning God made everything and said it was all very good. It is evident from the rich variety of interconnected living things in his created order that God delights in flourishing life. This thriving, teeming world brings God glory and reveals his power.

When we read the Bible in its ancient Near Eastern context, something else also becomes clear. The opening song of creation shows us that God intends for the entire cosmos to be his temple, the place where he makes his home. When the Bible says God "rested" on the seventh day, it doesn't simply mean he stopped working. In the ancient world, a deity "rested" in order to take up residence within a temple. So the new world God made becomes his creation-temple, and he rules over it, bringing peace and life.

This is the Bible's first account, and it forms the frame for everything else that happens. God's creation is the stage for all the acts of the Story going forward. And the role of others in the drama will determine whether or not the Creator's plan for flourishing life will be realized.

2. The Story of Humanity

Humans come into the creation story in a special way. They are portrayed as being formed from the earth itself, establishing their permanent connection with the rest of the creation. Yet they are set apart from the beginning with a unique calling: stewardship. Out of all the creatures, only humans are made in the image of God himself and are to bring God's intentions for his creation to fruition. Their job is to rule over all things, helping life to flourish. Humanity is God's plan for managing his world. As priests in the temple of God's creation, humans—more than any other creature—will determine the success or failure of God's purposes for the world.

However, there are also other forces at work. Evil powers exist and are in a position to influence humans, drawing them away from God and interfering with his aims. God's people are lured into self-assertion and rebellion. This disrupts not only their relationship with God but also the way they function in the world. Because of humanity's bond with the rest of creation and their special vocation within it, great tragedy comes into the world. As their own humanity is twisted out of shape, guilt, pain, violence, and death begin to wreak havoc throughout God's good creation. Human beings are made for worship, created to bring glory to the Creator. But when humans direct their worship elsewhere, the damage reverberates throughout the world.

You'd think this would be enough to make God reject humans completely. But instead, God makes a promise to Adam and Eve that he will continue to work in and through human beings. In fact, it will be an offspring of the woman who will defeat the powers of evil. God will overcome the moral chaos of the world, and he will do it in partnership with humanity. In the Bible's Story, the fate of humanity and the rest of creation are irrevocably bound together.

But the question then becomes: How will God do this?

3. The Story of Abraham and His Family

The book of Genesis reveals a surprising answer: God is going to mend the world and bring his blessing to all the families on earth through one man and his descendants. God calls Abram (his name is later changed to Abraham) to leave his home and go to a new land and a new future. God narrows his focus to one family for a time as the means for bringing restoration to all the world's families.

From this point on, the big stories of humanity and of creation will hinge on what happens in the smaller story of Abraham's descendants. God intends for this family to be an agent for the renewal of the world. This plan begins with God's making promises to Abraham—to bless him, to make his family into a great nation, and to bring blessing to all nations. Over time, God makes a series of these promises, or covenantal agreements, with Abraham's family. Each new covenant moves the story forward and makes God's ultimate intentions more clear.

Early in the narrative, Abraham's descendants go down to Egypt and are eventually enslaved there. But God comes down to set them free and bring them into their own land, an event known as the Exodus. This great act of liberation becomes the template, or pattern, for all the acts of deliverance that God will bring in the future. (The nation that comes from Abraham's descendants becomes known as Israel, named after Abraham's grandson.)

As part of the Exodus, God gives his Law to the people through the great leader Moses, and this Law becomes an important part of his covenantal agreement with Israel. In revealing his mandates to Israel, God expects Israel to become a light to the nations. God wants his people to show the rest of the world what it looks like to live well under God's rule.

Another critical event in the Exodus occurs when God's personal presence comes down and inhabits the Tabernacle (a great tent set up at the center of Israel's camp). This Tabernacle becomes God's house in the midst of his people and is filled with symbols of the earth and sky. It is thus a miniature picture of the cosmos, revealing God's desire to cleanse and renew the whole creation and to make his home with us here once again.

God is present with his people in their new land, keeping the promises he made through Moses. But Israel struggles to honor its covenantal obligations. Throughout the story of Israel, the nation turns away from God again and again. This breakdown threatens the covenant itself. God is committed to working through his people. So if they fail, then his restoration project cannot move forward.

But this story is full of God's surprises. Along the way, God establishes a further covenant with Israel's king David. God assures David of a dynasty of kings on which the promises and hopes of Israel will be concentrated. The destiny of Israel as the beginning of God's new humanity is now focused here.

However, the people of Israel persist in rejecting God's covenant—worshiping idols, inflicting injustice on the poor, and looking out only for themselves. In anger and frustration, God finally intervenes. He exiles his people from their own land and withdraws his presence from them. Others now rule over Abraham's family, and Israel's role in the divine drama seems to have disappeared. A key biblical truth is revealed here: There can be no renewal, for Israel or the wider world, until evil and wrongdoing are dealt with. Judgment is part of setting things right.

The failure of Israel is critical for the overall Story. Israel was called to be the means by which God saves the world, but now the rescue party itself needs rescuing. Everything God intended for his people—indeed, for the entire creation—now seems in doubt.

God sees everything that has gone wrong. But wrongdoing, violence, and death will not get the last word—not in God's Story. He has another promise. Through his prophets, God brings a vision of a new future, one aligned with his founding purpose. He will establish a new covenant, one that completes and surpasses all the covenants that came before. God himself will return to his people and restore them. They will be the light they were always meant to be. So the people wait—praying, worshiping, longing—for one more promise to come true.

4. The Story of Messiah Jesus

By the first century AD, Israel had been suffering under foreign rule for centuries. Now subjugated by the Roman Empire, God's people are divided about what to do. Zealous factions advocate violent rebellion. Many teachers and other religious leaders are urging people to get more serious about following Israel's distinctive way of life under God's law. And those running the Temple in Jerusalem survive by making compromises with their Roman overlords.

Israel's ancient prophet Isaiah had foretold a time when a messenger would come to Jerusalem proclaiming the good news that God is returning at last, that his people are being saved. But Rome had its own version of the good news, and it wasn't about Israel's God. The empire's gospel was about the great blessings brought by their own powerful leader, Caesar Augustus. He is, they said, "a savior for us and those who come after us, to make war to cease, to create order everywhere. The birthday of the god Augustus was the beginning for the world of the good tidings that have come to men through him" (from the Priene Calendar Inscription in Asia Minor, ca. 9 BC).

Into this world a child is born in Israel. He is a descendant of King David, but he comes from a humble family. An angel speaks to his mother, Mary, before he is born. He tells her that this child will be the long-promised and long-awaited Messiah, Israel's King, the One who will fulfill their history. Remarkably, Scripture's account of the ministry of Jesus echoes particulars of Israel's history.

Before Israel's Exodus, Pharaoh killed many Israelite babies, but Israel's deliverer, Moses, escaped; King Herod also kills many Israelite babies in trying to kill Jesus, but Jesus also escapes. The family of Israel went to Egypt to survive a deadly famine; the family of Jesus also survives by going to Egypt. Israel passed through the Jordan River to enter the Promised Land; Jesus is baptized in the Jordan River before beginning his ministry in Israel. Israel spent forty years in the wilderness, where they struggled with temptation; Jesus spends forty days fasting in the wilderness and is tempted by the devil. And as Israel had twelve sons who fathered twelve tribes, Jesus chooses twelve men to be his closest followers. In all of this, Jesus is reliving aspects of the ancient narrative of Israel, but now with a different outcome. Jesus is refreshing Israel's story and renewing Israel itself—through himself.

In his opening message to the people of Israel, Jesus calls them to be the light they were always meant to be, announcing the Good News that something unprecedented is happening in Israel's story. He demonstrates in powerful words and miraculous deeds what it looks like when God comes as King—teaching, correcting, and healing. Jesus is widely recognized as a rabbi and a mighty prophet in Israel, but the current religious leaders see him as a dangerous new problem. Jesus critiques their leadership, thus threatening their positions of power.

This tension between Jesus and the Jewish religious leaders rises until Jesus travels to Jerusalem for a final confrontation. His twelve disciples now recognize him as the Son of David, the Messiah, but they still don't understand his mission. They assume Jesus is going to fight his enemies and claim the throne. But Jesus talks about fighting a different kind of battle. He says his struggle is against the powers of darkness and the spiritual ruler of this world.

Then during Israel's annual celebration of the Exodus, Jesus shares a final Passover meal with his disciples. He tells them that his death will inaugurate the new covenant promised by the prophets. He is arrested by the religious leaders and handed over to the Romans for execution. He is nailed to a cross, with a mocking sign posted above his head that reads "The King of the Jews." It certainly looks as though Jesus has lost, that he is no king after all. But three days later, Jesus is raised from the dead and appears to his disciples.

It turns out that Jesus willingly went to his death as a sacrifice for the sins of his people. Through his sacrifice, he wins a surprising victory over the spiritual powers of darkness. He takes on sin and death directly—ironically, through death—emptying them of their power over humanity, and he rises from the dead to confirm his triumph. This unexpected story of Israel's Messiah reveals God's long-term plan. All the earlier covenants were leading to this one. The life and ministry of Jesus brings all the narrative threads in the Scriptures together into a single, coherent Story.

5. All the Stories in One

So we see that the story of Jesus does not simply stand alone. The Bible presents his narrative as intimately tied to all the plots and subplots that came before him. Jesus, crucified and raised, is God's answer to Israel's previous failure, humanity's wrongdoing and death, and the curse on all creation.

Jesus fulfills Israel's story and successfully plays the role of rescuer given to Abraham's family. He is Abraham's faithful descendant and David's powerful son, the Messiah. He is the light the nations have been longing for. People from every tribe, nation, and community can now join Abraham's family through belief in Jesus the Messiah. As the true Israelite, Jesus is also a new Adam, a fresh start for the human race. He has defeated our archenemies sin and death, restoring our relationship with God and ushering us into the life that is truly life. The new covenant in Jesus introduces a new world.

Jesus opens the doorway to the true worship of God, and we recover our God-given vocation to be his image-bearers through our stewardship of the world. As the new Adam, Jesus brings flourishing life back into the world. He embodies the new creation in his resurrection, blazing a path of future renewal for everything in heaven and on earth.

Jesus also launches a new community of God's people—the church—

creating the renewed humanity that God envisioned from the beginning. This community is the focus of God's work on the way to a completely restored and healed creation. The book of Acts and the letters of the New Testament record how the earliest churches continued the ministry of God's coming reign that Jesus had begun. The context of this ministry changes over time and in location, but the ministry itself remains the same for God's new family: to embody and proclaim the Good News of God's victory through the Messiah.

In the end, the discovery of the narrative unity we find in the Scriptures is not merely for the purpose of information. The Bible is an invitation. It calls us to join the Story and take up our own role in God's ongoing redemptive drama. We read the Bible deeply and well in order to learn the true story of our lives within God's bigger Story of the world. We read the Bible to grasp the cosmic scope and meaning of Jesus' victory. And we read the Bible to know what it means to follow Jesus ourselves. The path of the cross—selfless love and sacrifice—is the path for us, too. But that path also ends in our own resurrection when the Messiah returns.

> Yet what we suffer now is nothing compared to the glory he will reveal to us later. For all creation is waiting eagerly for that future day when God will reveal who his children really are. Against its will, all creation was subjected to God's curse. But with eager hope, the creation looks forward to the day when it will join God's children in glorious freedom from death and decay. For we know that all creation has been groaning as in the pains of childbirth right up to the present time. And we believers also groan, even though we have the Holy Spirit within us as a foretaste of future glory, for we long for our bodies to be released from sin and suffering. We, too, wait with eager hope for the day when God will give us our full rights as his adopted children, including the new bodies he has promised us. We were given this hope when we were saved.
>
> From Paul's letter to the Romans

The final theme of the biblical chronicle is life, the same theme that began the Story. Through the power of the Spirit and the action of the Son, the Father's intention will be realized in a new heaven and a new earth.

I M M E R S E
The Reading Bible

Many people feel discouraged in their Bible reading. The size and scope (not to mention the tiny fonts and the thin pages) intimidate new and seasoned readers alike, keeping them from diving into and immersing themselves in the word of God. The Bible itself is not the problem; how the Bible has been presented to readers for generations is.

Our Bibles currently look like reference books—a resource to put on the shelf and consult only when needed. So we read it like a reference book: infrequently and in small pieces. But the Bible is a collection of good writings that invite us to good reading—and it's God's word! There is an urgent need today for Christians to know the word of God, and the best way to do so is by reading the Bible. However, we need to understand the Bible on its own terms. We need to become deeply acquainted with whole books by reading them at length. And we can learn how to read the Bible well by altering a few of our current Bible reading habits.

First, we need to think about the Bible as a collection of writings written in various literary forms known as *genres*. Each literary form, or genre, used in the Bible—such as a poem, story, or letter—was chosen because, along with the words, it works to communicate truths about God to real people. (See "The Literary Forms of the Bible," p. 457, for a further explanation of some of these genres.) A complete book can be composed in a single genre, or the author may use several genres to tell one story. And even when books of the Bible are made up of several different compositions, as in the book of Psalms, those components are drawn together in such a way as to give each book an overall unity as a distinct work in itself.

Second, recognizing that the Bible is made up of whole books that tell a complete story, we should seek to understand the Bible's teaching and live out its story. To help readers better understand and read the Bible as whole books, we've removed any additives from the Bible text. Those additions, while inserted with good intentions, have accumulated over the centuries, changing how people view the Bible and, therefore, what they think they're supposed to do with it.

Chapters and verses aren't the original units of the Bible. The latest books of the Bible were written in the first century AD; however, chapter divisions were added in the thirteenth century, and the verse divisions we use today appeared in the middle of the sixteenth century. So for the majority of its history, the Bible had no chapters or verses. They were introduced so that reference works like commentaries and concordances could be created. But if we rely on these later additions to guide our reading of the Bible, we often miss the original, natural structure. This also puts us at risk of missing the message and meaning of the Bible. For this reason, we have removed the chapter and verse markers from the text. (We do, however, include a verse range at the top of each page, allowing for easy reference.)

This edition also removes the section headings that are found in most Bibles. These are also not original but the work of modern publishers. These headings create the impression that the Bible is made up of short, encyclopedic sections. So, like chapters and verses, they can encourage us to treat the Bible as a kind of reference work rather than a collection of good writings that invite good reading. Many headings may also spoil the suspense that the inspired storytellers sought to create and use to such good effect. (For example, a heading that often appears in the book of Acts announces in advance "Peter's Miraculous Escape from Prison.")

So, in place of section headings, *Immerse: The Reading Bible* uses line spacing and graphic markers to simply and elegantly reflect the natural structures of the Bible's books. For example, in the letter known as 1 Corinthians, Paul addresses twelve issues in the life of the community in Corinth. In this edition, double line breaks and a single cross mark off the teaching Paul offers for each issue. Single line breaks separate different phases of the longer arguments Paul makes to support his teaching. And triple line breaks with three crosses set off the opening and closing of the letter from the main body. By contrast, the section headings in a typical Bible divide 1 Corinthians into nearly thirty parts. These divisions give no indication of which parts speak together to the same issue or where the letter's main body begins and ends.

Modern Bibles also include hundreds of footnotes and often include cross-references throughout the text. While these features provide information that can be helpful in certain settings, there's a danger that they, too, can encourage us to treat the Bible as a reference work. Constantly going back and forth between the text and the notes doesn't really qualify as being immersed in reading the Bible.

Third, the order in which the books appear is another important factor in reading the Bible well and at length. For the majority of the Bible's history, its books were not arranged in any fixed order. Instead, they were placed in a great variety of orders, depending on the needs and goals of each presentation. In some cases, books from the same time period were put together. In other cases, similar kinds of writing were set side by side. And often the Bible's books were organized according to the way the community used them in worship.

The order of books that we know today didn't become fixed until near the time of the invention of the printing press in the fifteenth century. This ordering has many drawbacks. For example, it presents Paul's letters in order of length (longest to shortest) rather than in the order in which he wrote them. Also, in this order, the books of the prophets are divided into groups by size, and the smaller books are then organized based on phrases they share. This arrangement puts them out of historical order and sends the reader swinging back and forth between centuries. And there are many other similar concerns in what we know as the traditional order.

This edition returns to the church's longstanding tradition of arranging the Bible's books to best meet the goals of a given presentation. To help readers delve deeper into the Story of the Bible, it places Paul's letters in their likely historical order. The books of the prophets are arranged in similar fashion. Furthermore, the collection of prophetic books is placed immediately after the story of Israel because the prophets were God's messengers to the people during the unfolding of that story. The remaining books of the First Testament, known traditionally as the "Writings," are placed after the prophets and arranged by type of writing. The introductions to the various groups of books in this Bible will explain more about how they are arranged and why.

Finally, some complete books of the Bible were broken into parts over time. The books of Samuel and Kings originally made up one long book, but they were separated into four parts so they would fit conveniently on ancient papyrus scrolls. The books of Chronicles, Ezra, and Nehemiah are similarly the divided parts of an originally unified composition. In this edition, both of these two longer works are put back together as Samuel–Kings and Chronicles–Ezra–Nehemiah. Luke and Acts were written as a unified story of the life of Jesus and the birth of the community of his followers. These two volumes had been separated so that Luke could be placed with the other Gospels. But since the two parts were meant to be read together, they have been reunited here as Luke–Acts.

All of this is presented in a clean, single-column format, allowing each of the Bible's basic units to be read like the books they are. The lines of Hebrew poetry can easily be seen, and stories, proverbs, letters, and other genres can readily be identified. In short, *Immerse: The Reading Bible* takes full advantage of good visual design to provide a more authentic encounter with God's sacred words.

It is our prayer that the combined effect of these changes to the visual layout of the Bible will enhance your reading experience. We believe these changes serve the Scriptures well and will allow you to receive these books on their own terms. The goal, after all, is to let the Bible be the book that God inspired so it can do its powerful work in our lives.

THE LITERARY FORMS OF THE BIBLE

Just as God's word uses existing human language, the inspired authors also employ existing human literary forms that enable words to be arranged in meaningful ways. These different types of writing are called *genres*.

Today most of us are probably more familiar with the concept of genre from watching movies. By watching the opening scene, we can identify whether it's a Western, a science fiction thriller, a romantic comedy, or a documentary. Once we know what kind of film it is, we know what expectations we should have about what can or can't happen, how things are likely to develop, and how we should interpret what is being shown. These expectations, created by previous films and respected by filmmakers, are like an agreement with the audience about how its message will be communicated and should be interpreted.

Likewise, the Bible's authors and editors, through God's inspiration, used and respected the genres of their day. We may be able to recognize some of them as similar to genres we know today, but others may be less familiar.

Since understanding genres is critical to reading the Bible well, we will describe the key types below. The compositions that reflect these genres make up either whole Bible books or smaller sections of larger books, so some Bible books are written partly in one genre and partly in another. (Many of the genres introduced here will be further explained in the introductions to books or sections of the Bible.) As indicated below, the specific genres employed in the Bible can be divided into two general categories of writing: prose and poetry.

PROSE GENRES

- *Stories.* Narrative—or stories—weave together events in a way that shows they have a larger meaning. Typically, a story situates the reader in a place and time and then introduces a conflict. This conflict intensifies until it reaches a climax, which is followed by a resolution.

    Narrative is the most common genre used in the Bible, emphasizing that God primarily makes himself known through his words and actions in specific historical events. The Bible doesn't teach about God merely in the abstract; its historical narratives are intentionally shaped to highlight key points about God and how he relates to people and the world.

The Bible features two special types of stories-within-stories. Sometimes a person will tell a story to illustrate a point about the larger narrative that person is in. These stories are called *parables* and were a favorite teaching tool of Jesus. They usually describe real-life situations but sometimes can be fanciful, like Jotham's parable in the book of Judges, which uses talking trees as the characters. People in a story may also relate *dreams* and *visions* that they've had. In this case they're not making up a story but reporting one they've seen. This subset of narrative speaks in pictures and uses symbols to represent realities.

- *Apocalypse.* Meaning "unveiling," apocalypse is an ancient genre structured as a narrative but composed entirely of *visions* employing vivid symbols which a heavenly visitor reveals to a person. These visions disclose the secrets of the spiritual world and, often, the future. The book of Revelation is a complete apocalypse, while the book of Daniel is split between narrative and apocalypse. Elements of apocalypse also appear in Isaiah, Ezekiel, and Zechariah.

- *Letters.* About one-third of the Bible's books are letters that were originally written by one person to another person or to a group. Letters in the Bible, following the form of ancient letters, have three parts: the opening, the main body, and the closing. In the opening, writers typically give their name, say who they're writing to, and offer a word of thanksgiving or prayer. The main body deals with the business of the letter. In the closing, the writer extends greetings, shares prayer requests, and offers a prayer for God to bless the recipients. Letters in the Bible are typically used by leaders to present their authoritative teaching to a community when they aren't physically present.

- *Laws.* Also known as commands, these are instructions for what to do in specific situations in order to live as God intends. Less frequently, laws are statements of general principles to follow. Many biblical laws have been gathered into large collections, but sometimes they are placed within narratives as part of the resolution after a conflict. God's instructions are most often presented in the Bible as part of his covenantal agreements with his people, contributing to his larger saving purposes.

- *Sermons.* These are public addresses to groups that have gathered for worship or for the celebration of a special occasion. They typically explain the meaning of earlier parts of the Bible's story for people living in a later part of that story. Most sermons in the Bible are found within narratives, but the book of Hebrews comprises four sermons that were collected and then sent out in the same letter.

The book of Deuteronomy is a series of sermons by Moses to the people of Israel as they were about to enter the Promised Land. Parts of it take the form of a *treaty* that high kings would make with the kings who served them. The Ten Commandments are a miniature version of that kind of treaty.

- **Prayers.** These are addressed to God and are usually offered in a public setting in the Bible, though sometimes they are private. They can include praise, thanksgiving, confession, and requests.

- **Lists.** Many kinds of lists are found in the Bible. One of the most common types, *genealogy*, is a record of a person's ancestors or descendants. The Bible also includes lists of things like offerings, building materials, assigned territories, stops along journeys, court officials, population counts, and so on. Lists in the Bible are not merely informative but usually make a theological point or provide verification of someone's connection to God's people.

POETRY GENRES

Hebrew poetry is based not on the repetition of sound (rhyme) but on the repetition of meaning. Its essential unit, the couplet, features a form of parallelism. One line states something, and the next line repeats, contrasts, or elaborates on the first line, intensifying its meaning. This feature is sometimes expanded to a triplet (three-line unit) for greater emphasis.

Poetry frequently uses metaphors and other figurative language to communicate messages with greater strength and emotion.

- **Proverbs.** These are short sayings, typically two lines in length (though sometimes longer), that teach practical lessons for life in God's world. Proverbs are not necessarily promises about how things will work out; mainly they are descriptions of wise ways to live.

- **Songs.** Poetry set to music. In the Bible, songs are used primarily for celebration or for mourning (in which case they are called *laments*). They are often found within narratives, but some books of the Bible are whole collections of songs.

    Psalms are songs used by people gathered for worship. These songs are most often addressed to God as prayers set to music.

- **Oracles.** These are messages from God delivered by prophets. In the Bible, oracles are most often recorded in poetry; originally, they may have been sung. Some oracles are in prose, but even those often use symbolic language similar to dreams and visions. Most biblical oracles are found within larger collections from the same prophet; however, the book of Obadiah consists of a single oracle.

- *Poetic dialogue.* Utilized in a number of ancient writings, poetic dialogue is a conversation in which each participant speaks in a form of poetry. In the Bible, this genre is found only in the book of Job.

Reading the Bible well starts with recognizing and then honoring each book's genre. Following this practice will help prevent mistakes in interpretation and allow us to discover the meaning that the Bible's creators originally intended.

NLT: A NOTE TO READERS

The *Holy Bible,* New Living Translation, was first published in 1996. It quickly became one of the most popular Bible translations in the English-speaking world. While the NLT's influence was rapidly growing, the Bible Translation Committee determined that an additional investment in scholarly review and text refinement could make it even better. So shortly after its initial publication, the committee began an eight-year process with the purpose of increasing the level of the NLT's precision without sacrificing its easy-to-understand quality. This second-generation text was completed in 2004, with minor changes subsequently introduced in 2007, 2013, and 2015.

The goal of any Bible translation is to convey the meaning and content of the ancient Hebrew, Aramaic, and Greek texts as accurately as possible to contemporary readers. The challenge for our translators was to create a text that would communicate as clearly and powerfully to today's readers as the original texts did to readers and listeners in the ancient biblical world. The resulting translation is easy to read and understand, while also accurately communicating the meaning and content of the original biblical texts. The NLT is a general-purpose text especially good for study, devotional reading, and reading aloud in worship services.

We believe that the New Living Translation—which combines the latest biblical scholarship with a clear, dynamic writing style—will communicate God's word powerfully to all who read it. We publish it with the prayer that God will use it to speak his timeless truth to the church and the world in a fresh, new way.

The Publishers

A full introduction to the NLT can be found at:
http://newlivingtranslation.com/05discoverthenlt/nltintro.asp

A complete list of the translators can be found at:
http://newlivingtranslation.com/05discoverthenlt/meetthescholars.asp

UNITED AND DIVIDED KINGDOMS

UNITED KINGDOM OF ISRAEL

Aleppo

Euphrates R.

Tiphsah

N

Cyprus

Hamath
③
HAMATH

Arvad

Tadmor

Mediterranean
Sea

Lebo-hamath

②
Damascus

Tyre
Dan ARAM

Hazor

Megiddo
Sea of
Galilee

Shechem ①
AMMON

Joppa
Rabbah

Gezer
PHILISTIA
Jerusalem

Gaza
Dead Sea

Beersheba
MOAB

AMALEK

Kadesh-
barnea
②

EDOM

SINAI

Ezion-geber

Gulf of
Aqaba

DIVIDED KINGDOM

N

0   20 Miles

0   20 Kilometers

Orontes R.

HAMATH
Hamath

Arvad

Kadesh

Mediterranean
Sea

Lebo-hamath

PHOENICIA
Litani R.
Berothai

Sidon
Damascus

Tyre
Dan ARAM

Kedesh
Hazor

Sea of
Galilee
Ashtaroth

Beth-
shan
Ramoth-
gilead

Megiddo
Salecah

ISRAEL
Jordan R.

Joppa
Shechem
Jabbok R.
AMMON

Bethel
Rabbah

Gezer
Gibeah

Ashdod
Gath
Jerusalem

Gaza
Lachish

Hebron
Dead
Sea
Aroer

Beersheba
MOAB

JUDAH
Kir-hareseth

NEGEV

Brook of Egypt
PHILISTIA

Bozrah

Kadesh-
barnea

EDOM

WILDERNESS
OF ZIN

EASTERN DESERT

SINAI

Ezion-geber

Gulf of Aqaba

0   40 Miles

0   40 Kilometers

① Kingdom of Saul
② David's Expansion
③ Solomon's Expansion

EXILE AND RETURN
UNDER ASSYRIA AND BABYLON

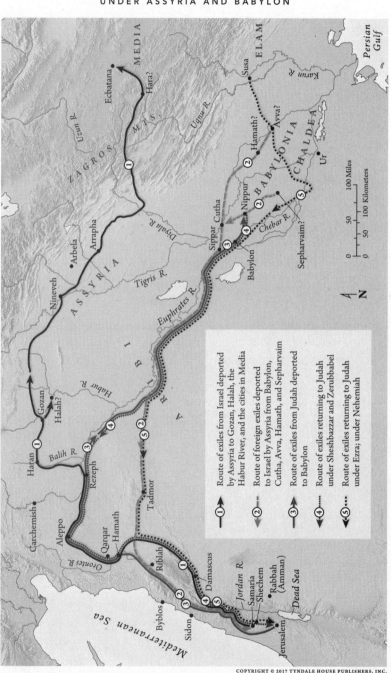

Route of exiles from Israel deported by Assyria to Gozan, Halah, the Habur River, and the cities in Media

Route of foreign exiles deported to Israel by Assyria from Babylon, Cutha, Avva, Hamath, and Sepharvaim

Route of exiles from Judah deported to Babylon

Route of exiles returning to Judah under Sheshbazzar and Zerubbabel

Route of exiles returning to Judah under Ezra; under Nehemiah

THE IMMERSE BIBLE SERIES

IMMERSE: THE READING BIBLE comes in six volumes and presents each Bible book without the distractions of chapter and verse numbers, subject headers, or footnotes. It's designed for reading—especially for reading with others. By committing to just two eight-week sessions per year (spring and fall), you can read through the entire Bible in three years. And online video and audio support tools make it easy to read together in groups. Step into this three-year Immerse Bible reading cycle with your friends; then do it again—and again—for a lifetime of life-giving, life-changing Bible engagement!

Immerse: Beginnings

includes the first five books of the Bible, known as the *Torah* (meaning "instruction"). These books describe the origins of God's creation, the human rebellion, and the family of Israel—the people God chose to be a light to all peoples. We follow the covenant community from its earliest ancestors to the time it is about to enter the Promised Land.

Immerse: Kingdoms

tells the story of Israel from the time of its conquest of Canaan (Joshua) through its struggle to settle the land (Judges, Ruth) and the establishment of Israel's kingdom, which ends in a forced exile (Samuel–Kings). The nation of Israel, commissioned to be God's light to the nations, falls to division and then foreign conquest for rejecting God's rule.

Immerse: Prophets

presents the First Testament prophets in groupings that generally represent four historical periods: before the fall of Israel's northern kingdom (Amos, Hosea, Micah, Isaiah), before the fall of the southern kingdom (Zephaniah, Nahum, Habakkuk), around the time of Jerusalem's destruction (Jeremiah, Obadiah, Ezekiel), and after the return from exile (Haggai, Zechariah, Malachi, Joel, Jonah).

Immerse: Poets

presents the poetical books of the First Testament in two groupings, dividing the books between songs (Psalms, Lamentations, Song of Songs) and wisdom writings (Proverbs, Ecclesiastes, Job). These writings all reflect the daily, down-to-earth faith of God's people as they live out their covenant relationship with him in worship and wise living.

Immerse: Chronicles

contains the remaining First Testament books: Chronicles–Ezra–Nehemiah, Esther, and Daniel. These works were all written after the Jewish people fell under the control of foreign empires and were scattered among the nations. They remind God's chastened people of their identity and calling to faithfully represent God to the nations and that there is still hope for the struggling dynasty of David.

Immerse: Messiah

provides a unique guided journey through the entire New Testament. Each major section is anchored by one of the Gospels, highlighting the richness of Scripture's fourfold witness to Jesus the Messiah. This creates a fresh reading of the New Testament centered on Christ.